Working-Class Cultures in Britain 1890–1960

Integrating a variety of historical approaches and methods, Joanna Bourke looks at the construction of class within the contexts of the body, the home, the marketplace, the locality and the nation, to assess how the subjective identity of the 'working class' in Britain has been maintained through seventy years of radical social, cultural and economic change. She argues that class identity is essentially a social and cultural, rather than an institutional or political phenomenon, and therefore cannot be understood without constant reference to gender and ethnicity.

Each self-contained chapter consists of an essay of historical analysis, introducing students to the ways historians use evidence and develop plausible ways of understanding change, as well as chronologies, statistics and tables, and selected further reading.

The book will be of interest to students of social history, labour history, sociology, gender studies and cultural studies.

Joanna Bourke is a lecturer in modern social and economic history at Birkbeck College, University of London. She is the author of *Husbandry to Housewifery: Women, Economic Change and Housework in Ireland, 1890–1914*.

Working-Class Cultures in Britain 1890–1960

Gender, class and ethnicity

Joanna Bourke

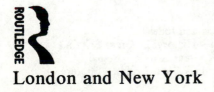

London and New York

First published 1994
by Routledge
11 New Fetter Lane, London EC4P 4EE

Simultaneously published in the USA and Canada
by Routledge
29 West 35th Street, New York, NY 10001

Reprinted in 1996

Transferred to Digital Printing 2002

Routledge is an imprint of the Taylor & Francis Group

© 1994 Joanna Bourke

Typeset in Times by Except*detail* Ltd, Lord Street, Southport

Printed and bound in Great Britain by Selwood Printing Ltd.

Printed on acid free paper

British Library Cataloguing in Publication Data

A catalogue record for this book is available from the British Library

Library of Congress Cataloguing in Publication Data
Bourke, Joanna.
    Working class cultures in Britain 1890–1960: gender, class, and
ethnicity/Joanna Bourke.
        p. cm.
    Includes bibliographical references and index.
    1. Working class – Great Britain – History. 2. Great Britain —
Social conditions – 20th century. 3. Great Britain – Social
conditions – 19th century. 4. Sex role – Great Britain – History.
I. Title.
HD8390.B68   1993
305.5′62′0941—dc20   93-18891

Contents

Chronologies

Tables

Preface

The aim of this book is to cover topics in the social history of the working class in Britain at a level suitable for university under-graduates. It attempts to make the reader approach social history as something requiring exploration rather than memorization. Thus, this book aims to go beyond the usual summaries of the discipline – although you will find some of that here – by integrating various historiographical approaches and methodologies. Each chapter consists of an historical essay, chronologies, statistics, suggested topics for discussion, and a selective bibliography. The self-contained chapters introduce ways to interpret the relationship between the working class and the body, home, marketplace, locality, and nation. These chapters are essays in historical analysis, introducing students to the way historians use evidence and compile plausible ways to understand change in the twentieth century. Incorporated into these essays are concise chronologies and statistics providing additional evidence. Students are encouraged to make use of the short bibliographies which follow each chapter to develop their own interests.

Acknowledgements

Since this book arose out of a course, taught at Birkbeck College, on the history of the 'working classes', I am grateful to my students for providing a stimulating forum for my ideas. In particular, thanks must go to my colleagues in the History Department for creating an environment conducive to research and writing. The staff at the British Library were consistently helpful in entrusting a greedy researcher with more than a respectable quota of books. Special mention must be made of those scholars and friends who have consistently encouraged and criticized me while writing this book: Nicholas Brown, Dominic Dumbar, Marianne Elliott, Richard Evans, David Fitzpatrick, Vanessa Harding, Alistair Lunn, Avner Offer, Anna Pierre, Dorothy Porter, Eric Richards, Peter Rickard, Edward Sands, Hilary Sapire, Michael Slater, F. B. Smith, Ros Tatham, Pat Thane, Kosmas Tsokhas, Jay Winter, Paula Woodley, and David Young. To my editor at Routledge – Claire L'Enfant – I owe a huge debt. Finally, thanks must once again go to my family: Stafford, Ella, Paul, Sharline, Mark, Lisa, David, and all my nieces and nephews.

1 Introduction
Class and poverty

Sex and violence have come to dominate modern historiography. It is surprising, therefore, to find that social histories of twentieth-century Britain have proven less susceptible to this allurement. In place of the body, these histories have substituted a concept: 'class'. This is true to such an extent that discussions of the sexual practices of the 'working class' are frequently dealt with in the context of 'trickle down' theories and 'embourgeoisement'. The intellectual fascination of British social history is found in elegant tomes elucidating the development of working-class consciousness as experienced in the waxing and waning fortunes of trade unions, workingmen's clubs, community pressure groups, and political parties. This book approaches the social history of the working class from a different angle: what does 'working class' mean when our vision focuses on the individual stripped of these institutional affiliations? The main sites of exposure are the body, the home, the marketplace, the locality, and the imagined 'nation'. Within these sites, working-class individuals constructed and reconstructed their states of desire.

It is a truism to say that, throughout the twentieth century, the British have thought of themselves in terms of class. Shifts in the levels of poverty and wealth, world wars, and burgeoning communication industries failed to diminish the almost intuitive awareness of one's own and other people's class position. As late as 1950, F. M. Martin's study of Greenwich and Hertford concluded that the 'great majority of our subjects thought in terms of a three-class system, and most of them described these classes by the same set of names – upper, middle, working'.[1] When asked to define precisely what is meant by 'class', there is much confusion and ambiguity. Within the space of one discussion, people may change their definition of 'class' a number of times, without being aware of inconsistency.[2] One study revealed that almost equal portions of 'working-class respondents' defined 'class' in terms of socioeconomic characteristics, socioprofessional categories, social prestige, and property.[3] Some working-class writers described 'class' structures in their area as 'feudal' with the 'Lady of the Manor sitting on top like a cock on a farm-yard midden and the tenant cottages at the bottom of the socio-economic scale'.[4] The profusion of definitions employed by historians, economists, and sociologists have further obscured the issue. Some definitions are quixotic: for instance, Jilly Cooper defines class as 'a group of people with certain common traits: descent, education, accent, similarity of occupation, wealth, moral attitudes, friends, hobbies, accommodation, and with generally similar ideas, who meet each other on equal terms, and regard themselves as belonging to one group'.[5] The weight given to the individual in such definitions precludes membership in any 'class' of more than one person.

More commonly, 'classes' are demarcated in terms of economic indicators, such as occupation, income, and a distinction between people who own the means of production and those who only own their labour power.[6] A person's class position is determined by his or her relationship to modes of production. This definition is not ideally suited to the historian's purpose. As a static concept, implying that there is a 'ladder' within which people can be slotted, no criteria are provided by which we can analyse *change* in the structure of class. It conceals antagonisms between different social groups within a specified 'class'. In addition, the high wages earned by some manual workers does not place that worker in the same category as university lecturers on an identical wage. Assigning people to their class positions on the basis of economic indicators alone neglects a human component: once subsistence needs have been met, the individual man or woman may be more concerned with *relative* incomes. 'Objective' definitions are problematical. Eric Hobsbawm pointed out the chief difficulty when he noted that if the 'working class' were defined as manual workers, the twentieth century witnessed a decline in this 'class' from 75 per cent of the population in 1911 to 70 per cent in 1931, and 64 per cent by 1961. If, however, 'working class' was defined in a more marxist sense, that is, as the proportion of the population who earned a living by selling their labour power (plus 'dependants'), then this 'class' had grown. In 1911, around 7 per cent of the workforce were 'employers and proprietors', compared with around 4 per cent by the 1960s.[7]

Other definitions – less concerned with precision and 'objectivity' – take account of shared social characteristics, such as similar life styles. In this way, the appearance and demeanour of an individual indicated class position. A stranger's accent was immediately noted, and the refusal of a person to adapt their accent to their 'social position' was frowned upon.[8] In a society where (at the turn of the century) 14-year-old working-class children were six inches shorter than middle-class children, visual indicators of 'class' were significant.[9] Clothes were another indicator. Elizabeth Fanshawe, the daughter of a fireman and train driver, won a scholarship to go to High School. Although her parents did their best to buy her appropriate clothes, on Elizabeth's first day at High School, her teacher asked her to stand in front of the class while she pointed out all the faults in her gym-slip. In Fanshawe's words, 'It was my first encounter with the "class" society; the types of clothing one wore was far more important than one's academic achievement.'[10] Another working-class writer, Kenneth Leech, agreed that an individual's 'class' was a matter of distinctions in material culture. His 'earliest consciousness of "class"' was connected with clothes, indoor lavatories, telephones, and books: 'The poor children – of whom I was one – whose parents could not afford new clothes at Whitsun, had no part in the processions.'[11] This view of 'class' reflected a world divided into minute distinctions based on status indicators. Thus, Johnny Speight lived in the Canning Town district of London between the wars. In 1932, when he was 12 years old, the family moved four streets away:

> It was almost a social upheaval. Some of the people in this new street even had aspidistras in the window. They all wore shirts. At the very top end they even wore collars and ties. The houses had bay windows. We still had an outside toilet. But now we had two rooms and a scullery downstairs and three rooms upstairs. . . . There were a lot of people a cut above us in the street. But we were a cut above the others.[12]

Although this understanding of the world was fundamentally concerned with interpersonal relationships, it must be regarded as distinct from other analysts who argued that an individual's 'class' position was inseparable from their state of consciousness. While interaction remained the key to a person's understanding of 'class', it required a form of political consciousness which was more than simply class awareness. In *The Making of the English Working Class*, E. P. Thompson argued that 'class happens when some men, as the result of common experience (inherited or shared), feel and articulate the identity of their interests as between themselves, and as against other men whose interests are different from (and usually opposed to) theirs'.[13] Thus, Louis Heren of Shadwell confessed: 'I was possibly dim, but was unaware of the British class system until I went to Sandhurst during the Second World War as an officer cadet and temporary gentleman.'[14] In this way, class was both the embodiment and expression of common traditions, experiences, and values.[15]

Prioritizing the political, the masculine, and the consensual in such definitions is unhelpful in analyses concerned equally with the private, the feminine, and the discordant. A more eclectic position – although offensive to theorists of both the political 'left' and the political 'right' – is the standpoint taken in this book. Claims to objectivity are rejected in favour of adopting the labels individuals give themselves as the final word on that individual's 'class' position. The label 'working-class' in this view need not imply class consciousness in the political sense – but it does imply class awareness. Realization of one's 'class' position emerged from routine activities of everyday life: it was the 'feeling of belonging' which was 'felt to be natural and was taken for granted'.[16] It was concerned as much with symbolic expressions of power in social relationships as with material realities. In this way, 'class' was intrinsically tied up with awareness of difference and experience of conflict.

Stressing individual perceptions of class position has an advantage for studies such as this one. It provides one way around the thorny problem of gender and ethnicity. Employing categories such as occupation, income, or relationship to modes of production as indicators of 'class' is clearly unsatisfactory when focusing on women and different ethnic groups. Ethnicity may override any 'objective' analysis of 'class'. Employed women may be categorized in terms of their own occupation, or that of the 'chief breadwinner' in the household. Women without paid employment are often allocated to the 'class' position of their husband or father (assuming – often wrongly – that women would be dependent on them). It is equally unsatisfactory to impute a wage to them. The advantage of allowing self-perceptions to predominate is that it allows a woman married to a manual labourer to classify herself in terms of her middle-class father's position, should she consider this appropriate. In a society where gender and ethnic relationships are unequal, there may be an incongruity of interests between men and women or between members of different ethnic groups allegedly sharing one 'class' position. Adding gender and ethnicity to a description of class awareness makes the process of attaining group identification a more complex negotiation among unequal partners.

Table 1.1 'Normal' real incomes of the British working class, 1850–1939

Year	'Normal' full-time incomes	Cost of living	'Normal' real incomes
1850	100	100	100
1880	143	121	118
1906	179	105	170
1913–14	200	105	190
1924	421	180	234
1935	421	119	354
1939	457	131	349

Source: John Benson, *The Working Class In Britain, 1850–1939* (London, 1989), 55.

POVERTY AND THE SOCIOLOGISTS

While eschewing the conventional reliance on social indicators in analyses of 'class', and rejecting exaggerated claims of 'objectivity' in the use of statistics, sociological surveys of levels of poverty in Britain, and, in particular, research into the fluctuating levels of poverty amongst a group labelled 'working-class' are valuable in depicting the broad expanse of economic relations in Britain. Although certainly not ideal, these studies cannot be ignored. Marxist, culturalist, and individualist definitions of 'class' all acknowledge that (in general) to be 'working-class' means to be less wealthy than 'middle-class' which, in turn, trails behind the affluence of 'upper-class'. Only 'working-class' individuals *must* retain the title 'working-class' despite any dramatic slump in their economic well-being. What we see in the twentieth century is that 'working-class' individuals retained their self-defined identity as 'working-class' despite impressive improvements in their material well-being. The 'class' structure has persisted as declining levels of absolute deprivation obscured the widening chasm in relative wealth between the rich and the poor.

In the twentieth century, absolute levels of poverty fell. In part, this was the effect of improvements in real wages. Historians differ on when real wages started to increase, and the magnitude of the increase, but one of the most reliable estimates suggests that real incomes increased by 90 per cent between 1850 and the First World War, and there were even more dramatic improvements between 1924 and 1935.[17]

Despite this reassuring scenario, in 1899 B. Seebohm Rowntree's investigation of poverty in York divulged that 43 per cent of the working-class population of this city were living in poverty. Of these,

15 per cent were living in 'primary poverty', that is, they were receiving insufficient income, irrespective of how it was managed, for 'merely physical efficiency'.[18] By the inter-war years, a number of studies revealed that levels of deprivation had shrunk. H. Llewellyn Smith's *New Survey* in the 1920s found that poverty had declined by two-thirds since the early 1890s. In the East End of London, the number of people living in poverty had dwindled from over 700,000 to 250,000. Using the same standard as Rowntree, H. Llewellyn Smith concluded that, in 1935, less than 7 per cent of the working class were living in 'primary poverty'.[19] This did not mean that the rich and the poor had identical levels of consumption. In 1938, a middle-class individual would consume two to three times the amount of meat, bacon, fish, cigarettes, electricity, hardware, and entertainments a week than a working-class individual; three to four times the amount of fruit, housing, footwear, and male clothing; four to seven times more sugar products, furniture, and reading matter; seven to ten times more female and infant clothes and postal services; two to fourteen times more personal services; and up to thirty times more wine and spirits.[20]

However, the causes of poverty had also changed. In 1899, over half of families lived in 'primary poverty' because their wages were insufficient to support an average sized family, even if the chief 'breadwinner' was fortunate enough to be in regular employment. Large family size and the death of the chief wage earner also significantly raised a household's risk of severe deprivation. Rowntree calculated that the family of a labourer with more than three children was liable to experience up to ten years of underfeeding. Most workers endured a financial crisis at some period in their life and their success in avoiding the stigma attached to using the Poor Law depended very heavily on luck, good health, a small family, prudence, and thrift. By 1936, low wages and large families were no longer the chief determinants in a family's welfare, and unemployment (followed by the illness or old age of the primary wage earner) had become responsible for much 'primary poverty'. Although the elderly have always experienced the highest risk to destitution, the fact that they became *relatively* more important in the risk tables was, ironically, the price of affluence. In 1890, the average expectation of life for a man was 44 years. Women were liable to live for an additional three years. By 1910, the respective ages were 52 and 55 years. Two decades later, it was 59 and 63.[21] Although the data refer to the entire population, manual workers reaped some of the benefits of improvements in living standards in terms of increased life expectancies. However, this also meant that more people were surviving through to the most risk-prone ages. In

Table 1.2 Proportion of the working class in primary poverty due to various causes, in York, 1899 and 1936

Cause of 'primary poverty'	1899 (%)	1936 (%)
Death of chief wage earner	2.4	0.6
Illness or old age of chief wage earner	0.8	1.6
Unemployment	0.4	3.0
Irregularity of work	0.4	0.4
Largeness of family (4 or more children)	3.4	0.5
In regular work, but low wages	8.0	0.6
Total primary poverty	15.4	6.7

Source: B. Seebohm Rowntree, *Poverty and Progress* (London, 1941), 116

addition, as working-class consumption patterns moved closer to their middle-class contemporaries they began dying of similar diseases: physical suffering shifted from typhoid and tuberculosis to diabetes, high blood pressure, and cerebral haemorrhage.[22]

More than any other group, infants were affected by the lowering levels of deprivation. For every 1,000 infants born in the 1890s, 153 died within the year, largely as a result of epidemic diarrhoea, respiratory diseases, and 'wasting disease' (such as premature birth and congenital defects).[23] These levels of infant deaths dropped steadily to 125 (to every 1,000 born) in 1911, then to 62 (to every 1,000 born) by the 1930s.[24] Plummeting infant death rates should not blind us to the persistence of the mortality gap between social classes. Between 1911 and 1930, the risk to infants born to fathers in some occupations remained extremely high and, for those born to agricultural labourers and coal miners, even increased. In 1930, for every 100 births in each class, three infants of the rich died as against eight of the poor.[25]

Levels of poverty continued falling for at least two decades after 1936. In 1950, the proportion of the York working class who were living in poverty was only 3 per cent.[26] Old age and sickness remained the chief causes of poverty, but unemployment and inadequate wages were no longer significant threats. This trend continued throughout the 1950s, and into the early 1960s. The personal consumption of manual workers increased by around 25 per cent in the decade after 1951.[27] The dramatic expansion in consumption goods was most obviously displayed in the domestic sphere. Working-class households were connected to electricity supplies. In 1920, only 720,000 houses were connected, but by the beginning of the 1950s, nine million homes

Table 1.3 Infant mortality by the social class of the father, in 1911, 1921–3, and 1930–2

Social class	Death rate per 1,000 legitimate live births			Percentage of rate for all classes		
	1911	*1921–3*	*1930–2*	*1911*	*1921–3*	*1930–2*
All classes	125	79	62	100	100	100
Class I	76	38	33	61	48	53
Class II	106	55	45	85	70	73
Class III	113	77	58	90	97	94
Class IV	122	89	67	98	113	108
Class V	153	97	77	122	123	125

Key:
Class I: Middle and upper classes
Class II: Intermediate classes
Class III: Skilled labourer
Class IV: Intermediate between skilled and unskilled labourers, includes agriculture
Class V: Unskilled labourer

Source: Richard M. Titmuss, *Birth, Poverty and Wealth* (London, 1943), 26.

Table 1.4 Causes of poverty, in York, 1936–50

Causes	1936 (%)	1950 (%)
Unemployed chief wage earner	28.6	0
Inadequate wages of earners in regular employment	32.8	1.0
Inadequate earnings of other workers	9.5	0
Old age	14.7	68.1
Death of chief wage earner	7.8	6.4
Sickness	4.1	21.3
Miscellaneous	2.5	3.2

Source: B. Seebohm Rowntree and G. R. Lavers, *Poverty and the Welfare State* (London, 1951), 35.

had been connected. In 1939 one-quarter of households had vacuum cleaners. By 1956, over half had vacuum cleaners, and by the 1960s, over 80 per cent.[28] Similarly, in the mid-1950s, nearly one-fifth of households had washing machines and only 7 per cent had refrigerators: within a decade the respective percentages were over 60 per cent and nearly half.[29] These are only a few examples: consumption of a much larger array of material goods flourished under the impact of 'post-war affluence'.

Table 1.5 Indices of average weekly wage rates of all workers in the United Kingdom, 1938–65

Year	Index	Year	Index	Year	Index
A. 1 September 1939 = 100		B. 30 June 1947 = 100		C. 31 January 1956 = 100	
1938	99	1947	101	1956	105
1939	101	1948	106	1957	110
1940	111	1949	109	1958	114
1941	122	1950	111	1959	117
1942	130	1951	120	1960	120
1943	136	1952	130	1961	125
1944	143	1953	136	1962	130
1945	149	1954	142	1963	134
1946	162	1955	152	1964	141
1947	168	1956	163	1965	147

Source: B. R. Mitchell and H. G. Jones, *Second Abstract of British Historical Statistics* (Cambridge, 1971), 144.

DEPRIVATION AND WELFARE PROVISIONS

High levels of insufficiency were a source of worry to contemporaries. Prior to the Second World War, the work of sociologists and medical inspectors in exposing the extent of impoverishment provides only one explanation for the earnestness with which many middle-class men and women rallied around movements for social reform. The political impetus was also present. The success of the London Dock Strike of 1889, the new militancy of the trade unions and their rapid growth from a membership of three million in 1911 to nearly seven million within ten years, high unemployment, and the spread of socialist associations at grassroots level were interpreted as indications that workers were no longer willing to tolerate persistently high levels of scarcity. A rhetoric, formed out of a loose bundle of ideas labelled 'social imperialism', provided individuals from a range of political persuasions with an ideological rationale for responding to 'the poverty question' in ways which could claim to be radical while being firmly located within a concept of 'national' well-being. Speakers on both the political 'left' and 'right' could press for direct governmental intervention into household economies on the grounds that workers' welfare was crucial to national efficiency upon which both local and imperial power depended.

The other impetus for social reform was the demise of philanthropy, extinguished as much by the allure of more vivid international crises as by the jealous accounting of an entrenching middle class. In 1904,

Joseph Rowntree lamented that it was easier to get money for Indian famine victims than to finance an inquiry into poverty in England.[30] The inefficient, sectarian reputation of many charities had led to considerable disillusionment, causing R. H. S. Crossman of the Workers' Educational Association to recall that 'all disliked the do-good volunteer and wanted to see him replaced by professionals and trained administrators. . . . Philanthropy for us was an odious expression of social oligarchy and churchy bourgeois attitudes.'[31] Although charities were becoming professionalized, the essential problem remained: how to reduce levels of poverty without either destroying the work ethic or discouraging thrift. There was also trepidation that certain 'reforms' would weaken familial obligations. Thus, in the debates over the provision of free meals for school children, a Royal Commission recommended against the meals on the grounds that the 'improved moral and physical state of a large number of future citizens' might be counterbalanced by the 'evils of impaired parental responsibility'.[32] Similarly, *The Times* claimed that a proposal by the London School Board to provide free meals to impoverished school children would 'inevitably tempt a large class of parents to starve or half-starve their boys and girls in order to escape a burden to which they are legally subject and which they are very well able to bear'.[33] Other men, inflamed with a new economistic message, contended that any increase in wages which was not related to worker efficiency would lead to either higher prices or soaring unemployment, both detrimental to working-class well-being. Fabian socialists countered these arguments with measured declarations that low wages caused poverty which in turn depreciated the stock of human capital, increased the burden of poor relief, and allowed inefficient industries to survive. Poverty was expensive. Philip Snowden in *The Living Wage*, published in 1912, argued that Britain paid for the neglect of the poor 'in infantile deaths, in the crippled and diseased bodies of the children who survive, in the inadequate return we get from the expenditure on education, in the creation of unemployables, in sickness and loss of work in consumption and other diseases, in pauperism, in the cost of public and charitable institutions for the support of the sick, the poor, and the insane, and in the incalculable loss of industrial and mental efficiency'.[34] For the Fabians, increased government intervention into the economy was a step in the direction of socialism – and this was not a bad thing.

The position eventually adopted by the Liberal government attempted to soothe the humanitarian itch irritated by socialist dogma while stopping short of satisfying it. Legislation was required to ensure

Table 1.6 Ages of people in England, Wales, and Scotland (age groups as a proportion of total population), 1901–61

Year	England and Wales 0–14	15–64	Over 65
1901	32	63	5
1931	24	69	7
1951	22	67	11
1961	23	65	12
Year	Scotland 0–14	15–64	Over 65
1901	33	62	5
1931	27	66	7
1951	25	65	10
1961	26	64	11

Source: Census.

that the poor received their share of the common wealth.[35] 'Reforms' were instigated on an *ad hoc* basis united only by their common purpose in being transfer payments to the poor as a right of citizenship and without forcing absolute destitution on the recipient. Edwardian welfarism was broad in scope: in some aspects, building on earlier reforms; in other aspects, providing new and radical forms of assistance. Labour exchanges, the Trade Boards of 1909, and the introduction of unemployment and sickness insurance in 1911 will be examined later, but the most important 'new' provision in this period was undoubtedly the introduction of old age pensions in 1908.

By the Old Age Pensions Act, single people over the age of 70 years were entitled to a pension of five shillings a week so long as their annual income did not exceed £21. Married couples were entitled to a pension of 7s 6d. People on an annual income of between £21 and £31 10s could be eligible for a pension of between 1s and 4s a week, calculated on a sliding scale. Aside from its importance in reducing the threat of destitution amongst the half-million people granted a pension in the first year, old age pensions gave the elderly a bargaining ploy, vital in a society where one in every four adults were directly helping to support an old age pensioner.[36] In the poorest households, it could be a significant bonus; in the words of one rhyme:

When the affairs of house or land
Go clean against her will,
She boasts: 'I have me Pension
And I'm independent still.'[37]

Table 1.7 Income of the elderly in Sheffield (proportions drawing their income from various sources), 1953

Source of income	Proportions (%)
Pension only, with or without national assistance	46
Pension, plus income from private sources or savings	19
Pension, plus income from current earnings	18
Current earnings only	6
Private sources or savings only	4
Other sources	7
Total number of individuals	303

Source: E. R. Bransby and Barbara Osbourne, 'A Social and Food Survey of the Elderly', *British Journal of Nutrition*, 7 (1953), 165.

According to one study, as late as 1953, the sole income of nearly half of elderly people was their pension.

The most significant area which Liberal welfare legislation built upon was related to structures of employment for wage-earning men and women: in particular, hours of employment. In the 1860s, the average length of the working week was between sixty and sixty-four hours. Between 1860 and 1878, the Ten-Hour Act was gradually extended to most branches of manufacturing. In terms of legislation, little else changed until 1902 when an amended Factory Act restricted hours of work for certain categories of workers, but still excluded men in sweated trades, retail, transportation, and agriculture.[38] By the end of the First World War, however, the average length of the working week had been cut from sixty or so hours in the 1860s to around forty-eight hours. In certain industries, this decline was dramatic; some men accustomed to working fifty-three hours a week just prior to the war, worked only forty-four hours a week in the 1920s.[39] In the 1920s and 1930s, hours of employment declined further, helped by the international movement towards the eight-hour day, trade union agitation, legislative directives in 1934 and 1937, and the economic turbulence of the inter-war years.[40] Although these figures take no account of overtime, the reduction in the number of hours working men spent on the job was significant. As I have already indicated, there were, however, significant differences across jobs. Thus, between 1924 and 1928, the average weekly working hours of manual workers in public utility services declined from forty-eight to forty-one while the hours of manual workers in food, drink, and tobacco industries actually increased by two hours a week.[41] These increases have to be viewed in the context of the spread of holidays with pay. By the end of the nineteenth century, Saturday was gradually becoming freed from the tether of waged labour. By the 1920s, one million manual workers had negotiated agreements with their employers providing for holidays with pay. Although some of these agreements were torn up during the slump, by 1939 four million manual workers were entitled to a paid holiday. Overall, manual workers experienced dramatic declines in the number of hours during which they were at work. Excluding holidays, for many workers this decline 'freed' an additional ten hours which they could invest in extra-employment activities.

Children also received special attention from public and private welfare agencies. Although subsidized municipal milk dispensaries had been introduced in 1899 and child labour had been restricted by legislation in 1903, the emphasis on children was intensified after 1906 when a number of investigations exposed the level of deprivation amongst the young. Of the 1,000 children examined in Bradford in 1906, only 3 per cent could be proclaimed 'clean' and over 70 per cent were decidedly 'dirty'. In Kent, 15 per cent of school children were verminous. In Ipswich, 26 per cent of girls examined in the schools were similarly infected. A doctor in Norwich announced that it was impossible to convince parents that head lice were not the natural inhabitants of the scalp.[42] Oral hygiene was neglected. In Flintshire, 68 per cent of both boys and girls in urban areas suffered from four or more decayed teeth – in rural areas, 66 per cent of girls and an outstanding 80 per cent of boys suffered from four or more decayed teeth. Free school meals (from 1906) and general improvements in nutrition were influential in improving the resistance of working-class children to infection and accelerating recovery rates from common childhood diseases such as diarrhoea and measles. Nevertheless, differentials by class remained. In a study carried out on 17 December 1910 by Dr F. E. Larkins, the Assistant Medical Officer of Health for Warwickshire, the average weight of children aged 13 or 14 was nearly 100 pounds if the child was born to parents earning over 25s a week and 71 pounds if born to parents earning between 12s and 14s a week. Eighty per cent of children living in the poorest households had their 'general condition' described as 'poor' compared with only 4 per cent of children living in the wealthiest households. In fact, no children born to households earning less than 20s a week could be described as being in 'very good' health while over half of the wealthier children fitted this category.[43] The School Medical Service was established in 1907, ambitiously aiming to eliminate the 'three Ds': disease, defects, and dirtiness. The Children's Charter of 1908 tackled parental abuse and the mistreatment of juvenile offenders. Notification of birth, adopted in some municipal areas as early as 1907, was made compulsory in 1915. Local authorities began employing Health Visitors in large numbers to police mothers and babies and, by 1914, they were employing 600 Health Visitors and had established 650 municipal and voluntary maternity and child welfare centres. By the end of the war, twice the number of welfare centres and over 2,500 Visitors were engaged in the struggle against poverty. By the late 1930s, there were over 3,600 child welfare centres in existence, 1,800 ante-natal clinics, and 6,000 Health Visitors.[44]

Chronology 1.1 Chronology of Acts regarding housing, 1885–1965

1885   Royal Commission on the Housing of the Working Classes exposed the state of housing

1890   Housing of Working Classes Act tackled the problem of insanitary houses and allowed councils to build houses from local rates

1903   Ebenezer Howard founded the company to develop the first 'garden city' at Letchworth

1909   Housing and Town Planning Act enabled urban local authorities to extend municipal boundaries for the purpose of housing

1915   Rent and Mortgage Interest (War Restrictions) Act introduced rent controls

1919   Housing and Town Planning (Addison's) Act provided grants to local authorities to spend on building houses. Any cost above one-penny rate was borne by the government

1920   Housing (Scotland) Act enabled councils to take over private properties for working-class housing

1922–3   Government withdrew from the housing market, on grounds of economy

1923   Housing (Chamberlain's) Act provided lump sum payments to private builders from councils

1924   Housing (Wheatley's) Act increased state subsidies on rented houses

1930   Housing (Greenwood's) Act provided for slum clearances

1933   Housing Act provided for more slum clearances

1935   Housing (Hilton Young's) Act obliged local authorities to act upon Overcrowding Surveys

1938   Rent Act removed some rent controls

1946   New Towns Act set up development corporations to build new towns

1947   Town and Country Planning Act compelled county councils to plan development and gave them powers of compulsory purchase

1951   Housing subsidies raised

1957   Rent Act abolished rent control (reintroduced in 1965)

The period from the 1910s to the Second World War saw an acceleration of welfare reforms, most importantly in connection with housing and unemployment insurance. The shift into council housing was initially prompted by the 1919 Addison Act which provided housing grants to local authorities. By promising to bear any costs above a one-penny rate in the building of houses, some 30,000 local authority houses were built in Greater London alone between 1919 and 1922.[45]

In this period, council housing concentrated on building suburban estates of good quality cottage houses. The houses were built for families (most had three or four bedrooms) and they possessed both front and back gardens.[46] After 1921, council housing was supplemented by the growth of private building projects. The number of new houses soared from an annual average of 150,000 in the 1920s to 200,000 in the early 1930s. In 1936, the number of newly built houses peaked at 350,000 and remained in excess of 300,000 until the outbreak of the Second World War.[47] Between council housing and the investment of private builders, four million dwellings were built in the inter-war years: one-quarter replacing slums.[48] At the same time, a marked shift towards owner-occupied residences can be detected. While in the middle of the nineteenth century, less than 5 per cent of working-class families owned their homes, by 1939, nearly 20 per cent could claim ownership.[49] In the entire population, the proportion of families owning the house they were living in increased from 10 per cent in 1914, to nearly half by 1966.[50] The significance of these shifts will be seen in Chapter 3.

By the 1930s, welfare provision was becoming increasingly focused on providing for the unemployed. In Chapter 4, we will be examining inter-war unemployment in more detail. It is sufficient to note here that, in these years, soaring levels of unemployment threw between 15 and 30 per cent of the population of Great Britain below the poverty line.[51] The shock of such high levels of unemployment destroyed optimism about the ability of the state to regulate the economy to benefit a large number of its members. The 'land fit for heroes' was a cruel joke. As one unemployed man pointed out to a Chief Relieving Officer in the late 1920s: 'I was fighting for the likes of such fuckers as you in the trenches when I was fifteen, while you sat behind a desk.'[52] While working-class men attacked the world with muscle and sweat, 'pen-pushers' sat behind desks and failed even to show gratitude.

The 'pen-pushers' did acknowledge that immediate governmental intervention was needed to remedy the inadequacy of existing

Table 1.8 Number of houses built by local authorities and private owners, in England, Wales, and Scotland (1,000s), 1919–64

Year	England and Wales		Scotland	
	Local authority	*Private owners*	*Local authority*	*Private owners*
1919–23	168.8	—	21.7	—
1924–28	298.7	637.7	48.6	27.9
1929–33	298.0	755.8	58.8	31.7
1934–38	345.4	1,324.6	83.1	36.4
1939–43	72.7	181.8	40.1	11.1
1944–49	423.3	128.0	62.1	4.8
1950–54	849.1	228.6	144.3	9.2
1955–59	652.7	623.0	134.0	19.9
1960–64	517.9	878.1	110.1	36.7

Source: Calculated from B. R. Mitchell and H. G. Jones, *Second Abstract of British Historical Statistics* (Cambridge, 1971), 117–18.

Note: Years 1944–49 are not comparable with earlier years since after 1944–45 enumeration changed to calendar years.

Table 1.9 'Owner-occupied' houses: proportion of working-class families in York who owned their home or were buying the house they occupied, 1950

Category	Owned their house (%)	Buying their house (%)
A	0.4	0.8
B	2.5	1.6
C	14.4	12.0
D	13.9	16.0
E	68.8	69.6
Number	4,005	1,125

Key:
A. Earning under 77s a week
B. Earning 77s–100s a week
C. Earning 100s–123s a week
D. Earning 123s–146s a week
E. Earning 146s or over a week

Source: B. Seebohm Rowntree and G. R. Lavers, *Poverty and the Welfare State* (London, 1951), 84.

provisions. Poor relief still harked back to the 1834 Poor Law Act (or, in Scotland, to the Poor Law Act of 1845). Not surprisingly, unemployment was most severe in areas least prepared. Since poor relief was organized on a regional basis, relief in Scotland (for example) was the responsibility of the local kirk and voluntary organization: councils were not even required to levy poor rates or build workhouses. By contrast, the workhouse played a dominant role in the relief of the unemployed in England and Wales. Before the severe crisis of the inter-war years, powerful local pressure groups had done their best to ensure that Boards of Guardians kept rates low by discouraging applications for aid. Although there was considerable protest about conditions within workhouses – particularly as exposed by the 1909 Royal Commission – the Liberal government in 1911 seemed content simply to tighten up procedures by making the performance of task-work compulsory.[53] It was this requirement which caused the most resentment in the 1920s and 1930s.

Chronology 1.2 Chronology of Acts regarding social welfare and factories, 1891–1919

1891	Factory and Workshops (Consolidation) Act extended safety and sanitary regulations and set the minimum working age in factories at 11 years
1901	Factory and Workshops Act increased minimum age to 12 years
1901	Trade Boards Act established Boards to fix minimum wages in some sweated industries
1906	School Meals Act permitted local Authorities to provide school meals (it became compulsory in 1914)
1907	School medical inspections became compulsory, and the school medical service was established
1908	Children's Charter established juvenile courts, probation services, and intervened increasingly in the lives of children
1908	Coalmines (Eight Hour) Act decreed an eight-hour day for underground workers
1908	Old age pensions introduced
1909	Old age pensions came into effect
1909	Unemployment Exchange Act established exchanges to help unemployed men and women find work
1909	Trade Boards Act set minimum wages in certain sweated industries
1911	National Insurance Act provided against sickness and unemployment
1911	Shops Act introduced the legal weekly half-day holiday
1918	Ministry of Health established
1918	Trade Boards Act extended to all low-paid trades
1919	Old age pensions raised to 10s per week

The Liberals did, however, introduce one major piece of legislation, the 1911 National Insurance Act. This Act provided insurance for some workers from sickness. Thus, workers would pay a contribution to an approved society, friendly society, or trade union, in exchange for which they could call on the services of a doctor appointed to the local 'panel'. Unemployment was also safeguarded. By this Act, some 2.5 million workers (chiefly in building, mechanical, engineering, and shipbuilding trades) were enlisted in a contributory system of relief through insurance. Workers and employers were obliged to contribute 2½d each, to which the Treasury added 1⅔d for each insured person. Although this fund was used to pay benefits to insured workers who were unemployed, help was limited: beneficiaries could not be on strike, their redundancy could not be due to dismissal or their own voluntary action, benefits could be drawn for no more than fifteen weeks, and the amount drawn had to be proportionate to the contributions paid by the insured worker. In 1911, this meant one week's benefit to five weeks' contribution. In effect it meant that the benefit – 7s a week – was well below that paid by the strictest Board of Guardians. Being insufficient for maintenance, it was intended to be supplemented by savings and trade union benefits.[54]

Under pressure of war and the downturn in the economy, the 1911 Insurance Act was modified. In 1916, provisions were extended to munition workers. More significantly, in November 1918, an Out Of Work Donation was instigated. This was a non-contributory benefit paid to unemployed ex-servicemen and unemployed civilians who had been employed for at least three months during the war. It entitled former servicemen to twenty-six weeks' donation in their first year after demobilization and it entitled civilians to thirteen weeks' donation between December 1918 and May 1919. The generosity of the scale, and its non-contributory nature, set a precedent which was to have ramifications during the inter-war depression.[55] As a response to escalating unemployment, insurance was extended to include all manual workers and all non-manual workers receiving less than £250 annually. Workers in agriculture, domestic service and certain groups of permanent employees were outside its provisions. By the 1920s, unemployed, insured men were allowed to claim 15s, women could claim 12s, and juveniles under the age of 18 years could claim half benefits. The maximum period an unemployed person could claim assistance remained at fifteen weeks a year. Benefits stood at 40 per cent of average wage in 1924, compared with 60 per cent in 1938. Although the relationship between benefits and earnings was improving, it was still insufficient to keep people above Rowntree's poverty line. The means test excluded many people from receiving any benefits. More to the point, the disparity in the standard of living for employed and unemployed people was growing. Between the 1920s and the 1930s, while benefits were being cut by 10 per cent and while more unemployed people were being refused any benefit, the standard of living of those in employment actually improved by about 16 per cent.[56]

Unemployment benefits always had conditions attached to them, and these conditions became progressively narrow. The requirement that an unemployed person had to prove that she or he was 'genuinely seeking work' caused the most resentment. Initially, it had been assumed that this condition would apply only to married women. However, between March 1921 and March 1930, nearly three million claims were refused on these grounds and, in some areas, one in three requests for help were refused.[57] It made no difference that the work they were supposed to be genuinely seeking did not exist. The 'anomalies' legislation of 1931 abolished this requirement for everyone except married women. In addition, by this legislation, married women had either to have made fifteen weekly contributions since their marriage and eight over the preceding six months, or to be able to demonstrate not only that they were seeking work but that they had a reasonable chance of acquiring a position. In the following two years, more than three hundred married women a day (200,000 in total) had their unemployment claims disallowed.[58]

In 1930, as the crisis worsened in response to the collapse of many European banks, further cuts were made in unemployment benefits: contributions to the Insurance Scheme were increased, the level of support was reduced by 10 per cent, the period for which a person could receive help was limited to twenty-six weeks, and a Family Means Test was imposed, recalling memories of the most punitive aspects of the old poor law. In 1935, E. Wight Bakke described it: 'The filling out of forms, the recurrent knocking of the investigator at one's door, the knowledge that all eyes in the street are on the investigator, the close association with the methods of the [poor law] . . . the experience of having the public eye on one's private affairs, all of these are symbols of one's new status.'[59] The means test signified the entry into the 'less eligible and less secure class'.[60] Its most odious feature was the way it was seen to break up families. By decreeing that unemployed people living in their parental homes would not be entitled to a benefit if anyone in the household earned 31s or more a week, the unemployed had to choose between becoming dependent on parents or leaving home. Homelessness suddenly developed into a serious problem. The means test also offended the sensibilities of 'respectable' working-class families proud of their independent family-based life. Interfering inspectors were anathema to this culture. An unemployed millwright from Derby rehearsed his resentment: 'Perhaps

I miss the cigarettes most, and I hate being chained to the home most. There is no substitute for work. After the monotony I hate most the visits of the Public Assistance Officer. He is very strict and gets to know everything about us. My wife is bad all day when he comes.[61]

The means test was not the only insulting requirement. From 1934, anyone claiming insurance benefit risked being required to attend a training camp. These camps had been restricted to young men under the age of 18, but, after the Unemployment Insurance Act of 1934, all unemployed beneficiaries of relief were at risk and, between 1929 and 1938, 190,000 men were consigned to camp.[62] These camps became the symbol of governmental callousness; as one youth argued: 'How anyone could expect an unemployed man to do physical jerks on 15s a week, or play ping-pong, while his wife was sitting at home before a half-empty grate with only margarine to eat.'[63] The second half of the Unemployment Insurance Act was just as repressive. Non-insurance benefits were placed in the hands of the Unemployed Insurance Board, benefits were reduced, and means testing became more restrictive. It was at this stage that the famous Jarrow Crusade occurred. Following in the footsteps of other – many much larger – 'hunger marches', the Jarrow march of 5 October 1936 attracted attention because of the scale of the unemployment problem in this town and because, unlike other marches, the Jarrow march could not be dismissed as a 'Communist demonstration'. Eighty per cent of men in Jarrow were unemployed. In a population of 35,000, some 23,000 claimed relief. The marchers carried 80,500 signatures in two petitions to parliament, asking the House to 'realise the urgent need that work should be provided without delay'.[64]

Chronology 1.3 Chronology of Acts regarding social welfare and factories, 1925–37

1925	Widows Pension Act provided contributory pensions for widows, orphans, and the elderly
1926	Old age pensions made contributory and qualifying age reduced
1929	Board of Guardians abolished
1930	Poor Law renamed National Assistance
1930	Mental Treatment Act made voluntary treatment possible for mental illness
1931	Means testing for unemployment benefits
1934	Provision made for subsidized or free milk at schools
1937	Factory Act regulated hours and conditions of employment for young persons

Although by the Second World War the economy was improving, optimism was short-lived. By the end of the war, Britain was again seen to be in trouble. Even more than the 1914 war, this war was a 'people's war', fought by conscripted civilians, and drawing attention to the dependency of the state on those who controlled the resources needed to win a total war. As a soldier in the 50th Division leaving for France addressed Ernest Bevin, the Minister for Labour: 'Ernie, when we have done this job for you, are we going back to the dole?'[65] The war (it was hoped) would lead to internal as well as international peace and good-will. In the words of an anxiously optimistic gunner: 'During the Blitz, men and women forgot the divisions and the snobberies of pre-war days, and worked together against a common danger. They told themselves, too, that this new companionship would not only continue during the peace, but would be extended to bind the human family in a fraternal compact.'[66] Disillusionment was rapid. Even during the war, there was little real coming together of the classes. As the social investigators, E. Slater and M. Woodside, summarized the attitudes of their working-class respondents: 'Both sexes were dominated by the distinction that is expressed in "We" and "They", and, even in this war in which all were involved together, by the feeling of a cleft between the two nations.'[67] The evacuation of children and mothers from the large cities did much to remind people of each other's differences. Men and women who had adopted the idea of narrowing class divisions in an attempt to sustain optimism during the worst days of the war and bolster spirits in times of rationing, deprivation, and hard work were the most disillusioned. Even more than in 1914, this war had not altered perceptions of inequality in the areas of health, employment, education, or general life style.[68]

Despite acknowledging that class distinctions had not diminished during the war, many people found comfort in dogmatically asserting that, given the scale of sacrifice, the world simply *had* to be better. In the words of J. B. Priestley, the war was being fought 'not so that we can go back to anything. There's nothing that really worked that we can go back to', but in the expectation of 'new and better homes, real homes, a decent chance at last – new life'.[69] Or, in the words of Peter Baker, a gunner during the war:

> During the war we lived on hope and on faith. We hoped for better days and had faith that they would come. The old world, we saw, had perished in the fire of the war, and the new world would rise phoenix-like from the ashes. The days of poverty, unemployment, and malnutrition, the queues of the Labour Exchange and the loungers on the street corner, the squalor of the slums and the misery of the depressed areas; all these, and the jerry-builders, the

petty entrepreneurs and the slick smart-alecs of Grub Street who thrive on the society that spawns them, were gone for ever from the earth.[70]

Disillusionment with old-style Edwardian liberalism was widespread: poverty was still in evidence and the potency of liberal social theory, with its emphasis on the equal freedom of all individuals, was weakened. Existing welfare services were regarded not only as inadequate, but also as retaining the odious traits of the past: charity, less eligibility, minimum standards, and a clumsy bureaucracy. There was widespread agreement that access to public services had to be widened: the question was only how this was going to be achieved.

In 1942, William Beveridge had released his famous Report, proposing the co-ordination of employment, education, health, and housing policy, and switching from a principle of selectivity to universality. Although it excited debate both within the Houses of Parliament and in the press, no legislation was brought forward until the late 1940s when a 'free' National Health Service was created, offering patients local medical care in addition to access to hospital and specialist services. At the same time, a comprehensive social insurance scheme was adopted. Under this scheme, everyone paid regular contributions into a fund, in return for which they became entitled to benefits in the event of unemployment, ill-health, pregnancy, and widowhood. Separate legislation introduced family allowances.

Chronology 1.4 Chronology of Acts regarding social welfare and factories, 1942–65

1942	Beveridge Report published
1945	Family Allowances Act provided 5s per week for every child after the first
1946	National Insurance Act provided benefits for sickness, unemployment, and retirement
1946	National Health Service Act provided free medical treatment
1946	National Insurance (Industrial Injury) Act provided injury and death benefits
1948	National Assistance Act abolished old Poor Law and provided benefits for people not covered by other schemes
1948	Children's Act appointed officers to protect children in care
1961	Graduated pensions introduced
1961	Factory Act consolidated safety regulations in industrial premises
1963	Offices, Shops and Railway Premises Act consolidated regulations for safety in commercial premises
1965	Redundancy Payments Act provided graduated redundancy payments according to length of service

The provision of welfare by the state was not accepted without much scepticism, criticism, and strife. As we have already seen, increased bureaucratic intervention into private and familial lives was resented: the knocking on the door of insurance agents, the endless filling out of forms, long waiting lists, delocalized social insurance, and the exclusion of wives and children from some health care peeved many working-class commentators. The low level of health and sickness benefits meant that many people still had to depend on the hated Public Assistance Committees for supplementary aid. As 'Mrs B', worker in a wholesale food distributors, remarked, 'everyone distrusts social welfare', believing that welfare officers were informers paid by the management to 'pry into' their private lives. When her firm arranged for mass radiography, hardly any of the employees consented to be examined: 'They were afraid if anything was found wrong with them they'd get their cards.'[71] Similarly, factory workers in the Potteries were opposed to the proposed provision of public creches on the grounds that it would 'take the bread out of the old peoples' mouths'.[72] The greatest opposition to the Beveridge reforms, however, came from wealthier people than these.[73] The secure middle classes expressed their views on how the government was investing their taxes. Opposition grew out of resentment about the alleged erosion of differentials between salaried workers and wage-earners. The new or reorganized welfare services were regarded by some as a profligate exercise which helped those who had already benefited from a redistribution of income in the 1940s. The *Economist* in January 1948 pointed out that the total amount paid out in wages had grown by 60 per cent during the war, yet the real purchasing power of the average salary had fallen by between 20 and 30 per cent. They concluded that 'At least ten per cent of the national consuming power has been forcefully transferred from the middle classes and the rich to the wage-earners.'[74] Social welfare schemes such as the National Health Service were said to disadvantage the middle classes and encourage exploitation of the schemes by healthy workers (including some 'foreigners') demanding spectacles, false teeth, and wigs.

The impact of these provisions was dramatic. The difference that the National Health Service made to the quality of life as experienced by the weak in body, the poor-sighted, the deaf, and the elderly is testified to by a generation of people. In 1951, R. Seebohm Rowntree and G. R. Lavers calculated the effect of welfare legislation for the poor by estimating how working-class individuals and families would have fared if their gain from welfare legislation had been at 1936 rather than

Table 1.10 The effect on families of welfare measures: percentage of working-class population in each class, comparing 1936 with 1950

Category	Actual situation in 1950	Situation in 1950 if welfare measures had been set at 1936 level
A	0.41	6.62
B	4.23	18.11
C	19.40	14.32
D	17.38	13.32
E	58.58	47.63

Key:
A. Earning under 77s a week
B. Earning 77s–100s a week
C. Earning 100s–123s a week
D. Earning 123s–146s a week
E. Earning 146s or over a week

Source: B. Seebohm Rowntree and G. R. Lavers, *Poverty and the Welfare State* (London, 1951), 37–9.

1951 levels. They calculated the value of food subsidies, family allowances, school milk, cheap milk for infants, and free school meals, added the difference between retirement or widows' pensions in 1936 and 1950, and subtracted the individual's weekly contribution under the National Insurance Act and the corresponding contribution in 1936. Their estimates must be regarded as lower-bound estimates since many of the benefits of the welfare provisions (such as housing) could not be calculated.

As table 1.10 shows, if welfare levels had been set at 1936 levels, the proportion of working-class families in the most desperately poor section of the working class (Categories A and B) would have increased dramatically. They added that three pieces of welfare legislation were crucial: family allowances, unemployment benefits, and housing. If it was not for the introduction of family allowances in 1945, the percentage of working-class families living in poverty would have been 6 per cent rather than 4 per cent. The removal of family allowances would throw nearly one-fifth of all families with two or more children into poverty. Similarly, if unemployment and unemployment benefits in 1950 had been at 1936 levels, nearly half of the population would be living in poverty. Housing subsidies enabled many working-class families to afford houses that their parents would scarcely have dreamt of.[75]

These declining levels of absolute poverty, which were profoundly affected by the extension of welfare provisions and declining unemployment since the 1950s, coupled with the related flourishing consumerism of working-class households in the 1950s, have resulted in some speculation about the 'embourgeoisement' of the working class. Thus, Carolyn Steedman spoke about the ambitions of her working-class mother in the 1950s: 'From a traditional Labour background, my mother rejected the politics of solidarity and communality, always voted Conservative, for the left could not embody her desire for things to be *really* fair; for a full skirt that took 20 yards of cloth, for a half-timbered cottage in the country, for the prince who did not come.'[76] The spread of consumption goods amongst the working class was made to bear its share of responsibility for the demise of the post-war Labour government and for an alleged 'deterioration' of 'working-class culture'. The sovereignty of the consumer was being swamped by what Denis Potter called 'admass' created by the 'pseudo-scientists of the new society' (that is, advertisers).[77] The dominant theorist in this debate was Richard Hoggart who argued that 'authentic' working-class culture was dying, corrupted by mass society.[78] As we saw at the beginning of this chapter, however, people continued to think of themselves and others in conventional 'class' terms. There can be no other criteria of authenticity. Furthermore, mass consumption was compatible with what has been termed 'working-class culture'. Distinctive modes of dress, language, and leisure may have retreated under the onslaught of materialism but there was still a mighty gap between bourgeois and working-class ideas about society and social relations. Welfare entitlements did revolutionize working-class lives, exposing their families to inspection in exchange for providing a buffer against absolute destitution, but the threat of poverty was disabled with a minimum demoralization of pre-existing systems of power.

CONCLUSION

Despite seventy years of radical economic change within Great Britain, and despite vast improvements in overall working-class well-being, 'class' identification remained a chief metaphor for defining oneself and other people. Crucial to this continuity was the power of historical construction. Men and women calling themselves 'working-class' were drawing upon an identity based not only on their current position within society, but also on a position inherited from their parents and grandparents. This book will be examining this historical construction of 'class' as it developed out of experience rooted in the intimate locale of the body, the home, and the neighbourhood.

SELECTIVE BIBLIOGRAPHY

Hopkins, Eric, *The Rise and Decline of the English Working Classes 1918-1990: A Social History* (London, 1991).
A chronological study which argues that the working class benefited politically and materially from the changes in Britain between 1918 and the 1970s. After this date, working-class political and industrial authority declined.

Jones, Gareth Stedman, *Languages of Class: Studies in English Working-Class History 1832-1982* (Cambridge, 1983).
Influential analysis of the relationship between culture and politics, placed within a theoretical framework. Should be read in conjunction with E. P. Thompson, *The Making of the English Working Class* (New York, 1966).

Stevenson, John, *British Society 1914-45* (Harmondsworth, 1984).
General social history of mainland Britain, including chapters on the two wars, the economy, population, employment and unemployment, health, housing, childhood, education, social policy, religion, crime, leisure, and 'culture'.

Thane, Pat, *Foundation of the Welfare State* (London, 1982).
Historical summary of changes in social policy between 1870 and 1945, including nineteen short documents and a useful assessment of the relationship between social legislation and declining poverty.

Treble, James H., *Urban Poverty in Britain, 1830-1914* (London, 1979).
Looks at poverty in British cities by focusing on causes of poverty (such as low pay and underemployment), public and private responses to poverty, and the effect of poverty on diet and housing.

Winter, Jay (ed.), *The Working Class in Modern British History: Essays in Honour of Henry Pelling* (Cambridge, 1983).
Divided into two sections: the outlook, organization, and politics of the labour movement, and the 'culture' of the working class. The latter half examines the working class in relation to hobbies, financial management, 'respectability', socialist education, the welfare state, images of class, and infant mortality. The introduction to the book draws the themes together.

2 Body
Making love and war

> Meet a body, greet a body,
> Crossing Peckham Rye;
> Meet a body, kiss a body,
> Need a body cry?[1]

Love is unexpected: blushing Laura in the story 'He Meant Business' (1911) stammered incoherently when Harry knelt in front of her, proposing marriage. Harry was prepared for her unnerved response: 'I have brought along a bottle of my unrivalled nerve anodyne. This preparation . . . will alloy any undue excitement, quiet the nerves, aid digestion, and restore lost appetite. . . . Take it, dearest.'[2] We must assume that Laura married her doting druggist and lived happily ever after. In the same year, the Women's Co-Operative Guild published a report dealing with the attitudes of working-class women to marriage and divorce. While castigating menfolk for their sexual promiscuity, all the respondents accepted that the marriage of a man and a woman relied on 'love'.[3] The romanticism of Laura and the Women's Co-Operative Guild were expressions of an ideal which many people never experienced. In a survey forty years later, barely two-fifths of respondents earning less than £12 a week claimed to have experienced 'love' at some time in their lives: slightly more than half of respondents earning over £12 a week could make the same claim. In other words, in 1950, three-fifths of working-class respondents had never (either before or after marriage) felt what they called 'love'.[4]

They had certainly been involved with 'something' which might be superficially reminiscent of 'love' and, in some commentators' views, they engaged in this 'something' much too eagerly. These commentators portrayed their generation as heralding in the 'permissive society': sexual prohibitions were violated, familial bonds repudiated. The twentieth century was represented as a time swamped by a tide of moral uncertainties which muddied the relationship between the individual and the group, the body and the family. On all sides, dangerous trends were identified. Declining church attendance was regarded with dismay, for where else were people to learn moral and religious ethics? Their alarm was vindicated in the blossoming of promiscuity amongst the unmarried. Even the sex reformer, Marie Stopes, refused to provide sexual advice to unmarried people for fear that wantonness would wreak great personal and social disorder. The spectre of concupiscence had been raised within the marital bed as well. 'The family' was portrayed as disintegrating under the strain of the sex 'obsession': delayed marriages and thwarted childbearing instincts rendered 'a throwback on the sex interest, divorced from family responsibilities', inevitable.[5] The declining birth rate threatened the 'survival of the white race'.[6] Birth control, abortion, and infidelity, not to mention the craving for sexual gratification with one's spouse, threatened familial mores. This disintegration of the family from within was typified by the lack of respect of spouses for each other and of children for their parents. People married with full knowledge of the procedures for divorcing. Children despised their elders. In the words of the Howard Association in 1898, 'The tendencies of modern life incline more and more to ignore, or disparage social distinctions, which formerly did much to encourage respect for others and habits of obedience and discipline . . . the manners of children are deteriorating . . . the child of today is coarser, more vulgar, less refined than his parents were.'[7] From within and from without, 'the family' was thought to have little chance of surviving the next generation. 'Victorian' morality found fewer and fewer defenders. Although evidence of moral decline could be witnessed throughout the century, many believed that there was major subsidence in the 1920s and 1950s.[8] Historians have noted that, in the 'careless twenties', the 'new free woman' displayed 'shameless abandon'.[9] The historian Stephen Humphries wrote that in the 1950s, 'the old era of Victorian condemnation of sex before marriage seemed to be coming to an end. The old taboos lost much of their former power. For the next quarter of a century more liberal attitudes towards young people and the sex life they chose for themselves were in the ascendant.' Summarizing the views of writers at the time, Humphries detected a feeling that their period was the 'dawn of a new era of sexual freedom'.[10]

Who, or what, was responsible? Some blamed the disruptions of two world wars: 'under the upheaval of the world upheaval, men and women departed from the old standards of sexual morality and began to exercise their elemental urge without the sanction of a priest or registrar'.[11] In the face of the horror and deprivations of war, people felt justified in grabbing as much pleasure as possible – including sexual pleasure.[12] The welfare state came in for criticism for the role it played in the disintegration of 'family' and 'morality'. In 1951, H. Mainwaring Holt wrote:

> The family is the repository of the qualities of our race, its countenance has been dimmed by the encroaching miasma of the welfare state. More and more is being done for the family by the State, children are brought into the world by the State, educated by the State in a manner which the State thinks best, their medical care is provided by the State, they will be employed by the State, the State will provide for their old age. Thus the initiative has shifted from the individual to the State.[13]

Others blamed the cinema for feeding the 'sex interest' and allowing it to 'run riot in an undisciplined way': while an indulgent cinema persisted, the stability of the family was 'in great peril'.[14] Although the future looked grim to these commentators, it is the purpose of this chapter to question their prognosis. Was promiscuity on the increase? This chapter reflects on the working-class body, observing the discarding of outdated 'forbidden fruit' and the fabrication of new sexual proscriptions. Despite world wars, the radical implications of birth control, widening access to divorce, and the advent of welfare state capitalism, rather than becoming redundant, the working-class family became irresistible.

PREMARITAL PROMISCUITY

The extent to which working-class people engaged in sexual intercourse prior to reciting the marital vows is impossible to calculate. The three sources an historian has available are: *ad hoc* evidence from working-class autobiographies and letters, sexual surveys, and the level of illegitimate births. All these sources are seriously flawed. Autobiographies are notoriously tricky to interpret.[15] People lie – especially about what they do with their bodies. Cohort-based studies have to cope with differing attitudes towards premarital sex by age. Levels of illegitimacy are affected both by the types of sexual activities favoured by a particular cohort and by information and access to birth control. What do these types of evidence, however, tell us? Eustace Chesser's cohort-based study indicated that premarital sex increased throughout the twentieth century. In his study, 19 per cent of married women born before 1904 engaged in premarital sex. For those

Table 2.1 Percentage of working-class couples claiming premarital sexual experience, 1946

Did you have any premarital sex?	Husband	Wife
None	36.5	51.5
None, but admitted by spouse	5.0	10.0
With others, not spouse	24.5	2.5
With spouse only	16.5	18.0
With spouse and others	12.0	4.0
No information	5.5	14.0
Total (numbers)	200	200

Source: E. Slater and M. Woodside, *Patterns of Marriage* (London, 1951), 288.

born between 1904 and 1914, the proportion was 36 per cent. It was 39 per cent for people born between 1914 and 1924, and for those born in the decade after 1924, 43 per cent. Although premarital sexual activity was a minority activity amongst all social groups, his survey indicated that young people from poorer households were much less liable to engage in it than those from wealthier households.[16] As late as 1946, a study of working-class couples showed that half of all wives and over a third of all husbands claimed to be virgins upon marriage (see table 2.1).

These data are sensitive to the sex of the respondent. Husbands were more liable than wives to admit to having had sex with their spouse prior to marriage. Many more were honest enough to admit that they had only been deterred by fear of consequences or lack of opportunity.[17] Even in the 1960s, young people (especially young women) remained wary of premarital sex. One survey in 1961 found that 81 per cent of sixth-form girls thought that premarital sex was always or usually wrong, compared with 56 per cent of sixth-form boys.[18] In this same year, the psychiatrist Dr Elizabeth Tylden read a paper entitled 'Teenage Attitudes to the Marriage Relationship' at a Family Planning Association conference. According to her research, young girls wanted to 'go out, have a good time, and get engaged' while boys only wanted to 'go out and have a good time'. For girls, marriage presented the only way to get a job which provided both status and 'a degree of freedom at present unknown to her'.[19] Irrespective of the fact that premarital sex was more likely to occur as the twentieth century progressed, attitudes towards premarital sex amongst the working population remained negative. 'Loose' women were liable to be ridiculed by local boys and publicly taunted as 'village bicycles', 'secondhand dartboards', and 'lavatory doors in a gale'.[20] The typical

Table 2.2 Illegitimacy ratios and rates in England and Wales, 1891–1970

Year (average)	Illegitimacy ratios (%)	Illegitimacy rates per 1,000 unmarried, widowed, divorced women aged 15–45 years
1891–95	4.2	10.1
1896–1900	4.1	9.2
1901–05	3.9	8.4
1906–10	4.0	8.1
1911–15	4.3	7.9
1916–20	5.4	8.4
1921–25	4.3	6.7
1926–30	4.5	6.0
1931–35	4.3	5.5
1936–40	4.2	5.6
1941–45	6.8	11.4
1946–50	5.5	11.7
1951–55	4.7	10.1
1956–60	5.0	12.8
1961–65	6.9	19.1
1966–70	8.3	22.0

Source: Peter Laslett, 'Introduction', in Peter Laslett, Karla Oosterveen and Richard M. Smith (eds), *Bastardy and Its Comparative History* (London, 1980), 17.

attitude was encapsulated in the words of a daughter of an unemployed miner when she said, 'A white wedding was the reward of a girl who had kept herself to herself and hadn't let anyone interfere with her. It was an incentive for virginity, for to the prudish but practical unemployed, a girl who "got caught" had not only squandered her only treasure but had depreciated her market value.' As married women reminded her, 'What man is going to buy a cow if he can get his milk for nothing?'[21]

The real offence, however, seemed not to be premarital sex as such (so long as the woman did not make herself 'cheap' and so long as the man did not show signs of remaining a 'rover' all his life) but the carelessness of being 'caught out' by pregnancy. From the 1870s to the First World War, illegitimacy rates had been steadily dropping. Although the war saw a temporary reverse of this trend, immediately after the war, the decline continued. However, by the 1940s, illegitimacy rates had increased, peaking in the middle of this decade when nearly 7 per cent of all births were born to unmarried women, then dropping again. The levels of illegitimacy recorded in the mid-1940s were not surpassed until the 1960s.

In addition, although the death rates of illegitimate babies remained high throughout the century, they moved closer to the rates of legitimate children. Thus, in 1918, out of every 1,000 legitimate births, 91 died prior to their first birthday, compared with 186 of illegitimate births. By 1949 the relative numbers dying before their first birthday were 32 for legitimate and 45 for illegitimate births.[22] These figures suggest that the problems of illegitimate children had more to do with the difficulties of raising a child singlehanded than with prenatal conditions.

For both sexual conservatives and sexual radicals, the relationship between premarital sex and illegitimacy was linked with debates about the efficacy of sexual knowledge. Both sides acknowledged that, far from information about sex permeating every nook and cranny, sexual ignorance persisted throughout the century. In 1929, one woman commented, 'I married knowing practically nothing of what married life would be – no one ever talked to me and told me things I ought to have known – and I had a rude awakening.'[23] Babies were thought to be made when 'a boy does a dribble in a pot and you do a dribble too'.[24] Kissing with an open mouth might cause impregnation.[25] Babies could be bought from jars in chemists.[26] Or found inside cakes, in cabbage patches, embedded in bellybuttons, or in midwives' bags.[27] Grace Foakes remembered her first pregnancy: 'I myself was never told anything about babies and when my first child was about to be born I was most shocked to find out how she would arrive. I had imagined my tummy would open to let the baby out.'[28] Although rural children might have watched animals copulating, they were not necessarily more knowledgeable about human sexuality than urban children[29] Even sleeping in the same room as adults did not guarantee any sexual knowledge. Catherine Cookson, an illegitimate child living in the Tyne Docks, slept in the same room as her grandparents: 'I would sit up and cry, "leave her be, Granda!" This would be after hearing me grandma whispering harshly, "Leave me alone, will you?" Yet I know now I wasn't actually aware of the reason for her protest, I only knew that he was "bothering her".'[30] Knowledge of differences in the genitals of males and females was equally enigmatic. In the words of one Scottish woman: 'I never was sure *exactly* what men had or hadn't until I met my first lover. . . . Nor can I say I was thrilled when eventually I *did* find out.'[31] As late as the 1960s, one-third of working-class girls were not given any information about the 'facts of life' until they had passed their fourteenth birthday. Only 8 per cent of girls from professional homes had to wait so long.[32] Michael Schofield's enquiry in 1965 into the sexual behaviour of 1,873 young people found that two-thirds of the boys and one-quarter of the girls had never received any advice about sex from their parents. Over half of the boys and 14 per cent of the girls had also not received any instruction at school.[33] A similar study a year earlier reported that only half of the 1,514 postnatal and expectant mothers interviewed had received sex education during childhood or adolescence.[34]

Although sexual knowledge was patchy, commentators could not agree whether this was good or bad. The crucial issue was power. Which would be more powerful: would the fear induced by ignorance restrain dangerous sexual impulses, or would the assurance prompted by accurate information induce people to act 'sensibly'? According to the first view, the problem of sex was a problem of the will. Although not the prerogative of religious thought, this view is best summarized in the words of a Joint Pastoral Letter in 1944. According to this report, sex education was doomed to fail

> since the evils concerned are the effect not so much of ignorance as of a weakness of will unsupported by the means of grace. Information alone will not produce a healthy and sound nation; much less will it be sufficient to prepare souls for their eternal destiny in the next time. It is not so much information as *formation* which is required – formation of character, the training of the mind, the heart, and the will with the necessary assistance of religion.[35]

Equally central to this view was the belief that the female sexual impulse was as potent as the male impulse. If a child was told that she could get pregnant by holding hands with a boy, she would be less liable to find herself in a position where she could become sexually excited. One girl remembered her sexual education:

> Milly, the one girl I did play with at school more than anyone, had already started [menstruating] at thirteen. She said it was something to do with having babies, and when you started 'monthly' you didn't play with boys anymore. It was dangerous. Her mother had strictly forbidden her to play with boys, without saying why. But Milly knew that if a boy kissed you when you had 'monthly' you would have a baby. This was absolutely dreadful, and the whole business frightened me beyond words.[36]

A girl's power over the licentiousness of 'adult' men lay in her ignorance and fear. Equally, a young man's ignorance would keep him away from the licentiousness of females. Male–female relationships were intrinsically antagonistic. Thus, in the 1910s, the adolescent Edith Hall was in love with the boy next door: 'Although everyone else thought Harry Hardman was a horror, I wished that I had been a boy so that I could have been a real friend to him and when I told him so, he said, "Never mind, we'll get married some day and that will be the next best thing."[37] Boys and girls could never be 'just friends'.

According to the second view, knowledge provided power. It was the view that sexual attraction was inevitable – occurring on a spiritual and aesthetic level irrespective of the excitations of touch. What was important, therefore, was providing 'rational' individuals with accurate information to alert them to the consequences of each and every action. Denying people access to sexual knowledge exacted heavy social and psychological penalties. Illegitimacy, abortion, and disease were the consequences of ignorance. In the words of Dr Van de Velde in the popular *Ideal Marriage*, 'Sex is the foundation of marriage' yet the fact that 'most married people do not know the ABC of Sex' resulted in an array of physical and psychological disorders.[38] The sexual ignorance of married people on marriage was frequently blamed for the lack of interest in sex. In the 1940s, 'Mrs H.', aged 25 years, remembered the first two disastrous years of her marriage:

When I married I didn't want to marry him, but he threatened he'd die of a broken heart, so I thought I'd better. I was more interested in joining the W.A.A.F. at that time. For two years I was desperately unhappy. It was a great mistake. I hated sex relations. Mother had told me nothing, and I was too shy to ask my mother-in-law. Anything I knew I learned in the crudest way. I was just cold. I had no feeling for him. I didn't care a hang about him.[39]

According to sex reformers, such responses to sexual intercourse could have been avoided.

Accurate sexual information was difficult to acquire. Responsibility was thought to rest properly with parents. Some parents performed this duty with aplomb. An East End girl, Elizabeth Ring, remembered a school friend in the 1920s telling her how her mother had 'admitted that sex was lovely' and explained it to her with the words: 'You know how you feel when you're talking about it? Well, it's like that, only better!'[40] The father of 'John V.' was a laundry proprietor and amateur boxer. He was domineering and 'fond of a drink', but was also 'broadminded', speaking to his children about sex and sexual practices, including homosexuality.[41] Other parents were unable to provide correct information. One adolescent in the 1930s recalled that she never received any sex education: 'The whole subject was absolutely taboo, but some mothers had already told their daughters that they would be having an "inconvenience" once a month, commonly called "monthly", without actually explaining why.'[42] Work friends were often informative.[43] For some girls, the information received from school and work friends was more helpful than advice from parents. Angela Rodaway lived in a North London working-class family. It took her months before she got up the courage to tell her mother that she had started menstruating. While school friends had given her all the practical advice she needed, her mother simply informed her that she must not eat ice-cream, swim, wash in cold water, or take a bath during menstruation, destroying Rodaway's confidence in maternal wisdom.[44]

The cinema was often mentioned as a sexual educator, perhaps justifying middle-class concerns about the relationship between the cinema and promiscuity. As one commentator announced, the cinema was calculated to draw crowds and unsettle moral certainties: 'Torrid Tunes! Glamorous Girls! Smashing Bands! – to quote a recent Metropolitan bill – all in exotic settings with money to burn, do not prepare the adolescent for the quiet tempo of what used to be called "getting married and settling down".' Instead, they 'add to restlessness and suggest a false standard of life which leaves little place for children, and promote a standard of values which rates "glamour", "Romance" (with a capital R) and instability generally far above the marital stability postulated by a family necessary to give children the right start in life'.[45] These commentators could have been right. A 21-year-old shorthand typist confessed, 'Films I think have made me more receptive to love making, sometimes I feel like kissing a stranger, but have never done this.'[46] An 18-year-old bank clerk noticed that films had increased her awareness of fashion and had made her 'despise the boys of about my age. . . . After seeing the polished lover on the screen it is rather disillusioning to be kissed by a clumsy inexperienced boy.'[47] Another young clerk agreed: 'Films definitely have made me more receptive to love-making and they have made me regard love-making as more of a technique than as an outcome of emotions.'[48] Despite the fact that many claimed to have received their sex education in the cinema, they were not fooled by the rituals of falling in love as depicted in the movies. Three-quarters of Geoffrey Gorer's sample were unconvinced by the cinematic depiction of love as progressing from 'love at first sight' to wooing to marriage.[49]

Books were almost as educative as the cinema. Nearly one-third of 14-year-old school girls in 1940 read 'erotic bloods'.[50] Others pieced the facts of life together through contemplative scrutiny of the Bible.[51] Unearthing medical books from obscure corners and high shelves was a favoured pastime: 'Whenever we were left alone in the house [my cousin] would climb up and secure the [medical] book, and together we would continue our education. At the same time, she would extract a volume of Foxe's *Book of Martyrs*. Childbirth and martyrdom were synonymous. We suffered the torments of the damned.[52] The East End son of a cabinet-maker, Sam Clarke, was forever grateful to Marie Stopes: 'The book was a bombshell.'[53] Similarly, Gladys Teal recalled how a draper's assistant in Yorkshire during the 1930s prepared for marriage by purchasing Stopes' book: 'I was glad that I was able to read it. I was never able to discuss sex with my mother or sister, the word was frowned upon.'[54] The book these people were reading was *Married Love*, probably the most influential sex manual in the twentieth century. In the first fortnight after it was published in 1918, it sold over 2,000 copies. By the end of 1923, sales amounted to over 400,000 copies. It continued to sell: by the 1950s, it had gone through numerous reprints and twenty-eight editions. Marie Stopes's vast correspondence attests to the demand for sexual information which people could not – or would not – get from their own doctors.[55]

Schools proved more reluctant to intervene directly in the sex education of children under their care. In 1918, the Department of Education report on *Natural Science in Education* mentioned that 'some knowledge of the main facts of the life of plants and animals should form a regular part of the teaching in every secondary school'.[56] In the Hadow Report of 1936 (which dealt with courses for children up to age 15), it was argued that instruction in elementary physiology and hygiene was 'especially important and should develop out of the biology lessons' in all schools. In their words, instruction in these subjects, 'if properly carried out, might well provide the basis for a right attitude on many social problems'.[57] Officially, sex education was not forthcoming in schools until after the Second World War. The Education Act of 1944 opened the way by declaring that it was the duty of Local Education Authorities to 'contribute towards the spiritual, moral, mental, and physical development of the community'. This was in line with public demand: the Wartime Survey in 1945 disclosed that there was substantial popular demand for more sex education in schools on the grounds that it would improve public morality.[58] These post-war educational debates were, however, characterized by anxiety about rapidly changing sexual ethics. The Crowther Report in 1959 expressed this apprehension, asking whether it was in fact possible for schools to establish a code of sexual ethics. Irrespective of the fluidity of ethics, the report concluded that teachers and youth leaders had a responsibility to 'bring to attention the personal bewilderment and disaster to which this public indecision over moral issues often leads the young'. By the 1960s a more forceful attitude was adopted regarding sex education in schools. The 1963 Newsam Report stipulated that boys and girls should receive guidance from their teachers on sexual morals. Four years later, the Plowden Report confessed that they had 'no doubt' that children's questions about sex should be answered 'plainly and truthfully'. Although they agreed that parents were the proper people to answer sexual questions, they recognized that many parents found it embarrassing and recommended that 'every school must make the arrangements that seem best to it and should have a definite policy, which, in consultation with the parents, covers all the children. It is not good enough to leave matters vague and open, hoping for the best.'[59]

This tortuous progression of widening access to sexual information was an expression of the trepidation felt about the risks involved in speaking openly about sex. Two threats – closely intertwined – were particularly potent: first, anxiety about the relationship between promiscuity and prostitution and, second, the fear of venereal disease. What would the effect of open sexual discussions in schools have on the 'prostitution problem'? Although criminal statistics showed a steady decline in the level of prostitution in England and Wales (between 1900 and 1904, nearly 11,000 women in England and Wales were arrested every year for soliciting compared with just over 3,000 by the late 1920s), contemporaries were not fooled, arguing that the statistics masked the rise of the 'amateur'. Wartime conditions had exacerbated the situation, as Brigadier-General Crozier explained in *A Brass Hat in No-Man's Land*: 'It is a fact that prostitutes and loose women always follow the big drum. The more big drums there are the more prostitutes abound.'[60] George Ryley Scott, in a book laying out the sexual dangers of war, was more blunt:

> It all began easily and simply enough. The girl, in the throes of sexual ecstasy for some passing 'hero', or as a means of securing a good time, gave herself to soldier or civilian as the case may be. Her companions were embarking upon these flirtations, and she saw no reason why she should not do the same. She probably dignified her erotic adventure by some such name as 'free-love', but it amounted to what, in all except name, was an act of prostitution. The barriers, once let down, there were repetitions of the initial act.

Scott had harsh words to say to the parents of these 'fallen' girls. Parents who allowed their girls to 'hie' to London and other large cities were culpable. The most irresponsible were fathers who ought to know 'their sex and breed'.[61]

This panic that working-class girls were sinking into 'amateur' prostitution through lack of understanding of the consequences of their actions, was not only a middle-class concern. Working-class girls were increasingly aware of their worsening situation as the hymen came to dominate discourses. The Contagious Diseases Acts of the 1860s and the subsequent 'tightening up' of the policing of working-class women both by the state and by middle-class reformers left a legacy of repression which lasted well into the twentieth century. The sexual mores of the prostitute and the rest of the working class never again coincided, and the prostitute herself was effectively isolated.[62]

It was in this context of the increased privatization of prostitution that women attempted to circumvent the alienation and isolation of their job through the establishment of 'monogamous' relationships with one man. Thus, 'Dollie' (a prostitute in Victoria, London, in 1955) had no associates who were not prostitutes. She 'said it was a lonely life for many of the girls and that's why they took ponces'. Women who were in the job for a shorter time often maintained their former associates: 'Christie', a prostitute in Hyde Park and East London, maintained good relations with her mother who looked after her child. In the inter-war years, Sidney Rogers married Irene, a woman he had got pregnant. He deserted them and was ordered by the courts to pay 17s 3d a week in maintenance. Later, he discovered that his wife had become a prostitute, and when he found her on the streets, he accosted her demanding to know what she was doing with their child. She explained that her mother was looking after the child, adding, 'Look, Sid, if it's the seventeen [shillings] and three [pence] you're worrying about, I don't want no more money off you. I can earn five pounds easy in a day. My friend has her own car and we take clients to her house.'[63] Others sought social mobility through prostitution, using the job to save money to buy a tobacconist shop, or simply to live at a higher standard of living than would otherwise have been possible. Prostitution gave working-class women a degree of independence of action lacking in the lives of many other women. In the words of 'Kathleen', a prostitute in Soho in the 1950s, 'I've a sort of pride in being independent.'[64] 'Mrs H.', separated from her husband 'because he could not earn enough to keep her in comfort', took up prostitution. Her husband 'would like her to return to him and is willing to overlook her present mode of life but she says that she prefers her freedom. . . . She sees nothing wrong in her way of life and maintains that she does good to her customers. She says, "I'm better than a Harley Street specialist for them, and I cost less."'[65] The Soho prostitute 'Margaret' never earned more than £3 a week before she went on the game.[66] As another prostitute reasoned: the financial benefits of selling the body made it preferable to working in a factory for fifty hours a week for a measly thirty shillings.[67] According to the police, in 1951, a prostitute would seldom earn less than £20 a day.[68] Low-grade, unskilled, monotonous employment was the chief alternative to prostitution. By contrast, prostitution was exciting, and could be sexually gratifying: when asked why they liked being on the game, 'Olive' replied, 'excitement and the thrill of being a "bad woman" '; 'Sadie' showed no sign of either remorse or 'frigidity', claiming that she 'enjoyed all aspects of prostitution'; 'Gwyneth' also declared that she 'thoroughly enjoys' the job; and 'Ada' was 'led by excitement and newness and money'. These women claimed that they 'applied themselves regularly'.[69]

Like other jobs, prostitution had its fair share of boredom and bullying. More important, the threat of venereal disease was sufficient to put off workers and customers alike. Ferdynand Zweig interviewed an unmarried maintenance engineer in the 1940s who, by working night shifts, earned a net wage of £5 2s. In his opinion, sex was 'over-rated' and he had avoided women for the past three years: 'He once met a doctor in a hospital for venereal disease who told him about [venereal disease], and this gave him a fright. After all, he says, you are a man and can surely control your sex.'[70] Such fears reached the level of a moral panic during and immediately after both world wars. As the *English Review* in May 1916 declared, the 'flapper on the streets' had become the 'flapper syphilitic' who went about 'infecting the soldiers by the dozen'.[71] At a time when the treatment for gonorrhoea was painful and syphilis was incurable, the Royal Commission on Venereal Diseases in 1916 reported that 10 per cent of men and 5 per cent of women had contracted syphilis and many more had gonorrhoea.[72]

However, the spread of venereal disease could no longer be blamed on prostitutes. Doctors recoiled in horror from the 'bare-faced manner' with which young women of 16 or 17 would approach them, calmly declaring, 'My boy has given me the clap.'[73] As the Medical Officer of Health in Portsmouth noted in 1921, 60 per cent of cases of venereal disease were the result of sexual intercourse with women who were not paid. In his words, 'I have been told that a whole lot of girls, on patriotic grounds, and probably with the thought that the men would come back to them, gave themselves free to the men.'[74] In 1917, Thomas Barlow had similar worries:

> Not only professional prostitutes have dogged the steps of soldiers in the public promenades, but the crowds of young, apparently respectable women, who likewise haunt the neighbourhood of the

Table 2.3 Number of cases of venereal disease dealt with for the first time at the treatment centres of England and Wales (annual rate: three-year averages), 1918–41

Annual average	Syphilis	Gonorrhoea
1918–20	37,284	32,139
1921–23	27,474	30,939
1924–26	22,383	33,262
1927–29	22,725	41,480
1930–32	22,756	42,904
1933–35	20,517	42,650
1936–38	18,609	42,597
1939–41	16,664	33,644

Source: Adapted from Sydney M. Laird, *Venereal Disease in Britain* (Harmondsworth, 1943), 71.

camps, have in a very large number of cases been the subjects of gonorrhoea, and having received this infection from soldiers, have passed it on to other soldiers. Indeed, clandestine or amateur prostitutes, as they are styled, have been one of the most painful and baffling factors of this problem.[75]

This venereal crisis was tackled by the Royal Commission on Venereal Diseases, whose report was described by one commentator as 'one of the most alarming, appalling and pathetic documents ever printed in the English Language'. It alarmed readers by exposing a 'race . . . threatened with grave danger'; it appalled them by revealing a 'mass of suffering which is largely preventable'; and it was pathetic because 'millions of innocent children, women and men are included in the multitude of victims of mankind's lower nature, ignorance, and irrational superstition'.[76] The Commission estimated that between one-third and one half of all cases of female sterility could be linked to gonorrhoea. Of registered stillbirths, at least half were due to syphilis. More worrying, the problem could not simply be laid at the door of the war. The Commission publicized data showing that one-quarter of the 1,100 blind children in London County Council schools prior to the war were blind as a result of gonorrhoea. For another third, syphilis was to blame. Naval statistics for 1912 showed that, for an average strength of 119,540 men, a total number of 269,210 days were lost as a result of venereal disease; in the army at home, with a strength of 107,582 men, there was a loss of 216,445 days due to venereal-stricken men.[77] They estimated that the treatment of lunacy caused by syphilis involved an annual expenditure in England and Wales of

£150,000.[78] The staggering emotional cost could not be ignored. In the words of one woman, 'I know myself of a case where a woman has suffered untold agonies through the disease given to her by an unfaithful husband. Her children also suffer from a skin disease, and are puny and sickly looking, and yet he has never struck her. Outwardly, he is apparently all that a man should be.'[79] This was no imaginary calamity: its effects brought misery to working-class lives throughout the century.

Unlike the educational debates concerning the 'facts of life', venereal disease was agreed to be a worthy – though embarrassing – topic of instruction. Silence had resulted in widespread ignorance. It was still believed by many people that a person could be cured of venereal disease by having sex with a virgin.[80] A doctor discussing the rape of virgins during the Second World War noted that most of these attacks had been carried out 'neither by a sadist nor as a means of satisfying sex hunger'. Rather, many were attempts by men to get rid of a venereal infection: 'It is a well-known fact,' he continued, 'that the venereally-afflicted individual, man or woman, has no conscience.'[81] Ignorance – whether naive or vicious – came to the attention of the Ministry of Health which decided (in 1942) to act. Press statements, radio broadcasts, parliamentary debates, a national conference, and a massive publicity campaign in newspapers and on public billboards were all part of their attempt to break the 'taboo' on public discussion of venereal diseases. In 1944, the Wartime Social Survey interviewed 2,587 people aged 14 to 60 years. When asked whether they knew what venereal disease was, one-quarter either replied 'no' or were uncertain. Poorer people, and those with fewer educational qualifications, were most liable to express uncertainty. While one-sixth of people with an education higher than elementary school or earning an income of over £5 were uncertain or ignorant about venereal disease, nearly one-third of people with only an elementary school education or earning an income of less than £5 were uncertain or ignorant.[82] The Survey concluded, however, that such levels of ignorance still represented a major improvement on earlier years. It was not until the AIDS crisis from the 1970s that a similar amount of concern was expressed about the prevailing ignorance of people concerning sexually transmitted diseases.

THE BODY AND POWER

The body was not, however, only a site of desire and disease: it was also an aesthetic object. The working-class body looked different from the middle-class body: it was leaner, shorter, and less healthy. In 1910, working-class children aged between 13 and 14 years who lived with fathers earning between 20s and 25s a week weighed more than thirteen pounds more than children living with fathers earning between 12s and 14s a week.[83] Forty years later, the differential had scarcely been reduced.[84] Working-class boys were less liable to be circumcised.[85] Working-class women were more liable to stem their menstrual flow with homemade sanitary napkins.[86]

In addition, what they did with their bodies was distinctive. From the turn of the century, but peaking between the wars, a series of related debates were under way concerning the aesthetics of the male body. These class-based debates can be represented in the campaigns organized by the Men's Dress Reform Party (an organization gathering support amongst professional middle-class men) and the League of Health and Strength (a lower middle-class and working-class organization). The Men's Dress Reform Party developed out of a response to the eugenics movement and the contemporary feminist movement. It encouraged men to create the ideal masculine body by imitating women's successes in freeing themselves from stuffy conventional clothing. Representative of its beliefs was the statement by J. C. Flugel, a professor of psychology at University College London, who argued that the past 100 years had been characterized by a 'remarkable repression of Narcissism among men'. According to him, modern men's clothing allowed few outlets for personal vanity: 'to be dressed "correctly" or in "good taste" is the utmost that a modern man can hope for; all originality or beauty in clothing (to say nothing of the even more direct gratification of Narcissism in actual bodily exposure) being reserved for women'.[87]

While adoration of the male body meant, for male professionals, fighting to reduce the number of constraints concerning states of dress and undress, for working-class men there was a surge of support for the revival of discipline over the body. The League of Health and Strength was established in 1906 as part of that flurry of concern about the poor state of the national body: 'Our German, French, Russian, Italian, and Turkish visitors easily demonstrated that our athletes were far behind foreign standards' declared one writer in their *Annual*.[88] In 1910, this *Annual* was circulated to 90,000 boys a week.[89] From a membership of 13,000 in 1911, by the First World War membership had doubled. In 1930, 86,000 young men belonged; five years later, 124,000.[90] The League declared itself to be 'catholic, impartial and independent', open to all who shared their aim: 'health and right living'. The cardinal principle was the 'sacredness of the body'. Members of this 'robust brotherhood' had to be over the age of 14, and capable of paying an enrolment fee of 1s 6d.[91] Although no further subscription was required, members had to pledge themselves to forward the cause of physical culture, to take 'judicious exercise' daily, to encourage fitness in others, to extend the 'right hand of friendship' to other members, to adhere to the principle of temperance and chastity, and to discourage juvenile smoking 'and all other evil habits'.[92] Although the motto on badges was 'Sacred thy Body even as thy Soul', members were reminded of a better motto which might help them 'order their lives': that motto was 'Brotherhood'.[93] For them, the body was to be 'built', or 'finely-tuned', to adhere to aesthetic as well as labour demands. The key words were maintenance and surveillance. Thus, in one seafaring family in the first decade of the twentieth century, the brother of a working-class autobiographer struggled to overcome his skinniness: 'At night he took off his shirt and washed in a bucket of cold water in the back yard. He had a loose page of print torn from an old copy of the *Boys' Own Paper*, which showed an expressionless gentleman with a pointed moustache illustrating boxing stances. Georgie propped it upon the scullery window sill and circled round the yard, pumping his skinny white arms and snorting fiercely down his nose.'[94] Like many other working-class boys, he idolized men such as 'Uncle Bob' whose booklets instructed boys in physical culture using language both highly romantic and deliberately archaic. A typical booklet (*How To Increase Your Height*) declared:

> Is it not the tall man who captures the very girl on whom the short man absolutely doted? The prospect of a win for 'five-ft-in-his-stockinged-feet' [*sic*] was favourable enough until a Knight of 'Commanding Presence' completely cut him out of the running. . . . To hang around and watch a taller rival make love to 'his' girl would be unpleasant. To seek forgetfulness in a watery grave would be ridiculous. Far wiser is he who, tormented by lack of inches, sets to with vigour and vim to gain height, when his luck in love as in every other sphere of life, will be enhanced considerably![95]

Indeed, if the cover to this booklet is to be believed, a boy earnestly observing the recommended exercises could gain a foot in height. 'Uncle Bob' and his imitators also produced booklets entitled *How To Gain Five Inches Chest Expansion*, *How To Develop Powerful Arms*, and *Muscles of the Body and How To Develop Them*. The message was clear: to be 'A Man', a person had to look 'manly' and this meant subjecting the body to the will.[96]

The stress on masculine chastity did not dilute the League's strongly erotic aspects. The working-class daughter of Conservative Party caretakers described a typical 'Physical Leaguer' who regularly visited the shop where she worked: he was 'a tall well made young male called Bob, I privately christened him Tarzan, he brought the weekly *Health and Strength* magazine and we became good friends, he was taking a practical agriculture course at a nearby farm'.[97] Homo-eroticism was more customary. In 1935, the Health and Strength Leaguers' *Guide* published a story describing the League's motto. At the beginning of the story, a young man lay in the darksome vale 'languid, feeble, suffering, yet content; content with the contentment of the brute creation, content with the contentment of despair. The vapours from a foetid swamp had lulled him into lethargy unrestful, unwholesome, and unholy.' Suddenly, beside him stood a man 'so beautiful, so strong, so noble'. The two men went on a pilgrimage together up the 'mountain of endeavour'. When they arrived at the 'City of the Strong', the young man suddenly recognized his companion: 'he had found the Spirit of the Perfect Man – for he had found himself'.[98] As the last stanza of the Leaguers' song expressed it:

> Sing the Body Beautiful as God Who made it planned;
> Sing the Body Supple, quick to move at His command;
> Sing the Body Strong to help a comrade heart and hand;
> Fill all the Earth with your singing![99]

This renewed emphasis on working-class masculinity and strength developed out of a number of shifts in male culture in the inter-war years. As we will be examining in Chapter 4, the link between masculinity and working-class employment was strong. When employment was fairly secure – as it was between the 1870s and the First World War – the masculinity of an individual could be based on waged labour. After 1920, this had become a fragile basis for masculinity. Not only were many working-class men increasingly at risk of having no job, but many sons of labouring men found themselves seated at desks performing equally menial – yet not so obviously 'manly' – jobs. Working-class men faced other threats to their masculinity in these years. No longer could they claim exclusive rights to the dignities of statesmanship: in 1918 some of their womenfolk received the vote alongside them, and by 1928 all other women joined. As one tramp argued:

> Well, just you remember as I fought in the bleedin' war. You lot might be bleedin' tramps, but I ain't, see? Fought for bloody king

and soddin' country. Land fit for bloody heroes they promised us what lived like rats in the soddin' trenches and here I am living like a stinking rat with no piggin' work and no bleedin' chance of any. Call this a bloody fair country? Bleedin' dictatorship's more like it! It's this shaggin' government, I tell you, and that sod Lady bloody Astor, a bleedin' woman MP. Women may be alright in bed but they're no bloody use any other bleedin' place.[100]

Feminism jeopardized conventional power relationships within working-class families.

In addition, these years saw the beginnings of what was to become a distinctive male 'youth culture'. While boys in 1900 had reached full height at 23 years, by the late 1950s boys reached full height at 17 years.[101] The masculine culture represented by organizations such as the League of Health and Strength drew on specifically 'young' forms of deviance. The other side of this culture expressed itself as juvenile delinquency. From the 1890s, there was a sharp rise in the number of males under the age of 19 prosecuted in the courts. One study of Oxford brings this into focus. In the 1870s and 1880s around thirty offences committed by young males came before the courts annually. By the turn of the century, however, this had soared to nearly 100 cases a year.[102] In the same period, the number of offences committed by adult males declined. Juveniles were committing certain types of crimes more frequently: theft and breaking and entering were on the rise as were non-indictable offences such as gambling, malicious mischief and trespass, loitering and dangerous play. The crucial point is not that adolescent boys were becoming more lawless, but that the authorities were becoming more willing to prosecute wayward working-class boys. The National Society for the Prevention of Cruelty to Children, Watch and Ward Committees, and a host of other organizations dedicated to the 'protection' of the young made sure that 'justice' was not meted out by the policeman's stick in the street, but in front of the judicial bench.

This rise of 'juvenile delinquency' was not new to the twentieth century: juvenile crime had a long history in which poor children featured strongly. What distinguished twentieth-century forms of delinquency from earlier variants was the blurring of the distinction between 'respectable' and 'unrespectable' adolescents. The problem of delinquency remained a dilemma of working-class youth: Cyril Burt's study of delinquency in London in the 1920s found that 56 per cent of delinquents came from households which never could claim more than irregular earnings or from households dependent on small wages (one-third of the general population in London came from such homes).[103] However, these were not only children of the unemployed, the starving, the rough – parents from the 'respectable' working class were also watching their adolescents rejecting 'respectable' values. Delinquency came to be associated with the stage of life and the term 'adolescent' came into popular usage.

The seeds for the 'generation gap' – a creation of the years after the Second World War – were planted in these years. By the 1960s, Michael Schofield could say without fear of contradiction that: 'There are clear signs of alienation between the young people of today and the adult generations.'[104] People began wondering what had 'gone wrong'. Some interpreted delinquency in the context of housing estates. Young people were bored. One Edinburgh offender complained that the new estate was an 'awful place; there was nothing to look at, not even a traffic light!', to which Winifred Elkin commented that while middle-class observers might deplore the extent to which young people played in the streets, 'a crowded street . . . provides a playground full of bustle and interest; it can never be dull. The transference from such surroundings to the suburban quietude of a new housing area requires an effort of adaptation that it cannot be easy for a child or a young adolescent to make.'[105] It was recognized that, because of the war, many children had older parents than the previous generation: 'this difference in age between parent and child may account for some difficulties in communication', declared Schofield in 1965.[106] Furthermore, these adolescents had money to spend. Between 1945 and 1950 the average real wage of youth increased at twice the rate of adults.[107] Financial pressures were lifted from the shoulders of both parents and youth. Although the total spending power of unmarried people under the age of 25 years was only 5 per cent of all consumer spending in 1959, this group bought 42 per cent of all records and record players, 37 per cent of all bicycles and motorbikes, and almost one-third of all cosmetics, toilet preparations, cinema admissions, and other entertainments.[108] They could afford the Edwardian suits and dandy accessories of the Teds. The attractiveness of this consumer culture for young people was so great that working-class children who won scholarships were often willing to forgo the advantages of increased educational opportunities to join it: without employment, they would have been unable to gain access to this youth movement. It was not until the late 1960s that Universities and Colleges became a site for a middle-class youth culture which could rival this working-class variety.[109]

PROMISCUITY AND THE MARRIED

There was one anxiety which prevailed over concern about the promiscuity and rebelliousness of the young: that anxiety was concerned with the perceived weakening of the marital tie. Corroboration that 'the family' was coming apart was flagrant. Divorce rates were the most obvious proof. Until the middle of the twentieth century, official divorce rates in Britain were low. In 1890, fewer than 700 divorces were granted. At that stage, in England and Wales, the 1857 law was still in force, decreeing that a man could be granted a divorce on the grounds of his wife's adultery while a wife had to prove adultery in addition to incestuous adultery, bigamy, cruelty, or desertion for two or more years. By the Divorce Act Amendment Act of 1896, the Church of England could not be required to solemnize the remarriage of the guilty partner. In Scotland, since the sixteenth century, both men and women could divorce on the grounds of adultery or desertion. It was, therefore, in England and Wales that pressure mounted for divorce laws to be relaxed. In 1911, when the Women's Co-Operative Guild conducted a survey about the attitudes of working-class women to divorce, they found that working-class women were demanding that women be granted the right to divorce on the same terms as men. Resentment was particularly sharp over the fact that husbands could get a divorce on the grounds of adultery whereas wives did not have similar rights. Divorce should not only be available to the wealthy: indeed, as one working-class woman commented, 'the law if anything should be made easier for the poor than the wealthy, seeing that in the majority of cases they are even unable to have separate bedrooms'. There was widespread belief that divorce proceedings should be cheapened and that mutual consent and serious incompatibility should be grounds for divorce. Working-class women were also opposed to the ruling that guardianship of children would be given to the father in the case where the mother was 'at fault'. Over 90 per cent of respondents thought that guardianship of children should be given to the parent 'most fitting on general grounds' and, for many of these respondents, this guardian should be the mother (unless she was 'irretrievably bad'). According to women in the Women's Co-Operative Guild, divorce reform would raise standards of morality amongst men, thereby having 'good indirect effects on family life'.[110]

Agitation from women's groups and law reform societies, in addition to the need to make some provision for the failure of many 'shotgun' marriages solemnized during the war, were influential in pushing through the legal changes in divorce law in 1923. By legislative

Table 2.4 Number of decrees for dissolution of marriage and divorce, in England, Wales, and Scotland, 1890–1965

	Number of dissolutions or divorces	
Year	England and Wales	Scotland
1890	400	87
1895	478	117
1900	494	144
1905	623	167
1910	581	223
1915	680	242
1920	3,090	776
1925	2,605	451
1930	3,563	469
1935	4,069	498
1940	7,755	780
1945	15,634	2,223
1950	30,870	2,196
1955	26,816	2,073
1960	23,868	1,823
1965	37,785	2,688

Source: B. R. Mitchell and H. G. Jones, *Second Abstract of British Historical Statistics* (Cambridge, 1971), 31–2.

Note: Prior to 1910, statistics for England and Wales refer only to decrees for dissolution. From 1910, includes number of divorces and nullity decrees passed. Scottish figures refer to divorce and nullity decrees.

decree in that year, women were allowed to divorce on the grounds of adultery alone. The Matrimonial Causes Act of 1937 allowed divorce if *either* spouse had committed adultery, deserted for three years, treated the other spouse with cruelty, or resided under care as insane for five years, and if the husband was guilty of rape, sodomy, or bestiality. In Scotland, a Divorce Act in 1938 added five new grounds for divorce: cruelty, sodomy, bestiality, incurable insanity, and presumed death. Not until the Divorce Reform Act of 1969 did the sole ground for divorce become the irreparable break-up of the marriage.

Levels of divorces did not cause much concern until after the 1937 Act when they rapidly escalated from fewer than 6,000 a year to well over 30,000 within a decade. Although Scottish men and women had access to free legal aid since the sixteenth century, in England and Wales, divorce remained the prerogative of the middle and upper classes until the 1940s. The main reason was financial: even uncontested divorces cost between £60 and £80. A person with an income of less than £4 a week with goods and property not exceeding

£100 in value (excluding tools of trade and clothes) could get a divorce for £10. However, the waiting list for a Poor Persons Certificate was so long that a petitioner would have to mark time for a number of years.[111] Solicitors were often reluctant to accept cases from wage-earners. Even more risky was accepting cases from wives. One woman complained that the cost of her divorce almost ruined her:

> I had a small business which I worked entirely myself. I was so crippled for money for two years afterwards that I often went without the necessities of life. Added to this, my late husband returned, and twice I had to go to the expense of taking him to the Police Court for threatening my life. My experience was such as no honest working woman ought to have, and had I not had a firm will, good health, and firm trust in the Divine help, I must have given up in despair.[112]

This woman was lucky in having access to an independent income. Even after the Married Women's Property Act of 1882 (and related Acts between 1865 and 1907) provided that the wife's property would not pass automatically to her husband upon marriage, most working-class women would have found paying for a divorce impossible: as one working woman explained, 'Where the husband is not true to home ties . . . his money finds many other channels, therefore the wife has no chance to save anything for herself. More often she can hardly make ends meet.'[113] Not surprisingly, working-class couples were more liable to have recourse to the Matrimonial Courts which charged 3s 6d for awarding separation and maintenance orders of up to £2 a week for the wife and 10s a week for each child. Remarriage was, however, forbidden and any subsequent amorous activity of the spouse who was awarded the order was grounds for it to be squashed. In 1923, some 13,000 separation and maintenance suits had been commenced. By 1943, 23,000 suits had been commenced.[114] Separation and divorce stakes changed dramatically when the Legal Aid Act was passed in 1949 and again in 1971 when the Divorce Reform Act of 1969 came into effect. Divorce rates spiralled upwards, seemingly confirming widespread fears of the demise of marriage. However, analyses which take divorce rates as an indicator of the decline of the family ignore the susceptibility of separated individuals to establish long-term *de facto* marriages and the readiness with which two-thirds of divorcees remarried.[115] If men and women were emancipated from the family by divorcing, then they eagerly submitted to renewed subjugation. Far from the family disintegrating, it was becoming increasingly crucial: in

Table 2.5 Average age of first marriage in Great Britain, 1901–61

Year	Average age	
	Male	Female
1901	27.2	25.6
1911	27.3	25.6
1921	27.6	25.5
1931	27.4	25.5
1951	26.8	24.6
1961	25.3	23.6

Source: Lawrence Stone, *Road to Divorce* (Oxford, 1990), 443.

1911, just over half of all women aged between 20 and 39 years were married – within forty years, nearly two-thirds were married.

Even couples who remained together came under immense stress. The more insidious menace was related to the intimate body. Squabbles about the degree of pleasure that both men and women were finding in the marital bed represented an almost prurient interest of sociologists and sexologists in the bodies of their contemporaries. However, the concern of sexologists with women's lack of orgasmic pleasure was, perhaps, misplaced. Many working-class women admitted to experiencing intense physical satisfaction from sexual intercourse. E. Slater and M. Woodside's interviews with wives of working-class soldiers are illuminating. These women responded to questions about sexual pleasure with comments such as: 'you've got to be playful sometimes, we're both loving like'; 'I do enjoy it'; 'that side of life is very very lovely'; and 'he need only hold my hand, and I want it'. One-third of these women said they experienced orgasm 'always', one-fifth said 'often or enough', one-quarter said 'infrequently or insufficiently', and only one-tenth had never experienced it. Of those women who claimed to have experienced an orgasm infrequently or never, most were indifferent and unworried by the admission, announcing, 'women never do'; 'should I be worried? – are other women the same?'; and 'it's just as enjoyable without'. Only a few expressed disappointment.[116]

Despite these high levels of satisfaction, the bedroom remained the central battlefield: the relative sexual needs of both partners required constant negotiation and renegotiation. Not only for wives, but for husbands as well, *limiting* the amount of sex demanded by the other partner was a steadfast ambition. Husbands and wives used different strategies. Working-class men often cited the 'hard' nature of their work to justify the draining away of their sexual desire. The attitude of one 39-year-old hospital porter was explained: 'He has no girl friends and feels no need of them. According to him the worker soon becomes less interested in sex, because his work leaves him very little surplus energy. The interest in sex, and especially the higher manifestations of sex, are really a matter for the "leisured" classes.' In his old age, he wanted 'companionship', but he felt no deficiency in his present stage of life.[117] A stoker in the London Gas Works agreed. He had a wife living in Ireland. Although he missed her, he was indifferent about the absence of sex. He explained: 'Sex wouldn't trouble you if you worked in a gas works. In this heat, all your juice is taken away.'[118] The advantage of this strategy was that he could simultaneously assert an absence of either licit or illicit desire while portraying it as a sacrifice he was making for the economic well-being of his wife and family.

A more sensitive issue for men was impotence. According to the two London branches of the Family Planning Association which catered exclusively for men, this was a common problem. Since the symptoms came 'heavily disguised', time had to be invested in encouraging men to relax and talk freely: 'the husband comes in, persuaded that his trouble is organic, and having something to show – a rash, an old deformity, a long foreskin, even glycosuria. If one can listen without looking surprised, and accept what the patient is trying to say, the real problem can be evaluated.'[119] The sympathetic response a man could expect from counsellors at these clinics was not always matched by other professionals. Take the case of a fifteen-stone docker 'of enormous strength' (aged 28) who attended a clinic in Birmingham. The report noted that he was 'a typical mesomorph with an amicable disposition and unquestioning self-confidence'. He had never consulted a doctor before nor would have if his wife's gynaecological problems had not forced it upon him: 'he himself did not think his sexual history was a proper subject for inquiry'. The doctors diligently reported that his puberty started early and street-corner intercourse had begun at the age of 15. Although he 'regretted that his wife had no enthusiasm for intercourse', he refused to acknowledge any responsibility: 'Were you too quick?', 'Dunno', 'How many thrusts?', 'About three or four.' He was sent away with tablets containing amphetamine sulphate, strychnine, arsenic, and yohimbine, a combination described as 'most helpful in bringing a man near to orgasm, though never to succeed'. We are told that the treatment was a success and 'though inarticulate, he was very grateful'.[120]

If male limitation of sexual intercourse focused on the flaccidity of the penis, female limitation stressed the frailties of the maternal body.

The pain of childbirth was frequently invoked: not surprisingly, since as late as 1946 only 3 per cent of wives of manual workers were given pain relief during their first delivery, compared with 65 per cent of the wives of professional or salaried workers.[121] In 1940, a miner's wife instructed a psychiatrist to impress upon her husband that 'instead of being proud of the fact that he's got two children and only twenty-two he ought to be sorry and that he shouldn't have any more for a few years at anyrate. Apart from the fact that he is ruining my health; I've got a job to keep my teeth now and my legs are very painful now with bad veins.' For the sake of the psychiatrist, she added: 'I've no guarantee that his children will be of much use to the country.' Finally, she declared:

> You have diagnosed my husband's trouble as Anxiety Neurosis to me it seems more like a case of excessive sexual indulgence, dishonesty and lies. He's home nearly all day long and if he leaves me alone for a day he thinks it's wonderful but he wants it twice as much the next day, whether I want attention or not.[122]

Another man ('E. G. B.') wrote to Marie Stopes: 'My wife is not passionate in the least and she tells me if I left her altogether she would be better pleased, but then I am the very opposite to her I feel that I need to cohabit with her every week or else I feel nervous and irratable, but after this child is born I feel I will have to leave her alone as we are both frightened that we may have another and I don't know what we would do if there was.'[123] This fear of harming one's spouse through indulging in sexual intercourse was matched by a sadness at hurting one's spouse by abstaining. Thus, a woman called 'E. B.' had five children. She wrote: 'Sometimes I have looked upon having another as a tragedy but my husband is very good and for three years has not had real "pleasure" in order to keep me right.'[124] The rewards for such a husband were not only in heaven.

One way around the delicate negotiations around sexual limitation was changing the centre of focus away from the genitals and towards a generalized notion of 'companionship' or 'children'. In 1946, M. Woodside found that when working-class couples were asked why they married, the reasons given were mainly trivial, concerned with appearance or behaviour. When sex was mentioned, it was in a negative context: 'She wasn't the flirting type', 'She was clean living', or 'He didn't try to muck about like the other chaps'.[125] Attention was refocused on the children of a union. In the 1940s, E. Slater and M. Woodside's study of 400 working-class men and women concluded that children were seen as the purpose of marriage. Some of their respondents said: 'I believe in children; you can't have a happy marriage without'; 'your children fetch happiness into a home'; 'there's not much point in marriage if you don't have a family'; and 'children make a marriage, what would you do and what would you talk about if you didn't have them?' They were a guard against divorce. 'Mrs S.', aged 27 years, was typical. She had pleaded with her husband to have a baby, finally threatening to leave him if he refused. Eventually, he gave way and she had a baby boy. In her words: 'the baby altered him; he stayed with me, and was quite content. It made a man of him.'[126] A childless marriage or small family was a tragedy. In the words of a 60-year-old unskilled woman in the 1940s: 'Unfortunately I've only got one. I say unfortunately because I should have liked more. . . . I don't know why I didn't have more, because we love children, but I expect it was the will of the Lord.'[127] Children provided more than security in old age: they were also a buffer between husbands and wives.

If attention could not be diverted from the body corporeal to the body corporate, other strategies were employed. By the twentieth century, the most effective rhetoric was that of science and modernity, accompanied by a rhetoric of Victorianism. Generational revulsion from the sexual activities of parents could be used effectively: accusations of frigidity could sting a 'modern' wife into her husband's bed. Women, however, had an advantage in these debates. They could employ the language of 'common sense' and the language of 'science' concurrently. The combined moral and scientific lever provided by Marie Stopes was effective. Although the ideology propagated by Stopes weakened the recourse women could have to arguments based on the fear of conception, the stress she placed on the integrity of each individual's body was a bonus. Any attempt by a husband to use his wife's body without her consent constituted rape. Sexology provided women with a useful axiom: men should adapt themselves to women's sexual needs with regards the timing and type of intercourse. However, the authority of the medical profession was employed by women only when it suited. A woman could claim that sex during menstruation was 'animal behaviour' which would result in the birth of a discoloured child.[128] She could employ religious injunctions, as did a friend of Margaret Powell who bragged about being able to spin menstruation out to last a fortnight since her husband was Greek Orthodox.[129] Equally effective, she could turn to scientific authorities, citing (for the benefit of less fastidious husbands) A. A. Philip and H. R. Murray's book, *Knowledge a Young Husband Should Have* (1911) which advised: 'Sexual intercourse during the menstruating period is not to be recommended, except in those cases where it would appear that the wife is in need of it. . . . Should the wife exhibit mental depression or nervous irritability to any marked degree towards the end of menstruation, it would be advisable for the husband to act entirely according to the missals of his wife in this respect.'[130]

By giving equal weighting to both 'folklore' and 'science' in the sexual debates, women were endowed with increased leverage. Thus, in the 1930s, a married friend of Elizabeth Ring attended a marriage advice centre in the East End. She described the occasion in the following words, 'Proper dirty lot they are there – said, "Tell 'im to play with yer nipples and yer privates, with 'is tongue if necessary, then you should enjoy it again."'[131] She wouldn't have any of it. Equally, a miner's wife could have her 'sexual promiscuity' excused by sexologists in 1947. She had been unhappy about her husband's excessive sexual demands: 'He was a miner and was not satisfied unless coition took place at least once a day. When on the night shift he would persuade his wife to go upstairs with him during the day. . . . [She] found it to be degrading.' In the end, she ran away with an Indian pedlar. The sexologists dealing with the case had no difficulty explaining her actions: 'It has long been held that other nations are superior in erotic technique to the British.'[132] The contradictions inherent in using 'traditional' and 'scientific' rationales were easily dealt with. An individual could always claim that *the* body' was not 'her/his body'. People were shy and confused about their own and their loved one's bodies and its functions anyhow. A study of 200 soldiers' wives in 1946 showed that minor gynaecological conditions were taken for granted and chronic conditions endured. The shyness many people felt about submitting their bodies to gynaecological examination meant that professional advice rarely needed to be taken into account.[133] This shyness was even more evident amongst men: as one woman writing for sexual advice curtly told Marie Stopes, 'My husband votes Labour but he is so shy regards getting advice on this matter I thought I would try myself.'[134] Women were more liable to be given advice – and, hence, given the power to choose which advice was most fitting.

This negotiation process was altered by the dissemination of more accurate sexual information, especially about the control of fertility. The complaint of a 36-year-old working-class woman ('A. J. B.') in 1929 that 'I have not had good Child births the last two being Breach Births which nearly cost me my life having hemorage very badly after it and the Matron in the Maternity Home said I must *not* have any more but she never told me how to advoid it and whats the good of telling a person it is more than their lifes worth to have any more

Table 2.6 Percentage of women in different social classes using any form of birth control at some time during their married life, before 1910 and between 1910–19

Date of marriage	Social class		
	I	*II*	*III*
Before 1910	26	18	4
1910–1919	60	39	33

Source: E. Lewis-Faning, *Report on an Enquiry Into Family Limitation* (London, 1949), 10.

without telling them how to advoid it' was becoming less common each year.[135] The respectability of birth control spread. The Population Investigation Committee's marriage survey revealed that the proportion of couples 'entirely disapproving' of contraception declined from 23 per cent amongst couples marrying prior to 1929 to 16 per cent amongst couples marrying in the 1930s, and 13 per cent of couples marrying in the 1940s and 1950s.[136]

Information on birth control was still not easy to come by. Family doctors were often as uncertain as their patients. As late as 1950, the Medical Women's Federation reported that out of the twenty-seven British medical schools, only Edinburgh, Aberdeen, Liverpool, and University College London provided lectures on contraception to medical undergraduates. Furthermore, over half of the 159 Medical Officers of Health interviewed reported that there were no facilities in their county or city for providing advice on family planning. They vindicated this neglect on financial grounds and on the grounds that they feared adverse criticism from resident Catholics.[137] Although information about birth control was largely through word of mouth, from the 1890s there developed a penny-press advertising contraceptive products. Literacy by this stage was so high that most working-class adults would have read about these products. In the 1920s there was a mushrooming of groups established to promote the use of birth control. Three prominent examples in the 1920s are Stopes's Society for Constructive Birth Control and Racial Progress, the Workers' Birth Control Group, and the National Birth Control Association. Also, women's organizations, such as the Women's Co-Operative Guild in 1923, the National Union for Equal Citizenship in 1925, the Women's National Liberal Association in 1927, and the National Council of Women in 1929, came out in support of birth control. Of course, the establishment of birth control clinics in working-class areas did not guarantee access of information to residents. One birth control clinic opened on a Liverpool housing estate in May 1955. The location of the clinic was defended on the grounds that families on the estate were large, the estate was ten miles from the central Liverpool clinic, and 'it was felt that if we did not take the service to them they would not come to us'. The first problem was finding suitable premises, but after a long search, a church hall was rented. Unfortunately, the prominent position of this building made potential customers quail. In addition, their finances illustrated the 'hard fact' that 'the more a clinic is needed, the less likely it is to pay for itself'. Similar problems were experienced by another clinic: 'Bad debts are numerous partly due to the fact that many husbands are employed on work which though not badly paid involves long periods of being "laid off". If we press for payment we lose our patients who revert to coitus interruptus and other unsatisfactory but cheap methods of contraception.'[138] It is not surprising, therefore, to discover that birth control clinics were used by a small proportion of the population. Outside London, clinics were few and far between and, even where they existed, women often avoided them. Thus, clinics in Wolverhampton, Aberdeen, Pontypridd, Rotherham, Exeter, and Bristol counselled fewer than five women (on average) a week; clinics in Glasgow, Manchester, Newcastle-on-Tyne, and Nottingham examined fewer than ten women a week; and only the clinics in North Kensington, East London, and Birmingham had to cope with as many as fifteen patients a week.[139]

Such small attendances indicate the extent to which birth control was a more general social – rather than institutional – issue, invented not by doctors, scientists, or sociologists, but by women themselves. Indeed, at the end of the nineteenth century, there was a greater variety of contraceptives on the market than there was in the 1960s. The problem working-class women faced was not availability but reliability. After abstinence, the most common form of limiting the number of births was by abortion. It was considered legitimate by working-class women so long as it occurred before 'quickening' – that is, about three months. The advantage of abortion over other forms of family limitation was that it had to be resorted to only in the event of 'bad luck'. Since sterility was high, many women never had to resort to it. Most importantly, it did not require the co-operation of the husband nor did it require any alteration in conduct or sexual relations. Legally, however, the woman wanting an abortion was in a difficult position. Abortion was illegal under the Offences Against the Person Act of 1861, although 'therapeutic' abortions were protected by the Infant Life (Preservation) Act of 1929 which permitted termination of pregnancy after twenty-eight weeks in order to save the woman's life. In practical terms, the 1938 Macnaughton judgement made abortions easier to obtain. This judgement made it lawful to terminate a pregnancy to safeguard the woman from 'being a mental and physical wreck'. In 1939, the British Medical Association estimated that between 16 and 20 per cent of all pregnancies ended in abortion.[140] The rate was higher in industrial areas. After the Second World War, the number of abortions increased, with about 10,000 legal abortions performed privately and 2,000 by the National Health Service each year. The physical cost was still high: in 1965, more than 3,000 women suffered from post-abortion sepsis and it was not unusual to have whole wards full of women with septic abortions.[141]

Private Members Bills to decriminalize abortion were introduced four times in the 1950s and 1960s until, in 1967, David Steel's Abortion Bill was finally passed, making abortion legally and safely available to the majority of women. By this Act, a person was not guilty of an offence when a pregnancy was terminated by a registered medical practitioner and if two registered medical practitioners agreed that continuation of pregnancy would involve risk to the woman's or family's physical and mental health. Abortion, consequently, became lawful on 'social grounds'.

Abortion was the most dramatic of all attempts to limit reproduction. Throughout the twentieth century, working-class women were increasingly liable to have recourse to abortion only if other forms of birth control failed. Coitus interruptus fell into disfavour (as one working-class woman complained, 'it feels like cold rice pudding in the morning').[142] Spermicides and barrier methods were not more widely used because of the fear of physical injury and mental disorder, aesthetic distaste, associations with prostitution and venereal disease, opposition from both Protestant and Catholic churches, their expense, and the number of bogus products on the market. More gradually, the condom was rejected. This had been the most popular form of birth control. In E. Lewis-Faning's study in the mid-1940s, 15 per cent of birth-controllers who were born prior to 1910 used the sheath, while 40 per cent of birth-controllers born between 1910 and 1919 used it. The increased popularity of this form of birth control was encouraged by the issuing of free condoms to the armed forces during the First World War. By the middle of the twentieth century, reliance was increasingly being placed on appliance methods, in particular a shift to female devices such as diaphragms and cervical caps which required overcoming the aversion to touching one's own genitals. This shift was

Table 2.7 Percentage of women 'at risk' using various methods of contraception, by year of first marriage

Method used	Year of first marriage				
	Pre-1951	1951–5	1956–60	1961–5	1966–70
Condom	38	38	40	35	31
Pill	13	16	17	30	38
Coitus interruptus	25	29	20	14	12
Safe period	5	9	7	4	6
Diaphragm	3	4	6	7	6
IUD	6	4	6	7	3
Spermicides	2	4	4	7	6
Abstinence	5	2	3	4	5
Douching	–	1	–	–	–
None	14	8	8	5	5
Total (number)	63	335	553	517	399

Source: M. Bone, *Family Planning Services in England and Wales* (London, 1973), 19.
Note: The percentages do not add up to 100 since some used more than one method.

encouraged by advances in the moulding of synthetic rubber and the growing use of quinine sulphate as a spermicide. The change also emphasized the role of the medical profession: these devices had to be selected and fitted by an experienced clinician to be useful. The rhythm method remained a minority practice, which was liable to increase chances of fertilization prior to the 1960s. The most significant change to contraceptive use was the switch to the pill after 1961 when it became available in Britain. In 1960, 97 per cent of patients were advised to use the cap: the remainder advised to use the sheath or chemicals only. Within ten years, 58 per cent of new patients were being prescribed oral contraceptives, 16 per cent the cap, and 13 per cent the IUD.[143]

The effect of birth control was dramatic. In the last decades of the nineteenth century, the birth rates of all social classes began to decline, although before 1900 the decline in working-class fertility was largely confined to the textile districts. Initially, declining fertility was most marked amongst the urban propertied class. Between 1901 and 1931, however, working-class birth rates were cut in half. In terms of the average number of children in a 'completed' manual worker's family, this meant a drop from 3.9 children in 1900 to 2.5 by 1929. Although birth rates rose in the late 1930s and during the Second World War, fertility again began falling in the late 1940s. The 'baby boom' of the 1950s lasted until 1965 when birth rates again descended steeply.

Table 2.8 Fertility trends in England, Wales, and Scotland, 1901–65

| Year | England and Wales | | Scotland | |
	A	B	A	B
1901–05	28.2	230.5	29.5	271.8
1911–15	23.6	190.7	25.8	233.2
1921–25	19.9	156.7	25.6	226.7
1931–35	15.0	115.2	18.2	159.3
1941–45	15.9	105.4	17.8	136.4
1951–55	15.3	105.0	17.8	131.5
1961–65	18.1	125.9	19.5	145.7

Key:
A. Average annual birth rate per 1,000 population
B. Average annual number of legitimate births per 1,000 married women

Source: A. H. Halsey (ed.), *Trends in British Society Since 1900* (London, 1972), 51.

Note: The Scottish data are for the following years: 1900–2, 1910–12, 1920–2, 1931–5, 1941–4, 1951, and 1961.

As birth control became more common, and emphasis shifted from size of family to quality of care, the fear of 'marital promiscuity' expressed at the beginning of the century lost its relevance. Indeed, it was the large family which displayed promiscuity – usually thought to be the result of over-indulgence of the husband rather than the wife. The working-class man who continued to reproduce after his house had been blessed with the average number of children was regarded as cruel: subjecting wife and children to a life of poverty and subjecting his wife to moral degradation. Unrestrained reproduction was an invitation to poverty. In a study in 1939 of 269 families in the Kingstanding estate in Birmingham, 5 per cent of families with one or two children were living below the poverty line (defined in terms of the ratio of income to minimum standard needs) compared with 40 per cent of families with three or more children.[144] Although these large families profited when several children were earning a wage, this period of relative comfort was not worth the long years of deprivation. As some working-class respondents told E. Slater and M. Woodside: 'people look back and see that big families mean hardship'; 'parents feel they've missed so much in their own lives'; 'you can do such a lot with two that you can't with six'; 'parents had a hard struggle, and grandparents a harder'; and 'the horror of not being able to find the money to keep 'em'. Slater and Woodside concluded that there was no nostalgia for the large families of the past. Far from representing fidelity and diligence, large families were attributed to 'lust', 'ignorance', and an absence of outside interests.[145]

CONCLUSION

Given the inevitable disruptions caused by two world wars, what is remarkable about the working-class family is the way it has survived – indeed, has strengthened – throughout the twentieth century. Legislative support for the family, in terms of family allowances, tax concessions, and welfare benefits had a relatively minor role to play in this process. More important was the flexibility of husbands and ,wives, and parents and children, to the demands of the life-cycle and generational shifts of focus. While working-class women frowned on premarital sex, they engaged in it with heightened vigour and took precautions; faced with the potentially demasculinizing effect of unemployment, working-class men drew women's attention to their superior physical prowess; parents nagged their adolescents, but gave them room to manoeuvre; husbands and wives selected elements from the new sexual theories and adapted them; and if they divorced, they remarried. In the 1940s, 80 per cent of working-class couples declared that they were 'happy' with their marriages.[146] Love was a bonus.

SELECTIVE BIBLIOGRAPHY

Hall, Leslie, *Hidden Anxieties: Male Sexuality 1900–1950* (Cambridge, 1991).
A lively analysis of male sexual problems in the first half of the twentieth century, making much use of Marie Stopes's correspondence and medical documentation.

Holt, Richard, *Sport and the British: A Modern History* (Oxford, 1989).
Examines sport in a broad context, in the nineteenth and twentieth centuries. Sensitive to class, gender, and regional differentials. As much a social history of modern Britain as a history of sport.

Humphries, S., *Hooligans or Rebels?: An Oral History of Working-Class Childhood and Youth 1889–1939* (Oxford, 1981).
Looks at the resistance of working-class youth within families, schools, neighbourhoods, gangs, and reformatories to middle-class culture.

Lewis, Jane, *The Politics of Motherhood: Child and Maternal Welfare in England, 1900–1939* (London, 1980).
The most useful analysis of women's and children's health during the first forty years of the twentieth century.

Rice, Margery Spring, *Working-Class Wives: Their Health and Conditions*, first published 1939 (London, 1981).
First-hand accounts of the attitudes of working-class women to their health, work, housing, and diet.

Weeks, Jeffrey, *Sex, Politics and Society: The Regulation of Sexuality Since 1800*, second edition (London, 1989).
Looks at the meaning given to sexuality, the construction of sexuality, and the relationship between sexuality and social policy. Particularly good on debates concerning state intervention and the response of people labelled 'deviants'.

Yeo, Eileen and Stephen Yeo (eds), *Popular Culture and Class Conflict 1590-1914: Explorations in the History of Labour and Leisure* (Brighton, 1981).
Important discussion of the usefulness of theories of 'social control' in understanding patterns of working-class leisure. Should be read in conjunction with F. M. L. Thompson, 'Social Control in Victorian Britain', *Economic History Review*, second series, xxxiv.2 (May 1981).

3 Home
Domestic spaces

In the 1920s, three domestic servants never tired of speaking about love. One of the servants dreamt of a lover like Valentino in *The Sheik*. Nothing less would do. The other two girls knew better:

> Real love wasn't riding off on a horse behind a, probably smelly, sheik. Real love was having a kind man who worked hard and handed over most of his wages. Real love was having children and bringing them up decent. It was growing old and having grandchildren. Real love was being a family.[1]

This vision of snug domesticity appealed to many women. Of all the dreams dreamt by working-class women, marriage followed by full-time housewifery was the most widely shared and showed little sign of fading prior to the Second World War. The extent to which women achieved this dream is difficult to quantify. The movement of married women in and out of the paid labour force is complex. Once we exclude the First World War, between one-quarter and one-third of all women were employed. Married women, however, were less liable to be in paid employment. Although in 1851 about one-quarter of married women were employed, in the censuses of 1901, 1911, and 1921, only 14 per cent of married women were employed. By 1931, the proportion of married women in employment had increased by only two percentage points. Within twenty years, these statistics abruptly swell. The burdens of war resulted in the cancellation of the normal census proceedings in 1941, but in 1951 the census enumerators reported that 40 per cent of married women were employed. In the next chapter the increased propensity of married women after the Second World War to take a paid job will be examined. This chapter is concerned with the first half of the twentieth century, when married working-class women were becoming less liable to take paid employment. In this period, although many working-class married women

continued to spend some time engaged in paid employment (usually at
the lower echelons of the market and frequently on a part-time or
casual basis), they generally defined themselves primarily as housewives. Furthermore, they seemed pleased to do so.

Historians have proven unwilling to believe that the decision of
working-class women to be full-time housewives (if they could possibly do so) was not involuntary.[2] Discriminatory practices by
employers and trade unions have been blamed for keeping women
within the home.[3] Both capitalists and male workers had an interest in
uniting to exclude women from jobs.[4] These explanations will be
discussed in the next chapter. Whatever explanation is adopted,
however, the overriding identity of married women as unpaid housewives is generally assumed to be oppressive. According to historians
representing a bewildering range of political and historiographical
traditions, most of women's ills can be traced to their being tied to the
household. Ann Oakley contends that the role of housewife in the
nineteenth century was a demeaning one, consisting of monotonous,
fragmented work which brought no financial remuneration, let alone
any recognition.[5] June Purvis argues that the lives of working-class
women were characterized by 'daily misery, poverty, and exploitation'.[6] Working-class housewives were 'manipulated consumers' who
practised 'self-denial' for the sake of their families.[7] They were
overworked and exploited by either patriarchy or capital (or both).

In addition to being portrayed as oppressed, the value of their
domestic work is discounted. Although the struggle to 'make ends
meet' is frequently acknowledged, it is portrayed as a rather pointless
struggle producing little intrinsic value.[8] Working-class housewives are
criticized for failing to join the socialist or feminist fight when things
were bad, or for uniting with their 'idle' middle-class sisters when
things were good. Thus, Rosemary Collins argued that 'Middle-class
women were now [by the middle of the nineteenth century] economically idle – their main role was to organize homes displaying their
husband's wealth. Working-class women continued to be economically active. . . . Towards the end of the Victorian period, working-
class women began to withdraw from industrial life into the home,
where they tried to emulate the domestic lifestyles of the wealthy.'[9] In
other words, they too became 'economically idle'.

How did working-class women understand their domestic lives?
Domesticity appealed not only to them, but also to their menfolk.
Working-class women became more prone to work full-time within
the home between the late nineteenth century and the First World
War, while working-class men inclined towards the domestic sphere in

the inter-war years. It is insufficient to see these wives and husbands solely as responding to outside forces: both actively determined their own history. In the words of Jean Comaroff, they were people who 'in their everyday production of goods and meanings, acquiesce yet protest, reproduce yet seek to transform their predicament'.[10] This chapter reviews the movement of working-class women into full-time housewifery. It considers the attempts working-class women made to improve their position within the home and explores the ways these women resisted unlawful power over them. Finally, shifts in the domestic lives of working-class men are investigated.

THE PLEASURES OF HOUSEWIFERY

Many working-class women thought that housewifery was something worth striving towards. The two spheres of labour – male and female, or paid and unpaid – was acceptable to so many women because it was seen as a better and less risky way of increasing their power over their own lives and the lives of their families. There was a price to pay for being a housewife: but the benefits were perceived as being cheap at the price.

As will be examined in the next chapter, bleak working conditions and low wages enhanced the allure of full-time housewifery. In the words of one Cockney woman, 'Work was a regrettable necessity to women [in the 1920s]; I never heard of any female *enjoying* her job.'[11] Even after the Second World War, when the employment of married women was on the increase, half of a sample of 1,093 women who had taken up employment between 1939 and 1947 did it either because they needed the money or for patriotic reasons. Only 15 per cent actually wanted to get away from the home. In the entire sample of 2,807 women, two-thirds thought that the only reason women took employment was financial.[12] If a woman could afford to avoid it, she did. However, working-class women were not completely free to choose whether or not they would be wage-earners in their own right. Financial constraints were eased with changes in the structure of wages at the end of the nineteenth century. A wage sufficient to provide basic food and housing needs was necessary if the household was to be supported by only one wage-earner. As one female labourer said in response to criticisms about women's work in the fields: 'if the farmer paid the men properly, the women could stop at home'.[13] When total household earnings reached a certain level (probably between 21s and 30s), the value of a woman investing all her time in unwaged domestic production outstripped the value of her wage.[14] As we saw in

Chapter 1, by 1900 rising real wages had pushed more working-class households into this higher bracket. Rising real wages for working-class men gave their wives an opportunity to move out of employment themselves and invest their time in managing the extra income and improving domestic production.

The consumption implications of these shifts in real wages were significant. Economists talking about the increased living standards of working-class households at the end of the nineteenth century focus on the 'benefits in terms of extra consumption' without acknowledging that consumption needs cannot be met without labour.[15] In other words, rising wages led to an increased demand for female labour within the home. It was no longer possible for a working-class household to maintain acceptable levels of domestic production and consumption without the full-time investment of the housewife's labour in the home, converting income into consumable goods. Thus, the increased prosperity of working-class households from the late nineteenth century was created not only by higher wages, but also by improved housewifery. Households containing employed women lacked 'domestic or material comfort', compared with those containing full-time housewives.[16] The productivity of household members earning a wage improved with proper domestic labour. In a report on Northumberland, it was noted that unmarried girls worked in the fields, but married women devoted most of their time to housework. The success of this division of labour bore testimony to the 'beneficial results of an active outdoor life when combined with good feeding at home' and was preferred to a situation where married women also worked in the fields without the back-up provided by domestic labour.[17] It was through improvements in health and nutrition resulting from changes in housewifery that productivity and general well-being was enhanced.

There were other advantages to be claimed by a married woman who devoted all her time to housewifery. Domestic labour was vital for the management of money. This was especially the case in households with children, since periods of high expenditure coincided with periods of lowest family income.[18] The mother could raise family living standards not by bringing in an additional wage, but by manufacturing rather than buying necessary goods.[19] Domestic manufacture was inefficient, but practical. Frequently, the calculations were marginal. Thus, housewives would walk extra miles to buy potatoes or bread which were a halfpenny cheaper than those sold locally.[20] According to economists like Gary Becker and Jacob Mincer, time costs money.[21] But people need not be profit maximizers. Indeed, the strategy of the working-class housewife was closer to that of the peasant: that of 'working the system to their minimum disadvantage'.[22] To such a way of calculating, time was the one free commodity.

The housewife gained status by competently managing scarce resources. The movement into full-time housewifery enabled the special needs and tastes of the individuals within the household to be catered for – and it was the housewife who created this collective identity. The great symbol was the parlour where the relationship between the housewife and her family, as well as the relationship between the family and the wider community, were symbolized and structured in subtle yet distinctive ways. In working-class England, it became the symbol of the housewife's power and control over her family. Desecration of this space by entering it at inappropriate times, or in unsuitable clothing, could bring swift retribution.[23] The parlour was a confirmation of the housewife's pre-eminent role in the management of resources, and symbolized her success in budgeting a limited income to allow for this 'surplus'.[24]

Although the parlour was the most sacred of the housewife's spaces, the entire home was her domain. Speaking about his mother at the turn of the century, Jobson recognized that 'she was the pivot around which our family life revolved. She dominated the scene, for without her we could do nothing. She did this not in a self-assertive manner but as the natural order of things.'[25] Or, as 'P. P.' wrote in the *Daily Herald* in 1922, the home was 'more a monument to the industry of the housewife than a comfortable place to live'.[26] The housewife was the 'Home Ruler', the boss.[27]

By investing time in the household, housewives were able to experience the pride and sense of well-being that comes from being in charge of the creation of beautiful things. Cooking a luscious assortment of dishes stimulated feelings of triumph.[28] Two of the main pleasures spoken about by women moving into full-time housewifery was the joy of spending more time nurturing children and the thrill of creating an environment capable of celebrating those aspects of the marital relationship which were thought to be unique. These pleasures did not have a money price – a point often lost on outside observers, especially those from a different class. Thus, in 1895, one landowner in Norfolk showed a lack of appreciation for domestic beauty when he complained, 'If you build a cottage with a good living room, and a kitchen containing a copper, oven, etc. they insist on living in the kitchen, and shutting up the front room as a "drawing room" to be entered probably only once a week. You put in patent ventilators and they promptly shut them up. They block up the windows of the sitting-room with a blind curtain, and flowers.'[29] The warm, close, cosy cottage with the parlour, blind curtain, and flowers was created by a woman with quite different tastes.

Although the main function of domestic arranging and rearranging lay in creating an environment which was both pleasurable to create and pleasurable to 'consume', there was some economic purpose to actions intended to keep up a good 'front' in the eyes of the neighbours. Maintaining acceptable standards of beauty and order were crucial to achieving good credit levels at the local shop, with the 'Uncle' or pawnshop, and the neighbours.

All this domestic work took a great deal of time, energy, and skill. Furthermore, relative to the other members of the household, the housewife did not get her 'fair share' of leisure. In one sense, *her* work facilitated *their* leisure. It was the housewife who was doing the work necessary for leisure: she made the comfortable kitchen in which the family could listen to the radio or talk; she packed the cold lunch for the trip to the seaside; she budgeted for the annual holiday. Yet, the full-time housewife reaped more of the benefits of increased leisure when compared with women working a double-shift in the factory and the home.

CONSOLIDATING POWER

There were serious risks involved in devoting one's time to unwaged housework. The family is a confrontational unit: husbands may be tyrannical, wages may be skimmed before reaching the communal purse, and women may get a smaller share of the daily bread. However, these problems were not intrinsic to the status of full-time housewife. Women in general were provided with less food and clothing, even if they were engaged in paid employment.[30] Employed wives and full-time housewives often colluded in the unequal distribution of domestic resources, keeping their husbands ignorant of their sacrifice.[31] For working-class women, power was something which had to be negotiated. It included limiting the scope of men's decision-making to consideration of only those issues which the housewife found non-threatening. It meant control as much as ownership. Owning an independent wage may provide the wife with certain rights *vis-à-vis* other (usually better-paid) wage-earners in the household. In exchange for giving up these rights, the housewife raised her standard of living and chiselled out an independent space in which her level of control was significant. The trade-off was worthwhile if the 'bread-winner' could be made dependent on the housewife. Attempts by housewives to *widen* the separation of 'his and her' kinds of labour were aimed at reducing their own powerlessness.

One way the spheres of labour were to be widened was by broadening the range and quality of domestic tasks through education in cookery, laundry work, and general housewifery. These classes in domestic education were organized by private organizations, local governments, and education authorities from the 1880s. By 1910, in elementary schools alone, nearly half a million school girls in England were attending domestic education classes annually.[32]

It is possible to portray education in housework as part of an attempt by the middle classes to disseminate a particular form of domestic ideology amongst working-class girls, ensuring that they knew their 'place' in society.[33] For working-class women, however, domestic education had a different meaning. They proved eager to attend the classes.[34] For the working-class Salford girl Emily Glencross, cookery lessons in school 'opened the world' for her.[35] Girls frequently stayed at school for an extra year in order to get training in housewifery.[36] They would walk long distances to attend the classes, and teachers were besieged with applications to admit older girls and women.[37] When given a choice, parents would send their daughters to schools which taught domestic education, as opposed to less well-provided schools.[38] Teachers discovered that the threat of removing a child from cookery classes was effective in enforcing good behaviour.[39] Girls were less liable to 'skip' cookery classes.[40] Scholars who missed out on domestic education at school 'lamented' their bad fortune and joined evening classes.[41] The passive acceptance of a middle-class ideology of domesticity does not explain the popularity of domestic education amongst working-class girls and women. For them, domestic education was a way they actively sought to redefine their status as women *within* the household.

More women accepted that it was the status of women as housewives that had to be improved than accepted that their status as waged labourers needed tackling. For housewives, the importance of education in the home was seen as necessary and obvious.[42] It was needed in order to dispel the idea that housework was 'natural' and therefore simple.[43] The taint of 'servitude' and 'domestic service' had to be removed from domestic labour.[44] Working-class homes were also suffering from a shortage of cheap 'dailies' to help with household tasks: increasingly the housewife had to do the most menial tasks herself. These tasks had to be reformed and redefined. People had to be made to acknowledge that housework required more than simply intuition.[45] The classes were popular because they provided an opportunity for girls and women to improve their status within the home by reducing the 'menial' elements of housework and emphasizing the more specialized and skilled forms of domestic labour.

Improving the quality of goods and services produced by the housewife seemed to be the key to raising the status of women. In part, the concentration of domestic education classes in working-class areas was a function of changes in consumption within these districts. The requirements of housewifery had increased dramatically. Housing improvements raised standards of cleaning.[46] Dietary diversification was a notable feature of working-class life from the 1850s, but especially from the 1880s.[47] As diet diversified, so did the degree of specialized knowledge required by housewives. Preparing and managing a variety of food took time. Women and girls in domestic classes were urged to invest in simple domestic technologies, such as gas cookers, a range of cutlery, pots, and bowls, simple washing and mangling machines, and cooling facilities, in part because such technologies conferred higher status on the domestic labourer. Working-class housewives did not use these 'labour-saving' devices to improve their efficiency; rather, they used them to raise their standards of domestic work which, in the long run, increased, rather than decreased, their labour.[48] Domestic technologies which could save time were largely unavailable to the working classes before the Second World War. As we saw in Chapter 1, before the 1950s, only a small proportion of households were wired for electricity, owned a refrigerator, or possessed a vacuum cleaner or carpet sweeper.[49] 'Labour-saving' devices were too expensive. A writer in the *Daily Herald* on 3 February 1922 was interested in the practicalities of two new inventions – the dishwasher and the clothes wringer. Both required an almost unlimited supply of nearly boiling water. In her words: 'It is singularly hard on the women of us that, just when the workers' wages are pushed right down to the fodder level and below, there should be such ingenious and delightful devices put on the market for easing kitchen labour. . . . As I say, excellent. But only the women who don't do their own washing can afford it. *A splendidly* arranged world, isn't it?'

Furthermore, during the first half of the twentieth century, there was considerable opposition from the older generation of housewives to new 'short cuts' to housewifery. The objection was not to the basic changes in, for example, stove technology, but to the insidious intervention of the capitalist marketplace into the home.[50] A typical example was the reaction of Eliza Edwards when a local baker started to mass produce Welsh cakes. Eliza would have 'nothing to do' with 'modern gadgets', believing that Welsh cakes could only be made on an old-fashioned bakestone on top of an open fire. She was scathing: 'Apart from the fact that the baker was an Englishman who thought he could cook Welsh cakes as well as he could eat them, all he could do was to fill them with "bi-carb" and to get a light appearance by what was really cheating. "No", said Eliza, "you've got to work the mixture, and work it again, and give it plenty of currants".'[51] Many of this older generation of housewives approved of domestic education classes precisely because they taught girls to respect traditional values and, by familiarizing students with 'first principles', were closer to conventional methods of housewifery.

Education in housework had an unforeseen consequence in bolstering the feminization of the more skilled and the more creative domestic departments, such as cooking. Housework became more specialized, progressively excluding male members of the family and enhancing the bargaining power of women. The marginalization of men was based not only on biological or psychological differences between men and women. It was an exclusion based also on the need of women to insure their eminence within the household. Thus, while none of the mainstream domestic classes included men, classes in cookery established for men working on ships and boats caused no comment.[52] Men were able to learn domestic skills, but only in contexts which did not threaten the predominance of women within the home. This can also be seen in the opposition of some working-class mothers to school meals. In the words of Anna Martin in 1911, 'The women have a vague dread of being superseded and dethroned. Each of them knows perfectly well that the strength of her position in the home lies in the physical dependence of her husband and children upon her and she is suspicious of anything that would tend to undermine this.'[53] It is not surprising to hear that housewives often resisted male intervention in the domestic sphere on the grounds that it disrupted their routine, resulted in the lowering of standards, and encroached on their power-base. For example, in Dipton (a Durham pit village) in the 1920s, male 'interference' in the domestic sphere 'wasn't wanted and very rarely given. Mother was in charge domestically, 100 per cent.'[54]

Of course, the position of housewife was threatened not only by the male members of the household. Women resisted sharing or subdividing power with other women as well. The failure of co-operative kitchens is well documented. Some daughters were not allowed to do housework because the mother was 'jealous[ly] clinging to power in every department of the house'.[55] P. A. Sheehan described an old woman unable to perform domestic labour, and forced to allow another woman to do it, with the words: 'one could see how the sense of her dethronement and subjection was telling on the old woman'.[56] Daughters were not thanked if they attempted to usurp the power of the kitchen-kingdom. In 1909, an Irish journalist, Robert Lynd, repeated the following story about the relationship between a daughter who had attended a domestic education course and her mother:

> A farmer's daughter in the south, having returned home with her training in cookery, was permitted amid some excitement to prove her gifts in getting ready the midday dinner. She prepared a magnificent steak pudding, the likes of which had never been seen in the house before. . . . 'We must always let Mary do the cooking after this!' [the father] cried. . . . The woman of the house, hearing this, suddenly lifted up her voice and wept. 'Oh!' she lamented, wringing her hands, 'After me cooking and slaving for you for 20 years! And now to have my own daughter put against me!' And she finished with a flood of tears. . . . No one ever dared to propose Mary as family cook again.[57]

Who produced *what* was important.

CONFLICT

Women may vie with each other for domestic authority, and men may attempt to superintend their labour, but the most serious threat to women's power lay in men's fists. Catherine Cookson's grandmother used to be beaten by her husband. She would sit Catherine on her knees, in their rooms in a tenement near the Tyne dock, and sing:

> Love, it is teasing,
> Love, it is pleasing,
> Love is a pleasure
> When it is new;
> But as it grows older
> And days grow colder
> It fades away like the
> Morning dew.[58]

Nancy Sharman asked her battered mother, 'Why do you put up with it?' Her mother replied, 'You just can't stop loving someone, like turning off a tap.'[59] Hitting those we love is an established tradition, although one which came increasingly into disrepute among the working classes from the 1890s.[60] In the middle of the nineteenth century, a working-class neighbourhood could sustain one conviction for aggravated assault on a woman for every two to three hundred houses, or, in different words, ten to twenty men in every neighbourhood would be convicted for common assault during any one year. Nevertheless, violence was dwindling, so that in London the number of aggravated assaults recorded in the police courts dropped from 800 in 1853 to 200 in 1889 and continued falling throughout the twentieth century.[61]

Wives were the favourite target, but indiscriminate blows often landed on children. As one boy put it, 'He could be the greatest dad in the world, and then destroy that world, shatter it to chaos and fear-sickness, by tipping the bottle. . . . Furniture smashed, windows smashed, self and brothers and sisters smashed. Snarling rages, huge volcanic eruptions.'[62] There were reasons for hitting one's loved ones. Perhaps the children had been noisy; perhaps they were not in bed when papa returned from the pub. Husbands thumped wives when their food was cold, or burnt, or unpalatable.[63] They hit out when taunted about their impotence.[64] Men thrashed women if their homes 'weren't as things should be' or if they complained.[65] A wife could be beaten because her parents were not sufficiently appreciative of the husband's sacrifice in marrying their daughter.[66] They struck wives for nagging ('My mother was a whiner and a nagger, there's no doubt about that, and, even if there was another woman in it, I reckon she drove him to it. After all, a man wants a smile or two from a woman sometimes').[67] Maybe they just slapped their wives because 'that was the proper thing to do'.[68]

Domestic violence was not random but was subject to legitimizing rites and rules. The distinction between 'legitimate' and 'illegitimate' violence was sharp. Wives caught *in flagrante delicto* deserved retribution: 'I reckon by the time Micah and Absy a' finished wi' their hides tonight they'll be too sore to lay about wi' anybody for a long time to come, an' serve 'em right' said a miner in Brierley (Forest of Dean).[69] Levels of violence were finely graded. Whether a man was too 'soft' on his wife or too 'hard' on her concerned neighbours. The 'soft', and sober, Englishman in a Glasgow street who handed over his entire wage packet to his wife was ridiculed by wives whose husbands were violent and stingy: 'Nae spunk at a'. . . . A Moose! . . . Of course he's English. Soft, that's whit he is.'[70] If a man wasn't the 'boss' of the home 'he wasn't considered to be a man'.[71] Equally, however, excessive violence dragged down everyone's reputation. Rules about 'legitimate' violence set the tone of a neighbourhood, and it did no-one any good to break them. Thus, Pat O'Mara's family were forced to move from lodging house to lodging house – each one worse than the one before – as his father's violence proved too monstrous even in areas where a considerable amount of violence was an accepted component of marital relations: 'The men considered it a traditional duty to beat their wives and the wives considered it a traditional penance to accept the continual beatings. Even in these surroundings my father was looked upon as more undesirable. The others occasionally did let up on their wives, but not my father – he was always drunk and at his task.'[72]

Beatings intended as punishment for some specific act might be received with stoicism. In the words of one woman, 'I'd take it if I know'd I was in the wrong or he didn't really mean it, but if he was in the wrong, or if he meant it – look out!'[73] Pat O'Mara's mother was frequently hospitalized as a result of the injuries sustained in domestic fights. She had a sense of being 'fated':

> The children must somehow be raised as good Catholics – that must come first. If she left my father, this would be impossible, for little economic help was furnished to husband deserters. . . . So my mother's choice lay between suicide and torture and as the former was impossible (since she was a Catholic), she had no recourse but to submit grimly to the latter.

The guilt of dependency on her sister during those times when she was separated from her husband lent a poignancy to her husband's periodic repentance.[74] There were worse things than living with a violent man:

> Some working men, quite decent and kindly fellows at ordinary times, will occasionally give their wives a black eye, especially if they are in liquor. What they are not so apt to inflict is the continuous mental torture which withers a woman's life, without visible bruises.[75]

Marriage was no picnic: 'We take 'em for better or worse, and it usually turns out worse, but a washing line needs a pair of pants on it as well as knickers. Look at Polly and Emma [two spinsters who lived together; when one died, the other went crazy]. That's what comes of bread and bread.'[76] And reconciliation could be exquisite:

> Next morning, the lady next door might say something like ' 'ad a bit of a "do" wiv yer ole man last night, didn't yer, ducky?'
> The going-ons had been plainly audible through the walls. The answer would be:

'Well, yes, it's the booze/kids yer know. But 'e's a good sort really: ever so good to me'.

Loyalty, you see. Or that very same evening the aggrieved husband might confide his troubles to pal George over a solacing pint. . . . What with that and time's healing hand, the husband might well take home a bottle of beer, the wife dry her eyes and unity be restored with 'What sillies we are' before climbing the stairs to bed.[77]

Chronology 3.1 Chronology of Acts regarding alcohol consumption, 1886–1939

1886	Children under 14 years no longer allowed to consume alcohol in public houses
1901	Intoxicating Liquor (Sales to Children) Act restricted 'off-sales' to children over 14 years
1902	Licensing Act punished drunken behaviour more severely and magistrates were given wider powers to refuse renewals of off-licences
1904	Licensing Act established a trade fund to compensate owners of off-licences who had been refused renewals
1908	Children and Young Person's Act prohibited the sale of alcohol (except in sealed containers) to children under the age of 14
1915	Wartime legislation led to the establishment of a Central Control Board to regulate the drink trade
1921	Licensing Act reduced opening hours
1923	Children under 18 years not allowed to be sold alcohol in public houses
1933	Brewers' Society began a campaign promoting beer ('Beer is Best')
1939	Wartime shortages began again and beer was diluted

THE RESISTANCE OF THE WEAKER

Whether the domestic persona of a man was quarrelsome, bullying, or savage, working-class housewives resisted. Strategies for asserting their autonomy and power within the household ranged from placid sabotage to fiery rebellion. Whatever the tactic, the site of conflict was the home: the kitchen, the bedroom. Domestic production is intimate: it is not surprising that housewives should protest in personal, individualized ways. The legitimacy of their resistance rested in a pervasive, but often garbled, set of shared values. A husband was 'good' if he let the housewife do her work without interference. If he attempted to oversee or intervene in the home, he was 'bad' and the housewife was justified in putting up a fight. This is not to deny that the housewife was less powerful than her husband; she had relatively less capacity to coerce and, when it came to the crunch, his superior physical strength and financial resources gave him considerable

Table 3.1 Convictions for drunkenness, in England, Wales, and Scotland (average per 10,000 population), 1901–51

Year	Number of convictions (per 10,000 population)	
	England and Wales	*Scotland*
1901	64.7	100.8
1911	54.3	86.7
1921	22.4	52.2
1931	12.3	27.7
1941	9.8	17.5
1951	12.2	10.5

Source: Calculated from statistics in Gwylmore Prys Williams and George Thomas Brake, *Drink in Great Britain* (London, 1980), 375–6, 380, 573, 585 and B. R. Mitchell and H. G. Jones, *Second Abstract of British Historical Statistics* (Cambridge, 1971), 3.

Note: 1901–31 are proceedings against persons for drunkenness offences; 1941–51 are convictions of persons for drunkenness offences.

bargaining advantages. However, the bullied housewife may not *feel* ill-treated or oppressed. For her, an important distinction was made between legitimate and illegitimate uses of power.

This concept of 'legitimate' and 'illegitimate' domestic violence was shared by other women. On one level, female neighbours developed intense support networks. The abused wife was entitled to sympathy: 'Someone would bring her half a loaf, another half a gill of milk. Someone else might bring a bit of butter and a bit of sugar. They rallied around. That man was thought of as less than the dust among his neighbours.'[78] Deranged attacks on a woman who was pregnant, ill, or simply too delicate to defend herself, justified outside intervention. Thus, in one Bristol family immediately after the First World War, neighbours tolerated domestic violence but would intervene when Ward's father punched his mother because she was 'too frail to stand up to him'.[79] On another level, however, the integrity of the family unit required solidarity. The wife had to defend her territory and interfering neighbours were not always thanked: 'I have heard many a woman screaming and shouting as a drunken man gave her a good hiding. The following day she would emerge with black eyes and swollen face, yet would not utter a word against her husband – and woe betide anyone who did! Not a word would she have against him!'[80] The status of the housewife was linked to maintaining the privacy of her home: as one battered woman told the Women's Co-Operative Guild in 1911, exposure of failure within that sphere 'has been my one dread'.[81]

The form of public defence of oppressive gender relationships did not connote acquiescence. In 1974, E. P. Thompson wrote that 'The same man who touches his forelock to the squire by day – and who goes down in history as an example of deference – may kill his sheep, snare his pheasant or poison his dogs at night.'[82] A woman may express contradictory opinions about her husband and family depending on the audience, the issue being discussed, and the immediate circumstances. One moment she may be heard approving; the next, denying. To one person she may express bitter resentment; to another, merely a desire to see things slightly modified. Occasionally (though not rarely) she uses violence to fight for what she considers to be her rights. Furthermore, subversion and resistance were part of the accepted reality of marital relations and were heralded in female-dominated mediums. Thus, common titles in women's magazines and in women's pages in newspapers are 'Strategy with Husbands', 'The Kingdom of the Home and How to Rule It', and 'Are Men Inferior?'[83]

Housewives sometimes physically fought men who did not appreciate the subtle balance between the rights of husbands to a degree of symbolic authority, and the rights of wives to rule the household. In the words of one poor London woman in 1906, 'I chastise my husband like a child.'[84] Violence was most frequently adopted by women in response to a man's attempt to assert his will aggressively. They would fight back when struck.[85] In 1908, when a district nurse expressed dismay to hear that a certain husband hit his wife, a working-class neighbour expounded, 'She isn't a bit afraid o' he. If he do give her a good smack, she do give he another.' The nurse recorded that 'this was the usual custom in the neighbourhood if husbands so far forgot themselves, which was rather rare'.[86] Violence was usually employed only after a wife's patience in 'talking him down' was exhausted. Then, in the case of Albert Jasper's mother, 'she would go berserk and clump the old man for all she was worth. She would threaten to "brain him"; a threat which always worked since no-one doubted that she would do it.'[87] Anyone who dared insult their children was at risk:

> Never for a moment was I concerned for mother, for to me the fight could only have one end – mother would win, for she had always won. And I was proud of her all-conquering powers. It was a great fight until neighbours intervened and ended it. My mother was Savage by name and she was savage by nature. She came of a race of giants on her mother's side – the Grahams of Cockermouth, famed in Border history as a race of wrestlers. And she was worthy of them.[88]

Husbands were liable to find heavy brass mats, irons, trays of toffee, brooms, loaves of bread, boxes of buttons, shovels, sheep's heads, and whatever else was at hand thrown at them if they arrived home late or drunk or were unappreciative of the wife's domestic efforts.[89] One East End woman was indignant that her husband preferred fiddling with his new wireless to coming to bed ('He seemed to forget he had a wife with a lovely little fanny just waiting for him') so she hurled a book at him.[90] More menacingly, knives could be waved in the face of stubborn husbands.[91] If he was unlucky, he could be locked out of his home.[92] Equally unlucky husbands might find themselves sleeping alone in bed every night if they refused to obey their wives.[93] Grumpy husbands – even those dying of TB – could simply be left until their manners improved.[94]

Less aggressive, but still daring, ways of resisting included lying about money or stealing from husbands. In the words of an old song from Rottingdean (Sussex):

When father came home at night and drunk we used to rob,
And after the course of a week or two we save up seven bob.
One day my mother did say, Come along with me, my boy,
We will go to Moses and Sons for a suit of corduroy
Right tiddy fol lol fol lol fol lol tiddy fol lol fal lay.
Right tiddy fol lol fol lol fol lol tiddy fol lol fal lay.[95]

A correspondent in the *Pawnbrokers' Gazette* mentioned a wife who stole her husband's wooden leg while he slept. She pawned his leg, saying, 'now he'll have to stop at home until he shells out'.[96] A domestic servant in London at the turn of the century justified the fact that she lied to her husband about how much profit she had made from a certain bargain by observing 'Now, if I do say I'll do a thing, I do do it, and everyone that do know me will tell you the same. Now me husband, he's not straight. If anyone do act fair with me, I do do the same with them.' Or, as another poor woman declaimed, 'If anyone tries to do me, I does them.'[97] In other words, certain forms of 'stealing' were legitimate, because wives have a right to the income earned by household members, and they have a right to be treated fairly and honestly.

Language was also used in a confrontational manner. Calm, determined words could reduce a husband to obedient acquiescence.[98] A shrill argument might help a housewife get her own way within the household.[99] It did not take much to shame a misbehaving husband. The failure of a husband to arrive back from the pub in time for his Sunday dinner might result in the reproof: 'and after me slavin' away all mornin' to make sure dinner's nice and hot while you're out enjoyin' yourself'.[100] Swearing was particularly defiant. That husbands interpreted swearing by their wives as deliberately provocative action is revealed in Nancy Tomes's work which disclosed that swearing was generally regarded by wife-beaters as the 'final straw'.[101]

These forms of open insubordination were, however, often dangerous and counterproductive. It is not surprising to discover that the most common forms of resistance for housewives were non-confrontational: manipulation, slander, and disdainful silence. At this level, the housewife was relatively 'safe'. She could be refused 'fringe benefits', but she was still liable to be maintained at a subsistence level.

Silence was a powerful (and frequently used) weapon, as Kathleen Behan depicted:

There was a ceremony in every house, when the man handed over the wages every week. My brother Peadar had a God Almighty row with his wife once. When he came in, he didn't *hand* her the wages, but put it on the mantelpiece. She wouldn't have that. Quite right too – it was degrading, as if she were some kind of lodging-house keeper, not the woman of the house. So, she wouldn't take the money off the mantelpiece, but waited for him to put it in her hand. They both sat there for a time, staring at this money, and at each other, and in the end, without a word, my brother took the money off the mantelpiece himself and took it down to the pub. That was it for the rest of the week for them.[102]

Just because her protest was counterproductive should not lead us to ignore her protest and the reasons for it. Silence seems to have been a common way wives responded to evidence of unfaithfulness on the part of their husbands: after such treachery, what was left to be said? Thus, Winifred Brown's mother maintained a long silence after her husband's extramarital affair was exposed. Her husband defended his entitlement to have an affair on the grounds that his wife withheld sex from him, a justification rejected as spurious by his wife who spurned the notion that male sexuality required expression. A similar response was elicited when Mollie Harris's mother uncovered her husband's infatuation with a young widow at a local pub: 'And that was that; she just never forgave him. Slowly, through the years, she grew further and further away from him and so did we children, not really knowing why.'[103] The errant husband was denied the affection of both his wife and children.

Much conflict, therefore, centred not around the allocation of resources, but around what E. P. Thompson has called the 'contest for symbolic authority'.[104] A favourite form of subverting the power of the male 'head of the household' was through unflattering or insulting references about him behind his back.[105] Gossip and 'slagging-off' could impose heavy penalties on a man by ruining his reputation within the community or household. Irrespective of the ranking of the husband in the 'wider' world, within the household and neighbourhood, women allocated social prestige and reputation.

Many women found the most effective way to govern was to use their domestic accomplishments to soften or persuade. A gentle, doting, or coquettish gesture could secure dominance.[106] As the women's columnist, L. Stoddart, instructed other housewives, 'It is an undisputed fact that man is an animal, therefore, he must have his creature comforts attended to, and these carefully, if you wish to keep him docile and tractable.'[107] If her sweetness was rebuffed, a housewife could retaliate by becoming super-obliging. Housework could be performed so efficiently that he suffered. His favourite clock could be dusted in such a way that it broke.[108] She could humiliate him by showing such concern with his diet that she would send his meal down to the all-male club or pub.[109] Less obliging, but equally effective, she could bungle housework. His meal could be burnt or fed to the dog if he came home late or drunk.[110] A plate of hash could be tipped over his head.[111] She could simply go 'on strike'.[112] In protest at a life of hard work, one day in the 1910s, Mrs Lane, charwoman and mother of ten children, struck: 'She stayed in bed all day and it was rumoured that Mr Lane poured cold water over her, but it made no difference.'[113] The refusal of a wife to cook a meal, apparently trivial, could be an important mechanism by which to enforce decision-making.

For the housewife adopting non-confrontational resistance, it was wise to wrap her words in the cloak of symbolic deference. In an 1890 article in the *Housewife*, entitled 'Strategy with Husbands', housewives living in homes where the 'master' considered that he 'knows best about all domestic matters' and intervened in domestic affairs in an 'irascible, overbearing and obstinate' manner were advised and reassured:

> By a constant series of little deceptions the tyrant is led to believe that his measures are carried out, whereas, in point of fact, they are quite properly ignored. I do not say that the wife is blameless, but I say that the fault lies first with the husband, whose tiresome tyranny forces his wife into subterfuges for the sake of the general good.[114]

When Richard Church's mother had succeeded in dominating her husband, she would 'contrive to restore his dignity and set him up again as the head of the house who could do no wrong and whose word was law'.[115] It was similar in Hannah Mitchell's family:

> Even my mother, who quite definitely ruled the roost in our home, paid lip service to the idea of the dominant male. She always spoke of my father as 'The Master', and when the dealers came to buy cattle, she always left the room while they bargained, as if leaving him to decide, although in reality she and my father had previously agreed the price to be asked.[116]

Different forms of address were adopted if a husband needed to be persuaded – forms such as 'my dear', 'love', 'darling', and so on.[117] Housewives may use appropriate linguistic forms of deference to get their own way, but this should not be taken to mean that they believe in the superiority of the 'master'. To his face, they may cajole; behind his back they may sneer. In working-class Salford at the turn of the century, Robert Roberts's mother responded to a visitor's question 'An' is the master at home now?' with 'I haven't one . . . but my husband's out'.[118] To get a man to do the housework while the housewife is ill, they may beg for his 'help' and praise his 'goodness', while knowing it is his duty. To get a husband to stop beating his wife, neighbouring wives could use the language of chivalry, but that does not mean to say that they believe in male loftiness. Significantly, when all other protests had gone unnoticed, a woman most commonly resorted to arguments based on an ideology of women's weakness. One day Richard Church's mother 'broke her usual policy of government by seeming acquiescence, and staged an open revolt': 'She referred to the disabilities of the female body and particularly of mothers of children, she pointed out the singular delicacy of her own children and enumerated several reasons for it, all connected with Father's heredity, personal stupidity and callousness. She called upon God to witness the universal unfairness between the sexes, with women as the eternal victim and slave.' He was duly snubbed.[119]

These 'risk-averse' forms of resisting made sense given the dilemma of working-class women subject to pregnancy, lacking good employment opportunities, and facing restricted sexual outlets outside marriage. Indirect subversion was appropriate: it did not require the co-operation of other people; advance planning was unnecessary; formal networks did not have to be brought into play (but if things went wrong, informal networks could be relied upon); it avoided direct confrontation; and, most important, it did not hold the *family* up to public ridicule. It is this sort of non-confrontational power that caused working-class autobiographers to assert the dominance of the mother, while simultaneously denying that the mother was actually domineering. For example, one working-class autobiographer apologetically wrote, 'It will have been noticed by now how every other object on the screen of memory fades back when my mother appears there. It was so in life, for she was dominant wherever she might be. I can't explain why, for she was never assertive.'[120]

These small acts of resistance should not be dismissed as somehow less 'political' than mass movements of resistance.[121] Risk-averse protests were not lower forms of resistance: they were the *preferred* response to oppression. For the housewife, the personal (sometimes anonymous) character of her resistance was not only an integral part of her position within society and the family, but was also an integral part of the very value system she was defending. Her goal was not to overthrow the family, but to protect it from the threats posed by 'breadwinners'. Her goal was not to drive away her husband, but to consolidate her role as housewife. It was no less radical for this.

DOMESTICITY AND THE WORKING-CLASS MALE

The 'breadwinner' against whom married women struggled cannot be portrayed as unchanging, unrepentant, and fundamentally undomesticated. Although the primary use of time for working-class men continued to be paid employment and, compared to their womenfolk, working-class men continued to spend little time doing housework, the home was also a masculine space.

The significance of the home for men was affected by shifts in structures of employment. As we saw in Chapter 1, the proportion of time that a man spent 'winning' the household's 'bread' declined, freeing some time for investment in either leisure or housework. Conventionally, economists investigating male working patterns predict that the demand for leisure will increase once total working hours are shortened. Certainly, in the case of manual workers between the 1890s and the 1930s, a portion of the 'freed' time was invested in leisure. As we examined in Chapter 2, the range of leisure activities expanded, with the evolution of more efficient architectural and organizational structures in sport and with the growing accessibility of new forms of leisure, such as cinemas, seaside resorts, bicycles, and popular forms of music and dance. With the proliferation of radios, gramophones, magazines and so on, the home also became a site of leisure.[122]

Not all the 'freed' time, however, was invested in leisure: some was invested in masculine forms of housework. This was not inevitable. As one woman complained in 1938, 'if you killed 'em, they couldn't spare time. . . . You'd think 'twas the harvest was calling 'em outside.'[123] Working men could have invested *all* of their 'freed' time in leisure. Some did. Time freed from employment alone was not enough to remind men of their domestic duties. The types of housework on offer to working-class men – do-it-yourself, repairs, redecorating, gardening – required a certain level of economic security. As in the case of their wives, the overall improvement in working-class living standards was crucial for the evolution of particular forms of masculine housework. As one commentator noted in a study of a working-class estate, do-it-yourself was popular with all men except for the poorest quarter: 'plaster ducks and poverty do not go together'.[124] Other historians have also suggested a link between economic security and the propensity of working-class men to spend time in the domestic sphere. For example, Geoffrey Crossick argued that it was the respectable, comfortably off artisans on the Evelyn estate in Deptford by the end of the nineteenth century who spent a large proportion of their time repairing things around the house, painting, building fences and so on. In his words, 'privatised and family-centred values were partially being absorbed by these [respectable] artisans'.[125] Masculine forms of housework required a little surplus. From the middle of the nineteenth century, more and more working-class households were managing to save this surplus. After the turn of the century, the introduction of state welfare provisions, in conjunction with changes in real wages, raised the general prosperity of working-class households. As more people were endowed with more time and income, masculine housework expanded.

Working-class men were increasingly willing to invest their labour in domestic production (once time and income were freed) because men were never excluded entirely from ideologies of domesticity. Although it has been said that cooking, cleaning, and childcare are 'almost universally *female* task[s],'[126] men were not *excluded* from these activities. Fathers looked after their children.[127] They were sufficiently concerned about their wives' health to write for advice to Marie Stopes.[128] Childcare was fraught with tensions for both mothers and fathers. As one unemployed Rochdale man explained in the 1930s: 'For a long time the little stranger was a real stranger to me. . . . It was months before I felt that he really "belonged" to my house.'[129] Once accustomed to the 'little stranger', many working-class fathers rose to the challenge. Men embroidered pincushions with the words 'For Baby, 1921' in celebration of a new birth.[130] In the words of a song sung to his children by a poor Sussex farmer,

When I get home at night just as tired as I be
I take my youngest child and I dance him on my knee
The others come around me with their prittle prattling toys
And that's the only pleasure a working man enjoys.[131]

In large families, fathers were often important in caring for older children while mothers nursed the newly born. As working-class children began spending longer hours in school, the father might have to help with those domestic chores previously the preserve of older children: 'He has his cross time early in the evening. I gen'lly have to trot him round for a nower or a nower'n'half while my wife's gettin' the supper and washin' up', bragged one father in 1908.[132] Fathers could trim their children's hair, and delicately plait it.[133] Sons sat 'companionably' on the loo with their fathers; they did Sandow exercises together each morning.[134] Fathers collected herbs for sick children and nursed them back to health.[135] During public rites, fathering could predominate, as Mass Observation reporters at Blackpool noted in the 1930s that well over half of fathers played with their children in the sand, compared with only 8 per cent of mothers.[136] Men cooked.[137] They cleaned, and not only during ritualized occasions of male domesticity, such as house cleaning before Lancashire's 'Mary Ann Night'.[138]

How should we square evidence of men doing housework with the frequent assertions that the fact that housework was woman's work was 'so obvious that it did not need to be stated. Only a "meek" man would descend to doing the chores "in his own home"?[139] In my study of over 250 working-class autobiographies dealing with childhoods between the years 1890 and 1930, for every writer who mentions a father *not* performing housework, fourteen declared that he *did*. There are obvious problems interpreting this evidence. The reliability of autobiographies could be doubted. Autobiographers with 'unusual' fathers who did housework might be more inclined to mention the fact. My impression is, however, that the evidence errs in the other direction. Nearly all mention of men performing housework is introduced as casual observation, in contrast to accounts of those fathers who are emphatically said *not* to do housework. The implication in the latter accounts is that here is an unusually inattentive father. If time and money could be budgeted to provide a surplus, certain domestic duties were expected of a husband and father. In addition, many of the autobiographers who declared that their fathers did *not* do housework often include contradictory internal evidence. While explicitly criticizing menfolk for neglecting the home, they include unselfconscious accounts of men working around the home. The example of men *not* doing housework which is cited most frequently by other historians would be Hannah Mitchell's bitter critique of different labouring requirements for boys and girls. She was forced to darn stockings for her brothers while they played: 'the fact that the boys could read if they wished filled my cup of bitterness to the brim'. Yet, scarcely a page later we are told how she negotiated with her brothers: she would do their domestic chores (cleaning boots and gathering firewood) if they would collect her library books.[140] Read as a whole, the testimony of this type of evidence strongly endorses the existence of a convention whereby men were expected to work in the home after returning from their place of employment.

Men did not necessarily do *more* childcare, cooking, or cleaning between the 1890s and the 1950s. In fact, with declining family size, running water, and gas stoves, they may have been doing less of these three activities. The real change was in the expansion of *other* forms of domestic labour for men. These changes required alterations in housing and the provision of allotments and gardens.

Improvements in working-class housing probably had the biggest impact on manly housework. The movement of workers into council housing, and into the suburbs in the inter-war years, favoured the further development of a family life for men. Since the history of this change is examined in Chapter 1, it is sufficient to notice in this chapter the dramatic effect these shifts in working-class housing had in promoting masculine forms of housework. The distancing of a working man's home from his place of employment – a trend which had begun in the nineteenth century – was accentuated. Progressively, 'home' became a separate sphere. Working-class estates were located at some distance from major working-class sites of employment: one study in 1946 disclosed that while nearly half of workers living in the central areas of cities could walk to work, only 14 per cent of workers living on working-class estates could do so.[141] The increased distance between home and employment was also a result of more general patterns of urban zoning. Thus, two-thirds of workers in Poplar lived and worked in the borough in 1921, but by the end of the decade half of the borough's workforce were commuting to other boroughs to work.[142] Changing patterns of working-class housing and spatial mobility encouraged a view of the home as a secluded, self-contained domain, or, in the words of a popular saying, a respectable external domestic front had to be maintained because 'there's more pass by than comes in'.[143]

Life on housing estates also affected the way work within the home was distributed between its members. In an article published in *Marriage and Family Living* in the early 1950s, J. M. Mogey revealed that 65 per cent of the 1,000 working-class households he examined in central Oxford had a rigid division of labour between husbands and wives, compared with 20 per cent of households on housing estates.[144] Another investigator, comparing the older areas of Manchester with the Wythenshawe estate, concluded that husbands on the estate were 'more cooperative than many working-class husbands tended to be: they helped around the house and the garden, took the children out on Sundays and rarely frequented pubs'.[145] Tenants on estates were liable to complain if their domestic ambitions were thwarted. Thus, in June 1939, the Bethnal Green and East London Housing Association received a letter of complaint about the thin walls in their flats: the writer grumbled, 'my husband's always got some job to do when he comes home, but he doesn't like to do much hammering because it disturbs other tenants'.[146] As a man living on the Dagenham estate explained: 'Down here a man makes an art of having something to do in his home when he gets back from work. He realizes he can do things he never thought he could do before.'[147]

Moving from rented accommodation in the inner city to council housing in the suburbs, combined with higher levels of home owner-ship, provided men with a rationale for investing more and more time in the home. The best documented examples concern the London City Council. Although this council redecorated their houses every five years, it was inadequate for many working men. Mr Barber, who redecorated his home annually, described the council's wallpapers as 'very antiquated, out of this world', adding, 'Myself I like something pretty modernistic, keeping up with the times.' Mr Wright agreed, refusing to allow the Council inside his home: 'I do all my own decorating and I prefer it that way.' His preferences were idiosyncratic: he had glued a grey, yellow, and blue-patterned wallpaper on three walls, contrasted with a red and white check wallpaper on the fourth; the woodwork had been painted grey; and he had fixed red plastic handles and finger panels onto the doors. Other men interviewed on this estate bragged about putting in water heaters, tiled fireplaces, superior sinks, efficient electric heaters, hot and cold taps, 'Ascots' or boilers, plastic handles, ball-catches on their doors, collapsible tables and stools, and additional light fittings.[148]

Changes in working-class housing were influential for another reason. As middle-class reformers had been saying from the nineteenth century, comfortable housing helped entice working men to spend time at home – that is, for both leisure and housework. In 1935, the

Bethnal Green and East London Housing Association received a letter from a woman relating her 'married life story of Houseing Accomadiation'. She started her married life occupying one front room, and 'removed' to two back rooms in Canning Town when she had children. Later, she rented a couple of rooms and a basement scullery in Bow Lane. About this home, she complained that 'the House was Let to Men Lodgers in different rooms they had to come into my Scullery at different times to get their water as it was the only Tap in the House and it was not very pleasant when we were having our meals'. According to her, life changed for the better only after she was allocated a flat by the Housing Association: 'I can honestly say I am more settled and Comfortable than I have been since I have been married. *We never knew the comfort of having my husband at home with us till we came here.*'[149]

Despite the considerable influence changes in housing stock had in nourishing a self-contained working-class family, it should not be exaggerated. At most only half of working-class families were affected by improved housing stock. More important (as we shall see in Chapter 5), it would be wrong to counterpoise the secluded life of the estates with an allegedly communal life in inner city areas. Even in established working-class areas, the sense of distance from neighbours was substantial and identification with a fairly small family unit pervasive. In 1933, the social investigator, E. Wight Bakke, discovered this when he invited some of his informants to his 'digs'. His landlord was outraged, explaining, 'An Englishman's home is his castle. I wouldn't want my next-door neighbour in here. No one but my very closest friends. This is where I live, and my family lives.'[150] Smaller families living in more spacious accommodation, the popularity of spouse and child-orientated leisure, decreasing alcohol consumption, and the creation of more aesthetically pleasing domestic environments were conducive to raising drawbridges against intruders.

The manipulation of wood, metal, and paint were not the only forms of masculine housework stimulated by housing improvements. Real men also messed about with dirt. Indeed, the allotment or garden may have been more favoured by working-class men than their homes. Since the Small Holdings and Allotments Act of 1908, it has been the duty of local authorities to purchase or lease land for allotments if the 'labouring poor' wanted them, and if they failed to provide allotments, the County Council might act on their behalf and send them the bill. As a result of this Act, the number of allotments grew steadily.[151] According to the 1913 Land Inquiry Committee, in almost every urban area the demand for allotments was strong.[152] Just before the

Table 3.2 Ratio of households to allotment plots, 1913 and 1918

Area	Number of households per plot	
	1913	*1918*
Burton on Trent	4	2
Leicester	5	3
Oxford	5	3
Gloucester	6	3
Reading	6	n.a.

Source: National Union of Allotment Holders, *Allotment Holders' Yearbook for 1923* (London, 1923), 65.

First World War there were between 450,000 and 600,000 allotments, and this number rose rapidly with the declaration of war. By 1918, there was one allotment for every five occupied houses. Although the number of allotments declined with the end of war, the number and size of allotments remained higher than pre-war levels. In the inter-war years, an allotment 'culture' developed, sustained by legislation in 1920, 1922, and 1925 which extended the rights of allotment holders, guaranteed them compensation for disturbance, made provisions against arbitrary ejection, established compulsory committees with tenant representation in every council, instituted compulsory acquisition of land, and extended provisions from the 'labouring poor' to everyone. This masculine 'culture' was also assisted by the introduction of daylight saving time in 1916. No longer were allotments a feature mainly of rural and small town districts; just prior to the Second World War, three out of four allotment holders were townsmen.[153]

Although there were 815,000 allotments in England by 1939, the total number had fallen between the wars.[154] The return of emergency land to its owners after the war, and suburban expansion which ate up much of the land formerly used for the allotments were partially responsible, but more important was the provision of gardens in the new working-class housing areas. Furthermore, these gardens were often not significantly smaller than allotments.[155] In a Mass Observation Survey of working-class estates, all homes had gardens, and 98 per cent had gardens between 12 and 30 feet long.[156] The provision of gardens enhanced the desirability of council housing. As a Kearsley collier and father of three young children replied to the Bolton City Council when asked in 1924 why he wanted a council house: 'Desireous of more sleeping accommodation. We are all strict teetottal and desire to live in a quieter place and ocupy our spare hours gardening.'[157]

The spread of gardens excited the National Allotments Society. In their annual report of 1931, they agreed that private gardens in council estates had 'given rise to a new problem and presented fresh opportunities' to them.[158] They were concerned with what they saw as gardening *naiveté*, so they immediately set out to establish branches in working-class areas and engaged in widespread distribution of cheap pamphlets and books aimed at the working-class man. Other organizations also took an interest in working-class gardening. Allotments and gardens were championed as a way of alleviating the worst effects of poverty by groups as diverse as the Society of Friends and the Conservative Party. Indeed, gardens did provide an important supplement to the household's diet. Few working-class men claimed to be enthusiastic gardeners; rather, the most common attitude was, 'My husband does the garden. Mind you, he doesn't like doing it – he does it to get the benefit of it – with the vegetables.'[159] B. Seebohm Rowntree's study of budgets in 1913 revealed that gardens and allotments could provide nearly one-quarter of the food consumed by families, and even poorly run or small gardens provided one-twelfth of the food consumed. As Rowntree summarized it, 'but for the fact that the majority of households were in a position to supplement the food purchased with product from their own gardens' underfeeding would be even more severe.[160] Local councils were always aware of this fact, and they attempted to foster the competitive urge by offering prizes for the attractiveness of the front garden and the productiveness of the back.[161] Gardening was introduced into the school curriculum.[162] The domestication of the working-class male may be represented in the shift from the tilling of root crops such as potatoes and carrots, to the cultivation of lettuces, peas, and runner beans.[163]

This domestication was limited: after all, allotments and gardens were masculine territories.[164] Thorpe's Committee found that only 3 per cent of allotment holders were women (and only 1 per cent were housewives). Women appeared only occasionally – as visitors or Sunday afternoon helpers and admirers. Arthur Ashby, who wrote a history of allotments in 1917, commented: 'in one thing the labourer of to-day fares worse than the labourer of the former generation – his wife gives less assistance on the allotment. This disinclination to engage in other than household work which spread very widely among the wives and daughters of farmers about 1870 spread later to the labourers' wives.'[165] The shortage of food and men during the First World War encouraged working-class women to move into allotments and gardens – but only for the duration of the war. It was not until the Second World War that working-class women got into gardening in a serious way.[166]

THE MARKETPLACE, THE STATE, AND WOMEN

Masculine housework was work, as B. Seebohm Rowntree paraphrased the words of Oxfordshire labourers in 1913: 'When all is said and done, life is a continual struggle. To be sure, the garden, as Mrs Mayne says, is "half the battle". But the garden can only be made to provide them with vegetables for the year by hard toil, given by a man who is already toiling hard through a long working day.'[167] However, it was portrayed as a form of leisure, never as an activity that extended working hours which they, their unions, and employers had reduced. Men were lured into performing domestic labour by the promise of reward. A man might raise his living standards more by working an extra couple of hours at home than by working an extra couple of hours at his employment. Indeed, one of the arguments made for reducing hours of employment was that it would enable men to invest more time in domestic production. The increased prosperity of working-class households was created not only by higher wages and the increased investment of women's time in full-time housewifery, but also by investment of men's time in certain forms of housework. Men also had to take a part in the process of domestic arranging and rearranging – under, of course, the supervision of the housewife. Husbands *had* to do housework to maintain acceptable standards of domestic production on which good credit levels with the local shopkeeper, the pawnbroker, and the neighbours depended. Working-class women had been greatly extending the quality and quantity of housework they were performing within the home; they required the help of their husbands.

The rewards were not only economic. Many working-class households – especially after the expansion of convenience foods – did not grow vegetables to supply deficiencies in the family's diet. Creativity cannot be ignored: men maintained standards of beauty, they enjoyed the touch of plants and wood, their domestic work symbolically reaffirmed their manly role as 'providers'. Masculine housework brought a new sense of accomplishment while enhancing men's masculinity. Creative manly housework was an acceptable way a husband could express love: the man who built his wife a sideboard was adored ('We were very happy and never quarrelled over anything').[168] Wives valued each other's menfolk according to their

Table 3.3 Number of pawnbrokers' and moneylenders' licences issued in England, Wales, and Scotland, 1905–48

Year	Pawnbrokers	Moneylenders
1905	4,727	—
1910	4,984	—
1915	5,022	—
1920	4,559	—
1925	3,973	—
1930	3,498	3,638
1935	2,981	2,940
1940	2,469	2,106
1945	1,932	1,563
1948	1,726	1,588

Source: Annual Reports of Customs and Excise.

Note: Statistics not published after 1948. Statistics for moneylenders not available before 1930.

domestic performance. For instance, the father who helped with the heaviest part of the weekly wash was 'held in the highest esteem and the wife who was forced to ask her children to help was pitied'.[169] Husbands also competed with each other. A man could lose status at work if he was exposed as being unable to control his children.[170] Men were rivals in the creation of masculine domestic goods: their fence had to be taller; their house paint more shiny; their vegetables superior to the 'passel o' rubbish' over the fence. Their allotment lettuces had to be plumper, their leeks longer, their children prettier.[171]

Extra spice was given to the competition between men by the development of an advertising and marketing infrastructure devoted to their domestic labour. Although the do-it-yourself revolution did not flare up until the late 1950s, preparations were being made in the earlier period with the establishment and spread of specialist stores catering for the domestic man, and with the coming onto the market of plywood. From the 1920s, cheap handyman books began to be published, justifying their existence by claiming that working men have 'more leisure time nowadays' in which to work at home.[172]

Masculine housework was also helped by changes in education. Housework is 'natural' to neither girls nor boys. Earlier in the chapter, the education of girls was examined; how did boys learn masculine housework? Obviously, other men provided training and male retreats such as the forge, the allotment, and the barbershop were important in this process.[173] Mothers were responsible for ensuring not only that their sons had a knowledge of masculine housework, but also could perform those tasks generally allocated to women. The son of a postman in the 1910s recalled, 'I lived in a home where scrubbing and dusting were a daily routine in which my brother and I used to play our parts. We never questioned these duties, any more than we questioned the round of mealtimes, or the ritual of going to bed.'[174] Mothers were proud of training their boys to do a wide range of domestic tasks.[175] This training of young boys in domesticity was part of the process of moulding a 'man'. In a book written in the 1930s by a former millworker, we are told that his mother taught him to do housework on the grounds that such lessons 'comes in so useful in after life, when a man has to or should help his wife in some of the harder of the household tasks'.[176] Until another man went to work in the mines, his mother 'always contended that working about the house was a necessary prelude to possible future circumstances'.[177]

As in the case of working-class girls, the state also intervened in the domestic education of boys. Manual training was explicitly introduced to dovetail with girls' domestic education: both were intended to teach gendered roles within the household.[178] Although the first classes began in 1862, it was not until 1904 that it became compulsory for boys in secondary schools to do at least two years of manual training. Since few working-class boys attended school to a secondary level, this legislation affected only a tiny proportion of working-class boys. Gradually, though, elementary schools were being affected. By the end of the 1880s, elementary schools in Sheffield, Manchester, and London were teaching manual education.[179] The Code of 1909 introduced manual education into most elementary schools in the country. Half of elementary schools also introduced gardening. By the 1920s, half a million elementary school boys were attending classes in manual education and well over 100,000 were also attending classes in gardening.

Working-class boys proved keen to attend the classes, and their parents were successful in pressuring their local school boards into providing instruction peculiarly suited to their local cultures. In the 1880s, when the classes were first being introduced, there was a considerable amount of interest in the usefulness of manual training in preparing working-class boys for employment in manual trades. From the turn of the century, educationalists were strongly opposing this rationale, arguing that the classes could only be justified by reference to the way they improved hand–eye co-ordination and trained boys in those things they would have to do about their homes. The classes were to teach boys to be 'more useful in their homes'[180] and to impart to boys 'the sort of handiness which is useful to them about their dwelling-house'.[181] As a report to the School Board of London concluded, manual training should be introduced because it would enable the future man 'to make his home . . . comfortable'.[182] When Rev. Patrick Finegan was asked in 1908 why manual instruction was important in local schools, he replied that the success of manual training was illustrated by the way 'they could turn it to immediately profitable account'. When asked 'Such as?', he replied: 'Working in their own homes; making gates and doors, and other things useful for the household.'[183] Male domesticity was promoted by the state.

Without the encouragement of working-class women, no educational campaign could have succeeded. Women created the domestic environment in which men could feel comfortable working. They organized. They instructed. Masculine housework needed the management of women: as Daisy Bumbelow bluntly told a young mother in the 1930s: 'What the hell do men know. . . . One poke and that's the end of it.'[184] In its feminine and masculine forms, housework is about power. As with girls' domestic education classes, boys' manual training threatened established power patterns within the household, as the *Yorkshire Observer* commented in 1913:

> Another thing which helps to make young lads bumptious is the manual training they get at school. To-day when a mother wants a job done in the house which requires the handy use of chisel, hammer and screws, it is to her big boy she appeals, not to her husband, because her boys are much more skilled in such tasks than the father whose vocation lies outside these lines. And the boy plumes himself no little on such skills and will presume upon it if not kept in hand.[185]

Relations of power based on sex also required maintaining. In reply to the question 'Did your father help in the house at all?', a daughter of a fisherman replied, 'No. I mean, the old girl used to say to him if he wanted to help, no, you sit down father, you've been at work all day long.'[186] Robert Roberts, in *A Ragged Schooling*, remarked that Salford husbands 'displayed virility by never performing any task in or about the house which was considered by tradition to be woman's work'. Their wives 'encouraged their partners in this and proudly boasted that they would never allow the "man of the house" to do a "hand's turn". Sneering names like "mog rag" and "diddy man" were used for those who did help.'[187] Housewives in one Yorkshire mining community would 'boast of their attention to the needs of their husbands and of how they have never been late with a meal, never confronted a returning worker with a cold meal, never had to ask his help in household duties'.[188] Good husbands did not interfere in those forms of domestic work which 'belonged' to women.[189] Thus, it was said in 1910 of a poor London woman (and mother of six children) that she had 'married a steady, industrious, good-tempered man, who rarely interfered in domestic matters except for the purpose of upholding her authority'.[190]

Childcare, in particular, was a sensitive area of control for women; as one woman who grew up during the First World War remembered, she did not know where babies came from but she knew that 'after babies were born they belonged to the mother, and I thought mothers very lucky that the babies belonged to them and not to the father'.[191] In the 1920s, Margaret Powell was married to a milkman who encouraged her to attend evening classes: 'He was quite capable, he said, of minding the baby. . . . So I demonstrated how to fold and pin the [baby's] napkin, and not to forget the vaseline and baby powder. I know I ought to have been pleased, but indeed I was rather piqued to find on my return that he'd made as good a job of nappy-changing as I did.'[192] Men had their domestic sphere: they were responsible for the more menial aspects of housework: scrubbing boots, dirty cleaning, carting water, and work connected with dirt, rough woods, and cold metals.[193] Significantly, most forms of masculine housework were also the preserve of children.[194] Men were also in charge of those aspects of housework which remained largely unaffected by technology. While working-class wives' domestic work was slowly becoming sanitized and mechanized through the sale of cleaning fluids, a diversification in kitchen and dinner ware, and the spread of gas, men retained those jobs connected with primitive dirtiness.[195]

Husbands and fathers would not always abide by the barriers erected by their wives. Some men responded to their wives clinging to domestic supremacy by secrecy. One brass caster relished long conversations with his children: 'but only when Mum wasn't about'.[196] Some men were more determined than others not to allow their wives to gain all the credit for bearing children. Mrs O'Calloran, who ran a small general store in Chelsea, did not suffer alone: throughout all six pregnancies her husband was tormented with boils.[197] Some men experienced morning sickness, as one pregnant woman in Hull recalled in 1919:

My husband suffered morning sickness, and each time I cooked a meal it was refused. His request was for [a tin of] salmon, this I supplied, but was at a loss to know why salmon? always be [*sic*] requested – when asked if any other fish would satisfy the answer was No. Alright! . . . After three weeks my husband was so ill he had to have medical attention, the result of the diagnosis being, he would be much better when a certain stage of my pregnancy occurred – that verdict proved correct.[198]

Other men cried out in pain during their wives' travail.[199] In the mining village, Bowers Row, everyone expected the pregnant woman's ailments to be shared by her husband: if he did not experience morning sickness, violent toothache, pain in the back, losing weight in ratio to his wife gaining it, and intense longings for certain types of foods, then he was thought to no longer love her, or to have been unfaithful. It was with these symbols and signs of both feminine and masculine domesticity that the working-class family created and re-created itself.

POWER AND MASCULINE HOUSEWORK

Between the wars, working-class men began spending more of their time in domestic production, but this made very little difference to the respective position of men and women within the home. An increased presence of men around the home does not necessarily imply greater equality between the sexes. There was little in the growth of masculine housework to promote equality between the sexes.

Masculine housework remained 'manly'. Certain jobs were reserved for them: heavy water carrying, emptying spittoons, painting, using tools, work connected with wood or metal, carrying coal, and (in the days of flock mattresses) turning mattresses.[200] Men and boys painted while womenfolk scrubbed and whitewashed.[201] Fathers made cupboards, fences, and swings and were responsible for interior decorating.[202] Only an unusual mother would cobble her children's shoes.[203] 'Wielding his weapons' (otherwise known as carving the beef) was a man's job.[204] In 1933, one-quarter of boys from poor or very poor households secured jobs through their fathers.[205] If any form of sex education was to be imparted to boys, the father would do it.[206] The division between the public and private was ever present. 'Feminine' chores had to be avoided, even if it meant hanging upside-down to scrub the hearthstone rather than risk being spotted by neighbouring boys.[207] While it was not unusual for a working-class father to spend his half-holiday at the washtub or to finish up his day's work with the heaviest part of the household cleaning, he might 'draw the line' at using the needle and cotton; that is, unless he was 'in seclusion'.[208] A man would be ill-advised to relax manly habits outside the home. Thus, one commentator in 1908 explained changes in children's clothing: 'I find one reason why children are short-coated so soon is that their fathers wish to carry them when they go out of doors, and no man but a sailor has the courage to be seen with an infant in long clothes.'[209] Or, as a 28-year-old working-class wife said, her husband was 'afraid of being thought a cissy; mine hates people to know he helps at all in the house; won't push pram'.[210] Pushing a pram was often cited as the most humiliating of tasks, although a grandfather could do it – but only if he used one hand and walked beside it as though it were of no concern to him.[211]

Furthermore, there were limits to the extent to which the masterful performance of housework might enhance the reputation of a working-class man: the jobless man was in a delicate position. Once the public sphere was withdrawn, domesticity was all that remained. Some unemployed men enjoyed the challenge of full-time domesticity; as one unemployed labourer from Stratford bragged, 'some nights, THIS NIGHT, I made them biscuits, no end o' little currant biscuits! . . . I cooked them in a tin over the fire, and the kiddies had a blowout.'[212] For other unemployed men, any suggestion of crossing full-time into the 'sphere' of the other sex carried the implied threat of emasculation. Until the inter-war years, the masculinity of a man could be located within the employment market: his domestic life was private and unthreatening. Inter-war unemployment menaced many forms of masculine housework. The house and garden were neglected. The economic surplus necessary for many forms of masculine housework no longer existed. Quarrels between unemployed husbands and their wives disrupted childcare. One man mourned the loss of his children who became 'less apt to consider me worthy of their love, or a fitting person to ask if they require advice or direction'.[213] As many wives took over responsibility for supporting the family, pressure was placed on unemployed men to perform conventionally female forms of housework. Unemployment clubs discovered that men would go to lectures on hygiene and food-values for poultry and pigeons, but studiously avoided lectures on hygiene and food-values for humans.[214] In 1934, an unemployed wire drawer from Ambergate described his life after his wife started work as a spinner for the English Sewing Cotton Company: 'I do the housework after my wife has left home at half-past seven in the morning, I read, I play with the child [aged five years], I go out for walks in the evening after my wife has returned at half-past six. Is this a man's life?'[215] Unemployed men resisted the blurring of gender roles, attempting to ensure that the domestic work they did was 'appropriate for men' and not for, as one unemployed man yelled at his wife, a 'bloomin' housemaid!'[216]

CONCLUSION

Both working-class men and working-class women were able to use their techniques of ordering and beautifying and surviving to adapt in positive ways to the twentieth century. No choice was ideal. For working-class women, housework was no easy option. Working-class housewives exiled to the suburbs were frequently lonely: without an obvious group of housewives with which they could compete, many were discouraged.[217] Clearly, the ability of a working-class housewife to make the most of her domestic power depended on factors such as the chief wage-earner's income, and the stability of that income. Crucial to her status within the household and within the community of housewives was her age, health, and number of children. In addition, many working-class men repudiated the male domestic ideal. Ivy Willis's husband in the 1930s refused to allow her to continue her paid job after their marriage: 'he used to say he didn't keep a dog and bark himself'.[218] Other men continued to treat their wives as their personal domestic servant: coming home drunk and hungry, stinting on housekeeping allowances, brutally copulating and refusing to take the consequences. However, for every negative, distant husband or father, there were dozens of warm working-class domestic men. Elizabeth Bryson could write of her father, a foundry worker: 'My greatest joy was my father. . . . My father put the two ex-babies, my brother and myself to bed. He told us endless stories, fairy stories and Bible stories and stories of his own; he made up little rhymes about us and added verses to the Old Nursery Rhymes just to please us. . . . Father tucked us up, secure from danger, and we said the prayer with the lovely words.'[219] Or, one wife confessed, 'my husband has always been husband, nurse, and mother'.[220] Housework was not 'invisible' work; it was very visible – especially to other housewives who competed with each other and punished (through social ostracism and gossip) other housewives who were seen as lowering standards. They worked to increase their power within the household in this period by focusing on the irreplaceability and indispensability of their skills and resources. For many, the home was a neighbourhood powerbase, but a powerbase none the less.

SELECTIVE BIBLIOGRAPHY

Bourke, Joanna, *Husbandry to Housewifery: Women, Economic Change, and House-wifery in Ireland, 1890–1914* (Oxford, 1993).
An analysis of the relationship between female employment, housewifery, and economic

growth in Ireland. Places stress on how poor women experienced and changed their lives. Compares what was happening in Ireland with changes within Britain.

Chinn, Carl, *They Worked All Their Lives: Women of the Urban Poor in England, 1880–1939* (Manchester, 1988).
Places emphasis on the role of women in maintaining poor households, matriarchy, and female forms of protest. Excellent discussion of domestic violence.

Daunton, M. J., *House and Home in the Victorian City: Working-Class Housing 1850– 1914* (London, 1983).
Combines a study of housing policy with the actual experience of living in working-class homes in the period to 1914.

Lewis, Jane (ed.), *Labour and Love: Women's Experience of Home and Family, 1850– 1940* (Oxford, 1986).
For the history of working-class women, see the chapters on mother–daughter relationships, mothering, state intervention, domestic violence, and marriage.

Roberts, Elizabeth, *A Woman's Place: An Oral History of Working-Class Women 1890–1940* (Oxford, 1984).
Perceptive oral history of working-class women in central and north Lancashire, focusing on growing up, youth, marriage, housewifery, families, and neighbours.

Rodger, Richard (ed.), *Scottish Housing in the Twentieth Century* (Leicester, 1989).
Historical studies of housing in Scotland, with emphasis placed on confrontation, evictions, rent strikes, national policies, municipal house building, housing associations, and landlords between 1880 and 1987.

Tilly, Louise A. and Joan W. Scott, *Women, Work, and Family* (New York, 1978).
Standard text on the impact of industrialization on women's work since the early modern period.

4 Marketplace
Public spheres

Germany had surrendered, but the menfolk were still on the battlefields. It was election time. On the front page of the *Daily Mirror* women were urged to 'Vote for Him': that is, to vote as their absent husbands would want them to vote. At least one reader responded favourably to this appeal: 'I shall vote for him. I know what he wants. . . . He wants a good house with a bit of garden. He wants a job at a fair wage, however hard the work may be. He wants a good education for the children.'[1] In the last chapter we looked at the first part of this reader's dream: the house and garden. This chapter examines the second half of her statement: a good job at a 'fair' wage and an education for the children. In the areas of employment and education, manual workers seemed to be prospering more in the second half of the twentieth century than in the first half. Welfare provisions not only provided a buffer against the risk of absolute destitution (as we saw in the first chapter), but also attempted to extend access to education and to reward individuals on the basis of ability rather than entitlement alone. Welcomed as revolutionary achievements, the significance of these shifts was deceptive: more fluid occupational structures concealed sluggish rates of social mobility for the children of the working classes, and burgeoning opportunities in white-collar jobs disguised extensive segregation by gender and class.

Whether we are concerned with absolute or relative levels of poverty, occupational structures underpin patterns of poverty. The major employing sectors in twentieth-century Britain shifted from primary and manufacturing industries into service provisions. Overall, for men, the number of professional, technical, and white-collar workers expanded while the number of manual workers shrank. In other words, in 1911 around 73 per cent of the male workforce were employed in blue-collar occupations: by 1961, this had fallen to 65 per cent.[2]

Table 4.1 Distribution of economically active male population, by occupational category, in Great Britain, 1911–61

Occupational category	1911 (%)	1921 (%)	1931 (%)	1951 (%)	1961 (%)
1.	13.1	13.6	13.8	15.3	16.8
2.	1.4	1.8	1.8	3.0	4.0
3.	1.8	1.9	2.0	3.3	3.8
4.	10.1	9.2	11.0	10.0	10.4
5.	33.0	32.3	30.1	30.3	32.3
6.	29.1	24.5	23.4	24.3	22.8
7.	11.5	16.7	17.9	13.8	9.9
Total (1,000s)	12,926	13,635	14,760	15,584	15,992

Source: Census.

Key: Occupational Categories
1. Professional, managers, senior administrators
2. Semi-professional, white-collar supervisors
3. Foremen, self-employed artisans
4. Routine white-collar
5. Skilled manual
6. Semi-skilled manual
7. Unskilled manual

Female employment has an utterly different history. While between 92 and 96 per cent of men aged between 15 and 65 claimed an occupation in the census, employment among the female population fluctuated more widely. In 1901 women constituted 29 per cent of the total employed population. This remained stable at around 30 per cent until after the Second World War when it slowly began rising. Even in 1971, however, women constituted only 36 per cent of the total employed population. The real change can be seen when looking at the proportion of women aged between 15 and 59 years who were employed. Between 1901 and 1931, 38 per cent of women in these ages claimed an occupation. There was no census in 1941, but by 1951 43 per cent of women were employed. This rose another four percentage points within a decade and passed the halfway point by 1971.

The importance of age structure can be seen even more clearly when broken down further. In the first third of the twentieth century, over two-thirds of women between the ages of 15 and 34 years were employed, compared with between one-fifth and one-quarter of those aged between 35 and 44 years, and only 5 per cent of those aged over 60 years. After the Second World War, however, there was a sudden jump in the female participation rates of women aged between 35 and 59 years. Between 1931 and 1951, the proportion of women with

Table 4.2 Percentage of women in each age group who were employed, 1901–61

Year	Total number of employed women (millions)	Percentage of women in each age group in the labour force		
		Under 35	35–59	Over 60
1901	4.2	73	22	5
1911	4.8	71	24	5
1921	5.0	69	26	5
1931	5.6	69	26	5
1951	6.3	52	43	5
1961	7.0	45	49	6

Source: Census.

Table 4.3 Percentage of each marital status in the labour force, 1901–61

Year	Single	Married	Widowed
1901	78	13*	9*
1911	77	14	9
1921	78	14	8
1931	77	16	7
1951	52	40	8
1961	40	52	8

(* Estimate based on data for ever-married women.)

employment in this age group jumped from 26 per cent to 43 per cent. At the same time, extended periods of education for young women resulted in declining participatory rates for women aged under 35 years. Related to this change are the participatory rates of married women. Up until 1931, 13 to 16 per cent of married women were employed. However, between 1931 and 1951, the proportions employed rose dramatically to 40 per cent, and continued rising throughout the century.

Similarly to their menfolk, there has been a trend of women workers out of manual occupations and into white-collar jobs. In particular, women have moved rapidly into clerical positions and into shops. The proportion of women in these jobs increased from between one-fifth and one-third of all workers in 1911 to between 50 and 65 per cent by 1961. However, within manual occupations, women have slipped out

Table 4.4 Number of women employed as a percentage of all employed persons, 1911–61

Occupation	1911	1921	1931	1951	1961
Employers, proprietors	19	20	20	20	20
White collar	30	38	36	42	44
manager, administrator	20	17	13	15	15
higher professional	6	5	7	8	10
lower professional, technician	63	59	59	53	51
foreman, inspector	4	6	9	13	10
clerk	21	45	46	60	65
salesman, shop assistant	35	44	37	52	55
All manual	30	28	29	26	26
skilled	24	21	21	16	14
semi-skilled	40	40	43	38	39
unskilled	15	17	15	20	22
Total occupied Population	30	30	30	31	32

Source: Census.

of the skilled jobs and have increasingly concentrated their paid activities in unskilled occupations.

The implications of this dramatic structural shift in occupational categories into the service sector are considerable. As work in manual occupations contracted, we would expect to see a substantial movement of individuals between occupations. Expanding employment opportunities in non-manual occupations should lead fewer working-class sons and daughters into manual jobs. To the extent that class affiliation is based on occupational categories, these trends hint at a class system in flux.

To what extent has the working class benefited from the structural changes in employment? John Goldthorpe has undertaken detailed research using data from the Mobility Study. He demonstrated that throughout the twentieth century there has been a substantial amount of social mobility as the sons of manual workers gained access to employment higher in the social scale (in particular, service class jobs). According to his researches, however, the tendency to 'avoid' manual labour was even greater amongst sons of non-manual fathers. In other words, the chances of a man of working-class origins finding himself in a manual job declined more slowly than had the chances of a man of non-working-class origins. More room had been made at the top of the occupational scale, but the higher economic classes benefited more than the lower economic classes. The working classes contributed less upward mobility than their proportional share. Manual workers continued to be the sons of the previous generation of manual workers and there was little downward mobility of professional or semi-professional sons into the manual sector. In Goldthorpe's words: 'once the perspective of relative mobility is adopted, [the overall trend] is no longer one of significant change in the direction of greater opportunity for social ascent but rather of stability or indeed of increasing *in*equality in class mobility chances'.[3]

Three economic and social crises were seen to fix or alter patterns of social mobility in twentieth-century Britain. The first two crises were the world wars between 1914 and 1918 and between 1939 and 1945, and the third crisis was the economic depression of the 1920s and 1930s. These crises will be examined in turn.

WAR AND GENDER

The impact of the First World War on working men was unmistakable. Half of all men aged between 15 and 49 years left their usual jobs and ended up toiling on battlefields or in war-related occupations. Of the eight million men who were mobilized, some 1.7 million were wounded and 722,000 were killed. In 1922, more than 900,000 war pensions were being paid out. In the words of factory worker, Jim Wolveridge,

> I didn't need to be told about [the war] any way, there were enough crippled and maimed around to bring it home to me. In our street there was a Mr Jordan who'd lost his right arm, my old man who'd been gassed, and the man at the top of the street who was so badly shell-shocked he couldn't walk without help. And there were always lots of one-armed and one-legged old sweats begging in the streets.[4]

Less deadly, but just as dramatic, were the changes on the Home Front. Many tributes have been paid to the First World War for transforming the lives of working women. In 1920, the suffragist Mrs M. G. Fawcett argued, 'The war revolutionised the industrial position of women. It found them serfs and left them free.'[5] Even at the time, women from a variety of backgrounds saw in this cataclysmic war a chance to elevate dramatically their economic and social status through radical reform of employment prospects. Between 1914 and 1918 an estimated two million women replaced men in employment, resulting in an increase in the proportion of women in total employment from 24 per cent in July 1914 to 37 per cent by November 1918.[6]

Table 4.5 War-related deaths by age group of the male population, aged 16–60 years, in England and Wales, 1914–18

Age group	War-related deaths
16–19	64,552
20–24	203,875
25–29	122,435
30–34	83,222
35–39	50,349
40–44	16,829
45–49	5,152
50–54	1,889
55–60	444
16–60	548,747

Source: Jay M. Winter, 'Some Paradoxes of the First World War', in Richard Wall and Jay M. Winter (eds), *The Upheaval of War* (Cambridge, 1988), 15.

Table 4.6 Numbers of women in paid employment, in July 1914 and July 1918

Employment	July 1914	July 1918	Percentage increase/ decrease
Self-employed, employers	430,000	470,000	9
Industry	2,178,600	2,970,600	36
Domestic service	1,658,000	1,258,000	−24
Commerce	505,500	934,500	85
Government and teaching	262,200	460,200	76
Agriculture	190,000	228,000	20
Hotels, pubs, theatres	181,000	220,000	22
Transport	18,200	117,200	544
Other	542,500	652,000	20
Total employed	5,966,000	7,310,500	23

Source: Adapted from *Report from the War Cabinet Committee on Women in Industry*, 1919.

The hope that the employment market would bolster women's social standing proved illusory. Even during the war, it was clear that women would have to pay a high price for the privileges gained by extended employment opportunities. Anxiety for the sexual security and survival of husbands or lovers, the pressures of employment combined with the need to perform housework in straitened circumstances, and the inadequacy of social services exacted a heavy toll and made the withdrawal of women back into their homes after the war less surprising. This return to full-time domesticity was not, however, wholly voluntary. In many instances, contracts of employment during the war years had been based on collective agreements between trade unions and employers which decreed that women would only be employed 'for the duration of the war'. Employed mothers were stung by the closure of day nurseries which had been vastly extended during the war.

Reinforcing these pressures were the recriminatory voices of husbands, lovers, and returning soldiers. As unemployment levels soared immediately after the war, anger towards women 'taking' jobs from menfolk exploded. Furthermore, women were divided, with single and widowed women claiming a prior right to employment over married women. Isobel M. Pizzey of Woolwich wrote to the *Daily Herald* in October 1919 declaring that 'No decent man would allow his wife to work, and no decent woman would do it if she knew the harm she was doing the widows and single girls who are *looking* for work.' She directed: 'Put the married women out, send them home to clean their houses and look after the man they married and give a mother's care to their children. Give the single women and widows the work.'[7] In some occupations, single women insisted on excluding their married sisters. For instance, in 1921 female civil servants passed a resolution asking for the banning of married women from their job. The resulting ban was enforced until 1946. There were other setbacks. During the First World War, hospitals had accepted female medical students: in the 1920s, women were rejected by the hospitals on the grounds of modesty. The National Association of Schoolmasters campaigned against the employment of female teachers. In 1924 the London County Council made its policy explicit when it changed the phrase 'shall resign on marriage' to 'the contract shall end on marriage'. When, in 1927, a Married Women's (Employment) Bill was introduced in the Commons, it was rejected as a 'travesty', threatening society with 'the reversal of the sexes, when the mother goes out to work and the father stays at home to look after the baby'.[8] Furthermore, the First World War did not result in a radical and permanent inflation of women's wages. Employers circumvented wartime equal pay regulations by employing several women to replace one man, or by dividing skilled tasks into several less skilled stages. In this way, women could be employed with lower wages and not be said to be 'replacing' a man directly. In 1931 a working woman's weekly wage rate was again, on average, half the male rate in most industries.[9]

The war did leave two valuable legacies. First, it opened up a wider range of occupations to female workers and hastened the collapse of traditional women's employment, particularly domestic service. From the late nineteenth century to 1911, between 11 and 13 per cent of the female population in England and Wales were domestic servants. By 1931, the percentage had dropped to under 8 per cent. Middle-class homes, as opposed to upper-class homes, were hardest hit. In the first two decades of the twentieth century, the number of female servants in wealthy homes declined by one-quarter (to forty servants per hundred families) while in middle-class homes, the proportion of servants declined by 60 per cent (to thirteen servants per hundred families).[10] For the middle classes, the decline of domestic service was facilitated by the rise of domestic appliances, such as cookers, electric irons, and vacuum cleaners. While the working class did not join in this appliances revolution until the 1950s, by the 1930s, the slogan 'Let electricity be your servant' represented a major shift of focus. The popularity of 'labour-saving' devices does not, however, explain the dramatic drop in the servant population. Middle-class women continued to clamour for servants, but working women who might have previously entered into service were being enticed away by alternative employments opening up to satisfy the demands of war. Thus, nearly half of the first recruits to the London General Omnibus Company in 1916 were former domestic servants.[11] Clerical work was another draw card. The number of women in the Civil Service increased from 33,000 in 1911 to 102,000 by 1921. The advantages of these alternative employments over domestic service were obvious: wages were higher, conditions better, and independence enhanced.

Trade unionism proved to be the second legacy of the war. Female workers have been less unionized than their male counterparts, partly as a result of their over-representation in part-time work and in small firms which proved to be a barrier to participation in unions geared to the working patterns of men. In addition, unions had a history of ambivalence towards female workers. During the latter part of the nineteenth century and the early decades of the twentieth, trade union halls were active participants in a series of debates about the 'family wage'. This meant altering wage or employment structures to enable male workers to support a family. The most effective way of achieving this 'family wage' was disputed, with one group contending that the employment of women (especially married women) should be banned, thus forcing employers to pay their workmen a wage sufficient to support women, while a more benign group placed the onus on employers to raise the wages of male workers irrespective of the employment status of women. Of course, this latter group reasoned,

Table 4.7 Trade union membership by sex, 1911–61

Year	Membership (millions)		Women as a percentage of union membership	Percentage of potential membership	
	Women	Men		Women	Men
1911	0.3	2.8	10	6	23
1921	1.0	5.6	15	18	44
1951	1.8	7.7	19	25	56
1961	2.0	7.9	20	24	53

Source: Michael Webb, 'Sex and Gender in the Labour Market', in Ivan Reid and Erica Stratta (eds), *Sex Differences in Britain*, second edition (Aldershot, 1989), 182.

raising wages would inevitably result in the removal of wives, mothers, and daughters from employment as their fathers, husbands, and sons realized their potential as sole 'breadwinners'. The arguments of both groups were problematical for working-class women. Everyone accepted that it was wrong that women were forced to work long hours for a pittance. The proposed 'reforms', however, were impractical. Anna Martin worked among women in London's dockland. Her book *Mothers in Mean Street*, published in 1911, gave instances of husbands receiving a 'family wage' who failed to share the extra money with their dependants. She documented how mothers and children did not benefit from increases in male wages and how they continued to live at a much lower standard of living than the 'breadwinner'. More obviously, many women could not claim the support of any 'breadwinner'. The First World War forced unions to deal with the issue of women's work: the scale of women's employment could no longer be denied; feminist pressure on established unions and the formation of separate women's unions threatened to destabilize men-only unions; and rising levels of women left unmarried or widowed by the war forced their hand. The increase in female trade union membership from only 357,000 in 1914 to 1,086,000 by 1918 represented an increase in the number of unionized women of 160 per cent compared with an increase of 45 per cent among men.

In terms of women's lives, the impact of the Second World War and the economic boom which followed was also limited. As with the First World War, women of all classes were encouraged into the paid workforce. In 1943, at the height of wartime mobilization, women made up 39 per cent of the total occupied population, compared with less than 30 per cent in 1931. Furthermore, they were young women.

Fifty-seven per cent of women employed in the 1940s were aged between 25 and 44 years, compared with 43 per cent in 1931. As we have already seen, the most important change occurred in the proportion of married women in employment which jumped from 16 per cent in 1931 to 43 per cent in 1943. The movement of these women into the workforce was partly the result of administrative dictum. Young, single women and young childless wives were conscripted into industry and the services. From April 1941, all married and single women aged between 18 and 45 years (later 50 years) were compelled to register at a labour exchange. Many women managed to ignore the pressures, citing domestic responsibilities. State ambivalence about the desirability of female employment also tipped the balance in favour of housewives. Government departments vied with each other. For instance, the Ministry of Health obstructed the Ministry of Labour's plans to open more nurseries for working mothers on the grounds that children should be cared for at home. As late as 1944, there were nursery places for only 6 per cent of all children aged under five years. Rather than improving facilities, a campaign was launched exhorting neighbours to come to the aid of employed women by assisting with housework and childcare. Through a blend of government pressure, union manoeuvring, and employers' hiring policies, female employment during the war did not imperil male workers. The extension of part-time and shift work only formalized women's role as second-class workers. Again, at the end of the Second World War, pressure was brought to bear on employed women to return to full-time housewifery. Many were pleased to do so, enabling E. Slater and M. Woodside to conclude in 1943 that:

> Most women are uninterested, regarding their jobs as a short-time expediency until marriage. With the married women who had been brought out of their homes to work during the war, the increased income was not felt to compensate for disruption of the normal pattern of family life. There were exceptions to this among some older women, often those who lived in suburbs, who enjoyed the new social contacts of part-time work in a factory. For the younger childless women, full-time war work meant considerable hardship in physical endurance and monotony.[12]

While more women have combined motherhood with paid employment since the Second World War than before, the majority continued to work in low-paid, low-skilled jobs.

Table 4.8 Number of women employed in industry (1,000s), 1939 and 1943

Industry	1939	1943
Distributive trades	999	993
Service industry	975	1,037
Textiles	601	436
Clothing	506	357
Administrative and clerical	449	929
Engineering, aircraft, and shipbuilding	438	1,635
Manufacturing	384	336
Food	263	245
Chemicals	73	293
Agriculture	66	168
Transport	50	197
Auxiliaries	–	531

Source: John Costello, *Love, Sex and War* (London, 1985), 10.

UNEMPLOYMENT

For many individuals and families in the working class, the period between these two world wars was bleak. In the winter of 1920, one and a half million workers were unemployed. Within six months, the number of unemployed had rocketed to over two million, and numbers fluctuated between this figure and one million throughout the decade. Worse was to come. In the early years of the 1930s, unemployment peaked at three million, never dropping below one and a half million. These bald statistics disguise the even more dramatic extent of unemployment. It was obvious that officially declared levels of unemployment were under-estimates. No account was taken of short-time working, although this was a major way employers coped with the crisis, particularly in South Wales, Yorkshire, Lancashire, and parts of the Midlands. The secretary of the Tailors' and Garment Workers' Union explained, 'It is not customary or usual to dismiss the women outright, the firms will retain the staff of women in the hope that they will eventually get busy again. They may work them a day a week, or a day and a half, or two days, and where there is no proper organization in the factory on the trade union side or on the employer's side, they may have the same girl calling 5 or 6 days a week yet having only one full day's work.' In the 1920s almost one-third of wholesale tailors were working short-time. Unemployment statistics also referred only to insured workers: the levels of unemployment in agriculture, council employment, and certain types of railway work were unknown. Conservative estimates add between one-fifth and one-

Table 4.9 Percentage rate of unemployment in Great Britain (range each five years), 1900–69

Years	Percentage (annual range)
1900–04	2.5–6.0
1905–09	3.6–7.8
1910–14	2.1–4.7
1915–19	0.4–2.1
1920–24	2.0–14.3
1925–29	9.7–12.5
1930–34	16.0–22.1
1935–39	10.8–15.5
1940–44	0.7–9.7
1945–49	1.2–3.1
1950–54	1.2–2.1
1955–59	1.2–2.3
1960–64	1.6–2.6
1965–69	1.5–2.5

Source: Adapted from A. H. Halsey (ed.), *Trends in British Society Since 1900* (London, 1972), 119.

quarter to the official figure to take account of short-time work and unemployment among non-insured people. Furthermore, women had trouble signing on unemployment registers. Eighty-seven per cent of unemployed men registered, compared with 45 per cent of unemployed women.[13] Since housework was considered to be their 'normal' work, women who had been employed in munition and other industries were not allowed to register as unemployed. Added together, therefore, about half of all people were touched personally by unemployment.

Ironically, however, these bleak years of unemployment improved the chances of upward social mobility for one section of working-class youth. This section was working-class *boys* of a certain age. Their sisters were not so lucky. Not only were they more liable to find themselves unemployed due to agreements made by employers and unions during the war, but they were also more liable to be in part-time jobs which were not protected by unemployment legislation. Furthermore, they lacked political ammunition to counter the claims of ex-servicemen (who constituted one-third of the unemployed in 1919) that those who risked their lives in battle had a greater entitlement to employment than those who remained at home. These claims of ex-servicemen were sometimes aggressively asserted, as in 1919 when female tram conductors in Bristol had their trams attacked

Table 4.10 Percentage unemployed in the staple trades, 1929–38

Occupational sector	1929	1932	1936	1938
Coal	18.2	41.2	25.0	22.0
Cotton	14.5	31.1	15.1	27.7
Iron and steel	19.9	48.5	29.5	24.8
Shipbuilding	23.2	59.5	30.6	21.4
Average (all industries)	9.9	22.9	12.5	13.3

Source: J. Stevenson, *British Society 1914–45* (Harmondsworth, 1984), 270.

and pushed off the rails. Other times, ex-servicemen relied upon their political allies, as when the Lloyd George government advised local authorities to employ ex-servicemen in preference to women.

Their brothers could claim more social and political support. In the 1930s, the proportion of sons from manual backgrounds being recruited into non-manual jobs increased. Explanations for this phenomenon lie in the distribution of unemployment between groups and districts. Manual workers (and especially those in casual and seasonal employment) suffered higher levels of unemployment than white-collar workers. Employees in textiles, steel works, shipbuilding, and coalmining industries were hit hard, especially when compared with female teachers, the only group of white-collar workers to experience large-scale unemployment. The old, the sick, and those suspected of being weaker were liable to be made redundant first, and were less liable to be re-employed, leading to an increase in the incidence of long-term sickness, disability, and vagrancy – all of which declined during the Second World War when the demand for labour once again increased. Some historians, rejecting the picture of inter-war Britain as a place of unremitting poverty, have argued that widespread unemployment was caused not by economic collapse but by extensive industrial restructuring, which workers were slow to adapt to.[14] Although their argument has been overstated, it has forced historians to look more carefully at the rise of new industries and the resulting changes in the scale of organization. While older workers suffered disproportionately, young workers benefited. In both the First and the Second World Wars, conflict opened up jobs for men not yet old enough to be in the armed forces. The mobility chances of younger men were helped by the growth of 'essential industries' and the running down of older industries.

Furthermore, unemployment was geographically concentrated. In

Table 4.11 Regional variation in unemployment (percentage of insured workers who were unemployed), 1929–38

Area	1929	1932	1934	1936	1938
South-east	5.6	14.3	8.7	7.3	7.7
Midlands	9.3	20.1	12.9	9.2	10.0
North-west	13.3	25.8	20.8	13.1	17.7
North-east	13.7	28.5	22.1	16.8	12.9
Scotland	12.7	27.1	23.1	18.7	16.8
Wales	19.3	36.5	32.3	29.4	25.9
Northern Ireland	14.8	27.2	23.4	22.7	24.4
UK (average)	10.4	22.1	16.7	13.2	12.9

Source: G. McCrone, *Regional Policy in Britain* (London, 1969), 100.

the 1920s, 70 per cent of all unemployed people came from only nine counties.[15] Fearing that the concentration of the unemployed could promote class action (a fear exacerbated by the 1926 miners' strike), the government attempted to encourage unemployed men and women to migrate to more prosperous districts in the Midlands and the south-east. While not being a viable option for women or men with families, it was a proposal many single, working-class youth accepted. Most of this migration occurred on an *ad hoc* basis, but official schemes also played a part. The most important of these schemes was the 1928 Industrial Transference Scheme which resulted (between 1928 and 1935) in the placing of over 24,000 boys and girls from depressed areas into jobs in the more prosperous parts of the country. These possibilities for social mobility did not survive the end of the war and the onset of economic depression. However, the post-war flow of 'new' immigrants into the lowest types of employment squeezed 'locals' up one step. From the 1960s, growth in the non-manual sector occurred within the service sector and educational qualification came to be the key to upward mobility.[16] These qualifications (as we shall see later in this chapter) were dominated by those already in the non-manual sector.

SEGMENTATION AND THE JOB SEARCH

For members of the working classes, for women, and for ethnic minorities, the risk of getting 'blocked' in jobs characterized by fluctuating wages, insecure prospects, and unpleasant working conditions lay in the process of the job search, structural inhibitions, and cultural traditions.

The more sluggish rate of social mobility experienced by working-class children in the twentieth century was exacerbated by the decline in apprenticeships from the turn of the century. Although apprenticeships remained important in printing, bookbinding, bootmaking, shopkeeping, tailoring, and various branches of the building trade, they were out of favour in the new and expanding branches of the economy. Legal restriction on the employment of the very young pushed those unskilled jobs which had previously been performed by under 14-year-olds into higher age brackets where apprenticeships were regarded as less justifiable. Long-term trends, such as subdivision of various branches in trades and the growth of industrial units, combined with increased competition in periods of high unemployment, hastened the death of the apprenticeship system. With this decline of apprenticed jobs, the labour of adolescents came to depend increasingly on 'dead-end' jobs, that is, jobs which offered no prospects. Well over two-thirds of van-guards, vanboys, day servants, messengers, porters, watchmen, newsboys, and news-vendors were adolescents trying to earn a living through working in these jobs which had a high turnover.[17] Employers were reluctant to continue employing such workers indefinitely since, after the worker's sixteenth birthday, employers were required to pay contributions under the National Health and Unemployment Insurance Schemes. In the words of Barclay Baron in 1911, 'Time and time again a young man of nineteen is told one morning that his services are not required, and a boy of fourteen takes his place.'[18] In A. D. K. Owen's study of 500 male school leavers in 1933, 27 per cent held their job for less than one year. Of 470 female school leavers, 40 per cent moved on within a year. Less than half of the boys and girls managed to keep their job for two years.[19] In a Lancashire-based study of 2,000 boys in the mid-1930s, one-fifth had three or more jobs in the two years. In most cases, the change of job was the result of dismissal from a dead-end job, or simply due to aimless drifting from one job to another.[20]

For young working-class boys and girls, so-called 'non-progressive' jobs could be gratifying. In the short term, they paid well and offered school leavers a taste of freedom. In 1906 the Committee of the London County Council lamented that the low wages of errand boys and messengers were more attractive than the low wages paid during industrial training: 'Earning looms larger in his imagination than the laborious and less remunerative learning.'[21] As one boy employed in a scrubby job bluntly declared in 1911, 'I don't care, so long as the money's all right.'[22]

The 'problem' of youth labour was exacerbated by transformations in the role of parents in directing the labour of their offspring. In terms of the household economy, it was crucial that siblings were efficiently dispatched into the paid labour markets at the earliest legal age. In 1932, Jack Lawson testified to the difference the wages of his siblings made to the household. Their 'hungry days were almost ended' when two of his brothers accepted jobs in the mine: 'It is astonishing how a little helps at such a time. Struggle to make ends meet there still was; clothes and clogs were still sometimes just out of reach; but hunger as we had known it was left behind. We had indeed entered the Promised Land.'[23] The ability of parents to 'place' their children in satisfactory jobs, however, was waning. Periods of high unemployment thwarted expectations which were already low. In Welsh mining areas, boys demanded 'any job on top' and girls asked to be placed in shops, dressmaking, and clerical posts, but the main jobs on offer for boys were as miners' assistants or errand boys and, for girls, as domestic helps.[24] In 1936, when discussing employment opportunities for youth in Wales, Gwynne Meara confessed that 'the static position of trade and industry' meant that most vacancies were 'nonprogressive in type' and all superior jobs were reserved for the sons and daughters of employees or customers.[25] Only a few trades (such as mining and work in tin plate and galvanizing works) maintained a hereditary pattern of recruitment.[26] Despite the continuing dominance of locality in deciding type of employment, familial traditions of employment could not be maintained.[27] When Reginald Bray analysed the employment of 4,000 children leaving London County Council schools in 1909, he found that it was very rare for father and son to follow the same occupation.[28] In most occupations, parents possessed little power to give sons jobs, although many tried.[29] In the words of the Consultative Committee of the Board of Education in 1909, the large majority of parents 'would be both able and willing to accept rather lower wages at first for their children for the sake of bettering their subsequent position, but . . . are not sufficiently acquainted with the prospects of the various trades and occupations to be able to make a wise selection of them'.[30] As E. Llewelyn Lewis put it in 1924, unskilled fathers were rarely able to seek apprenticeships for their sons owing to their lack of contact with potential employers from other classes of society: unskilled parents were 'obliged to inhabit very poor localities and to dwell among people of similar habits'.[31] In the words of Miss F. H. Durham, inspector of technical classes in West Southwark, 'An artisan has often no knowledge or influence by which he could put his boy into any trade except his own, which he is rather apt to think the worst there is; and a labourer has practically no power to get his son into a skilled trade.'[32]

Parents in some industries were opposed to their children following in their footsteps. Although parents in mining industries could use their influence to place their sons in mining employment, few parents were willing to do so. Sons were equally unwilling. In 1929, the Pontypridd Juvenile Advisory Committee noted that 90 per cent of the boys interviewed definitely refused to consider coalmining jobs, although in the past, over three-quarters of boys leaving school in this area would have entered the mines.[33] If boys continued going into mining, it was only due to the shortage of alternative employment. Sixteen years later, the same was true; one-third of miners interviewed in Scotland wanted a different job, one-quarter admitted that there was no future in mining, and one-fifth said that they would remain in mining only because they had no other prospects.[34]

Anxiety about the fate of working-class school leavers prompted the establishment of advice bureaux and employment exchanges aimed at improving the flow of information. The government established two types of committee to direct the labour of youth: juvenile advice and juvenile employment committees. Juvenile Advisory Committees were created when the Labour Exchange Act of 1909 established separate juvenile departments in the Labour Exchanges to give advice and information to parents and young people about choice of employment. The Board of Trade was responsible for the working of the Act until 1916 when the Ministry of Labour assumed responsibility. Meanwhile, Juvenile Employment Committees had been appointed in 1907 by certain education authorities to advise school children on their choice of career and to help place these children with local employers. In 1910, by the Choice of Employment Act, all local education authorities were empowered to follow their example. The Employment Committees had an advantage over the advisory committees in that they maintained a close link to the schools and could, therefore, recommend that children continue in higher education rather than seek immediate employment. The success of these exchanges is disputed, with investigators arguing that anything from 13 per cent to one-third of young people found jobs through the exchanges, but more agreed that they were particularly important in placing working-class girls in jobs since a high proportion of boys entered jobs in retail, coalmining, and cotton factories which made little use of official agencies.[35]

State-inspired bureaux were not alone in offering employment advice and information to working-class adolescents. In 1909, there were twenty-seven committees affiliated to the Apprenticeship and Skilled Employment Association (seventeen in London) giving work to nearly 1,500 boys and girls annually. The Post Office, in response to censure for their policy of sacking telegraph messengers once they turned sixteen, started their own Labour Bureaux. The scheme had some success: of the 3,000 boys fired between June 1907 and March 1908, one-third were found work by the Post Office bureaux. Boys' clubs (especially those in Manchester and London) often had labour exchanges attached. One of the more successful of these exchanges was the Jewish Lads' Employment Committee which exacted a promise from boys that they would remain in their chosen job unless given permission to leave by the director of the bureau. At a time when female domestic servants were scarce, the Metropolitan Association for Befriending Young Servants also had a high success rate. It was founded in 1874 to locate safe and secure jobs for young girls. In addition to serving as an employment agency, the Association provided lodgings for unemployed servants, clothing and training for servants entering new posts, and care in sickness. By 1910, it had twenty-nine branches, eight training houses, and eleven lodging houses to which the girls could go for advice during periods of unemployment. In the more popular branches, over 600 domestic servants used the facilities annually. Nearly half of the servants they placed hailed from poor law schools or charitable associations. Each year, they found places for 5,500 girls.[36]

Although staffed by enthusiastic, well-meaning staff, the limitations of these employment bureaux were obvious even to the most fervent organizer. The problem of youth labour was simply too big. Furthermore, while they attempted to place working-class youth in secure jobs, they were unable to improve chances of social mobility. Indeed, they never attempted to do anything more than reproduce existing class divisions. By focusing on the issue of unemployment rather than social mobility, they aimed to bestow patronage, formalize contracts, and facilitate connections between employers and employees within a range of low-skill jobs.

EDUCATION

The failure of employment bureaux to improve the chance of a working-class youth finding *good* employment was largely a problem of education. Higher-level educational qualifications – either in a private school, at a selective secondary school, or at some institute of further education – were essential if a person aspired to a middle-class job, as the Oxford Mobility Study's interviews of 10,000 men aged between 20 and 64 years in England and Wales disclosed. According to this study, about one-third of men in stable middle-class jobs had a private primary schooling, or some further or university education. While one-quarter of all men sat school examinations, 82 per cent of men in stable middle-class jobs had sat such examinations compared with less than 5 per cent of men in stable working-class jobs.[37] This link between education and occupation was a central plank in debates around the access of working-class children to schools. The first important governmental move to harness the three 'Rs' for the poor was the Education Act of 1870 which theoretically guaranteed a minimum level of elementary education to everyone. Since education was acknowledged to be a public service, provision for more generous grants were made available to Church schools and permission was given to school boards to spend up to threepence in the pound of rateable value on elementary education. Although it was left to the discretion of local school bodies whether school attendance was to be compulsory, by the middle of the 1870s about half of the total population (more in urban areas) was under compulsion. School attendance over the entire country was made compulsory in 1880, and fees were abolished in 1891.

For the working classes, the next important legislative move occurred in 1902 when Balfour's Act established Local Educational Authorities and encouraged these authorities to extend educational provision at both elementary and secondary levels. 'Able' working-class children were encouraged to climb the social ladder by acquiring a secondary education. One outcome of the fiery debates about social inequality during the period of Liberal rule between 1906 and 1914 was the Free Place Regulations, introduced to ensure that all secondary schools aided by grants 'shall be made fully accessible to children of all classes'. Grammar schools offering at least one-quarter of their places free to pupils from elementary schools were rewarded with higher grants. All the same, the numbers of working-class children affected remained small. Only four or five working-class children out of 1,000 could hope to win scholarships to secondary schools. Although the proportion of children attending secondary school doubled between 1902 and 1907, four-fifths of children aged between 14 and 18 years in 1912 never attended secondary school.[38]

The damage done to the education system during the First World War was tackled by H. A. L. Fisher's Education Act of 1918. The Act stipulated that one-quarter of places in grammar schools had to be reserved for scholarship children, it increased the school-leaving age to 14, and it abolished exemptions and the half-time system. All children in England were to share nine years of education – although some would spend those years in superior institutions. Despite this clear resolve in 1918 to expand education, the inter-war period witnessed a series of setbacks. Mass unemployment, particularly in South Wales, the Black Country, Clydeside, and Northern England, combined with the inability of children to help mitigate poverty by their own labour, resulted in severe ill-health and malnutrition among many children. In Rowntree's poverty survey in 1935, 43 per cent of York's working-class children under the age of 14 years lived below the poverty line.[39] Despite vigorous appeals by unionists, educational reformers, and economists, education was cut.[40] In 1932, the official size of school classes was fifty pupils, and in the following two years expenditure on education declined by two-thirds.[41]

By the 1940s, it was clear to most commentators that the education system was in crisis and radical reforms were needed. The Education Act of 1944 was advertised as 'Free Secondary Education for All'. Based on the principle that every child should be educated 'according to his age, aptitude and ability', Butler's Act abolished tuition fees at state maintained schools, raised the leaving age to 15 years, and introduced the tripartite system of secondary schools (grammar, modern, and technical), which in the 1950s became bipartite (grammar via 11-plus, and secondary modern). As a result, there was a significant increase in the proportion of 15- to 18-year-olds in education from 6 per cent in 1931 to 20 per cent in 1961.

Chronology 4.1 Chronology of Acts regarding education, 1889–1960

1889	Board of Education established
1891	Assisted Education Act provided capitation grant, enabling schools to cease charging fees
1893	Education (Blind and Deaf Children) Act established special schools
1902	Education (Balfour's) Act abolished school boards and established local educational authorities which were given powers to establish secondary schools (followed in Scotland in 1908)
1903	Association to Promote Higher Education of Working Men (from 1905 called the Workers' Educational Association) founded
1907	All secondary schools receiving local authority grants had to reserve between 25 and 40 per cent of free places for children from elementary schools
1918	Education (Fisher's) Act raised school-leaving age to 14 and abolished fees for elementary education
1926	Hadow Report was published, recommending the division of schools into primary and secondary tiers

1936	Education Act raised school-leaving age to 15 (not enforced until 1944)
1944	Education (Butler's) Act raised school-leaving age to 15, provided free secondary education, and divided schools into grammar, technical, and secondary modern (in Scotland, 1945)
1951	General Certificate of Education (GCE) replaced School Certificate
1959	McMeeking Committee stressed the need for technical education
1960	Robbins Committee on higher education established

Despite these attempts to promote greater social equality in access to education, class differentials persisted. For boys born between 1899 and 1910, 27 per cent of those from middle-class homes received a secondary education compared with 4 per cent of boys from working-class homes. For boys born between 1910 and 1929, this differential actually increased to 39 per cent of boys from middle-class homes and 10 per cent of boys from working-class homes.[42] In the mid-1950s, 40 per cent of children aged 17 years or over from professional or managerial households remained at school, compared with 3 per cent of children aged 17 years or over from semi-skilled manual backgrounds.[43] Access to the most prestigious schools, colleges, and universities also reflected disparities in wealth, despite early beliefs that the abolition of fees in local authority grammar schools and the increased primacy of examination results would equalize opportunities. In Scotland, for example, sociological surveys examining access to university by class consistently repudiated the mythology that Scottish education was 'classless'. In a study of entrants to Glasgow University in the 1930s, Adam Collier revealed that although entrance to the University had widened due to improvements in working-class incomes, declining family size, and increased demand for professional workers (especially teachers), significant differences in the access of various classes to university persisted. Thus, in Social Class I, the number of children per entrant for law was 200 to one: in the lowest social class, it was 20,000 to one.[44] Ian J. McDonald's study in 1967 agreed, showing that the economic groups which benefited from the major legislative changes since 1910 were the children of clerks, commercial travellers, and policemen. Children of manual and lower skilled workers were scarcely affected.[45]

The situation was no better in England where, in the early 1960s, 18 per cent of entrants into university came from independent schools, which educated only 6 per cent of children and which drew children mainly from higher social classes. Only one-quarter of undergraduates were drawn from families which were headed by a manual worker.[46] As the Robbins Committee noted in the early 1960s, the only reason

Table 4.12 Class background of entrants into Glasgow University, in 1910, 1934, and 1960

Occupation of father of entrant	1910 (%)	1934 (%)	1960 (%)
Class I	19.2	18.2	17.7
Class II	38.7	38.6	35.9
Class III-a	10.3	11.8	13.6
Class III-b	23.2	19.9	23.6
Class IV	7.6	9.3	6.7
Class V	0.6	2.6	2.2

Source: Ian J. McDonald, 'Untapped Reservoirs of Talent?', *Scottish Educational Studies*, 1.1 (June 1967), 53.

Key:

Class I:	Higher professionals
Class II:	White collar
Class III-a:	Clerical, commercial travellers, policemen
Class III-b:	Skilled manual
Class IV:	Manual workers
Class V:	Unskilled manual workers

Table 4.13 Percentage of children in different age groups attending school, in England and Wales, 1901–68

Year	12 to 14 Years	15 to 18 Years
1901	2.8	0.3
1911	–	1.5
1921	–	3.2
1931	8.8	6.0
1938	10.0	6.6
1951	7.7	12.5
1961	10.8	19.6
1968	10.7	30.0

Source: A. H. Halsey (ed.), *Trends in British Society Since 1900* (London, 1972), 163.

there were more working-class students at university was that the total number of students had doubled: the proportion of working-class as opposed to middle-class students remained undisturbed.[47]

Educational policy ignored some of the fundamental reasons for the under-representation of working-class children in higher education. Scholarships relieved only a portion of the educational burden. Uniforms, gym slips, hockey sticks, and footballs still had to be purchased and the cost of postponing the child's monetary contribution to the household considered. Financial stringencies affected female students more than male students: the attitude of many parents was that 'girls didn't need educating', even if a scholarship had been won.[48] Schools within working-class areas were under-funded. The selective system of secondary schools following the 1944 Act was supposed to achieve parity of esteem among grammar, technical, and secondary schools. In reality, the 30 per cent of students attending grammar schools received almost half the total expenditure allocated to the secondary sector.[49] Comparing the cohort of boys born between 1913 and 1922, and between 1943 and 1952, the average son of a professional had seven times as much money spent on his education as the son of an agricultural labourer in the earlier period – and six times as much in the later period. While the average professional's son was credited with an extra £566 a year for education after elementary school, the average agricultural labourer's son received an extra £102 a year.[50]

The financial cost of education was not the only problem: there was a more personal price to pay. Working-class scholars found themselves in danger of being estranged from relatives, neighbours, and friends. In the 1950s, Valerie Walkerdine won a scholarship to attend grammar school. She described her experience:

> They held out a dream. Come, they told me. It is yours. You are chosen. They didn't tell me, however, that for years I would no longer feel any sense of belonging, nor any sense of safety. That I didn't belong in the new place, any more than I now belonged in the old. So around every corner of apparent choice lurked doubt and uncertainty. My mother described its pejorative connotations as typified by a change of accent which she referred to as 'lasting and pasting'. The fear in this working-class morality of putting on airs and graces was the fear of being found to be an impostor. The terror was not a simple matter of working-class pride. It was all right to talk like that if you had a right to belong to that class.[51]

Educational policy failed to convince working-class parents that education was the key to upward social mobility. Indeed, much educational policy resulted in a fall in the economic ladder as the household was deprived of the earnings of children. Experience taught parents that there was no guaranteed relationship between level of education and wages after leaving school. E. Slater and M. Woodside's working-class respondents felt that education was 'theoretical, and had little practical bearing on everyday life. Beyond what was immediately useful, the ability to read, write and reckon, it was nearly all forgotten. It formed no cultural background for reading and study in later life; and most of them felt that all they had learned that was worth learning had been from their experience of life itself. Their schooldays had been irksome and irrelevant to the real business of living.'[52] More relevant to working-class experience was the development of 'all round' characteristics, as one mother explained in connection with her son: 'I am not going to let him learn anything; I want him, if need be, to be able to put his hand to everything.'[53]

Part of this disaffection with 'learning' arose out of the oppressive class nature of schools. Ron Barnes recalled that his teachers in the 1930s were 'as remote as shit from sugar' from the students:

> I hated school. Everything was so orderly, correct and restricting. Self-expression seemed to be alien to the whole grey, antiquated building. The male teachers were nothing like my father and the female ones nothing like my mother, or any other relatives, come to that. My lot sounded, and even looked friendlier than these beings. They looked as though they had just been taken out of a showcase. Their tone and accent had an aloofness about it which made it impossible to strike up any sort of relationship whatsoever.'[54]

Another working-class autobiographer, Len Wincott, had similar things to say about his teachers: 'They were aliens to us and I suppose we were to them. They lived in another part of the city, the "posh" part, and when lessons were over they jumped on their bicycles and sailed away to it.'[55] These tensions occasionally flared into full-scale strikes. Between 1889 and 1939, there were strikes at over one hundred schools.[56] The strikers wanted schools to respond to the needs of local communities, demanding that schools catered for the welfare needs of children, that flexible attendance was tolerated, and that teaching methods became less coercive. In imitation of the tactics of the labour movement, school children struck, picketed, demonstrated, and negotiated. These were not simply generational conflicts, but won the approval of some working-class parents. The crucial variable was class. Concessions were won in some schools, and the strikers succeeded in encouraging educational authorities to question the effectiveness of coercion in school policy, so that by the Second World War, corporal punishment had been severely restricted in two-thirds of all schools.[57]

The under-performance of working-class children within the school system was not only a result of cultural tensions between the authorities and teachers on the one side, and parents and children on the other. Students were distracted from education by ill-health and part-time employment. Some children were so badly nourished that they could not concentrate on schooling. At the turn of the century, Dr Thomas, the Medical Officer of the London County Council, found that 61 per cent of wage-earning schoolboys showed signs of fatigue, 36 per cent were anaemic, 63 per cent showed 'nerve strain', 64 per cent were suffering from deformities from carrying heavy weights, over half had severe heart strain, and 27 per cent had severe heart disease.[58] According to the Chief Medical Officer of the Board of Education in 1915, around a quarter of a million school children were seriously crippled, invalided, or disabled. No fewer than a million school children were too ill or mentally unsound to be able to 'derive reasonable benefit from the education which the state provides'. More than 10 per cent of school children were suffering from malnutrition.[59]

Legislation was only marginally more effective in dealing with child labour than it had been in the educational field. The 1911 Coal Mines Act limited the number of hours for certain categories of young persons employed on surface work at mines to fifty-four hours a week and ten hours a day. Underground work was restricted. The Shops Act of 1934 set the working time for persons under the age of 16 years at forty-four hours and for persons aged between 16 and 18 years at forty-eight hours. Overtime was forbidden to the younger children and curtailed for the others. Provisions were also made for weekday half-holidays, intervals for meals and rest, ventilation, lighting, heating, sanitary washing, feeding accommodation, and the provision of seats for female assistants. In 1937, a Factories' Act extended these provisions to other occupations, and further restricted the hours between which young people might be employed. A year later, the Young Persons' (Employment) Act was introduced to cover young workers employed in the collection and delivery of goods, in carrying messages and running errands, in residential hotels, clubs, and places of public entertainment, and in receiving or dispatching goods in connection with laundries or dyeing and cleaning works. This legislation only attempted to regulate conditions within and between low-skilled jobs, not to promote the movement of young working-class children into more prestigious employment.

Despite good intentions, the legislation failed to effect more than a slight improvement in working conditions for working-class youth. As late as 1942, education authorities throughout the country attested to its failure. The Middlesex Education Authority found that many boys and girls worked an average of twelve hours daily. In Kent, boys were reported as being unable to join youth groups because of long working hours and shift work. In Smethwick, the young girls were employed for an 'excessive' number of hours 'to the detriment of their health'. The Coventry authority found that 42 per cent of boys worked more than fifty-six hours a week and some worked for seventy hours. A similar situation was reported in Lincoln and Caernarvonshire. The Wallasey account testified to the long hours worked by boys in shipbuilding and engineering firms, and of girls in cinemas, laundries, and canteens. Southampton revealed that 20 per cent of boys worked long or difficult hours. The Education Authority in Hertfordshire listed one hundred cases where boys were engaged for a sixty-hour week. The worst instances occurred with children employed by parents, especially on the land and in small shops. Young people in restaurants and in golf clubs usually worked a twelve-hour day. The Ipswich report summed up the general feeling when it complained that the practice of employing lads for up to fourteen hours a day was 'devitalizing the nation'.[60]

Part of the reason for the failure of the legislation was its exclusion of many occupations from legislative control. In 1930, the Minister of Labour invited the National Advisory Council for Juvenile Employment in England and Wales to enquire into the employment of young persons in occupations whose hours of employment were not limited by statute. Out of 127,000 juveniles investigated, more than half worked over fifty-four hours a week, and 21 per cent worked over sixty hours.[61] During the debates on the Shops Act of 1934, it was estimated that 700,000 young workers were not covered by the Factory Acts. The Shops Act was intended to deal with 400,000 of these, leaving 300,000 unprotected.[62] Ten years later, young clerical and office workers, agricultural workers, male young persons employed on repairing work, and most dock workers were still not covered by labour legislation. Even within controlled occupations, enforcement was difficult. Illegal employment had to be detected, reliable evidence which could stand up in court had to be amassed, and the magistrate had to designate a penalty. At each step, it faltered. There were other practical problems, including the fact that timecards were the private documents of the firm and could not be used as evidence, and that much of the documentation was subject to 'cooking'. The nature of some work made regulation impossible. The most difficult to regulate were those jobs involving travel where employers could claim that lorries had broken down or that young employees had been left stranded because of dependency on only one lorry. Since local authorities rarely had the proper staff to check hours, responsibility for policing infringements lay with an already overworked police force. Local politics also posed difficulties, as many councillors were shop proprietors unenthusiastic about enforcing rules which might affect their own businesses. The complexity of the Factory Acts, coupled with the fact that hours were becoming much shorter, lessened employers' sense that the evasion of the law was a serious matter.

FEMININITY

For both male and female workers, the chief factor influencing their ability to make choices about the type of work they were going to do was their sex. As we have seen, men and women worked in utterly different sectors of the economy. Employed women concentrated in certain 'women's occupations', and this segregation declined only slightly over time. Only in a few jobs (such as school-teaching, nursing, and retail sales staff) was there actually any competition between women and men in the employment market. Occupational segregation declined in the twentieth century, but it remained important. The total number of women in employment may have increased, but a dual labour market whereby women provided the bulk of workers for low-status jobs was maintained. Contrary to popular opinion, the number of women in jobs recognized as 'skilled' declined since the nineteenth century, and there were not many more women in 'top jobs' in the 1980s than there were in 1911.[63]

No explanation for this perpetuation of sex-typed occupations with women in the least-favoured jobs can ignore the widespread public disapproval of female employment. Disapproval was expressed at every level – from Parliament to the pub. From the 1840s, Parliament had responded to what had come to be seen as the 'problem' of female employment by introducing 'protective' legislation. The Mines Act of 1842, the Ten Hour Act of 1847, and Factory Acts of 1844, 1853, 1860, 1867, 1878, 1891, and 1895 all limited the number of hours women could work and dictated their conditions of work. Shops Acts of 1906, 1907, and 1913 laid down maximum hours for female shop-workers and brought an end to the living-in system. Although these legislative interventions improved the employment lives of women, they also restricted women's options in the paid sphere. Thus, the prohibition of Sunday and night work meant that women could not become electrical engineers or telephonists. The expanding 'new' industries of the inter-war period did not lead to an increase in female employment, despite the fact that 'light' industries requiring stamina and dexterity were conventionally seen as suitable for women. In part, their exclusion from these industries was due to the creation of marriage bars and the

Table 4.14 Occupational segregation, 1901–61

Year	*Percentage of women working in occupations employing specified proportions of women*			
	100%	*90%*	*70%*	*50%*
1901	11	52	71	82
1911	3	45	64	78
1921	0	40	56	72
1931	0	41	62	73
1951	0	31	50	68
1961	0	21	53	79

Year	*Percentage of men working in occupations employing specified proportions of men*			
	100%	*90%*	*70%*	*50%*
1901	47	74	89	95
1911	44	70	86	93
1921	29	70	83	92
1931	22	69	84	94
1951	20	61	82	92
1961	22	62	77	85

Source: C. Hakim, *Occupational Segregation* (London, 1979), table 12.

availability of other low-paid groups, such as young males and ethnic minorities, to do the work. In addition, 'Fordist' employment policies, adopted by these new industries in an attempt to reduce the turnover of labour in capital-intensive industries by offering high wages, operated against the employment of women who were perceived as having a high turnover for reasons of marriage, pregnancy, and child-rearing. The best workers were men – even better, 'family men'. Despite female suffrage, the burgeoning of the feminist movement, labour shortages, world wars, and social changes in the perceived role of women, the employment market remained highly discriminatory.

Although employment for married women was not an ideal, many women depended on it for survival. The women obviously requiring paid work were married women deserted by their husbands and women living with low-waged husbands. In Bolton, Miss Norah Darbyshire wrote to the Public Assistance Officer on 15 November 1935 with the plea: 'I am writing to ask you a favour. I work in the Laundry at Fishpool Institute as an ironer, and I understand that if I get married, I should have to cease work. As my intended husband only gets 22s. a week as a side piecer, we could hardly manage on that.' She asked to be allowed to continue in the job after her marriage until her husband was promoted. Permission was granted. It was to her advantage that her job was unskilled, unpleasant, and poorly paid. Female employees in the same Institute who held skilled positions were less fortunate. Thus, Mrs B. Brislee who had been working as an assistant Bookkeeper for over nineteen years was dismissed on the grounds of marriage: she was a senior employee and men were clamouring for her job.[64] Women workers did not always respond to restrictions on their rights to both marriage and employment in ways their employers predicted. Alice Foley was an activist in the weaving industry in Bolton. She noted that 'much of the objection to the employment of married women comes from single women' but commented that 'as every single woman is potentially a married one, her point of view alters entirely when she realizes that she cannot marry unless she gives up her work'. According to Foley, women responded by establishing 'a more questionable form of union'.[65]

Many people – including those in the working classes – were ambivalent about the employment of women, especially in jobs shared with men. The implications of the integration of women workers into previously male terrain were wide, including fears of promiscuity. One woman complained in her diary that her husband had found a condom on his toolbox at work. She blamed the lack of 'moral tone' in factories on the influx of women workers: 'Wives of serving soldiers, women with little self control and fewer scruples, act as magnets to silly young men, and to silly older ones too.' Her husband 'saw red' and complained to the management 'saying that if the factory were to become a brothel, let it cease to produce aircraft'.[66]

Objections to the propriety of women's employment were even more adamant in the case of married women. Even the cohort of women swelling the labour markets after the Second World War were uneasy about their employment status. One survey in 1947 asked 2,807 women detailed questions about employment. Less than one-fifth of full-time housewives thought that female employment was a good thing. Even amongst women who were employed, only one-third approved. Surprisingly, disapproval of women's employment was greatest among single women: 82 per cent of employed single women were unfavourably disposed to female employment compared with 63 per cent of employed married women. One-fifth of the employed women lived with husbands who disapproved of their going out to work on the grounds that women's place was in the home and that domesticity was a full-time job upon which men's comfort depended. Wives often agreed with their husbands. One-quarter of full-time wives lived with husbands who would not object to their employment.

The interviewers concluded that, since no full-time housewife mentioned the husband's disapproval as one of the disadvantages of employment (although 20 per cent said he did disapprove) the husband's attitude was not the telling factor in deciding whether a wife would or would not find employment. In answer to the question 'should wives work?', 65 per cent of the wives said that it depended on the circumstances, especially the presence of young children. Although younger women, those living in the north-west, and women in the lower and middle economic groups were most liable to be favourably disposed towards the idea that wives took paid employment, the assumption that women's paramount duty rested with the care of husbands and children prevailed.[67]

For most working-class women, the attractions of waged employment were meagre. Employment doubled their workload. Employed women did as much housework as full-time housewives, although they did it at different times. Thus, a study in 1943 on cake-baking revealed that employed women did not bake fewer cakes than full-time housewives but their timetable shifted to the weekends when they baked for the entire week.[68] Not surprisingly, employed wives and mothers were 'too exhausted by having to live two lives in one'.[69] The working-class women interviewed by the historian Elizabeth Roberts also made this point: 'Women who worked full-time were certainly not regarded as emancipated by their contemporaries, rather as drudges. Women whose husbands earned sufficient money to clothe, feed, and house the family preferred to have a reduced work load rather than extra income.'[70] In a study in 1911 of the reasons working-class wives gave for being employed, 85 per cent said that they worked to supplement a small income, another 12 per cent worked because their earnings were the sole income, and only 3 per cent declared a preference for employment over full-time housewifery.[71] This made economic sense. Employment could be more expensive than not being employed. In Geoffrey Thomas's survey of women in industry in 1948 it transpired that female wages were so low that, once the cost of going out to work had been calculated, the net gain was negligible.[72] Besides paying for wear and tear on clothing and shoes, childcare costs had to be considered. The 'free' childcare provided by older children was often unacceptable. Fear that one's child would be injured through the carelessness or the ignorance of the baby-minder grew as family size shrank and the investment in each child swelled. The nineteenth-century comment, repeated by a number of poor women throughout the country, that 'between the woman that works and the woman that doesn't there is only 6d to choose at the year's end, and she that stays at home has it', still applied in the twentieth century.[73]

There were social as well as economic reasons for the reluctance of many women to find employment. Husbands might simply reduce the housekeeping money in proportion to the amount their wives earned. Albert Jasper's father delivered furniture in Hoxton: 'I don't ever remember my mother having a week's wages off him – six or seven shillings was the most she ever received. The reason he never gave her regular wages was he knew my mother could always earn a few shillings with her [sewing] machine.'[74] Once Pat O'Mara's mother got a job as a cleaner in a Liverpool doss-house in the 1910s, his father's efforts on the docks dwindled 'now that he saw the barest necessities being provided by her'.[75] The words of one East End woman in the 1930s were appropriate: the employment of wives had an unfortunate effect on men – 'it saps their ambition, gives them nothing to strive for'.[76]

At a more general level, it was in the postwar period that public proclamations of domestic ideology reached a new height. Exhortations addressed to women to move back into the home reflected concerns about the way family life had been disturbed by the war. A revival in the rhetoric of the sanctity of the family, plummeting birth rates, and debates about the psychological need of children for mothering ('Bowlbyism') confirmed the view of many women and men that motherhood had to be protected.[77] The architect of the postwar welfare state, William Beveridge, contended that industrial growth required high quality and regular servicing by women of male workers. He acknowledged that married women had to be regarded as 'occupied in work which is vital, though unpaid, without which their husbands cannot do their paid work and without which the nation cannot continue'.[78] Concern about the birthrate and the level of unemployment among ex-servicemen cannot totally explain the backlash against female employment: after all, after the war, a baby boom coincided with declining mortality rate, and (by the mid-1950s) a labour shortage had prompted the Ministry of Labour to appeal to married women to return to employment. The attitudes of employers and women themselves were crucial: part-time work seemed to be the answer, so that in 1951 the most conservative estimate shows that 23 per cent of employed wives were working part-time.[79]

However, irrespective of these forces opposed to – or ambivalent about – the employment of married women, after the Second World War there was a remarkable movement of these women into the employment markets. This was not fuelled by improved wage rates. In the 1950s, full-time female workers in Britain received only 51 per cent of the average weekly earnings of male workers. By the end of the 1960s this had increased slightly to just under 54 per cent and women had to wait until the Equal Pay Act of 1970 to earn 64 per cent of the average male wage. The impact of changes in marriage patterns on women's work cannot be ignored. Declining family size and the accompanying changes in patterns of child-rearing were important. Chapter 2 examined the decline in working-class fertility from the end of the nineteenth century. The practical implication of declining fertility was that while less than one-fifth of all late Victorian families had fewer than three children, by the 1930s only 19 per cent of children grew up with two or three siblings.[80] A typical working-class mother in the 1890s experienced ten pregnancies and spent about fifteen years of her life pregnant or nursing a child less than one year old. By the 1960s, the average working-class mother spent only four years of her life engaged in these activities.[81]

The shifts in fertility were not the result of restrictions in marriage or alterations in the age of marriage. Between 1930 and 1960, increasing numbers of people in Britain had been marrying – indeed, after 1960 a higher proportion of the population were married than at any time in the previous century. Malthus's attention to delayed marriage as a way of reducing family size also cannot be held responsible for fertility changes. People were marrying at younger ages. Thus, in 1911, 55 per cent of women in their twenties were married while, by 1951, 73 per cent of these women were married.[82] Because of this relationship between fecundity and age, total family size can be just as effectively reduced by increasing the intervals between children ('spacing'), as by 'stopping' childbearing abruptly. Although the 'spacing' of children may have been important for some households (particularly in the nineteenth century), in the twentieth century a woman was much more liable simply to stop childbearing at a certain age resulting in a clustering of children into the early years of marriage. In the middle of the nineteenth century, the median age of a woman at the birth of her last child was 39 years. Even in the 1930s, it was around 32 years. Those marrying after the Second World War, however, completed childbearing by the age of 28, leaving women with another expected half-century of life after the birth of their last child. The implications of early childbearing combined with increased life expectancies for female labour-force participation since the 1950s are obvious.[83]

MASCULINITY

Just as the femininity of a job was at the centre of attitudes of women to employment, for working-class men the coincidence of masculinity and class was just as direct. For the young working-class male, his masculinity was reaffirmed by manual labour, suffused as it was with ideas of potency and heroism. The prize for the convincing exhibition of manly qualities (such as strength, inventiveness, endurance, and cunning) was the wage packet. For instance, Jack Hilton turned 12 on 21 January 1912. Being legally able to work a half-day made this 'the historic workday of my life'. In his words:

> I wanted to be like the other men-boys, to look down on errand, lather, and newsboys [who worked after school]. I wanted to be able to wear my cap on one side, to smoke a cigarette, and to use language that would become my manhood. I wanted to be a half-timer, and still more to be a full-timer. I'd have regular hours and nights to myself. I'd be a little somebody at home, and mother would give me the deference due to a worker. I'd be able to open my mouth, and my younger brothers and sisters would not have to give me their lip. Soon I'd be full-time, and then would follow my new suit. I dreamed it all rosily.[84]

Newly employed boys proudly described their new status: 'When I started work of course I was the big he-man'; 'I now wanted to tell the world I was now a man'; 'it was not the money which encouraged me to work. I think it gave me a sense of manhood'; and "Going out to work", in fact, was an important milestone on the road to manhood and the source of some pride. I remember the feeling of self-importance as I stepped out of the cottage all fitted out for my first day's flint-picking on the hills.'[85]

While gratifying, the new manly status could be extremely wearing, as Jack Hilton discovered after he started working half-time in the mill: 'At tea-time I found that my first half-day's work had been given a special treat. I was given thinner bread, an egg, and some marmalade. My spirits rose, and I looked down on my brothers and sisters, feeling the elation of a worker. I knew that I must live up to my status, and though it would have been better to go to bed, I stayed up. . . . By the end of the week I was a tired lad, doubting my manliness.'[86] It was this link between masculinity and a 'living' wage that required defending. Thus, Winifred Foley explained her father's willingness to strike during the coal miners' strike in 1926 with the words: 'The strike was really a desperate cry for the status of manhood – to be able to do a full week's work in the pit, to be paid enough to fill the bellies of their families.[87] The preferential treatment bestowed by mothers, sisters, and other women depended on masculine employment.[88] Husbands and fathers could only be assured of their entitlement to be the 'boss' of the home if they were employed.[89] The young miner, Fred Craddock, started work at a time when his father was unemployed. Each day when he returned from work, 'everything' in the household stopped until he had his bath in front of the fire: 'He had Mother running round like a scalded cat fetching hot water or scrubbing brushes or towels and she had to answer his roar of "Wash my back" whatever else she might be doing. The best that was in the house was offered to Fred and his word was law.'[90] This worried middle-class commentators. In 1911, Alexander Paterson fussed about the relatively high wages and more secure employment of young men compared with their fathers, pointing out that this tended to weaken the father's traditional position and make children of 16 'openly independent': 'This abdication of the father in favour of his children is even more marked in the poorer quarters. There a boy of eighteen will often be found to be the main, if not the entire support of a small family. He will without comment, expect and receive two kippers for his tea, while his unemployed father will make the most of bread-and-butter.'[91]

As we saw in Chapter 2, the masculinity of a man could be securely fixed to employment prior to the First World War when 'manly' jobs were to be had. Inter-war unemployment changed all of this. Complex and increasingly restrictive unemployment benefits combined with the sudden economic deprivation and emotional stress of joblessness was devastating. For many, the fact that the loss of income could be supplemented by welfare agencies and provisions was little consolation. In the words of an unemployed blast furnace worker: 'There is nothing quite like the dole. It is the final and irrevocable disaster to working-mankind.'[92] Fathers and husbands returned from the labour exchange or pub or club, 'surly with shame', asking themselves, 'Is this a man's life?'[93] In the words of an unemployed electrician:

You get so finally you leave the last thing that gives you pride in yourself, your job as a skilled man, and you take up something else. No one who hasn't gone through it knows how that tears you up in here. I haven't gone through it completely yet; but I see it coming. And I lay awake at nights, and it's a nightmare. But you have to work you see, even if it's at something else, to keep your self-respect.[94]

In such circumstances, the role of women in buttressing the masculinity of men – whether they be fathers, husbands, or sons – became more overt. In the words of a wife of an unemployed miner: 'we wives have to keep buoying up our husbands, which is not easy, when we ourselves are at our wits' end to feed our family'.[95] Some women refused this role, and responded by punishing menfolk who failed to bring in a regular wage packet. Asked to cheer up her unemployed husband, one woman tossed her head and retorted, 'Let him get a job and we'll see.'[96] An usherette in the Globe Theatre (London) in the 1930s expressed her resentment at the lowering standard of living consequent on her husband's unemployment by defying his commands and attending a party at work. Her husband was so stung by this act that he immediately accepted a job as a costing clerk at a builders. She described his return from his first day at work:

> We looked at each other. In his eyes, just for a second, I glimpsed something unsure. Burt was never good at playing the masterful male. He needed help. I smiled and capitulated, 'Does this mean I'm going to be a lady of leisure again?'
> 'That's about it.' He nodded at the vanity case on the table, 'You can sit at home and do your face up all day long.'
> We both started to laugh. It was the best kind of ending to a lovely day.[97]

This usherette's husband was not unusual in resenting the ability of his wife to find employment when he was having so much trouble. An unemployed engineer in the 1930s also admitted that tension within his marriage became marked only when his wife took a job. Eventually, the wife and son asked him to leave.[98] Another unemployed man – a wire drawer from Ambergate – confessed that he was so ashamed about his wife being the breadwinner, that they kept the fact a secret from their child for three years.[99] A husband might prefer a lower standard of living to such mortification. In the 1930s, Eileen Slade's father was an unemployed furniture salesman. Although her mother was a qualified teacher with a degree in music and literature, when it was suggested that she teach, her father was incensed: 'Perhaps it was hurt pride, perhaps it could have been called foolish pride, but he firmly refused to allow her to even consider this action, even threatening to leave home if she did, and he thereby condemned us all to dire poverty.'[100]

This sense of shame emanated from the relationship not only between the wage packet and masculinity, but also between the wage packet and marital love. Stripped of the ability to buy gifts for the wife and children, husbands and fathers were challenged to resort to 'feminine' ways of expressing love. One unemployed colliery banksman told that 'the bitterness, the irritation and gloominess that I experience are merely the result of being unable to give my wife and son the family life which is their right and which they really do deserve'. He spoke movingly of his wife's bravery and optimism, but noted that 'being mortal and normal, with strong feminine instincts, persistent disappointment must inevitably take toll. For myself it would be easy to answer an enquirer as to my reaction to our lower level of subsistence. I should say that we still shared the sun and air, the fields and the woods, the Public Libraries. But, of course, other people, including my wife, have other levels of satisfaction.'[101] The 'breadwinner' had to *earn* the love of his family; the inability to do so risked his status within the family. In 1934, a London house-painter explained the effect of unemployment on the relationship between himself, his wife, and six children:

> My wife, not at first realizing the difficulty of obtaining employment, used often to make unnecessary remarks implying that I not only did not seek work but was lazy. These remarks, with both our tempers ruffled, naturally led to quarrels. These quarrels were overheard and impressed themselves on the minds of the children. The idea seemed to be created in their minds that mother's view was correct, with the consequent result that they are less apt to consider me worthy of their love, or a fitting person to ask if they require advice or direction.[102]

Or, in the case of a Jarrow family, the writer connected the long-term unemployment of his father with the withering of love: unemployment had 'stripped my parents long since of any kindness or love for one another, or of any reticence about their relationship'.[103] An unemployed millwright from Derby acknowledged that his wife looked upon him as 'a useless piece of goods, and worse than our old table'.[104] Unemployment made him not one of the prized possessions, but an object with little meaning attached. Shame could be followed by impotence as the man found himself no longer capable of making love, either figuratively or physically.[105] As we saw in the last chapter, the adoption by working-class males of more domestic roles during the employment crisis between the wars was resisted and 'house-husbands' or 'house-fathers' remained a negligible portion of the population.[106] As one young husband used to say, he 'didn't keep a dog and bark himself'.[107]

CONCLUSION

Inflexibility in the marketplace exacted a heavy toll. Legislative intervention into the education of working-class children raised expectations which were then thwarted. Although the threat of unemployment as it was experienced between the wars was removed, it never lost its power to compel workers to adopt defensive economic and political strategies. After the years of depression, the good job at the 'fair wage' seemed a possibility. Ferdynand Zweig's *Worker in an Affluent Society* (1961) argued that advanced capitalism was leading not to the polarization of classes, but to their disappearance.[108] In the first chapter, however, we looked at the failure of the 'years of affluence' to alter the balance of well-being between the rich and the poor. As Zweig discovered, women were much more sensitive to class distinctions than men: moving between discriminatory employment markets and rapidly changing domestic economies, it is not surprising that women should aspire for material well-being, leaving the political arena for the more naive.

SELECT BIBLIOGRAPHY

Clarkson, L. A. (ed.), *British Trade Union and Labour History: A Compendium* (London, 1990).
Composed of four essays on British trade unionism between 1780 and 1875, and between 1875 and 1933, and the aristocracy of labour prior to 1914. The last essay – by Elizabeth Wilson – is a fine, short survey of women's employment between 1840 and 1940.

Constantine, Stephen, *Unemployment in Britain Between the Wars* (London, 1980).
A concise history of the background, effects, and policies of inter-war unemployment. Contains 30 short documents.

Cronin, James E., *Labour and Society in Britain 1918-1979* (London, 1984).
Concerned with the link between workers and the Labour Party. Most interesting when dealing with the post-1950 period.

John, Angela (ed.), *Unequal Opportunities: Women's Employment in England, 1800–1918* (Oxford, 1986).
Examines women's employment in hosiery, bookbinding and printing trades, tailoring, textiles, domestic service, clerical work, and mining. Also looks at social feminism and trade unionism.

McKibbin, Ross, *The Ideologies of Class: Social Relations in Britain 1880-1950* (Oxford, 1990).
The chapters on gambling, hobbies, class and poverty, and the psychology of unemployment provide challenging perspectives. The first chapter asks the question, 'Why was there no Marxism in Great Britain?' and the final chapter concludes with a discussion of the Conservative Party and 'conventional wisdom'.

Whiteside, Noel, *Bad Times: Unemployment in British Social and Political History* (London, 1991).

Establishes the social and political constructions of unemployment in an historical context and the effect these constructions had on governmental policy. Links inter-war unemployment with contemporary economic crisis.

Winter, Jay M., *The Great War and the British People* (London, 1987).
The most insightful analysis of the impact of the First World War on British social and demographic history.

5 Locality
Retrospective communities

Typing onto a few crumpled pages, the mill worker Annie Hukin described life in Bolton when she was a child in the 1890s. Girls played hopscotch, skipping rope, jacks and bobbers, shuttlecock and paddle, and 'breezy' bowls. Itinerant traders did a brisk trade in ice-cream and hokey-pokey, bears danced in the streets, German bands played for clumps of neighbours, and blind men sang for their living. Community life in working-class Bolton was alive and well.

The typescript, however, does not end with Annie's words: a neighbour and friend added a postscript. Without any sense of irony, this postscript destroys the friendly communal atmosphere by attesting that Annie 'never had a childhood'. When she was three years old, her father (a cabinet-maker) made her a little chair from which she nursed her numerous brothers and sisters. When she was five years old, a taller stool was constructed, enabling her to reach the kitchen sink. At the age of ten, the educational authorities exempted her from attending school so that she could attend to the increasing demands of her siblings and father. Finally, we are told that Annie was an 'undersized child with a disfiguring squint'.[1] Instead of spending her time playing jacks and bobbers on the streets, Annie worked within the home, rearing her siblings and doing the housework. The 'community' she eulogized existed in her imagination for over eighty years.

Annie's memory of communal sociability may not have been experienced by her, but she knew what a 'working-class community' would *feel* like. Many other working-class writers looking back into their childhood seek to convey their nostalgia for a past 'community'. In a handwritten memoir, Margaret Brown wrote that Coventry was 'populated with mostly Coventrarians and they all seemed to know one another, they were kindly people, always ready to help a neighbour in sickness and distress'.[2] Dorothy Tildsley remembered that when she was a child, Granville Street in Swinton was 'full of friendly people who would always help you when you were down'.[3] In Poplar, John Blake recalled that 'anyone feeling lonely only had to stand at the door, and in a short time someone would come along and have a chat and cheer their neighbour up'.[4] Charles Forman agreed, arguing that the sense of 'community' was strongest among women: 'If anyone was sick or needed any kids minded, someone would say "send them here" '.[5]

Attempting to define this feeling of 'community' more precisely has proved difficult. In 1955, George Hillery listed ninety-four major ways of defining a 'community' and, in the subsequent decades, definitions have continued to proliferate.[6] The word 'community' is popular in twentieth-century histories of Britain, yet historians tend to be vague about what constitutes a 'community' or 'communal feelings': generally, it is said to include elements of identification with a particular neighbourhood or street, a sense of shared perspectives, and reciprocal dependency. More commonly, the term is used without any attempt at definition. This has proved possible because of the resonance of the phrase 'working-class community' within two quite separate discourses: one, a backward-looking romanticism, and the other, a forward-looking socialism. The romantic use of the phrase has been fostered in working-class autobiographies and oral histories, where social relations are often recalled through a golden haze: conflict is forgotten in favour of doors that were always open; the neighbour who was never seen is neglected in favour of the neighbour who always shared; tiring workdays are ignored in favour of nearly forgotten games which diverted children even during difficult times. Socialist debates are equally responsible for the popularity of the term 'working-class community'. For them, the 'community' represented the innate socialism of the workers. Contemporary socialists, such as George Lansbury and John Scurr, found solace in the 'traditional helpfulness' and 'splendid comradeship' of the poor, declaring that they found 'more loving kindness' in an East End slum than in a Hampstead drawing room.[7] Socialists noted the way workers used the term 'community' as a weapon against the power of other classes and as a defence against the encroachments of the police and other authorities. In the competition for local jobs, residents pleaded for the exclusion of immigrants from their 'community'. In the scramble for council houses after the First World War, people would evoke their connection to the 'community' to improve their chances of securing a house.[8] Workers in industry argued that the survival of the 'working-class community' depended on the granting of a family wage. Activists such as Alice Foley opposed the introduction of shift work in the Bolton factories on the grounds that 'the community' was not organized on the basis of a shift system.[9] Within local districts, residents could unite as a 'community' to fight a particular cause: afterwards, they could disband.[10] As a rhetorical device, the 'working-class community' flourished.

Modern socialist historians have been loath to give up the concept. As with their predecessors, 'community' represented resistance to capitalism. It was conducive to class consciousness. The 'community' was the neighbourhood which was, in turn, the class. Thus, Jeremy Seabrook believes in the working-class 'idea of neighbourhood' with its 'values which the best of the working class forged in opposition to the poverty and insecurity of capitalism – the mutuality and the sharing, the imaginative understanding of other people's sufferings'. For him, the alleged 'retreat from community' in recent years was lamentable.[11] In a similar vein, Martin Bulmer describes mining districts, seafaring neighbourhoods, logging camps, and textile towns as separate 'communities' with 'their own codes, myths, heroes and social standards'. According to him, it was precisely these 'solidaristic ties' which created class consciousness.[12] More recently, historians such as John Benson devote major sections of their histories of working-class Britain to a discussion of the continued existence, or disintegration of, 'working-class communities'. Nowhere, however, is there any clear analysis of what could possibly constitute a 'working-class community'.

COMMUNITY

There are two assumptions central to the defence of the concept of a 'working-class community'. The first assumption is that the physical features of the city influence the social construction within it. Thus, Robert E. Park wrote:

> In the course of time every section and quarter of the city takes on something of the character and qualities of its inhabitants. Each separate part of the city is inevitably stained with the peculiar sentiments of its population. The effect of this is to convert what was at first a mere geographical expression into a neighbourhood, that is to say, a locality with sentiments, traditions, and a history of its own.[13]

This notion of shared experience leading to shared ideology is amplified in the second assumption which declares that, under certain circumstances, working-class individuals residing within a particular locality will grow to identify themselves *as a group*. This is liable to happen if the locality has a stable population or if people within a locality are forced to defend themselves against attacks by other groups, either from outside the locality, or even by other groups (or classes) within the locality.[14] This sense of 'community' is exemplified in the way its members identify their well-being with that of the group, establishing elaborate principles of the mutual rights and duties of each member towards each other member.

Given these assumptions, localities consisting predominantly of manual workers seem well placed to develop a consciousness of themselves as a 'community'. Important prerequisites for the development of communal consciousness are said to be physical and social impediments to spatial mobility. By restricting the individual's activities and social relations to a single locality, low spatial mobility consigns the individual to membership of a local group. If we exclude Ireland, Scotland, and Wales from our analysis, and if we look only at major urban centres, from the end of the nineteenth century, spatial mobility within predominantly working-class districts was sluggish.[15] Restricted geographical mobility meant that many individuals both lived and worked in the same district. Thus, the 1921 census revealed that two-thirds of the people who worked in Poplar also lived in the borough.[16] In many working-class districts there was a core of long-term residents. For instance, in 1934, fewer than 5 per cent of the residents in Bermondsey, Deptford, Bethnal Green, Hackney, Poplar, Stepney, and East and West Ham were not born in those boroughs or in adjoining boroughs.[17] In Michael Young and Peter Willmott's study of Bethnal Green, just over half of their sample were born in the borough.[18] In Geoffrey Gorer's sample of 1951, even in the relatively young group, nearly one-third had lived at the same address for ten to twenty years, and 10 per cent had lived there longer.[19] Even in 1982, in the London Area Regional Authority housing district, 85 per cent of the indigenous South Londoners still had parents living within the boundaries of South London, a third of them in the same district.[20] According to one historian, it was this restricted mobility which created the 'quintessential working class neighbourhood'.[21]

Not only were these predominantly working-class localities stable in terms of population, the residents also lived in close proximity. According to adherents of the 'community' concept, the development of 'communities' was helped by the physical closeness of neighbours and kin. In working-class neighbourhoods, crowded streets and houses made this inevitable. Whether an individual liked it or not, she

Table 5.1 Percentage of working-class families in York sharing a house with another family, 1950

Category	Number of families sharing house	Percentage of families in that category
A (earning under 77s a week)	18	22.2
B (earning 77s–100s a week)	—	—
C (earning 100s–123s a week)	936	26.6
D (earning 123s–146s a week)	792	25.2
E (earning 146s or over a week)	2,412	22.7
Total	4,158	22.9

Source: B. Seebohm Rowntree and G. R. Lavers, *Poverty and the Welfare State* (London, 1951), 89.

Note: earnings calculated on the basis of a husband, wife, and three children.

or he could not avoid other local residents: houses were close together, rooms crowded, privacy difficult to achieve. A substantial proportion of working-class families shared a house with another family. Most people could hear noises from neighbouring homes.[22] In a working-class street in Coventry it was 'possible to sit in the Cannings's living-room and to tell the time by the clock in the house over the way' and one 8-year-old boy whimpered that he was spied wearing pyjamas by the girl across the road.[23] Individuals would have had to strive hard to be alone since 'You cannot live in a court without knowing a good deal about your neighbours and their concerns, even without deserving the title of a gossip.'[24]

It would be a mistake, however, to conclude from low spatial mobility and high population density that there was an identifiable 'working-class community'. It is easy to exaggerate the extent of spatial immobility within predominantly working-class districts. Even if spatial mobility had declined in the twentieth century, structural changes in communications technology, such as the penny post, the printed press, the radio, and the spread of car ownership increased the ability of individuals to reach outside the immediate locality. Furthermore, for every working-class district where spatial mobility was low, another working-class district could be found where it was high. For example, in a study of Hackney in 1944, although 13 per cent of the women had lived in their homes for more than ten years, 56 per cent had lived in their house for less than five years, and nearly one-third of these women had moved to Hackney from another part of

Table 5.2 Migration in England and Wales (proportion per 1,000 residents of net inward and outward population movement), between April 1960 and April 1961

Region and conurbation	Migration
Northern region	+1
Tyneside conurbation	−7
Remainder of region	+3
East and West Riding region	+2
West Yorkshire conurbation	+2
Remainder	0
North West region	+3
South-East Lancashire conurbation	0
Merseyside conurbation	−4
Remainder	+9
North Midland region	+7
Midland region	+6
West Midland conurbation	0
Remainder	+11
Eastern region	+20
London and South East region	+7
Greater London conurbation	+1
Remainder	+23
Southern region	+21
South Western region	+13
Wales	+1

Source: Census (based on the 10 per cent sample).

London.[25] Unfortunately, information about internal migration is notoriously unreliable. The conventional way of estimating such movements on a regional basis has been to compare the resident population with data referring to births and deaths. The obvious problem with this method is that it fails to indicate movements *both* in and out of an area. In 1961, however, census enumerators included a question to a 10 per cent sample on changes of usual address, making possible the calculation of the proportion of people whose 'usual' address on 23 April 1961 differed from their 'usual' address on 23 April 1960. Not surprisingly, perhaps, what this revealed was sizeable out-migration from the conurbations of Tyneside and Merseyside and significant in-migration in the south and east, particularly the Eastern region, London region (excluding Greater London), and in the south-west. Although such data provide no detailed analysis of neighbourhood-based migration, the substantial population movements on a regional basis indicate anything but an immobile population.

The mobility assumption also confuses the *fact* of spatial immobility with the *desire* to stay in the same place. For a sense of 'community' to emerge from a stable population, residents need to be (at the very least) resigned to their locality. Yet, many immobile individuals were restless, desiring motion. In a Sheffield estate in 1954, a substantial proportion of working-class respondents wanted to move, yet the annual departure rate from this area was less than 3 per cent.[26] In Willesden, 62 per cent of respondents yearned to leave, yet, due to uncertainties of employment opportunities elsewhere, only 5 per cent thought they had a chance of moving within the next two or three years.[27] In a survey of mothers residing in a Hackney street in 1944, only one-third said they wanted to move elsewhere: when they were asked whether they would like to move if employment was not going to create problems, nearly twice as many proved keen.[28] In a Scottish survey, 39 per cent of working-class housewives had tried to move but had been unsuccessful. Many of these respondents jeered when asked about whether they would be willing to move: 'we have had our name down for one [a council house] for ten, fifteen, or twenty years'.[29] A stagnant housing and employment market kept people in place, even against their will. A spatially immobile population consisting of a considerable proportion of people anxious to leave may not be the best locality for the development of either communal responsibilities or pride.

In addition, close proximity to neighbours does not necessarily promote a sense of identification between the individual and the group. For some, close living may be a celebration of conviviality: for others, stifling and alienating. Kin may resent interference into their private lives, especially if it took the form of censuring sexual intercourse between married couples.[30] Neighbours complained about knowing too much about each other's intimate lives: 'you can even hear them use the [bedside] pot' blushed one woman.[31] A Coventry woman grumbled that her neighbours could see when she went to the toilet: 'I may only be going to clean it [the closet] or wash it, but it's all the same to them. For all they know, I may be going to the toilet.'[32] Others deplored hearing neighbours talking in bed: 'You sometimes hear them say rather private things, as, for example, a man telling his wife that her feet are cold. It makes you feel that *you* must say private things in a whisper.'[33] 'Mother Goose-Gob' or 'Old Mother Murphy' with their 'thin pointed nose between the aspidistra and the nets' were familiar, despised characters.[34]

Individuals coped with the lack of privacy by various distancing mechanisms. Neighbouring children were allowed to run in and out of each other's houses, but they were forbidden to mount the stairs.[35] Beds were turned away from the party-wall, so that 'embarrassing' noises would not be heard.[36] Keeping 'oneself to oneself' was effective.[37] Neighbours were bluntly rebuked when they used their first names.[38] The breakdown of distancing devices was one of the things which angered Mrs Freeman when she was moved from an inner-city neighbourhood to a Liverpool estate. She said of her new neighbours: 'They won't leave you alone with their mischief and their gossip, not like where we were before; just friendly like – "good morning" and "good night" – and you didn't see any more of your neighbours from one year's end to the next.'[39] Friendships with neighbours were considered to be dangerous. As two Coventrarians said, 'It's best to have your friends a distance off' and 'you won't be able to get rid of [neighbours]' or, as another man declared, 'if you go out you want to go further away from home than to your neighbours'.[40]

The isolated working-class family living in a predominantly working-class street was not as rare as the 'community' theorists would have us believe. A railwayman in Willesden explained:

> Social intercourse does not bother us much; as a family [three children] we get very little of it and what does enter our lives is usually in the family circle. We very rarely visit a place of amusement, picture house or theatre, neither have we any particular pub or club which we visit. If we are out for a walk and fancy a drink, we have it.[41]

For this family, and for many others (as we saw in Chapter 3), leisure was centred within the home, rather than within the locality. While much work has been done establishing patterns of sociability within localities, there has been little attempt to illustrate the extent of socializing which takes place by the same individuals outside the immediate locality. Yet, a significant proportion of an individual's relationships were based outside the locality. Letters to friends and relatives provide one indication of this, as does participation in other leisure activities. In one working-class district in Liverpool in 1954, between one-fifth and two-fifths of residents left the locality at least once a week to participate in some form of leisure.[42] The presence of cinemas may encourage socializing between people living in the district – or it may do the opposite, as in the case of parents who sent their children to the cinema to keep them *away* from neighbouring children.[43]

The pub and the church were also ambiguous uniters of neighbours. In the 1940s, a Mass Observation survey revealed that people did not necessarily go to the nearest pub. Nor did they necessarily attend the nearest church or chapel of their chosen denomination.[44] On the Sheffield estate in the 1950s, just over half of the housewives visited a public house weekly or more frequently. Half of the 'regulars', however, went to public houses outside the estate. In the words of one 'regular', it was easy to get 'fed up with seeing the same old faces'.[45] Pubs were chosen for a variety of reasons – the game of darts or dominoes, credit facilities, the presence of a piano, spaciousness, an agreeable landlord or barmaid, or the advantages of having some say in the management (for instance, in Workingmen's Clubs): the presence of 'locals' was only one possible reason.

One potentially important institution for socializing between residents was the church. Yet, this seemed to fail. Even in the sectarian city of Glasgow, religious identification was ambiguous. Thus, Jimmy Reid remembered, 'We were Catholics yet I was never conscious of any religious influences. Some days, coming home from school, boys would stop and ask me, "Are ye a Billy or a Dan?" You did a quick calculation and hoped you guessed their religion right before answering. If you got it wrong you got battered for your trouble. Looking back now it seems more tribal than religious.'[46] Religious observance was out of favour, most notably after the agricultural depression in the 1880s which reduced the clerical profession to a shabby gentility.[47] In Bristol on the first Saturday night of 1882, over 104,000 people (that is, half of Bristol's population) entered a drinking place.[48] Religious leaders were appalled, despite the fact that, in the same year, on a Saturday night in October, 116,000 people entered a place of religious worship. Those were good days. In 1901, the nonconformist magazine *Christian World* admitted that the average congregation consisted of 'six adults, four children, and fifty-seven gaslights'.[49] By the turn of the century, religious training colleges were having a difficult time recruiting any students. Not only were the sons of Anglican clergymen opting for more lucrative jobs, but even nonconformists were struggling to attract enthusiastic young ministers.[50] What's more, the absolute decline in the clerical population occurred at a period of overall population expansion; the shortage of clerics became annually more pronounced. Novel-reading crushed the market for religious books. Less than 9 per cent of books published in 1893 had religious titles, compared with nearly 19 per cent twenty years earlier.[51] Churches even failed to convince local educational authorities of the value of religious instruction in schools. By 1908, one-third of Local Education Authorities in England and Wales had substituted 'moral education' for 'religious education'.[52] In 1943, one-

Table 5.3 Number of adults attending places of worship, by denomination, in York, in 1901, 1935, and 1948

Denomination	1901	1935	1948
Anglican	7,453	5,395	3,384
Nonconformist	6,447	3,883	3,514
Roman Catholic	2,360	2,989	3,073
Salvation Army (indoor)	800	503	249
Total attendances	17,060	12,770	10,220
Total population	48,000	72,248	78,500

Source: B. Seebohm Rowntree and G. R. Lavers, *English Life and Leisure* (London, 1951), 342–3.

quarter of all male teachers and 18 per cent of all men favoured the exclusion of religious education from schools. Even though women and female teachers were much less liable to want religious instruction excluded entirely from the school curriculum, the rationale for such instruction was moral rather than religious. As one female teacher who did not believe in God replied when questioned about religious education, 'Quite frankly, I think that perhaps they should [have religious education] because it gives children an idea of what's right and wrong.'[53] The lament of the Commission on Evangelism in this same year is appropriate: 'It is open to question which is the more alarming feature, the failure of the Church to attract or its failure to repel.'[54]

York provides an example of the trends in church attendances between 1901 and 1948. In this city, 35 per cent of the adult population attended church in 1901, dropping to 18 per cent in 1935, and then 13 per cent by 1948. In other words, the proportion of attendances at church in 1948 was a little over one-third of the proportion of attendances in 1901. The only exception to the rule of general decline was the Roman Catholic Church. Although Catholic attendances were also declining relative to population growth in York, relative to other churches, it improved its position. In 1901, 14 per cent of adult church attenders in York attended a Roman Catholic church: by the middle of the century, nearly one-third were Roman Catholic.[55]

Many parishioners were unsympathetic to calls for a return to shared religious certainties, failing to congregate in religious buildings for love of either neighbours or priest. The Polish journalist Zygmunt Nowakowski reassured Poles in Britain that if they could 'learn to more or less put up with the English Sunday' where everything (including the churches) were closed, they would 'be able to bear almost anything else with ease'.[56] The church was seen as a place for elderly women: in the words of one 30-year-old man, '[Religion] doesn't touch me much – it's all right for women, especially when they're getting on a bit – but I don't think I need it yet, thanks.'[57] Even the example of the non-Catholic clergy, 'many of whom have raised large families of high qualities under conditions of poverty and self-sacrifice, not to say hardship', excited pity rather than a desire to 'go and do likewise'.[58] 'Class' proved a barrier. One Irishman recalling life in London during the 1930s said that he rarely met a fellow Irishman: 'Occasionally, we might meet an Irish architect or doctor at some Church function, but they always struck me as being embarrassed when we met and when I told them I was a carpenter.'[59] In the words of one working-class housewife in 1951, 'A working-class family that is religious is working against its own interest. Everyone knows religion isn't true, but the nobs try to make working folk believe it is, so that they won't kick up a fuss.'[60] Or, as a working-class widow exclaimed, 'Don't talk to me about parsons! They've got a pretty soft job, if you ask me. Telling decent working folk how to behave! What do they know about it? Never done an honest day's work in their lives, most of them.'[61]

Discussing her work in the East End at the turn of the century, the district nurse Margaret Loane warned against misinterpreting signs of working-class religiosity. She noted:

> To count up the churchgoers and the chapelgoers, compare the resulting number with the population, and then if there should be a great disparity, argue that the neighbourhood is without religion . . . is a more serious error. It is a confusion of formal outward signs and inward spiritual graces. Many of the poor rarely attend church, not because they are irreligious, but because they have long since received and absorbed the truths by which they live; while the idea that attendance at public worship is a duty does not occur to them. . . . To put on one's best clothes, to be surrounded by neighbours in theirs, to sit in a large, well-lighted, well-warmed and beautifully decorated building, to hear the organ, to join in the singing, all this differs from anything they are accustomed to call duty. It is a pleasure, and, like most other pleasures, must be left chiefly for the young.[62]

Indeed, the care, training, and discipline of children was the main role left for the church in working-class districts. Loane spoke about one town where:

Table 5.4 Proportion of children who occasionally attended Sunday School or a religious service, by economic group, 1947

Type of service	Lower class		Middle class		Upper class	
	Boys %	*Girls* %	*Boys* %	*Girls* %	*Boys* %	*Girls* %
Sunday School	49	66	53	59	52	57
Religious service	42	41	44	48	46	48
Sample size	55	76	461	389	321	330

Source: J. C. Ward, *Children Out of School* (London, 1948), 30.

all spoilt and wilful children, regardless of creed, were sent to the Roman Catholic day school, because the discipline was more indulgent than at the Board school. The mother of one of these little rebels proudly asked me to hear 'what a lovely lot of textes [*sic*] our Gertie can say, and her on'y six last August'. The 'textes' were the prayers invariably taught to all young children of that faith, and implied doctrines which the mother nominally held in abhorrence.[63]

The social and educational value of religion had priority over any more fundamental spiritual purpose. Even this function was waning. The working-class convention of sending children to Sunday School in order to evoke the pleasures of early matrimonial solace was becoming less important as working-class housing came to cater for the need for marital privacy. As late as 1947, working-class girls were still more liable to attend Sunday School than boys or girls from any other economic group, but the explanation for this lies less in 'communal solidarity' and more in the shortage of alternative leisure activities for young girls.

The failure of local churches in predominantly working-class areas to provide a centre of social communion was tackled directly by religious authorities. Young men and women were targeted. Thus, the YMCA and YWCA built gymnasiums in the 1880s, and witnessed dramatic growth in membership. The Boys' Brigade, established by William Alexander Smith in 1883, was followed by the Anglican Church Brigade (1891), the Jewish Lads' and Girls' Brigade (1895 and 1903), the Catholic Lads' Brigade (1896), the Boys' and Girls' Life Brigades (1899 and 1902), the Girls' Guildry (1900), the Church Girls' Life Brigade (1901), and the Girl Guides (1910). Most of these organizations placed dual stress on military and spiritual values. Henry Drummond, a Scot, theologian, and ardent supporter of the Boys' Brigade argued: 'Call these Boys, BOYS, which they are, and ask them to sit up in a Sunday School class, and no power on earth will make them do it; but put a fivepenny cap on them and call them soldiers, which they are not, and you can order them about till midnight.'[64] The theory seemed to work. Taking the example of the Boys' Brigade: beginning in 1883 with thirty boys, the Boys' Brigade had grown to 16,000 by 1890. After stagnating in the late 1890s, by the end of the Boer War it could claim 41,000 members in the United Kingdom. In 1933, it had 97,000 members.[65]

Despite such clear success, working-class boys were not being effectively wooed. Working-class boys were not excluded from the movement, but they were a minority. In the Glasgow Boys' Brigade, less than 1 per cent of boys enrolling between 1890 and 1895 had fathers who were unskilled. Seventy-two per cent of these boys had parents in skilled manual trades, and 27 per cent had fathers in the lower middle class.[66] In a poll of adult males in 1966, 44 cent of middle-class men had been scouts at one time, compared with 25 per cent of working-class men.[67] Typically, working-class attendance tended to fluctuate more widely and to be more short-term. Thus, Rowntree and Lavers tell a story of a Methodist parson who ran a thriving club for young people in the East End. Although he was careful never to wear clerical dress in the Club nor during Sunday evening services, he was once spied wearing a 'dog collar' by one of the lads attending the club. The boy was indignant, telling his mates, 'Boys, we've been had. He's a bloody parson', and the club was emptied from that day onwards.[68]

The demise of adult religious practice has been accounted for in similar ways. Explanations range from the churches' inability to cope with theological questions (especially those concerning the infallibility of the scriptures) to internal population movements resulting from the First World War. Christianity by the turn of the century had to compete with other institutions and organizations which fulfilled similar functions to the churches: trade unions, leisure societies, workingmen's clubs, and self-help societies all provided working-class members with alternative pursuits which were both personally satisfying and socially confirming. State intervention into education and poor relief relieved the church of much of its function in working-class life. By the First World War, it was clear that religion provided little to unite 'communities' torn by questions of poverty, racial tension, or class antagonism.

Whether in the local church or pub, adults, as well as young people, might be 'fed up with seeing the same old faces'. These faces represented ties of responsibility. The strongest argument in favour of the 'community' concept refers not to any notion of the innate desirability of socializing with those in close proximity but to the 'culture of poverty': that is, 'community' consciousness was a strategy for coping with low and unpredictable incomes. Reciprocity was crucial. By adhering to a 'community', individuals could claim a right to receive help, in exchange for their duty to give help. In 1947, when Tom Burns attempted to explain what he saw as a lack of 'traditional working-class communality' in the housing estates, he argued that the 'special neighbourliness' of the slums could not be exported from the slums: 'neighbourliness, regard for the feelings of others, mutual help, the closely-knit social groupings around pub and corner-shop, come from the pressure of poverty or hardship'.[69] Those who adhere to the 'community' concept acknowledge that there were high rates of failure in the way 'communities' looked after their members. Poverty did not necessarily encourage people to share. There was no contradiction between declarations of neighbourly closeness and a vast array of familial secrets. For instance, a worker in Farnsworth recalled that 'neighbours were neighbours then', before cataloguing the lengths to which her mother went to hide the family's poverty from these very neighbours.[70] The reciprocal help exchanged between families is undeniable and will be discussed later, but it is important to note here that neighbourliness can be separated from the sense of 'community'. Indeed, workers often made this distinction themselves. In the 1950s, Mr Askew was employed in a Liverpool factory and lived on a housing estate. He spoke warmly of his neighbours, but was at pains to point out that communication was maintained at a 'chatting level'. One of his neighbours, Mr Bowden, was a skilled worker. Although he had previously lived in a congested city area, he said that the estate was 'chummy' and his neighbours helpful in times of crisis (he always reciprocated). However, he added, 'we don't have a lot to do with people, we have only casual friends'. As a woman living on the same estate explained, 'it doesn't do to get too friendly with people, for then they like to borrow and you never see your things again. I don't mind doing a good turn for people, the only thing I disapprove of is running in and out of people's houses.'[71] The distinction between neighbourliness and 'community' was not only made on housing estates. A resident in an inner-city tenement in Liverpool argued that 'Good neighbourliness is, of course, not uncommon but there is no widespread feeling of community.'[72] This was also admitted in a study of two working-class neighbourhoods in Liverpool and Sheffield. Although the writers had been anxious to establish the existence of a 'working-class community', they were forced to conclude that 'such ties as exist to bind people together appear to arise out of a need to deal with common problems and frustrations, rather than to make possible new and enjoyable experiences'.[73]

A problem with the concept of 'community' based on reciprocal rights and obligations is the need for its members to share a set of moral values. It is doubtful whether any consensus existed. Even neighbouring kin may not share similar social values. A letter by a working man to Marie Stopes in 1929 provides an example of the failure of kinship networks to provide basic information about controlling fertility. He claimed to be writing on behalf of his wife:

> She has had nine children of whom three are alive only her sisters keep tell her to stop having Children but they wont give her any knowledge they just say they can stop from having them i have asked there husband and they say they dont do anything my wife has two sisters each has one Child only so if they have any knowledge they keep it to themselfs so i appeal to you for the sake of the Children we have and my wife to let us have the knowledge we ought to have.[74]

In this case, the brothers-in-law prove to be more willing to co-operate than the sisters, yet the couple still had to go outside the working-class neighbourhood and kinship networks to seek information. High levels of conflict within 'communities' are also a problem for this consensual model of working-class culture. Violence was endemic; neighbours hated the sight of one another; the ferociousness of gang warfare was tame compared with brawls between 'friends' at local public houses. Given high levels of conflict, it makes more sense to assume an absence of consensus, rather than assume that conflict was indicative of some unidentified rapport. There could be no consensus because there was no homogeneity: in the words of a tenant on a London County Council estate, 'Although it is almost entirely "working class", every subtle gradation within that class is represented.'[75]

Stress on conflict rather than consensus has been adopted by some defenders of the 'community' model. Gerald Suttles, for example, argued that the concept of 'community' makes sense only in the context of defensive groups. That is, neighbourhoods identify themselves as a group only when they are attacked by other groups.[76] However, the group attacking (even in Suttles' account) are just as liable to *share* the values of the neighbourhood they are attacking as are the members within the attacked neighbourhood. There may be very little to distinguish between the members of gangs from adjacent streets. In addition, in response to being attacked, residents may *reject* their neighbourhood. For instance, as a child in Bolton, Alice Foley became aware of the uniqueness of her neighbourhood when the Court and Alley Consorte Society set up their instruments on the corner of her street in an attempt to subject the poor to classical music. Although Foley enjoyed the music, she resented their presence in her street: 'for there arose the first uneasy awareness that our home and surroundings were of a kind to invite the attentions of a more cultivated section of the community, and the new knowledge forthwith dimmed my spontaneous acceptance of things'.[77] Individuals responded in different ways to being attacked: some rejected the values of the attackers, others adopted them. The concept of 'community' cannot help us understand these diverse responses.

NETWORKS: NEGOTIATION AND POWER

Focusing on the 'community' obscures both minority groups and individual action, and provides no mechanism by which we can know *who* at any one time belongs or does not belong to the designated group. Foreigners may be excluded for lacking 'neighbourly feeling'.[78] The woman who ran away with another man may be shunned ('We have t'put up wi' our men, why shouldn't she put up wi' hers?').[79] The handicapped may be isolated, as the spastic Louis Battye commented in his autobiography: '[Other children] lived in a different world, a world of school lessons and football in the streets, of rough-and-tumble and gate-climbing, of hopscotch and good hidings, of catch-phrases and esoteric repartee: I was not one of them.[80] Unemployed, unmarried women 'live alone in rooms . . . very lonely'.[81] *At what stage* did the Indian, the woman who did not adhere to certain cleaning norms, the homosexual, the prostitute, the Roman Catholic, the handicapped girl, the aged, the very young, the unmarried woman and so on 'belong', and *who* decided whether an individual would be accepted? Living in a particular neighbourhood does not simply entitle an individual to access to specific spatially restricted resources, such as friendships, schools, shops, and leisure activities. Rather, it enables individuals to *bid* for these resources by increasing information and raising the costs of searching for resources elsewhere. By examining networks between individuals, we can expose a complex of power relations instead of merely describing a broad stratum of alleged consensus. This approach also enables us to investigate constantly shifting networks between neighbours and kinsfolk, in addition to those between individuals who are relatively near and those who are relatively distant.

Individuals use collaborative ties to achieve particular needs, which vary significantly over the life cycle. To discover how these ties are negotiated, individual transactions are just as important as social institutions. It is not enough to specify the interaction of two individuals as being between two members of a particular class who belong to the same 'community': rather, we must look at how these two individuals define their relationship (as an acquaintance, a neighbour, a friend, or a member of the family) and how the exchange is conducted (through latent exchanges of rights and obligation, gifts, or the cash nexus). Finally, we need to know whether the links are dense or diverse, loose or strong, frequent or infrequent. Because links between individuals are almost unlimited, encompassing not only people with whom the individual has contact, but also people who are related in some way to the immediate contact, this chapter will be concentrating on the two relationships central to the 'community' thesis: kin and neighbours in inner-city slums and housing estates.[82]

RELATIONS AND RELATIONSHIPS

While kin were crucial, kinship ties were not of equal intensity. Parents, siblings, children, and grandchildren were usually as far as active relations with kindred extended, while latent ties (which could be activated in certain circumstances) included cousins, aunts, and uncles. The sex of the relative also influenced the weighting, with the most important familial member being the mother. Only she could compete with her children's spouses and her power could even extend to the sexual activities of her married children.[83] For instance, during the trial of a young man accused of an act of indecency, it was reported that in his family it was customary for the married couple to go to bed on Sunday afternoons. However, his wife disliked the habit, 'not because – according to the husband – she had any grounds for disliking it, but solely on account of family tradition'. It was pointed out that 'her side of the family had never heard of such a thing, and when she visited her parents' home enquiries were regularly made to see if she was conforming to her husband's family behaviour patterns. If she was, she came in for a certain amount of criticism which she passed on to the husband on her return home.'[84] The importance of the mother was often instilled into the children at an early age by the mother herself: as a Liverpool slum-child of 13 said, 'Me mother says "You can get another father but you can't get another mother": and that's true, isn't it? You can't get another mother.'[85]

Although – as was argued earlier – proximity did not necessarily breed intimacy, it could make contact easier. Kin were liable to be physically closer for working-class families than for middle-class families. In a national sample of households in the 1950s, 28 per cent of the working-class families had relatives living within five minutes' walk of their home, compared with 18 per cent of the middle-class families.[86] Kin who lived nearby were visited more frequently. Nearly 60 per cent of kin living on one estate visited each other at least twice a week, while only one-fifth visited kin living elsewhere in the city as frequently.[87] Again, there were significant gender differences in the amount of attention paid to kin. Elderly female relatives were more welcome than elderly male relatives: as Margaret Loane explained, 'the woman is less exacting and makes less work, and even if in feeble health can give household help in a hundred small ways'.[88] The age gap at marriage meant that wives would be more likely than husbands to have surviving parents. Women had better knowledge of kin than men.[89] Even if both the husband and the wife had kin residing nearby, women saw their own relatives more frequently.[90] In Michael Young and Peter Willmott's survey of East London, one-third of the men had seen their parents in the preceding twenty-four hours while half of the women had seen their parents.[91]

Not surprisingly, therefore, the female side of kin relationships dominated. In a working-class district in central Oxford, it was usual for daughters to move into rooms near their parents after marriage, resulting in a situation where over half of wives were born in the district in which they lived. This was true for only one-quarter of husbands.[92] A woman asked why she got married replied, 'There was a flat going next to mothers.'[93] The expectation that a marrying woman would live close to her mother was so pronounced that one elderly woman lamented, 'A son married is a son lost.'[94] In effect this made it more likely that a husband would be drawn into his wife's extended family than vice versa.[95] Not only did the wife's relatives live closer to each other, they were also more important than the husband's relatives for other reasons.[96] The mother's mother (called 'Nan' rather than 'Gran') was the family's nucleus.[97] She was crucial in giving advice, helping during confinement, looking after the grandchildren, and sharing the housework. Indeed, the grandmother was nearly as important as the father in looking after young children while the mother was employed.[98] Furthermore, it was customary to pay her for these services.[99] In a study of 'South Borough' in 1956, it was concluded that wives and mothers were key figures: 'In terms of emotional relationship, communication and services . . . the tie between the mother and her children is normally very strong and tends to remain so throughout her life. Mother and married daughter are commonly in frequent, often daily, contact, if possible.'[100] As one young wife said, 'I couldn't do without Mum; the day wouldn't seem right if I didn't pop in to see her.'[101] It was the mother's mother who kept the female siblings together. Mrs Rank was 34 years old and had been born on the Dagenham estate after her parents moved from Stepney. Her parents and two married sisters lived 'just round the corner'. She described her day thus: 'I see Mum pretty well every day. It's on the way to the shops, so I usually call in there to have a cup of tea and see if she wants anything. I sometimes call on my sisters or I see them out shopping, but mostly I see them round at Mum's.'[102] Daughters all gathered at the mother's home and, once the mother died, it was not unusual for daughters to gradually stop meeting, each one eventually becoming the head of her own family.[103]

Although kinship relationships could be intense and intimate, neighbours were also important. Since neighbours were liable to become kin, it was better not to antagonize them too much. Gillian Rose examined parish registers in All Hallows (Bromley-By-Bow) and St Stephen's (Bow) in every second year between 1919 and 1929. From these records, she concluded that between 42 and 51 per cent of marriages were between partners living in the same street, and an additional quarter were between partners living in the same parish.[104] Neighbours were crucial when speed of reaction was required or when the need was dependent on a shared territory (as in keeping an eye on children playing in the street). On one Sheffield estate, if an individual suddenly ran out of bread, nearly one-third of respondents said that they would be unable to turn to anyone for help, while nearly two-thirds would turn to a neighbour. Very few turned to a relative or another person. In the case of serious illness, almost equal proportions would turn to neighbours (48 per cent) as would turn to relatives (41 per cent).[105] Borrowing and lending was entered into warily, however: 'My mother laid down the rule: never borrow, then you'll never be under any obligation to anybody.'[106] It was acceptable only in emergencies which would not reflect badly on the autonomous family unit.

In the case of neighbours, as well as kin, women were the most important actors. Husbands played very little part in their wives' neighbourhood networks.[107] John Allaway was born in 1902 to a mother who worked as a cleaner in a Sheffield canteen and a father who was the storekeeper for an engineering firm. He describes the relationship of his father and mother to their neighbours:

Our neighbours were all working people, but how different they were from each other! The Ealands belonged to the unskilled working class. Harry, the father, was a drayman, but he and his large family were easy-going folk who kept an open house and were ever ready to help anyone in trouble. My father despised them for their untidiness and improvidence and was appalled by their familiarity. By contrast, the Lemons belonged to the skilled working class. Albert, the father, was a centre-lathe turner, with two daughters. They had a well-furnished and well-kept home, but were not very neighbourly. He was an active Trade Unionist, Co-Operator, Socialist, and Atheist. To my father the Lemons were no more acceptable than the Ealands for he detested everything they stood for. My mother's relations with the Ealands and the Lemons were widely different. She was very friendly with Harry and Lizzie Ealand and with Mary Lemon. But of Albert Lemon she stood in awe.[108]

At first sight, this passage could be used to bolster arguments about the 'communality' of the unskilled working class, as opposed to the skilled working class. What is more interesting, however, is that the father rejected both the values of the neighbour slightly lower on the social scale than him, as well as those of the neighbour slightly higher on the social scale than him, while the mother had befriended both neighbours, but remained aloof from Mr Lemon because of his rejection of religion.

THE OLD NEIGHBOURHOOD AND THE ESTATE

In the 1940s and 1950s, a number of commentators began agonizing about the destruction of 'working-class communality' on the new housing estates. According to them, working-class streets in well-established districts had supported thriving 'communities', in stark contrast to the impersonal relationships on council estates. The Second World War was a crucial dividing point due to the dramatic changes in housing. Bombs had destroyed hundreds of thousands of houses. The crisis was exacerbated by the fact that new house-building had been at a standstill for six years. Between 1945 and 1964 there were three phases in government housing. Under the Labour government, council housing and short-term solutions were offered to the housing shortage. They supported building prefabs and the repairing or converting of existing homes. By 1951 over 1.5 million units of council housing had been provided, compared with only 25,000 privately built houses. The proportion of households living in council homes increased from 12 per cent to 18 per cent between 1945 and 1951. The first postwar Conservative government stepped up the building of council housing. Each year between 1952 and 1954, over 200,000 council houses were built. The third period, from the late 1950s to 1964, saw a switch to private building and owner-occupied housing. Council housing had fallen to 100,000 built annually by 1959. Private sector housing increased from 25,000 in 1951 to 150,000 by 1964. Owner-occupied houses increased from 29 per cent of the total number of houses, to 41 per cent. Most studies, assuming that a high level of 'communality' existed in well-established working-class localities, concentrate on exposing the 'individualism' of the estates. Others concentrate on estates which were in the process of being built or were still too new to make any comparison between them and established areas persuasive. To what extent can we argue that the dramatic changes in housing destroyed what might have existed in terms of 'community' feeling?

A distinction must be made between types of estates. Certainly, the postwar estates did tend to separate families from their wider kinship networks. Thus, Mrs Simpson on the Dagenham estate noted that she had been ill a few weeks earlier and had to stay in bed during the day, struggling out of bed only when the children returned from school. Comparing her former life in an established working-class area with her current life on the estate, she said, 'It's not like up there, where you've got someone to help you – you could always go to a sister or sister-in-law if you wanted anything. That's what you miss most.'[109] Such seclusion must be seen within an historical context, however. Isolation from kin was a new development on the Dagenham estate. Before 1945, when tenancies on the Dagenham estate were easy to acquire, there was a considerable amount of chain migration by relatives. For example, Mr Bedford's parents moved to the estate from Stepney in 1937. They were followed by his sister with her husband, then Mr Bedford followed with his wife, and finally another brother joined them: 'Eventually we were nearly all here.' Similarly, Mrs Gale arrived on the estate in 1929: 'My mother and father were dead and I didn't like leaving my sisters, but two of my sisters and one of my brothers followed me here.'[110] The postwar estates were less responsive to chain migration.

The assumption that residents in established inner-city localities were friendlier than those on estates was widespread. For instance, in the 1950s, residents in an inner-city slum in Oxford who were being rehoused were unhappy about the move because they expected that 'community relations' would be more chummy in their slum than on the housing estate. However, when pressed, few could admit that they were actually friendly with the folks next door.[111] Antagonism between neighbours was common to people on both the new estates and the old communities according to a 1943 Mass Observation report.[112] Comparing Bethnal Green with the Dagenham housing estate, Peter Willmott concluded that most respondents claimed that the estate was just as friendly as Bethnal Green.[113] Respondents in Bethnal Green were clear: 'We're friendly . . . but we don't get too involved because we've found that causes gossip and trouble.'[114] Other studies expose as mistaken the idea that residents living in inner-city slums were more 'communal' in their relationship with neighbours than estate dwellers. Gitta Meier was so struck by the lack of 'neighbourly co-operation' in the older working-class areas of Manchester that she embarked on a project to establish whether this was equally true on the estates.[115] In a Mass Observation survey, fewer than one person in one hundred engaged in any form of leisure activity that involved co-operation with other people.[116] In 1958, Madeline Kerr established that although most of the residents in Ship Street (in a Liverpool slum) were Catholics, few adults attended church or took part in social activities centred around the church.[117] Casually dropping in for a cup of tea in the afternoons was acceptable practice for some 'mums' living in Ship Street, but this was the exception rather than the rule. In this street, length of residence and associations over a lifetime did not necessarily lead to contact. Thus, 'Mrs A.', 'Mrs M.', and 'Mrs N.' went to school together and were almost neighbours, yet they were not on visiting terms. Similarly, although 'Mrs B.' lived in Ship Street all her life, and went to school with 'Mrs F.' who lived opposite, she had no friends. 'Mr L.' lived in the street for forty-six years, yet he confessed that he and his wife kept to themselves and never visited anyone. 'Mrs S.' had always lived in the street, and swore she would never leave it, although she had no friends in the locality and was not on friendly terms with her neighbours: 'we keep our front door shut'. Of the sixty-one families interviewed by Kerr, only five expressed any (even half-hearted) desire to move, but this desire to remain in the same locality was not due to the presence of friends or 'human relations in general'; rather it was due to a 'vague undifferentiated feeling of belonging and the security of moving around in a well-known territory'. Thus, 'Mrs E.' had an opportunity to move – her husband had been offered a better job elsewhere and they had a chance of getting a larger house – but she refused. When asked if she had friends in the locality, she replied, 'Not particular. I don't make friends with all. I go to Mrs F.'s yard sometimes.' When she was asked what tied her to the neighbourhood, she simply repeated, 'I've always lived in this neighbourhood!'[118]

There were many structural reasons for this lack of socializing in established working-class residential districts, the chief one being the size of families and the lack of space in homes, making social intercourse very difficult. In both the inner-city slum and the estate, socializing was a low priority. Lulie Shaw noted this in 1954:

> With so large a circle of relatives to visit, T. V. to watch and the pools to do, there was not much time or money left for social life with other people – particularly for the women who had jobs to do as well as homes to run. Neighbourhood relations were, on the whole, limited to 'passing the time of day' and to helping in time of trouble; such help as running in to light the gas under the dinner for a neighbour who was working was taken for granted and did not form the basis for friendship.[119]

Established working-class districts were not the desirable neighbourhoods portrayed in many accounts. According to a survey carried out by Mass Observation interviewers in 1943, four out of the five 'most liked' areas were housing estates or Garden Cities while four of the five 'most disliked' areas were established housing areas.[120] During the scramble for council houses in Bolton in 1930, applicants had to declare why they wanted to move from their old neighbourhoods. Some wanted to move because of their leisure preferences: the collier Arthur Lever lived in Radcliffe but he wanted to move closer to the Kearsley bandrooms. The two most common reasons given for wanting to move, however, reflected a dislike of the existing neighbourhood. 'Don't like neighbourhood' wrote Emma Davies, the caretaker at Clinic Longcausey in Farnsworth. Fred Wright, a horizontal borer of Farnsworth, explained, 'Present accommodation insufficient and Neighbourhood very unsuitable'. John Johnson, a miner in the Manchester Colliery, simply noted, 'Wife expecting Motherhood and Unsuitable Nieahbourhood'. James William Thoraley, Clerk of Works for the Little Hulton Council, replied, 'Undesirable neighbour'. Charles F. Mather, electrician in Clifton, complained, 'Pestered to death. Life miserable. Searched and applied for houses for miles around for the last 2 years.'[121] Surveys in the 1940s and 1950s reveal a similar willingness to move, particularly among residents in central areas of the city.[122] In addition, those who had moved to the new estates were frequently pleased with their decision. In 1939, Mass Observation interviewers found that nearly half of the people being cleared from a slum in Ocean Street were keen to leave. When they looked at those who had already moved onto estates, levels of satisfaction were even higher. On both the Cable Street estate in Stepney and the Kensal House estate in North Kensington, between 90 and 94 per cent of the people were thrilled with their new location.[123] In a survey of Glasgow and North Lanarkshire in 1948, respondents were generally willing to move in an attempt to improve their housing: those who were reluctant explained their ambivalence in terms of satisfaction with their houses, rather than with their relationships with local family, friends, and neighbours.[124] In Middlesbrough, approximately 70 per cent of residents wanted to move. Of those not wanting to move, 70 per cent gave as their reason the fact that they liked their house. Less than one-third wanted to stay because they liked the neighbourhood or the people in the locality. Satisfaction with present accommodation was explained in terms of custom ('they were born there and were used to it') or employment.[125] Sixty-two per cent of residents in Willesden wanted to move elsewhere but since over half of the population of Willesden remained within the borough to work, and only 8 per cent went further than adjoining boroughs to work, many residents were reluctant to move. Although those who had lived in Willesden the longest were the ones who were most reluctant to move, this was not due to the existence of strong social ties in the district. Irrespective of social or communal ties, older people were less inclined to move.[126]

CONFLICT AND COMPROMISE

Relationships with kinsfolk and neighbours cannot be categorized simply as expressions of 'community'. Rather, they were expressions of a series of negotiations whereby individuals combined over one issue and dispersed over others. As we have already noted, neighbours were useful as allies, rather than as friends. Thus, between 50 and 60 per cent of people in Willesden claimed that they bestowed and received help from neighbours while less than one-quarter would socialize with them. In fact, in this locality, the poorer housewives were significantly *less* liable to visit or help neighbours than wealthier housewives. Friends and neighbours were clearly differentiated: 'We are all very neighbourly in this district, and we would always help each other – but we wouldn't make friends with each other.'[127]

What was the cause of so much distrust and dissension within localities? Conflict generally centred over access to scarce resources. Competition for resources only led to conflict when these resources were in short supply. In relation to the 'bottomless coffers' of the

County Council, conflict was unnecessary: all claimed their 'rights' and once the council had acceded to the demands of one, they had to assent to the rest. The council tenants in Mossfield Road, Kearsley, were unwilling to allow one neighbour to tap council resources alone. Thus, on 15 January 1955 Miss Kelly in No. 116 Mossfield Road wrote to the council asking that a glass panel be put in her back door, and that the door be changed to stop flooding in rainy weather. The council agreed to the improvements. Within a fortnight, tenants in houses 161, 173, 175, 177, 179, 181, and 183 had made similar requests. In the following nineteen days, the council received further requests from tenants at nos. 11, 13, 15, 104, 108, 110, 114, 135, 141, 143, 145, 149, and 163. In the words of Joseph Murphy of no. 175 Mossfield Road: 'I am writing these few lines to you to ask if you would consider putting a back door on for me when you are putting on for my neighbours.'[128]

A different set of rules applied in the case of access to scarce resources such as the communal water pump.[129] Neighbours would 'forget' to tell each other about free jam for miners on strike.[130] Other conflicts focused on rights of sovereignty. In the Dagenham estate, one-quarter of houses had a shared porch. One woman explained how the shared porch became the focus of local feuds:

> This morning I was scrubbing my side of the porch and I thought I'd better scrub hers as well to make it look the same, and she came out and said, 'Why do you have to scrub my half?' Well, she's found out *I won't* quarrel, I never will quarrel, and I didn't say anything. I suppose it made her angry, because she banged me on the top of the head with a broom. Well, I thought, I'm not going to put up with that, so I paid her. I hit her back.[131]

Goods representing status could also be the focus of intense competition. For example, particular armchairs on either side of the fire were reserved for parents, who could not be held responsible for their actions if a child or neighbour sat on them.[132] The type of curtains represented the difference between Irish Catholics and Irish Protestants in a community.[133] The colour of one's shoes revealed the status of the wearer and 'no-one was tolerated who tried to rise above it'.[134] One horrified person circulated the story that her neighbour had paid only 7s for a garment, but gave the price as £1.[135] In Bethnal Green in the 1910s, an 'Old Clothes Man' would present valued customers with either an aspidistra or an ornamental vase. The vases were coveted, for obvious reasons since they stood about two feet high and had 'more curves on them than on an undulating belly dancer': 'On the belly itself a pre-Raphaelite painting of semi-nude maidens, arms entwined, against a background of verdant foliage, stood admiring their reflections in a mirror-like pool at their beautiful unblemished feet. The design was framed in an oval cartouche of gold and stood out vividly against the deep blue of the main body.'[136] Housewives dreamed of displaying these vases in the parlour, and competed with each other for them. The piano and (by the 1920s) the radio were other objects around which competition flourished.[137] The unemployed unmarried mother living near the Tyne Docks in the 1920s bought her daughter the best new piano on the market in an attempt to raise her daughter's standing in the eyes of the neighbours and her sister.[138] Whether or not she was successful, many others followed suit so that, by 1950, one-quarter of households where the chief wage-earner earned less than £3 a week owned a piano.[139]

Objects alone did not bestow power. Amongst women, solemn appraisal of each other's housewifery provided the rhetoric which decided the hierarchy of women within the street.[140] The whiteness of curtains revealed the 'kind of woman' inside.[141] The shade of a family's underclothing on the line was noted and the judgement passed concerned the housewife's morals as much as her skills at the wash-tub. 'Cleanliness was next to Godliness.'[142] Women low in the hierarchy were called names associated with uncleanliness ('dirty Kate') and were 'considered very common'.[143] For mothers, children played an important role in these cleaning rituals. Indeed, as one maltster's wife put it, having children could be justified only in terms of the way they kept wives 'clean and up to the mark'.[144] It was the mother who was humiliated if her children had lice. In Bethnal Green schools, children would be given a number '3' if lice were discovered in their hair. The distress of a mother whose daughter returned home with a '3' was sharp: 'Shut up, all the court'll hear you! . . . You can't have three, you can't. . . . Your Dad'll kill me.'[145]

Children were also vulnerable to claims of dirtiness in the fight for local power. Molly Weir lived in a Glasgow tenement in the 1910s. Having caught ringworm from a school friend, Molly had to have her head shaved and iodine poured on it: 'Oh the shame and misery of that shaved head! To be a skinhead in our tenements meant only one thing – ringworm! It shouted aloud as though I had carried a bell, and intoned "Unclean, unclean".'[146] In Rotherhithe, children sent to the delousing clinic would find their bus surrounded by local children shouting, 'Unclean! Unclean!'[147] The higher in the status hierarchy, the 'cleaner' an individual had to be. Households where people washed in a tin-tub before the fire were inferior to households where the family

washed in the scullery 'and closed the door'.[148] When, in the 1910s, a
son of a miner successfully courted and married the under-manager's
daughter, conflict within the miner's family centred around their son's
sudden use of scented soap and hair cream.[149] In the words of one boy
after bathing in Walworth in 1912: 'I came out of Manor Place Baths
with a clean body in clean clothes and felt like a toff.'[150]

The most ostracized of local men were those in charge of the most
'dirty' forms of cleaning, that is, 'night-soil men', whose job it was to
remove human excrement. James Kirkup, from a working-class family
in South Shields, remembered waking up at night to the sound of the
scavenger's wagon preparing to shovel out the night soil from the
middens, or earth closets: 'They were strange beings, those unknown
men toiling at their lowly task. No one ever knew who they were: they
preferred to work at the dead of night so that their identities would not
be discovered. Some said they were convicts, and some children I
knew said they came up out of the sea, or out of the harbour round the
Black Rocks each night to do their dirty work.'[151] He thought of them
as 'bogles' or bogey-men, terms which were used to threaten misbehaving children.[152] In the mining village where James Bullock lived in the
1910s, however, the identity of the 'muck man' was known: he was a
village outcast, forced to live in an isolated cottage out of the village,
and never seen in chapel or at any social function in the village.[153]
Night-soil men were 'indeed solitary men'.[154]

Districts, as well as individuals, were ranked according to rites of
cleaning. In an essay, written in 1938 and entitled 'My Home and Who
Lives There', a 13-year-old boy declared that he would not want to
move: 'I think Id never get used to it living in a new house besides I
would get used to sissy boys street I am rough and ready and taugh
and the people who live in my hous are very clean in body and clean in
mind.'[155] Neighbours informed the landlord if other tenants did not
keep their houses scrubbed.[156] They would accuse each other of being
slatternly, inebriated, rough, dishonest when narrating their familial
background, and – the most hurtful thrust of all – only capable of
'dragging up' children.[157] Mrs O'Grady and Mrs Hemming of Coventry were amicable, until O'Grady's son threw dirt at Hemming's baby
as it sat in the kitchen. Hemming threw some dirt back into O'Grady's
kitchen, and so on. Things reached crisis point when O'Grady's
broomstick 'inadvertently' crashed through Hemming's kitchen door.
O'Grady calmly defended her actions to her hysterical neighbour and a
growing crowd of curious locals: 'I never interfere with her. I don't
notice her on the street. She says my kids wasn't brought up proper,
just dragged up. When I was pally with her, she wouldn't let the

children fight it out, as I said they should.' Hemming declared that she was unwilling to pay 22s 8d a week to live next door to her former friend, yet *she* refused to move. Just when the argument reached this impasse, Mrs Hemming's husband (a shift-worker) appeared, in his pyjamas, and promised to put up a trellis between the two side entrances. Seven months later, this still had not been built.[158] Local women earnestly attended to the shifts in these two women's relationship, ever mindful that who they spoke to and what they said depended on knowing what stage the feud had reached. Individuals had to be careful who they snubbed: any affront would start up a chain reaction amongst neighbours and friends.[159]

NETWORKS AND THE LIFE CYCLE

The development, clustering, and intensity of networks varied within an individual's (and a family's) life cycle. For instance, when the Poplar couple, John Blake and his wife, married, their chief link was with Mrs Blake's mother with whom they shared a house. After their first child, the council allocated them a two-bedroom cottage in Dagenham. This 'meant the breaking of all our ties, with both our families, and the neighbours of many years, and we could only hope that it would be for the best'. Each morning, Blake had to commute to Poplar to his job on the railway. This caused problems: 'When I got home at night, the wife was miserable, not being used to the new surroundings and strange people.' So, after a few months they returned to Poplar where they lived until three things happened: the wife's mother died, the children grew up, and their home was damaged during the Second World War. At this stage of their life, they were quite happy to return to Dagenham.[160] Marriage, employment, child-rearing, middle age, and retirement were key determinants in the arranging and rearranging of interpersonal relationships.

The way the life cycle affects networks of relatives, neighbours, and friends can be examined by looking at four estates (two in Liverpool and one each in Sheffield and Oxford) in the 1940s and the 1950s. In these estates, the immediate locality was most important for children and youth. It was they who defined group loyalty, colonized particular streets, defined the boundaries, and dictated appropriate expressions of sociability. Children's friends tended to live close. Of 297 children on a Sheffield estate, 88 per cent claimed that their 'best friend' lived on the estate. In fact, 37 per cent were fortunate to have their closest friend living within one hundred yards of their home.[161] This close proximity of friends encouraged the establishment of youth gangs to defend territories. Although these gangs were most important for young boys, girls were not always excluded, as one boy recalled the 'goings on' of his gang in the Dowlaid district:

> Sometimes my tea would be interrupted by the crashing open of our front door, and the shout, 'Quick Reg . . . the Sand Street Gang' which meant a war party had been sighted. . . . Outside, the runner had done his job well and kids poured out of houses to defend our domain. Our street, comprising of Spanish, Irish, Welsh and me [half Welsh, half Chinese] were more clannish than all the clans, and would fight to the last man or girl.[162]

In many districts, clubs and gangs for the young were the only locally based groups. For example, the housing estate of Canterbury Gardens sustained a Boys' Club with its football and boxing teams, an 'unofficial' football team, Saturday night dances on the club premises, and a gang of 'tough guys'. In Kearsley, as well, most of the 'community services' were for the young: youth clubs (linked to schools), a playground, cricket and football pitches, a park, and a tennis court.[163] Of course, the loyalty given to friends was not entirely dependent on close proximity. In the 1948 rehousing of families from inner-city slums in Liverpool, a young man (John Smith) was moved three miles from his former home. Many of his friends were rehoused in Paddington which was half that distance. Rather than making new friends, John would cycle to his old neighbourhood to socialize with his former friends and attend a Boys' Club. He was also a member of the cricket and football teams run by the friends who had been shifted to Paddington. These networks were only broken three years later when John was called up for National Service.[164]

The other stage in the life cycle where the immediate locality was decisive was for the woman bearing and raising children. The closeness of their children's 'best friend' was relevant to the lives of their mothers. Shared educational facilities were also compelling, as the 64-year-old Mrs Kemp testified: 'I started talking to the neighbours when my children went to school. . . . You started talking to other mothers when you're waiting outside the school. And then later on, as your children are growing up, people stop you and tell you, "My daughter is getting married" and that sort of thing. You've more or less all gone through it together.'[165] Reciprocal help between neighbours was crucial in these years, especially if the neighbours were at the same stage in their life cycle. Little help was received from elderly neighbours.[166] In the words of two women on the Sheffield estate: 'Both neighbours are old – we haven't become as close as if they were younger' and 'No, I don't call her by her Christian name, she's a bit older than me. It wouldn't be right.'[167] Women aged between 20 and 39 were most liable to ask for help from neighbours for minor emergencies, such as a shortage of bread, and mothers of large families relied more on neighbours than mothers with small families.[168] The dependence of child-rearing mothers on neighbours was due, in part, to their restricted mobility and in part to the need for immediate advice, general help, and emergency assistance. As one Poplar woman described it, the one time when female neighbours would rally around was childbirth: 'No one ever went without any help, especially when they were having their babies. They would pop into each other's houses, helping the midwife, preparing all the things that were needed, getting the children off to school and feeding them.'[169] Help between neighbours was facilitated by their 'minute acquaintances with the circumstances of those whom they assist': it was not only the poor who were more liable to need help – they were also more able to police it.[170]

Patterns of friendship also depended on whether a woman was employed or not. Less than half of the housewives interviewed by Mark Hodges and Cyril Smith claimed to have friends other than relatives or neighbours. Most of these friendships were longstanding: indeed, over half had lasted for more than fifteen years. However, friendships of short duration were more frequent among employed women and ceased when they left the job. Furthermore, nearly two-thirds of those working full-time claimed to have friends, compared with just over half of those working part-time and one-third of those not employed.[171] In another study, a variant pattern was seen, with one-quarter of married or widowed women who worked full-time having visited a non-relative in the past twenty-four hours, compared with around one-third of women having part-time employment or no job at all. All women – whether they were employed or not – were more liable to have visited a non-relative than men.[172]

THE NATION, LOCALITY, AND INDIVIDUAL

This emphasis on negotiations of power does not entail a rejection of localities altogether. For example, Chapter 3 was concerned with sketching out the general pattern of male and female roles within the domestic sphere. However, crucial to patterns of both male and female forms of housework was geographic location. Although women living in housing estates may have found it easier to create a 'space' separate from the masculine world of employment, they were also more cut off from other housewives. Women living in crowded accommodation in

London lacked the symbolic power of the parlour and women in small towns possessed advantages not shared by their sisters in the cities. However, although the concept of neighbourhood identities was uppermost in these women's minds, their situation was not radically different in other parts of England. Housewifery was essentially local in nature, while national in overall form. There were also different traditions of men and housework in various parts of the country. The most obvious distinction would be between rural and urban men. In Yorkshire, village men often held a 'common share' of land where they would shoot rabbits for the family dinner.[173] In Wales, unskilled workers were more liable to have possession of a small plot on which they could raise poultry or pigs.[174] Gardens were not common in mining villages (even when there was ample space), while even the poorest houses in East Anglia had gardens and artisans in East London were famous for their displays of flowers.[175] In Ireland, the high proportion of never-marrying men changed the nature of masculine housework: it was not unusual for two or three old brothers to live together, with one allocated the tasks of baking, cooking, mending, and washing.[176] This was not unusual in Britain as well.[177] And there could be very different traditions within the same neighbourhood. Robert Roberts, in *A Ragged Schooling*, noted that, on the whole, Salford husbands did not do feminine types of housework, yet he also admitted that there was 'one quiet street in the village where several husbands dared help their wives regularly', and this street became known in the pubs as 'Dolly Lane' or 'Bloody-good-husband street'.[178]

People's experience locally was essentially their experience of national politics, institutions, and structures. People did not experience the 'Education System', they experienced neighbourhood primary schools: they did not experience the 'Health Service', but local clinics. The significant locality may be an entire district ('I am not an Englishman: I am a Londoner') or part of a street ('We did not go down the Other End').[179] When these 'Londoners' left their districts, either in search of leisure, for employment, or to escape bombs, their hosts in other districts agreed that they were 'foreigners'.[180] People from different parts of the country, or different parts of the same town, felt that they had little in common: they may not even laugh at each other's jokes.[181] The 'stranger' from another part of Britain was liable to fall foul of local rules. Elizabeth Riley broke one of these housing rules when she moved into 'The Island' in 1948. She was allocated a council house which locals had decreed as 'belonging' to the neighbour's daughter, an 'Island native'. Elizabeth described the reaction of her neighbours to her presence: 'I used to go into shops and people would be talking. They'd stop as I walked in and wait until I left. It was resentment. They couldn't understand my next door neighbour's sister having the house before us and Mrs. Bailey's daughter not getting it, because she was an Islander.' Her two children were the only ones in the neighbourhood not invited to the party when the Queen was crowned in 1953.[182]

Strangers from other parts of Britain were treated with distaste.[183] For instance, in a Kent village during the hop-picking season, the local shopkeeper would spray Jeyes Fluid over everything as a form of 'barricade against the horde of invaders': after all, 'who could tell what horrible germs were lurking in the clothes of those scruffy looking cockneys? He was quite sure they never took a bath.' However, while the local Kent people found the Cockneys filthy, the Cockneys jeered at the gypsy pickers: 'Dirty gypsies! lousy gypsies!'[184] Some were more 'strange' than others. Because indicators such as accent, dialect, and obedience to local manners were important, children tended to be accepted before their parents. The main rituals through which this 'belonging' was achieved were those associated with sport, music, and marriage.[185] One working-class youth from Canning Town explained the hierarchy in the following terms: 'Southend was only thirty miles or so away from where we lived but it was like going to an outpost of the Empire for us. We knew the natives were hostile but there was always enough of us so we didn't really have to mix with them. . . . I preferred hop-picking in Kent to Southend. The natives were just as hostile but there were less of them.'[186] Prejudices were often harsh: as one Hampshire girl told her new friends in Yorkshire, 'my mother has taken a lot of settling in. You see, she didn't want to come to Yorkshire. She has always said it's all incest and buggery up here.'[187] No wonder neighbours felt they needed to give advance warning of any stranger entering their street.[188]

Outsiders may never be accepted, irrespective of how long they stayed.[189] In the Yorkshire mining village Bowers Row, during the first decade of the twentieth century, Lancashire miners were regarded as 'complete foreigners' for months, but it took years for Scottish and Irish miners to be accepted. A girl from Bethnal Green in the 1920s explained that she lived in a cul-de-sac which was a favourite place for games: 'there were often fights when our own gang turned on those from neighbouring streets and told them to get back where they belonged. An Englishman's home may be his castle, but the cockney fellow's street was his kingdom, and not lightly trampled on by outsiders. Even we small girls felt this bristling pride of belonging.'[190]

Tensions between localities were most forcibly expressed in the context of male–female relationships.[191] In 1940, a woman from 'The Island' married a man from another part of the city:

> The other Islanders treated Jim alright, although he didn't really feel one of them at first. He was treated all right, but not really accepted. It took a long time for him to be accepted. He was always 'Someone that married Nellie Kohler'. When he went round to Farmer's shop, Frank Farmer said, 'Hallo, Jimmy Kohler, what do you want?' 'My name's not Kohler. It's Priest', said Jim. We used to give all the boys the girl's name when they got married, if they came from outside The Island.[192]

The ambiguous relationship between the nation and the locality is most clearly exposed when we look at the way ostensibly 'national' rituals were actually experienced and celebrated. For instance, Dorothy Rockett described the celebration of 'Empire Day' in Streatham during the 1920s in the following way:

> One of the 'great days' I remember at Hitherfield Road was Empire Day. This took place on 24th May each year, and we would march around the playground (or Hall, if wet) waving Union Jacks and singing 'Land of Our Birth'. I think we all enjoyed Empire Day . . . it gave us a sense of belonging, and thus of security, very precious to a child. Besides, we had a half-holiday in the afternoon. It was a tradition in our family to go 'blue-belling' on Empire Day.[193]

Was Dorothy celebrating belonging to the nation, or the locality, or the family? Was there any distinction for her? Similarly, on Coronation Day in 1937, the men and women of Mass Observation who were collecting the opinions of people in the street, noticed that at the street level, gaily painted barriers were erected to keep 'strangers' from neighbouring streets from gate-crashing. They concluded that while the effects of the Coronation were nationwide, localities jealously guarded their own ceremonies: 'All have in common a reference to the central celebrations at Westminster Abbey, but it would seem that in quite a number of cases this reference was not as marked as might have been expected, and the celebration tended to reflect the local loyalties more than the central ones.' Hence, an Observer in a Scottish town recorded that there was no mention of the Coronation or of London throughout the day; the 'success' of the town itself was the general theme.[194] While the content of such ceremonies may be national in form, in character, identities were based on the locality or family. This was not because the locality was generalized to represent the national, but because, for the individual, the distinction was irrelevant.

CONCLUSION

The 'working-class community' as it survived in the writings and in the political discourse of working-class commentators was a retrospective construction. Faced with interlocking and sometimes discordant networks, individuals chose to give their allegiance to neighbours, kin, friends, and acquaintances on a more *ad hoc* basis. Their choices were restrained not only by limited alternatives and restrictive resources, but also by cultural norms: but these norms are not so fixed as to constitute a shared 'identity'. This flexibility was central to the struggle not only to 'make ends meet' in the working-class slums of the pre-war period, but also to the urge to 'keep up with the Joneses' in the housing estates of the post-war years. A shared identity as 'working class', even if rooted in a single geographical space, could not surmount the difficulties inherent in competitive society.

SELECTIVE BIBLIOGRAPHY

Benson, John, *The Working Class in Britain, 1850–1939* (London, 1989).
The book is divided into three sections: material conditions, family and community, and responses. Contains the best discussion of the relationships between family, kin, neighbours, and the 'working-class community'.

Currie, Robert, Alan Gilbert and Lee Horsley, *Churches and Churchgoers: Patterns of Growth in the British Isles Since 1700* (Oxford, 1977).
A detailed study of church attendance in Britain.

Johnson, Paul, *Saving and Spending: The Working-Class Economy in Britain, 1870–1939* (Oxford, 1985).
Indispensable analysis of the strategies for 'making ends meet'. Argues that 'mutuality tended as much to strengthen the particularism of local communities as to mould a national working-class consciousness'.

Scannell, Paddy and David Cardiff, *A Social History of British Broadcasting: Volume One 1922–1939. Serving the Nation* (Oxford, 1991).
Comprehensive study of the social history of broadcasting in terms of politics, the production of information and entertainment, and audiences.

Young, Michael and Peter Willmott, *Family and Kinship in East London*, first published in 1957 (Harmondsworth, 1990).
The classic study of working-class families in Bethnal Green and Greenleigh. Packed with fascinating comment from working-class respondents.

6 Nation
Britishness: illusions and disillusions

'The world that I regard is myself.'[1]

In the 'ramshackle ruins' of Stepney in the 1920s, a child daydreamed
of the cottage in the country she wanted to live in one day, 'complete
with roses round the door, a handsome husband, beautiful children
that were always clean and a kitchen that smelled of my delicious
baking'.[2] It was a dream of a 'new England': familial, harmonious, and
picturesque. Reality was unlike the dream. English roses vied with
Scottish thistles, Irish shamrocks, and Welsh leeks. Visions of a
harmonious 'nation' were aroused by ugly denunciations of groups
identified as interlopers. Illusions evoked subsequent disillusionment,
as the 'nation' fractured into its many parts.

An individual's fabrication of the 'nation' is multipartite, hurriedly
stitched together out of a medley of relationships, rites, and symbols
which have to be unravelled to answer the question: is there a 'we' and
who are 'we'? Although clumsy, the term 'national identity' is used to
refer to the way individuals or groups characterize their nationality.
Following the usage of European scholars, this term gives precedence
to the political imaginings of nationhood, despite the fact that
nationalism or patriotism does not inevitably result from a person's
identification with any particular 'nation'. Furthermore, class and
gender are central to the development of a 'national identity'. An
individual's consciousness of nationality is always in flux. What it
means to be 'British', 'English', 'Cockney', or 'Welsh' depends on
whether it is peace or war time, whether the discussion is taking place
in a pub or at home, and whether the individual is black or white, male
or female, rich or poor, young or old.

The ambiguity and multiplicity of 'identities' can be illustrated by
the Heren family. Born in 1919, Louis Heren spent his early years
helping his widowed mother run a humble coffee house for dock

labourers in Shadwell. His mother had a 'very strong sense of personally belonging'. Louis declared that her patriotism was 'personal', then listed a number of very public symbols: 'She believed in the monarchy, the church and the Empire because she saw herself as part of it. This explained her classlessness and mine.' This sense of self-recognition could be maintained in Shadwell but it broke down when they went hop-picking in Kent: there, no-one doubted that 'we Cockneys were a *race* apart'. For Louis, his original sense of what it meant to be 'British' evaporated further when, during the Second World War, he went to Sandhurst as an officer cadet and a 'temporary gentleman'. Looked at again, his mother's concept of 'belonging' to a nation united by the monarchy, the church, and the empire did not even apply within Shadwell: she excluded 'Catholics, Jews, Nonconformists, and foreigners' from her vision of Britain. For Louis, there was a fuzziness about whether 'American' was also 'British'. At school, Louis and his Cockney classmates sang 'Jerusalem' enthusiastically: with equal fervour they sang 'Marching Through Georgia' and it was years before he realized that this was an American song ('but then the United States was somehow an extension of empire'). Other countries impinged on his sense of nationality. As a child playing games where either Germans or French were 'enemies', Louis was secretly proud that one of his grandfathers was French and the other German. As he put it, 'However you looked at it, we Herens were unbeatable.' For Louis and his mother, the sense of nationality which was harnessed to 'big' symbols such as the monarchy was realigned in day-to-day life by the rituals and symbolism of the locality and the family.[3]

The stress in this chapter is on working-class individuals such as Louis Heren and his mother. Because the language used by the middle and upper classes is politically explicit in its appropriation of the 'nation', it is often assumed that 'national identity' is expressed in and through its elite. This position is defended by writers such as Peter Boerner who argued that 'attempts to define a national identity generally originate with the intellectual elite of a people, or, viewed in social terms, with the upper and middle classes'.[4] The conflation of one class-based version of nationality with that of another class is usually less deliberate. For instance, during the Coronation celebrations in 1937, a letter was published in the *Daily Telegraph* commenting upon the aesthetic tastes of different socio-economic groups. According to the writer:

> In the East End practically every house is gaily decorated. Families with little to spare have saved up to express their feelings of loyalty

in a burst of colour. The emotion aroused in richer homes by the Coronation is surely no less profound – but it is apparently 'bad form' to express it openly. The nearer one gets to the West End the more meagre are the decorations on the larger private houses. . . . At such a time cannot Englishmen forget their dread of giving vent to their feelings in public?[5]

For this writer, 'Englishmen' live in the West rather than in the East End. To take another example, the turn-of-the-century exposure of physical degeneracy is commonly reputed to have provoked a crisis of 'national identity'. Of the 20,000 volunteers for the Boer War, only 14,000 were fit to join.[6] The national body was even more ominously found to be wanting in some urban areas: for instance, in Manchester, out of 11,000 volunteers, 8,000 were rejected outright and only 1,200 were accepted as fit in all respects.[7] In the words of Arnold White, 'our species is being propagated and continued increasingly from under-sized, street-bred people . . . the Empire will not be maintained by a nation of out-patients'.[8] What did imperial glory matter if Britain was unable to 'flush its own sewers', lamented the young Winston Churchill?[9] The situation had improved little by the First World War. Medical inspectors examined over 2.5 million recruits between November 1917 and the end of the war, categorizing the men into four groups: Grade One being men who were fit, Grade Two being 'adequate' men, Grade Three consisting of men unable to walk five miles and unsuitable for combat, and Grade Four composed of men in even worse health. In the final analysis, 42 per cent of recruits were revealed to be in the last two grades. The virility of the Briton was unauthenticated.

Although such revelations led to much distress and calls for remedial action were incessant, the sensation of living through a 'national crisis' was endured by only a segment of the 'nation': that is, the wealthier members. Thus, around the time of the Boer War, the general labourer Walter Barrett lingered outside the Turk's Head pub in the Fens to listen to the men inside singing, 'The monument of England is the British working man'. He mused: 'This filled me with a sense of self-importance, for was I not a member of that society?'[10] No irony was intended, despite the fact that a more objective observer would have been justified in pointing out to Barrett that a lifetime of deprivation was the cause of his endemic ill-health. The working classes did not encounter any 'crisis' since the experience of their own bodies was not of degeneration but of stasis or regeneration.

The parochialism of statements about the 'nation' was widespread,

Table 6.1 Percentage distribution of men, examined by National Service Medical Boards, in four grades of fitness for military service, 1917–18

| Region | Grades of fitness | | | |
	One	Two	Three	Four
London, South-east	28.2	23.2	36.1	12.5
South-west	30.8	23.6	31.6	14.0
Eastern	31.8	25.1	31.3	11.8
West Midlands	37.1	22.1	31.4	9.4
Eastern central	40.9	22.4	29.2	7.5
North-west	31.0	25.1	32.6	11.3
North	43.6	16.8	29.6	10.0
Scotland	44.2	19.3	28.2	8.3
Wales	46.0	21.3	25.2	7.5
Great Britain	36.0	22.5	31.3	10.2

Source: Ministry of National Service, *Report Vol. I Upon the Physical Examination of Men of Military Age by National Service Medical Boards From November 1st, 1917 – October 31st, 1918* [Cmd. 504], P. P. 1919, xxvi, 13.

as reported by C. Delisle Burns at the end of a BBC broadcast on 7 February 1930: 'We still speak as if England were a single person and France another. But we might discuss how many Englands there are in social custom or economic interest or intellectual outlook.'[11] 'Britishness' often excluded social inferiors and people from the peripheries of the kingdom and empire, as another commentator disrespectfully pointed out:

Each member of the mass, secure in the orthodoxy of our unassailable fair play, is perfectly aware, and would readily admit in conversation, that there are among our acquaintances individuals who cannot be trusted to act chivalrously, that in his time, fellow-countrymen have let him down, taken advantage of him, played sly and cunning tricks upon himself or those known to him. In private he clearly recognizes that such conduct is to be expected from inferior Englishmen (not to speak of Welshmen, Ulstermen, Scots, Australians and South Africans). In public he forgets it or, if constrained to refer to it, calls it un-English.[12]

Cultural rules may be confused, as Lord Morley failed to recognize when describing how certain 'English' characteristics had been broken down by the Second World War: 'It is quite common now to see Englishmen speaking to each other in public, although they have never been formally introduced.'[13] Linking 'Englishness' with adherence to certain social rules excluded most of the population.

Another example would be the commonly asserted importance of 'fair play' in the construction of 'Britishness', which ignored the fact that many of the institutions which the middle classes saw as the epitome of British fair play – for instance, the police force – were adjudged by some sections of the working classes to be the epitome of unfair play.[14] Jim Wolveridge of Stepney described his reactions when listening to the activities of the police in dispersing an anti-fascist protest: 'I was horrified. . . . I'd been influenced by the books I'd been reading and was a firm believer in British justice and British fair play, and as far as I was concerned beating up women and the helpless simply wasn't British.'[15] The impossibility of escaping class-based interpretations of 'fair play' may be summarized by quoting a street entertainer's patter in St Martin's Lane on 12 May 1937. While wrapping chains around his partner, the entertainer complained about the audience's parsimony in expressing appreciation of the act. He declared that 'he is a white man (this with much feeling) and points to the Union Jack above. He says it covers four corners of the universe and it does not matter if you are yellow or white or black, if you are British, you are a sportsman and expect a fair wage for your work. He is not getting that; if any gentleman will change places with his partner he will get the wage and he himself will give him one pound besides.'[16] The gender, class, and regional affiliations of individuals led them to identify with a huge array of very distinctive (and sometimes contradictory) symbols and rites of the 'nation'.

Place of residence and accent were probably the chief superficial characteristics signalling the 'nation'. In a hesitant statement on British national character, Geoffrey Gorer puzzled over the close relationship between the characteristics of the southern elite and the 'national' identity, noting that although the domination of the south had been strengthened by centralized mass communications and standardized education, regional differences in accent, vocabulary, and diet were undiminished.[17] This point remained unrecognized by commentators like the Fabian Margaret Pease, who explained to children in 1911 why they could 'understand the soul of England much better than the soul or character of France, or Germany, or Italy, or Russia'. According to her, this was because:

all Englishmen talk the same language as we do, so that we have no difficulty in understanding what they say. But it is also because men whose fathers for many hundreds of years have lived in one country side by side grow like one another in character and think alike. When we read about some such great Englishmen as William Pitt or

Charles Dickens, we notice that he has some qualities like those of
the men we know. And that makes us feel we understand him. So it
is as easy to love our own countrymen as it is to love our own
family.[18]

Leaving aside speakers of Welsh and Gaelic, Britons do not 'talk the
same language' and they often barely understood each other. Elizabeth
Blackburn's mother was from Northampton and, when she moved to
her husband's home town in Lancashire, he had to accompany her
when she went shopping because she required a translator.[19] At least
this husband and wife hailed from the same class. Margaret Pease's
glib comment about the importance of 'living together' in the formation of national identities breaks down just as rapidly. Members of
different classes had very little to do with each other; sometimes to the
extent of not being aware of the existence of other classes until late in
life.[20] The degree of social segregation increased as the century
progressed.[21] In the same years as Margaret Pease was writing, the
prison reformer Alexander Paterson noted that 'rich and poor are at
cross-purposes; neither can understand why the others say and do such
unaccountable things, wear such odd clothes, or have such absurd
tastes and prejudices'.[22] The 'nation' was truly an 'imagined community'.[23]

EMPIRE, WAR, AND 'NATION'

The empire provided one of the sites of exposure to different 'nations'.
The apocryphal story of the 1914 volunteers in a London regiment
who declared that they were fighting 'for the Empire' (meaning the
Empire Music Hall) was not an indication of imperial *naiveté* but of
the extent to which imperialism permeated British life.[24] Even after the
actual physical composition of England, Britain, the United Kingdom,
and the empire (as learnt by rote in elementary schools since 1888) had
been forgotten, its awesomeness was enshrined in the memory,
alienating as much as generating pride in a broad but vague conception of the 'nation'.[25] The empire was most illusive. In 1929, when
Mary Wade's school class visited the North East Coast Exhibition on
Newcastle town moor, she recalled that her finest thrill occurred when
she and her friends visited the 'African village': 'Despite all the poverty
around us, perhaps this was our first injection of a superiority
complex. With furniture in our homes and desks in our classrooms,
surely we were very fortunate! Home cooking did not vary much, but
leek puddings and tettie hash was certainly more appetizing than

anything the Africans were eating.'[26] At school, children learnt about the 'far-flung countries of our British Empire' and, in Sunday School, about missionaries who 'saved savages in darkest Africa', but 'in contrast to the solid reality of our own circumscribed world these were . . . as awesome and as unreal as a story from *Grimms Fairy Tales*'.[27]

Yet, many people continued to find in the idea of the empire salutary blessings. For some members of the working class, the empire was a personal experience. Elizabeth Fanshawe's family lived in Zimbabwe in the 1910s. Her father's favourite saying was: 'Illogical prejudice is the dearest possession of the ignorant', and he used to remind her that the African heart was 'as white as ours'.[28] With the dismantling of the empire, working-class men and women returned from distant lands with new customs and prejudices. As we will be examining later, one of the legacies was a particularly virulent variety of racism: in the words of a writer to the *Spectator* in March 1931, 'The growing colour prejudice against the Indian in England is due, among other things, to the fact that the Britishers retired from overseas dependencies and now permanently settled in England are increasing in numbers from year to year.'[29] Children were named after imperial heroes, like Haig and Kitchener. An East End boy described a geography lesson in the 1920s where they were taught about self-governing dominions and the promised gift to India of independence within the Commonwealth. He noted, with hindsight, that the African colonies were hardly mentioned but the effect of the lesson was to confirm him in the belief that he was a 'freeborn Englishman and the world was my oyster. I developed an expansive and proprietary view of the world which has never quite left me.'[30]

Negative definitions of the 'nation' could claim the widest agreement. For many, to be 'British' meant not to be French or German. France is often said to be 'a kind of blackboard on which English character draws its traits in chalk'.[31] During both the First and Second World Wars, the antithesis of 'Britishness' was German, to such an extent that the British aristocracy anglicized their German-sounding names. Under the provocations of war, the balance of interest in national symbols and rites shifted, focusing on a few issues regarded as particularly pertinent. 'Englishness' was forced to give way to more inclusive terms: in the words of an advertisement in *The Times* in November 1914, 'Englishmen! Please use "Britain", "British", "Briton" when the United Kingdom or the Empire is in question – at least during the war.'[32] Threats from without inspired spasmodic declarations of unity. During the First World War, more men volunteered in Wales (as a proportion of the population) than in England. Scotland could boast of distinguished regiments in the British Army. Despite the inability of the British government to impose conscription in Ireland, almost a quarter of a million Irishmen enlisted within Ireland (and many more travelled to England to enlist), eager to defend the United Kingdom in its 'darkest hour'.

Even in the midst of war, however, expressions of concord were confused. Had the Easter Rising of 1916 not occurred, the broadly 'British' patriotism of Irishmen would have remained the dominant memory of this period. Even in 1916, many Irishmen and women remained hostile to the Rising at a time when their loved ones were fighting in France – as one person released from prison recalled, 'there were still thousands of Irishmen fighting in France and if you said you had been out in Easter Week one of their family was liable to shoot you'.[33] During the First World War, a man from Jarrow remembered: 'Everything German was bad. We passed a house on our way home where Germans were said to live, and never failed to shout insults at its dirty windows. Sometimes a mild bewildered face appeared between the ragged lace curtains.' Years later they discovered that a Scots recluse had lived there. The children in this community also confused the local Mayor in his ceremonial dress for the Kaiser.[34] The signs by which people distinguished the 'insider' from the 'outsider' may be misconstrued.

During times of war, cross-class understanding was intermittent, and never implied unconditional patriotism. For instance, during the Clydeside Rent Strike of 1915 (during which 20,000 tenants – mainly munitions workers – refused to pay rent increases in protest at their living conditions) a labour pamphlet quipped:

'What did you do in the Great War?' asked the boy whose father was an engineer . . .

'I did munition work, my boy', the father answered.

'What did you do in the Great War, Daddy?' asked the boy who was the son of a factor.

'My boy', answered the factor, 'I *did* munition workers.'[35]

The willingness of some workers to strike during 'national emergencies' was incomprehensible to other patriots.[36] During the war, the government intervened forcefully into the marketplace, passing the 1915 Munitions of War Act which established compulsory arbitration procedures and effectively made strikes illegal in war industries, setting up industrial conciliation councils from 1917 to allow for consultation between employers and employees, and drawing into government trade union and labour leaders. Radical

Table 6.2 Proclamations of states of emergency called under the States of Emergency Acts of 1920 and 1964, 1921–66

Date of proclamation	Nature of dispute
31 March 1921	Coal miners' strike
28 March 1924	Bus and tram strike in London
30 April 1926	General Strike and coal miners' strike
28 June 1948	Dock strike
11 July 1949	Dock strike
31 May 1955	Rail strike
23 May 1966	Seamen's strike

Source: Keith Jeffery and Peter Hennessy, *States of Emergency* (London, 1983), 274–5.

intervention of the government into industrial relations had some effect in reducing levels of industrial conflict: working days lost through disputes halved between 1911–14 and 1915–18. However, the growth of the shop stewards movement and general discontent amongst workers resulted in a number of serious strikes, involving engineers in Clydeside, miners in South Wales, cotton workers in Lancashire, electrical engineers in Birmingham, munition workers in London and the Midlands, railwaymen in the West Country, and policemen in London. In 1919 the number of trade disputes recorded by the Ministry of Labour reached 1,413, and involved nearly 2.6 million workers. In 1920, there were 1,715 disputes recorded, involving 2.0 million workers. As a response to industrial discontent during the war, the strengthening of the Triple Industrial Alliance of miners, railwaymen, and transport workers, fears of a Russian-style revolution, and the miners' strike of 1920, the government passed the Emergency Powers Act in 1920 providing for the declaration of a state of emergency if strike action threatened to interfere with the 'essentials of life' (that is, food, water, fuel, light, and transport). Since this date, states of emergency have been called on seven occasions prior to 1970.

The inter-war years witnessed the most serious unrest in twentieth-century British history. Striking workers, however, had no problem interpreting their actions in terms of the 'national interest'. The most dramatic of these strikes was the General Strike of 1926 which occurred when the Trades Union Congress voted to support the coal miners' dispute over reduced wages and longer hours of employment. Although the TUC later called off the strike, and the strike had little effect in reversing the trend of declining union militancy, it was of immense political importance, resulting in the passing of the Trades

Disputes Act of 1927 which banned sympathetic strikes, forbade civil servants from aligning themselves with TUC unions, and forced trade unionists to contract in to pay the political levy to the Labour Party. In terms of the striking miners, this strike emphasized the disjunction between themselves and non-strikers of both the working and middle classes. The presence of 'blacklegs' from within the mining community was traumatic: in the words of one miner, even after the strike 'it was a dreadful thing if you spoke to a blackleg's wife or his children'.[37] Equally, however, a working-class man – such as Thomas Jones – could identify himself as both a 'blackleg' and an 'ardent socialist'.[38] Patriotism was confused by questions of nationality, class, and politics. Another miner talked about being forced to confront the contradictions inherent in his own patriotic service in the army, in the empire, and in the mines:

> In November 1919 I went out to India with the Lancashire Fusiliers. I never had a days leave in my life until February 1926 that [*sic*] was over six years, until I got home at the end of March 1926. Only to find in this very house my father's on strike, my uncle's on strike, brother-in-law's on strike, and my two brother's is on strike. Shortly after I got a letter from the War Office asking me if I would volunteer for services to run the country, to defend the right. I thought that's bloody good that! I'm an ex-collier myself kind of thing and they were asking me to drive lorries for them and I'm on leave at that.[39]

Or, in the words of a miner during the 1921 lockout, 'well, lads, we're all out on strike but remember this, we are fighting for a just cause, we're fighting for a living wage. We are not the same as these people as owns the mines.'[40]

Strikes during the Second World War were also not an indication of a lack of patriotism on the part of workers. That period saw the highest level of strike action since the General Strike. Nye Bevan told the House of Commons during the strikes in the coalfields:

> These 130,000 patriotic Yorkshire miners at a critical stage of the war came out on strike and the nation lost some 1,000,000 tons of coal in consequence. These men have got sons, brothers, fathers, daughters, and sisters in the fighting forces. Are we seriously asked to believe that those stolid Yorkshire miners came out on strike and the South Wales miners also struck because of a number of evilly disposed Trotskyists? The fact of the matter is that these mines came

Table 6.3 Number of working days lost through industrial disputes, 1895–1964

Years	Average number of days lost each year (1,000s)
1895–99	7,470
1900–04	2,888
1905–09	4,204
1910–14	16,120
1915–19	10,380
1920–24	30,276
1925–29	36,207
1930–34	3,980
1935–39	1,978
1940–44	1,814
1945–49	2,235
1950–54	1,903
1955–59	4,602
1960–64	3,179

Source: Calculated from Chris Cook and John Stevenson, *The Longman Handbook of Modern British History 1714–1980* (London, 1983), 152–5.

out on strike because of grievances which were subsequently remedied.[41]

Mass Observation interviewers in November 1943 came to similar conclusions. As one of their respondents argued,

> I have sympathized with the strikers, although I have felt perhaps they are mistaken in striking when production is so urgent. On the other hand, the 'strike' is really their only weapon. And it is a weapon that becomes really effective only in wartime. . . . People say 'Suppose the Army went on strike, what would the workers do for them?' But the point is that the soldiers and sailors and airmen are not employed by the capitalists. They don't feel that half their toil goes to put money into the pockets of people at the top. . . . They know that this war doesn't mean 'equal sacrifice for all'.[42]

Although wartime profiteering was labelled 'unBritish' by workers, employers regarded it as lying comfortably within the bounds of capitalist tenets. During the wars, the conscription of labour rather than capital provided ample cause for periodic bouts of cynicism to be expressed by working-class men and women remaining in Britain. The threat that war posed to the 'nation' did not result in any diminishing of 'class' as a focus for identification.

The dignified mantle of that unwieldy 'nation' composed of locality, country, and empire could slide onto the shoulders of individuals, emboldening them to actions of audacious patriotism. Working-class virility – in contrast to middle-class chivalry – bound them to defend the 'nation'. Their patriotism was sparked during the war. If the middle-class man volunteered in a fit of chauvinistic fervour, working-class volunteering formed part of a rationalist struggle to raise a penny and stir the spirit.[43] In the words of a warehouseman in 1901:

> I know it is the rule to expect all soldiers, volunteers, or servicemen to exclaim, 'Why I went to fight for dear old England, my Motherland, against the foreign foe'. Well, to tell you the truth, those who go say nothing of the kind. . . . What they did talk about was where the next bit of 'bacca was to come from or the desire for beer or when the war would be over, and a word or two about dear old Dad and the Ma at home. . . . I did not care tuppence about the merits of the dispute, and the rubbish about 'fighting for the dear old flag', and our desire to kill Boers or anyone else, for the glory of old England . . . it was to escape for a time the monotony of existence.[44]

This was acknowledged by military officials who responded by introducing general educational classes for army men in an attempt to stimulate recruitment by improving their chances of finding employment after leaving the army.[45] In particular, they targeted recruits in categories D and E – that is, men who were unable to read or write more than a few words (at the time of Munich, over one-third of recruits belonged in these two categories).[46] It was a man in Category D who, when asked why he joined the army, wrote: 'I was grwom I was delar I soled stawbies I never got no scwooling I had to wotk al the time for my kwep at the age of 14 I got gop in a ridinal school in Belfast I got the sick I mead up my ming to jgoned the army I had a gop in form at 5/- a weaf for sest monst I left and jot a nother in a bldr at dricer a horse and fan for to jartes.' As army officials acknowledged, 'Jack Frost' may have driven such men into the army, but the army had a duty to the 'nation' to ensure that education in patriotism went hand-in-hand with the teaching of basic literacy and industrial skills.[47]

Once at the Front, patriotism was a different issue. The fighting soldier faced the more stark choice of clinging to his companions in slaughter or giving way to those trying to spill his blood. With the belittling treatment of returned working-class soldiers after the war, the patriotism of ex-soldiers edged closer to working-class men and women on the home front, leaving behind returned servicemen associations to safeguard war-induced patriotism, not solely for the sake of those who had fought and returned, but in honour of the values of those who did not return.

To some extent, militarism did provide working-class men with a set of symbols and rites which were broadly shared with men of other classes. Even by the beginning of the twentieth century, 22 per cent of men aged between 17 and 40 years in the United Kingdom had some personal experience of military life.[48] As the century progressed, men of every class were increasingly forced to participate in comparable rites within the army, navy, or air force. Excluding the obvious periods of world conflict, this was particularly true for the generation of men living in Britain between 1945 and 1963 when National Service was instituted. Initially, the rationale for this legislation arose out of the hostilities of the Second World War. The National Service Acts in 1948 consolidated the wartime legislation, demanding that men over the age of 18 served in the forces full-time for eighteen months followed by part-time service for four years. In 1950 the period of full-time service was increased to two years while the period in the Reserves was reduced to three and a half years. Thus, between 1945 and 1960, 2.3 million men were called up. British subjects in government posts abroad, mental defects, the blind, clergymen, and men employed in important industries were exempt. In addition, young men could have their Service deferred if they were an apprentice completing indentures, a student, or could prove exceptional domestic hardship. Only 0.4 per cent of those called up avoided service by citing conscientious objections. A much higher proportion – 16 per cent of those examined – were rejected by the services for being physically unfit.[49]

As we saw in the context of strikes during wartime, the extent to which the 'nation' of men could be drawn together through the imposition of a common militaristic training was undermined by prior 'class' identities. Thus, Jimmy Reid believed strongly in national service and, when his turn came up in the late 1940s, he loyally signed up. The crisis came only when he discovered that he was going to be required to unload ships in strike-bound London docks in 1951. He recalled his conversation with the Commanding Officer:

> 'Well sir, if I had known when I agreed to do my national service that I would be used in an industrial dispute in the capacity of a strike-breaker, then I would have been a conscientious objector.'
>
> 'Do you really think that we are going to allow those bastards to dictate to us?' he asked.
>
> 'Who are the "bastards" you're referring to. Who is "us" I asked.

'The dockers are the bastards, and by "us" I mean "us"?', the people, the nation.'

'Well sir, I don't think the dockers are bastards, and it's my opinion that the people who are really dictating to us are financiers, bankers, and a tiny handful of men who control our political and economic life.'[50]

The 'nation' was restrictive.

Class was only one of the three limiting criteria. Ethnicity was also important. Military education in citizenship taught that to be 'white' and British were the measures of civilization; Africans were 'as primitive as the ancient Britons' while West Indians were 'almost completely Europeanised'.[51] Not surprisingly, until 1948, a colour bar was maintained at all levels of military service, including the Women's Land Army. Gender was the other criterion. Military service not only forced men to discharge the responsibilities of their nationality, it also required acknowledgement of masculinity. New members strutted and marched and saluted themselves in the mirror.[52] The uniform gave them 'an equality of opportunity in their relations with girls. It gave them manhood, virility, and acceptability if not a sexual glamour, it made the path of their amatory adventures the easier.'[53] When David Morgan was conscripted into the Air Force in 1957, he experienced a buzz of randiness when dressing himself for the first time in his 'best blue' uniform. He noted that 'although I entered the service a virgin and came out in exactly the same state, something had changed. I had learnt, although not through direct experience, that heterosexual intercourse was something to be desired. Not just having a girlfriend, holding hands or snogging in the back row of the cinema.' As the recruits were informed on arriving at the training camp: 'you won't have your mothers here'.[54] The army was for men.

Although working-class women were encouraged to identify with the struggle engulfing the 'nation' during the wars, their identification with this 'nation' was different from men's. For some women, the broadening of their horizons was intoxicating, as Marjory Todd confessed during the First World War: 'We had to write "compositions" on such themes as "How can a schoolgirl help England?" and I actually can remember some of the cliches they contained. I really *did* write, "The future of our country is ours to make or mar", and was very proud of this expression, which I thought I had invented. It seemed to have the dew fresh on it when *I* wrote it.'[55] The grieving woman became the central motif against which an individual measured her integration within the 'nation' and evaluated her rights to make demands upon the services of the wider community. Thus, after both wars, the claims of widows, of women remaining single because of the death of actual or potential lovers, and of married women prematurely aged through the trials of the war years gained additional force. The wars did, however, separate the imagery of the 'nation' as expressed by women from that expressed by men: the militaristic focus of men's 'nation' was shared and public and although women's rites of grieving were also often public events, their focus remained intimate.

THE FAILURE OF COMMUNICATION

If war failed to unite classes and genders under the common auspices of the 'nation', the type of agreement reached during other times was even more specious. From the late nineteenth century, technological advances in communication infrastructures seemed to forecast a narrowing of class and regional differences. Penny postage, the telephone, and the spread of road and rail transport were said to be promoting communication between geographically dispersed individuals. The number of private cars in use increased from 16,000 in 1905, passed the million mark by 1930, and reached nearly nine million by 1965.[56] Newspaper reading also was seen to be having an effect. In 1920 there were only two newspapers with a circulation of more than one million – within the decade, five could make this claim. Between 1937 and 1947, total daily sales of newspapers rose from less than ten million to well over fifteen million and Sunday sales doubled to almost thirty million. Between 1890 and 1960, the number of telephone calls increased from eight million to 4,287 million, and the number of letters, postcards, and packets processed by the Post Office increased from 2,237 million to 10,200 million.

According to some, however, these technologies did not cross class barriers. Newspapers, for instance, remained divided on socioeconomic lines. Thus, Stephen Reynolds argued that communication networks brought working-class individuals 'more in touch with us – more "like the likes of a fellow's self" – than people of other classes who have lived in the neighbourhood all their lives'.[57] Others hoped that expanding communication networks would eventually bridge the gap between classes. In 1931, Dr Harry Roberts, who had lived and worked in the East End since 1906, pointed out that while in the past the middle classes regarded members of the working class as 'a distinct species of animal, or, at any rate, a distinct variety of man', the

Table 6.4 Number of telephone calls made, and number of Post Office mail deliveries, in England, Wales, and Scotland, 1890–1960

Year	Telephone calls (millions)	Post Office deliveries (millions)
1890	—	2,237
1900	8.1	3,304
1910	26.7	4,708
1920	902.2	5,420
1930	1,323.3	6,400
1940	2,215.4	7,460
1950	3,175.0	8,350
1960	4,287.0	10,200

Source: Adapted from B. R. Mitchell and H. G. Jones, *Second Abstract of British Historical Statistics* (Cambridge, 1971), 110–14.

Note: Telephone calls include trunk and private calls. Post Office deliveries include letters, postcards, newspapers, and packets.

combination of the spread of education, improved real wages, the wireless, and the long-distance motorbus was changing their minds.[58]

Many historians concur. The spread of a uniform education system was influential in creating a homogeneous sense of national identity. Not only did more working-class children share a similar school curriculum to their middle-class contemporaries, but the shared subject matter – particularly in history and geography – promoted patriotic values.[59] Educational authorities explicitly promoted the development of 'national consciousness' in schools. In 1913, a Fellow of the Royal Historical Society defended teaching school children the names and actions of British patriots 'until the burning, active love of one's own country' became a 'powerful factor in the daily life of every true son and daughter of England'.[60] However, even given shared textbooks, different conclusions were drawn by their readers.[61] The manner in which children were taught and the way they reacted to the syllabus prevented a uniform response.[62] Furthermore, the information conveyed was often distorted. For instance, Peter Vigor was born in 1911, and was brought up by his father, a car factory worker. He described the disjuncture between his history lessons in Luton and what he saw on the streets of Tunbridge Wells:

> History was taught solely from the British point of view and dwelt on the wars we had won and the countries we had occupied by force. . . . Illustrations usually showed the natives in 'fancy dress' and these pictures were inserted in an effort to popularize the factual

text. For these reasons I thought Africa was peopled with savages, and I was quite shocked and stared in disbelief when at about twelve years of age I saw walking towards me in the Pantiles, Tunbridge Wells, a negro wearing a well-cut lounge suit and a white collar and a club tie.[63]

Others learnt in schools that Englishmen were worth ten Frenchmen, that Frenchmen were 'a lot of frogs and were a little sissy as they had a great pull with the opposite sex', and that Germans had square heads, crew cuts, and fancy braces, and were totally without initiative.[64] The violence of 'Chin Chin Chinaman' was frightening, the beards and side-curls of Orthodox Jews eerie, and Polish and Yiddish speech disconcerting.[65] 'Britishness' excluded difference.

Educational establishments were only one locus for the attempted merger of a disparate people. Probably the greatest hope for binding together the 'British' was through shared familiarity with cinematic and radio broadcasts. The cinema was credited with extensive powers. Although Thomas Edison invented the movie picture camera in 1889, it took seven years before the first screening of motion pictures occurred in Britain and another eighteen years before the introduction of 'talkies'. By the First World War, there were 3,000 cinemas in the United Kingdom. This medium was particularly important in the lives of women and children, as the new 'Picture Palaces' came to dominate their leisure activities. It had many advantages over alternative leisure pursuits: the cinema did not share the dubious reputation of the Music Hall, it was comparatively cheap, and it encouraged the attendance of everyone in the family. By the inter-war years, in many working-class districts it was conventional for the entire family to go to the cinema together.[66] Films were an appealing form of leisure for these people. Jessie Blenkinsop recalled her life in a working-class family in the 1930s: 'Times were certainly hard, but we were young and life had its enjoyments. The cinema was a favourite "escape" for many of us, and perhaps the enormous popularity it possessed is explained by the contrast between our everyday lives at work and the luxury it afforded.'[67] It was no wonder the Pictures were agreeable: for the price of 6d, a person could listen to an orchestra, and watch two major films, a cartoon, and a news reel, while seated in well-padded seats with wall-to-wall carpet. By 1937, twenty million people (or 40 per cent of the population) went to the cinema at least once a week.[68]

However, all was not well with the cinema industry. Peak cinema audiences occurred in 1946 when there were 1,635 million admissions to 4,709 cinemas. In 1950 there were just under 1,400 million

Table 6.5 Number of broadcasting receiving licences, 1925–65

Year	Sound (1,000s)	Television (1,000s)
1925	1,350	—
1930	3,091	—
1935	7,012	—
1940	8,951	—
1945	9,711	—
1950	11,876	344
1955	9,477	4,505
1960	4,535	10,470
1965	2,794	13,253

Source: B. R. Mitchell and H. G. Jones, *Second Abstract of British Historical Statistics* (Cambridge, 1971), 114.

admissions and, ten years later, this had dropped further to 581 million. In 1963, 357 million people entered the remaining 2,181 cinemas. In other words, between 1955 and 1963, two-thirds of the audience and half the cinemas disappeared.[69] Competition came from the radio and (in the later period) the television. The radio furnished a more uniform message.[70] Although patented in 1896, it only began realizing its potential during the First World War. In 1922, when the BBC started transmitting, there were barely 36,000 wireless licences in England. By the Second World War, over nine million people owned licences.[71] By this time, more than two-thirds of families in Great Britain possessed a wireless set and members of the working classes were just as enthusiastic as anyone else.[72]

More than any other medium, radios acquainted people throughout Britain with how other people in the country lived. In the words of two historians of broadcasting in Britain, 'A sense of belonging, the "we-feeling" of the community, has to be continually engendered by opportunities for identification as the nation is being manufactured. Radio and, later, television, were potent means of manufacturing that "we-feeling". They made the nation real and tangible through a whole range of images and symbolism, events and ceremonies, relayed to audiences direct and live.'[73] Despite programming attempts to divide audiences by socioeconomic categories, it was a profoundly democratic medium, allowing everyone to share not only in the same presentation of facts, but also in the cultural 'facilities and opportunities for the enjoyment of music, drama and oratory, which formerly were the privilege of comparatively few'.[74] It could have an effect on day-to-day life. Thus, when discussing handicraft schemes in

Lancashire for unemployed men, the Reverend Cecil Northcott boasted that 'decorative schemes of this sort have given ideas of art and colour to many men, and a lot of cherished ugly things have been swept off the mantelpiece because somebody on the wireless said they were tawdry'.[75] Speaking about a working-class district in east Bristol in 1939, Hilda Jennings and Winifred Gill agreed that the radio had cultural implications: 'The fact that millions are listening into the same programme gives them the sensation of being part of a nation in a way that was experienced rarely and for shorter periods only in the past.' Proudly, they announced that, in time, everyone would share in the launching of a new battleship or the opening of a national exhibition.[76] In the words of the founding father of the BBC, John C. W. Reith, 'There is a grumble and a cause of complaining if the crofter in the North of Scotland or the agricultural labourer in the West of England has been unable to hear the King speak on some great national occasion.'[77]

Chronology 6.1 Chronology of broadcasting events, 1901–66

1901	First transatlantic radio message
1922	British Broadcasting Company established
1924	John L. Baird transmitted the first successful television pictures
1926	The British Broadcasting Corporation established
1929	Experimental television broadcasts began
1936	First regular television broadcasts
1939	Television suspended for the duration of the war
1946	Television resumed
1954	Television Act established commercial television under control of the Independent Broadcasting Authority
1955	First commercial television transmissions
1962	Pilkington Committee criticized trivial nature of television programmes
1964	BBC 2 began transmitting
1966	Colour television introduced

Source: Chris Cook and John Stevenson, *The Longman Handbook of Modern British History 1714–1980* (London, 1983), 120–1.

At the very end of the period dealt with in this book, television began to compete with cinemas and the radio, particularly in provincial areas. In 1950, 4 per cent of the adult population had a television at home. This had jumped to 40 per cent within five years. By 1960, 80 per cent of families owned a television set and the hours of transmission had increased from six hours a day in 1954 to sixteen hours in 1963.[78] This rapid increase in the number of households with televisions represented not only a rise in working-class prosperity but also a massive change in working-class recreation. Although it was not inevitable that the television was to be a domestic medium (between the 1920s and the 1950s, many critics argued that television would be more important *outside* the home, in, for instance, cinemas), the family took radio and television to its bosom: they were to become domestic goods, triumphs of individualism and self-improvement.[79]

Although the cinema, radio, and television did encourage some degree of cultural consistency, they also brought American (and European) culture into the living-room. People were increasingly watching American films. Some protection was offered to the British film industry by a quota system which dictated that at least 20 per cent of first features shown in cinemas had to be British, but the crowds were more anxious to see Bette Davis gliding down staircases in glamorous gowns than the more dour British productions. Films and radio programmes were just as likely to draw attention to irreconcilable differences between groups residing in Britain as to confirm any common heritage. Examples may be drawn from reactions to the BBC's 'Children's Hour', which occupied 6 per cent of the total programme time.[80] As a number of working-class men and women remembered it, birthday greetings during the 'Children's Hour' served only to remind them of their estrangement from wealthier, consumer-conscious contemporaries.[81] Major national celebrations might ostracize the individual rather than draw them into wider networks. Thus, a wife and mother in Cricklewood summarized her feelings on Coronation Day in 1937: 'Drink sherry at midday meal, rest of family gloomy, decide broadcasting of big events brings feeling of isolation'.[82] In addition, the ability of programmes to *change* political attitudes was limited. The British Institute of Public Opinion in 1950 revealed that half of all voters had listened to the speeches of Churchill and Attlee on the radio. However, fewer than one in one hundred was affected by them to the extent of changing his or her vote, and as many changed from socialist to conservative as a result of Churchill's broadcast as turned from conservative to socialist as a result of Attlee's.[83] Even when communication between diverse members of the 'nation' existed, its effects were ambiguous.

THE 'PERIPHERIES'

Despite sharing a centralized communications network, a coherent system of law and administration, and a single dominant language, many people directed their loyalties not to the whole nation but to specific regions which (according to some) make historical claims to be regarded as separate 'nations'. Wales, Northern England, and Cornwall had all been incorporated into the English state by the sixteenth century, and Scotland was integrated by treaty in 1707. Although there were separatist parties on the Isle of Man and in Cornwall and Northern England, only Scotland and Wales developed any significant ethnic organizations.

As we saw in the last chapter, high levels of internal migration have meant that arguments based on 'blood' have failed to provide a coherent basis for unity between individuals living in Scotland and Wales. Rather, 'culture' – broadly defined – took precedence. Devolutionist politics and the preservation of language have provided the chief foci. Particularly in Wales, movements calling for a devolution of the centralist structure of the United Kingdom have received a sympathetic response from successive British governments. From 1889, a distinctive system of secondary education was established in Wales. In the first decade of the twentieth century, a Welsh Board of Education, National Library, and National Museum were set up. Although Cymru Fydd, or the 'Wales To Be' movement, of the late 1880s and 1890s failed to survive the decline of the Liberal Party and its inability to reconcile demands from the south-east, in 1925, Plaid Genedlaethol Cymru (later called Plaid Cymru, or the Welsh Nationalist Party) was founded. Its immediate concern was with Welsh language, spoken by 37 per cent of the Welsh population in 1921.[84] By the 1930s, they were demanding 'self-government'. However, popular approval in Wales for their initiatives was not forthcoming either in terms of electoral success or in terms of more general cultural influence. Although 360,000 people signed the Welsh Language Petition (presented to Parliament in 1941), these were the years when Welsh bilingualism fell most rapidly. The campaign 'Parliament for Wales' enlisted a quarter of a million signatures in 1950, but failed to win political support. In the elections of 1959, Plaid Cymru's share of the vote was only 5 per cent.[85] The language issue was, however, revived in the 1960s when Welsh-medium schools opened their doors to students. The Welsh Language Society began demanding that Welsh was given equal status to English in Wales, and the Welsh Language Act of 1967 recognized the 'Principle of Equal Validity' of Welsh and English in courts and on official forms. Irrespective of these achievements, since the 1970s, only one-fifth of the Welsh population claimed to speak Welsh.

The relationship between language and Scottish nationalism was even less clear. In 1891, 11 per cent of people in Scotland spoke Gaelic. Even at this stage, Gaelic speakers were predominantly female and elderly. In Argyll in 1911, nearly half of children who were too young

Table 6.6 Number of Welsh speakers in Wales, 1901–61

Year	Number (1,000s)	Percentage
1901	930	50
1911	977	44
1921	922	37
1931	909	29
1951	714	29
1961	656	26

Source: Charlotte Aull Davies, *Welsh Nationalism in the Twentieth Century* (New York, 1989), 39.

to be attending school spoke Gaelic – while 1 per cent of 10-year-olds spoke Gaelic.[86] In the entire population, by 1961, only 3 per cent spoke the language. More worrying, the proportion speaking Gaelic in non-industrial counties was scarcely higher. As in Wales, not all language revivalists were nationalists and not all nationalists regarded language as a prime demand. The language revival, which began with the founding of the Gaelic Society of Inverness in 1871, was brought into the political arena in the early years of the 1900s, but for many nationalists, the language issue was potentially dangerous, threatening to split their movement into Highland and Lowland factions. Balancing calls for the encouragement of Gaelic with assurances that Lowland Scots would also be promoted proved difficult. Not surprisingly, therefore, when the Scottish National Party was established in 1934, language was not a central issue as it had been in Wales. Between 1931 and 1951, bilingualism in Scotland declined by 67 per cent. As in Wales, political power eluded Scottish nationalists. Between 1945 and 1959, they won less than 2 per cent of the vote at national elections and despite a rush of popularity in the 1960s, they won only 5 per cent of the vote. In a country which boasted of having one million communicants in a population of five million (compared with England's two million communicants in a population of forty-five million), the support of the Presbyterian Church for nationalist institutions, including the Scottish Rights Society, Home Rule for Scotland, the Scottish Patriotic Association, and the Scottish National Party, failed both to promote Gaelic or to elicit mass support for nationalist parties.[87]

IMMIGRATION

Confusing discussions about the independent 'cultures' of Scotland and Wales were a series of parallel debates around what were seen as

Table 6.7 Percentage change in the bilingual population, as a percentage of the entire population, in Wales and Scotland, 1891–1961

Years	Wales	Scotland
1891–1901	–5.3	–18.1
1901–1911	–5.5	–11.1
1911–1921	–1.9	–12.5
1921–1931	–0.0	–14.2
1931–1951	–18.0	–66.6
1951–1961	–4.8	–25.0

Source: Victor Edward Durkacz, *The Decline of the Celtic Languages* (Edinburgh, 1983), 226.

clearly discrete cultural groups. Although both sets of deliberations remained distinct, the overlap in content – though not in tone – was considerable: both reformulated ideas of 'race', 'culture', and 'nationality', and both questioned the resulting implications in terms of 'rights'. But, whereas in the Scottish and Welsh debates, political ascendancy was paramount, in the discussions concerning immigrants, political authority was subordinated to cultural autonomy.

From the late nineteenth century, debates about immigrants have centred around three groups: the Irish and Jews in the first half of the twentieth century, and 'blacks' (predominantly West Indians) in the second. Numerically, Irish migration to Britain was the most significant of these movements. Migration from Ireland has a long history, with numbers escalating after the Great Famine. The seasonal migration of agricultural labourers was maintained at a level of between twenty and thirty thousand every year throughout the 1890s and 1900s before tapering off by the First World War.[88] Permanent migration was even more significant, especially in the histories of London, Lancashire, the West Midlands, Yorkshire, and West Scotland.

By the First World War, the Jewish population was almost as large as the Irish population. From the late nineteenth century to the First World War, the Jewish population in Britain increased from around 60,000 to some 300,000. Most of the newcomers were Eastern Europeans fleeing anti-semitic regimes; they hailed from the lower middle-class or artisan strata, and their religion, language, and clothes embarrassed the wealthier, 'assimilated' Jews who had a long history of settlement in Britain.[89]

Until the Second World War, the immigration of Irish and Jews dominated the debates about levels of immigration, despite the

Table 6.8 Irish-born population of Great Britain, 1891–1966

	Number	*As percentage of population*
England and Wales		
1891	458,315	1.6
1901	426,565	1.3
1911	375,325	1.0
1921	364,747	1.0
1931	381,089	0.9
1951	627,021	1.4
1961	870,445	1.8
1966	878,530	1.8
Scotland		
1891	194,807	4.8
1901	205,064	4.6
1911	174,715	3.7
1921	159,020	3.3
1931	124,296	2.6
1951	89,007	1.7
1961	80,533	1.6
1966	69,790	1.3

Source: Census.

Table 6.9 Number of Jews in Great Britain, 1901–61

Year	*Number*
1901	157,090
1911	237,760
1921	300,000
1929	297,000
1940	385,000
1951	450,000
1961	450,000

Source: *The Jewish Year Book* (London, 1901), 177–8; 1911, 267; 1921, 168; 1929, 283; 1940, 334; 1951, 324; 1961, 189.

Note: Data not available for 1930, 1931, and 1941. Data include England, Wales, Scotland, and Northern Ireland.

longstanding presence of 'black' localities in Bristol, Cardiff, Liverpool, and London. These areas only came to be seen as a threat after 1945 with the arrival of Afro-Caribbean and Asian migrants. The post-war labour shortages (agreed to be in the region of 1.3 million at the end of 1946) was a major factor in determining the Labour

Table 6.10 Approximate numbers of West Indian migrants entering the United Kingdom in substantial parties, 1952-61

Year	Number
1952	2,200
1953	2,300
1954	9,200
1955	24,400
1956	26,400
1957	22,500
1958	16,500
1959	20,400
1960	52,700
1961	61,600

Source: Sheila Patterson, *Dark Strangers* (Harmondsworth, 1965), 359.

government's urgency in encouraging older workers and women to return to paid employment and tapping new sources of labour, such as prisoners of war and Polish ex-servicemen. In 1946, the government also began recruiting European Volunteer Workers from Displaced Persons camps in Germany and Austria, for employment in agriculture, mining, textile factories, and domestic service. This scheme alone involved the settlement of some 80,000 men and women in Britain during the first two years of its operation.[90] The government strongly preferred 'white' European workers on the grounds of their alleged 'suitability' and ease of assimilation. Trade unionists also saw in the employment of European workers some safeguards to the employment and wages of 'indigenous' workers. However, labour shortages were so severe that the efficacy of utilizing non-European workers had to be reconsidered. Workers from the Commonwealth were favoured: they were already British subjects and therefore free to enter the United Kingdom and, in the wars, they had proved their loyalty both on the battlefields and in British factories. Furthermore, they were relatively cheap, arriving in Britain on their own initiative and, by being British subjects, absolving the government of the duty to provide special housing or welfare facilities for them – indeed, to do so would be to discriminate against the 'indigenous' population. As the *Economist* pointed out in 1959, taxpayers did not have to pay for the breeding and rearing of imported Commonwealth labourers and, with luck, these labourers could be disposed of during recessions.[91]

The numbers of Commonwealth immigrants arriving soon escalated. In the immediate postwar years, there was no regular passenger service from the West Indies to Britain, so migration was slow. In 1948, however, the *S. S. Empire Windrush* brought the first large group of migrants. By the mid-1950s, more than 20,000 West Indians were arriving annually and some 150,000 persons born in the West Indies were living in Britain, over 60 per cent being men and the largest proportion settling in London. Colonial propaganda had led these Commonwealth workers to expect to be welcomed by a 'mother country' devoid of what the Colonial Office called 'the prejudice against colour'.[92] Like the earlier Jewish immigrants, what they found was different.

Chronology 6.2 Chronology of 'black' immigration and settlement, 1947–68

1947	End of Overseas Volunteer Scheme
1948	*S. S. Empire Windrush* brought immigrants from Jamaica
1948	British Nationality Act distinguished between citizens of the Commonwealth and citizens of the colonies
1956	London Transport Executive established a liaison with the Barbados Immigrant Service
1958	Nottingham pub riots and the Notting Hill riots
1958	Institute of Race Relations established
1960	Standing Conference of West Indian Organizations established
1960	Withholding of passports declared illegal by Indian Supreme Court
1961	Committee of Afro–Asian–Caribbean organizations set up to oppose legislation restricting Commonwealth immigration
1962	Commonwealth Immigration Act made entry subject to holding employment voucher
1964	Campaign Against Racial Discrimination set up following visit by Rev. Martin Luther King
1965	Malcolm X visited Britain
1965	Racial Adjustment Action Society established
1965	Race Relations Act passed, setting up the Race Relations Board
1968	Race Relations Act established the Community Relations Commission

From the beginning of the twentieth century, immigrants faced a barrage of restrictions to their entry into Britain. In 1905 the Aliens Act was passed, directed at what was seen as disturbingly high levels of Jewish immigration. The justification of this legislation rested with arguments about the nature of 'Englishness'. In the words of William Joynson-Hicks, the Home Secretary between 1924 and 1929:

> If two brothers come to this country and one of them settles in a district where only aliens live, continues to speak his native language, marries a woman from his own country, sends his child to a school where only foreign children are taught, keeps his account in a foreign bank, employs only foreign labour, while the other

marries an Englishwoman, sends his children to an English school, speaks English, employs British labour, keeps his account in a British bank, it is the second brother, not the first who will stand to obtain naturalization.[93]

The Aliens Act in 1905 refused entry to any potential welfare claimant and any person unable to prove that they would be self-supporting. It also set up a mechanism by which immigrants found to be homeless, living in crowded conditions, or dependent on poor relief within a year of entry could be deported. Irritation that immigrants might capitalize on welfare provisions was succinctly expressed by Bruce Glasier of the Independent Labour Party when he declared that 'neither the principle of the brotherhood of man nor the principle of social equality implies that brother nations or brother men may crowd upon us in such numbers as to abuse our hospitality, overturn our institutions or violate our customs'.[94] In the first four years of the Act's operation, 1,378 'abusers of our hospitality' were deported.[95] Many more were refused entry, most frequently on grounds of health.[96]

In 1914 and 1918, the Aliens Act was extended from its focus on Jews to all other 'foreigners'. In addition, the issue of patriotism came to the fore. The exemption of Jews from active military service during the First World War and indignation that Jews were profiting from the absence of 'British boys' during the war provoked Stepney Council's General Purposes, Staff and Education Committee in June 1918 to demand the calling up, internment or repatriation of all male 'aliens' of military age.[97] In the words of 'Justitia', writing in 1917:

Thousands of fine lads from the East End have volunteered to serve their country – many have paid the great sacrifice – but whilst hundreds of homes mourn the loss of a dear one, the price is cheerfully paid. Nevertheless, that our own folk should sacrifice their sons – their businesses – in order that the Jew and the alien may occupy their place is an injustice to the population and not to be tolerated. . . . If enlistment is not possible, work on the land under army conditions would be an experience for the alien with his patent boots, spats, and Homburg hat who openly avows, 'It may be your king, but our country'.[98]

The Jewish Lads' Brigade – an organization established in 1895 to help 'Anglicize' newly arrived Jewish boys in the East End – responded to such attacks by reminding people that British Jews were also being killed at the Front (indeed, one-third of those killed were former members of this Brigade). They failed, however, to convince either

East End Jews or writers such as 'Justitia' that their members could be 'at the same time a good Jew and a good Englishman'.[99] The Aliens Act of 1919 required all Jewish 'aliens' to carry identity cards, to notify the authorities if they were to be absent from home for more than a fortnight, to eschew designated 'protected areas', and to sign special hotel registers.[100] The power of medical inspectors in admitting 'aliens' into Britain was enhanced by the Aliens Act of 1920 and in the Aliens Order of 1953 (in force until 1973).

In the context of these debates about 'nationality' in the 1920s, the situation of the Irish Free State – or Eire (from 1937) or the Republic of Ireland (from 1949) – provided a remarkably non-controversial counter-example. Prior to the establishment of the Irish Free State in 1922, Irish-born persons were British subjects. As such, there were no restrictions upon their movement or employment within the United Kingdom. In 1922, however, the establishment of Irish citizenship potentially threatened this status. By the Irish government's Nationality and Citizenship Act of 1935, citizens of nation states in which Irish citizens were treated as if they were 'nationals' would be granted equivalent rights in the Irish Free State. This applied in the case of Irish citizens residing in Great Britain because the Irish Free State was granted the same constitutional status as Australia, Canada, New Zealand, and South Africa. So citizens of the Irish Free State remained British subjects and were not subject to immigration control. Although the Republic of Ireland left the Commonwealth in 1947, by the British Nationality Act, citizens retained the right to enter, work, and vote in Britain.

Irish citizens were the exception. After the Second World War, demands for the tightening of controls over non-Irish immigration became increasingly shrill. While the 1948 Nationality Act had confirmed the right of 'colonials' to settle in Britain, the Commonwealth Immigration Act of 1962 withdrew the *right* to live in Britain from citizens of independent Commonwealth countries and the colonies. Negotiations to join the European Economic Community reflected the shift away from a concept of Britain as an imperial country, towards an image of Britain as part of Europe. From 1962, immigrants from independent Commonwealth countries and the colonies had to apply for work vouchers. By granting immigrants from the disintegrated former empire an indefinite right to live in Britain and to bring in their families, these work vouchers were still more generous than the work permits 'aliens' required. In 1965 the Labour government reduced the number of work vouchers available to 8,500, that is, a reduction by two-thirds, and three years later, removed the right of free entry into Britain for people from the colonies who had not been born in the country or who lacked a parent or grandparent born in Britain. Acts in 1971 and the British Nationality Act in 1981 progressively removed the automatic right of all children born in Britain to be British citizens. Citizenship became a gift of the state.

One element has, however, been left out. In all these debates, gender was significant in deciding the extent of inclusion in the 'nation'. British lineage was male, and remained so in law until 1983. Naturalization Acts in 1844 and 1870 decreed that 'foreign' women marrying British subjects automatically became British while 'British' women marrying 'aliens' were divested of their Britishness. By the British Nationality and Status of Aliens Act of 1914, women were allowed to retain their nationality – but only if their husbands relinquished British nationality *after* marriage or if 'alien' husbands were separated from them by divorce or death. The British Nationality and Status of Aliens Act of 1918 allowed British-born wives of 'enemy aliens' to resume their British nationality in times of war (at the discretion of the Home Secretary) but it also allowed the Home Secretary to deprive women of British citizenship as a result of their husbands' misdemeanours. In response to the matrimonial attractiveness of American men, British women were allowed (after 1933) to retain their citizenship of birth if the laws of the husbands' country (such as America after 1922) did not allow them to take their husbands' nationality. Finally, by the British Nationality Act of 1948, women obtained the right to retain their nationality on marriage, although they had to wait until 1983 to be allowed to pass on this nationality to their children. The implications of 'nationality' laws could be harsh. Irrespective of the equality argument, they increased the risk to women of becoming 'stateless' and they withheld entitlements to vote and to gain access to many welfare provisions. These legal restrictions – affecting Jewish women in the East End more than any other group within the working classes – comprised the public aspect of the question of nationality.[101]

RACIALIST GROUPS

Although restrictive and discriminatory, legislation aimed at 'aliens' and 'foreigners' was the governmental reflection of a more expressive ideology of hatred shared between individuals from diverse classes, genders, and localities. Racism has strong backing in British institutions and explicitly racist organizations have won considerable support within working-class districts. Its twentieth-century history can be said to have started in 1902 when the British Brothers League

Table 6.11 Estimated membership of the British Union of Fascists, 1934–39

Date	Estimated membership
February 1934	17,000
July 1934	50,000
October 1935	5,000
March 1936	10,000
November 1936	15,500
December 1938	16,500
September 1939	22,500

Source: G. Webber, 'Patterns of Membership and Support for the British Union of Fascists', *Journal of Contemporary History*, 19 (1984), 577.

(an organization based in the East End and claiming a membership of 45,000) pressured for immigration controls to (in the words of its president) discourage grafting onto 'English stock' and diffusing into 'English blood' the 'debilitated, the sickly and the vicious products of Europe'.[102] Such arguments gained widespread appeal between the wars when competition for employment and welfare provisions reached a critical stage. Politically motivated assurances in the early 1930s by the British Union of Fascists that 'religious and racial tolerance' ('part of the British character') would be preserved were no longer regarded as necessary within a couple of years.[103] In a bid for popularity, the politician and leading fascist, Oswald Mosley, attacked 'big' and 'little' Jews for their role in impoverishing the economy and swallowing up 'British' cultural identity with foreign customs and allegiances. In the Albert Hall, in October 1934, Mosley declared war on Jews in Britain for daring to 'challenge the conquering force of the modern age . . . we take up that challenge. They will it! They shall have it!'[104] In this same year, the first East End branch of the British Union of Fascists was opened in Medway Road, Bow, followed by branches in Bethnal Green, Shoreditch, and Limehouse within a couple of years. Jew-baiting, the impaling of pigs' heads on poles wrapped in Union Jacks and placed in front of synagogues, fascist graffiti, and the destruction of Jewish property expressed the willingness of many East End residents to make Jews into scapegoats for local social and economic ills.[105]

Although the British Union of Fascists gained popular support in Manchester, Liverpool, and Leeds, the East End (which accommodated one-third of the Jewish population of Great Britain) remained their homeland. In the London County Council elections of March 1937, the British Union won 23 per cent of the vote in North

East Bethnal Green, 19 per cent in Stepney (Limehouse), and 14 per cent in Shoreditch. In the municipal elections (held six months later) it fought eight seats, finishing second in six. Membership figures are unreliable, but, according to the best estimate, total membership rose from 17,000 in the first few months of 1934 to a peak of 50,000 by July of that year. After dropping back to 5,000 within a year, there was a slow recovery to 15,500 through 1936, reaching 22,500 by the declaration of war.[106] An enormous variety of people were attracted by its dual claims of patriotism and radicalism. In South-East Lancashire, 'cotton campaigns' attracted textile workers frightened by threats of redundancy. Self-employed workers were lured by promises to stabilize the economy. The protection of trade was compelling bait for shopkeepers, taxi-drivers, furniture traders, and other small entrepreneurs. Housewives were guaranteed new and better homes while, on the streets, gangs pursued each other within the forum provided by the Union. Whatever the motive, members tended to be young and male. When a Gallup Poll in 1937 asked people to choose between fascism and communism, 70 per cent of respondents under 30 years of age chose fascism compared with just over half of the entire sample.[107] The depression had politicized the working-class young man. As Mosley recalled, 'the vigour, vitality and warm responsiveness to any appeal for personal action or high idealism' drew men into his party.[108]

Racialist sentiments were not the sole preserve of extremist organizations such as the British Union of Fascists, the League of Empire Loyalists, or the British National Party. In 1933, the Scottish Protestant League won 23 per cent of the total municipal vote in Glasgow after promising to 'Kick the Pope' and after distributing leaflets entitled 'The Life of a Carmelite Nun', 'Why Priests Don't Wed', and 'The Horrible Lives of the Popes of Rome'.[109] Less frenzied, perhaps, but with equal vehemence, the trade union and socialist movement pressed for control of 'foreigners' on the grounds that Jews were detrimental to the welfare of the British worker. In the Trade Union and Labour journals *Clarion*, *Labour Leader*, and *Justice*, Jews were identified as a threat to British self-preservation and a menace to the working class. As one editorial said, 'alien' immigration would 'besmirch the fair name of England and corrupt the sweetness of our national life and character'.[110] Many members of the 'white' working class concurred. In Anthony Richmond's survey of 'race relations' in Bristol, 80 per cent of respondents favoured further restrictions on immigration.[111] In the words of a shop-owner in Bradford in the first decade of the twentieth century: 'They should put every German on a Jew's back and make 'em swim to Ireland.'[112]

The Jewish and the 'black' working class confronted settlement in Britain in a variety of ways. Responses reflected not only the diversity of settlement in Britain, but also differing attitudes to settlement itself. Sam Clarke, born to Russian parents in Bethnal Green in 1907, had one dream: to be the flyweight boxing champion. Shadow boxing in front of the mirror, he liked what he saw, describing himself as a 'thin hairy-chested stylish boxer with the Union Jack on one side of my boxing shorts and the Sign of David on the other'.[113] This second-generation Jew's pride in his dual identity contrasts with the experience of – for example – a West Indian labourer anxious to distinguish himself from West African labourers: '[Employers] think we all like those African boys – we just drop down from the trees in the jungle like black monkeys and never wear shoes before. The foreman ask me how come I speak English so good if I only here two years.'[114] No unified response was possible, but faced with racial violence, protest was initially conducted through conventional channels. Lobbying MPs and petitioning the Home Secretary were methods supported by established Jewish groups, notably the Board of Deputies. Although they won some victories (such as persuading the London County Council in 1928 to award scholarships to certain Jewish children and reversing their policy of employing only British-born citizens) the class bias of the Board was resented by the predominantly working-class Jews in the East End. The paternalism of the Board was exacerbated by their tendency to work in secrecy, their abhorrence of populism, and their anxiety to avoid the mobilization of Jews. Assimilation, not confrontation, was their slogan – but this could not reassure the East End Jewry who were increasingly forced to respond to violence by violence.

In response to racialist threats, many young working-class Jews joined the Communist Party, the most visible group fighting anti-semitism because of its threat to democracy rather than specifically to Jews. As the *Jewish Chronicle* admitted, young Jews were being drawn into the Communist Party, not because of any strong Communist conviction, but 'in the desperate belief' that the Communists were the only group vigorously defending their general interests.[115] The Communist-inspired 'Battle of Cable Street' was decisive for East End Jews and fascists alike. In 1936, when Oswald Mosley announced his determination to march through predominantly Jewish areas of the East End on 4 October, the Jewish People's Council against Fascism and Anti-Semitism mobilized, collecting in two days 77,000 signatures objecting to the march. When the council took no action, more than 100,000 protesters gathered to block Mosley's 1,900 fascists. At Cable

Street, rising levels of violence compelled the police to forbid the fascists from proceeding. In the resulting excitement, over one hundred people were injured and eighty-five arrests were made. A week later, avenging the anti-fascists for stalling their march, a group of youths assaulted local Jews and smashed windows of Jewish shops and houses along Mile End Road. The Public Order Act of 1 January 1937 was rushed through Parliament, enhancing police powers to ban and control demonstrations and marches, forbidding uniformed paramilitary groups, proscribing the use of stewards at open air meetings, and outlawing public use of insulting words liable to cause a breach of the peace. The Act restricted the activities not only of fascists, but also of communists and the National Unemployed Workers Movement. After the Cable Street disturbances of 1936, Jewish 'defence' organizations multiplied in the East End, including the Jewish Council of Action (a small, short-lived organization), the Jewish Ex-Servicemen's Legion (supporting the Board of Deputies), the Ex-Servicemen's Movement Against Fascism (a left-wing group), and the Jewish People's Council Against Fascism and Anti-Semitism (a broadly based council challenging the pre-eminence of the Board of Deputies). Established groups, such as the Association of Jewish Friendly Societies, joined the fight against fascism and the East End trade union movement urged Jewish workers to fight 'with their English comrades' against 'capitalism and reaction'.[116]

'Blacks' also mobilized in protest at the discrimination they experienced. Prior to the 1960s, their protests tended to be informal, but rising tensions and the enhanced political power of Afro-Caribbean and Asian migrants stimulated the establishment of a variety of organizations to defend their interests. These organizations included the Indian Workers' Association, the West Indian Standing Conference, the Cardiff Coloured Defence Association, and local 'black' groups responding to neighbourhood-based hostility such as the Notting Hill Riots of 1958. The conditions leading up to the riots of 1958 came into being in 1956 when the fascist Union Movement decided to target North Kensington. By August 1958, tensions were running high, attacks on 'blacks' were mounting, and 'white' youths were being arrested for engaging in 'nigger hunts'. Stimulated by a wave of racial violence in Nottingham in August, in the first weekend of September, a crowd of 700 'white' men gathered around the area from Bromley Road to Blenheim Crescent and Westbourne Park Road smashing windows of 'black' homes and attacking any 'blacks' they met. Violence spread to Brixton, Hackney, Southall, and Harlesden. By 5 September, 150 arrests had been made. Perversely,

Oswald Mosley chose this time to announce that he would stand for North Kensington in the General Election. Despite the fact that 'whites' were attacking 'blacks', these riots were used within Parliament and in the press to argue against further immigration. In the words of *The Times* on 3 September 1958, 'There are three main charges of resentment against coloured inhabitants of the district. They are alleged to do no work and to collect a rich sum from the Assistance Board. They are said to find housing when "white" residents cannot. And they are charged with all kinds of misbehaviour, especially sexual.' Extreme right groups joined with conservative factions to mount an attack around these three issues.

The riots had an immense effect on 'blacks' in Britain: no longer could they pretend that they were 'oversea British' living in Britain – they were 'blacks' in a 'white' country. 'Black' organizations sprang up. The Racial Brotherhood Movement fought against restrictions being placed on the movement of 'blacks'. The People's Progressive Association and the Afro Asian Club (run by the Association for the Advancement of Colonial People) provided community centres where 'blacks' could band together and speak for themselves. By the end of 1958, a co-ordinating committee had been established, called the Committee for Inter-Racial Unity, which was representative of eighteen trade union branches, six Labour Party branches, and several local 'black' organizations. In 1964, the most powerful of organizations to fight racist movements directly was established: the Campaign Against Racial Discrimination, or CARD, dedicated itself to fighting racial discrimination at a national as well as a local level.

THERE AIN'T NO BLACK IN THE UNION JACK

Fascist organizations, and the establishment of groups dedicated to fighting them, remained a minority response. More typically, racist and anti-racist activity was carried out on the humdrum level of day-to-day interaction. 'White' working-class rejection of the 'foreigner' did not seek justification within a rhetoric stressing biological inferiority, but the opposite: 'foreigners' were proving themselves superior in the fight for scarce resources. In particular, the fight centred around three sites examined in this book: the body, the home, and the marketplace. Although no one 'racial' group was regarded as threatening one of these three sites exclusively, racialist rhetoric tended to link Irish 'dirtiness' and vulgar fecundity with fears relating to the body, West Indians and Africans with the menace to housing, and Jews with the challenge to 'British' standards of employment. Racialist polemic, centring on territorial claims based on the body, home, and market-place was flawed: hatred focused on issues of scarcity and competition, even where none existed. Thus, when Mass Observation compared the attitudes of non-Jews in a district of Liverpool where there were no Jewish residents with two London districts with a high Jewish population, they disclosed almost identical resentment towards Jews.[117] In their analysis of racial attitudes in two districts in the East End, they made a similar discovery. In the district where very few Jews lived and worked (Silvertown), nearly one-third of the people questioned were 'definitely anti-semitic', compared with 15 per cent of the people questioned in the district which housed a large number of Jews (Limehouse). Gender was also a factor, with men much more liable to be anti-semitic than women.[118] However, irrespective of locality or gender, 'difference' was a curse.

'Foreigners' were seen to threaten local constructions of the 'body', and all the rules of respectability which followed these constructions. As one commentator argued in 1928, 'where the foreigner has taken up his abode, respectable neighbourhoods become evil colonies where the most elementary laws of sanitation are disregarded. The alien drives away the clean-minded natives and fills the vacant space with double the number of human beings for which it was originally intended.'[119] The Irish, in particular, were portrayed as 'dirty' and 'dragging the neighbourhood down' by non-adherence to cleaning norms and rules concerning crime and drunkenness. Given that they were five times more liable to be sent to prison as the English population, and ten times more liable in Scotland, it is not surprising that the Irish were accused of being responsible for most of the crime: 'Wheresoever sneak thefts and mean pilfering are easy and safe, wheresoever dirty acts of sexual baseness are committed, there you will find the Irishman in Scotland.'[120] Their large families were non-respectable, signalling their allegiance not only to a 'foreign' religious authority, but also to a perverse love of the haggard and exacting Lady Poverty. As we saw in the last chapter, local pride depended on resisting such temptations. The Irish were a serious threat in part because their 'invasion' was insidious: they were 'doing by peaceful penetration what no previous invaders were ever able to do by force'.[121] As a Glaswegian man reminisced about life in the Calton district in the 1880s, 'The less we had to do with [the Irish] the better. Their religion was not our religion; which was the best; and their customs were different from ours, as was their speech. Doubtless there were good folk among them, but the unruly and turbulent ones showed us what we might have become if we did not keep to our own people.'[122] As this Glaswegian recognized, unrespectable traits were contagious: working-class men and women had to remain 'on guard' against infection.

Immigrants were accused of exploiting the powerlessness of local working-class men over the labour market. Thus, the 1919 race riots occurred in the context of the demobilization of men after the war and the closing down of munition factories. The riots broke out on 10 June in Bute Town, Cardiff, when 2,500 'white' men took to the streets armed with chains, knives, and sticks, and destroyed a house lodging 'black' seamen. Riots also occurred in Liverpool. Ernest Marke was living in a seaport town during these riots. He had been born in Sierra Leone but had stowed away to England during the First World War. At the time of the riots, a friend advised him not to walk the street looking for work because of the level of violence against 'blacks'. Looking for employment was pointless: 'The unemployment situation is getting worse and if there's a job to be had, you won't get it. The John Bull is the boss, he isn't going to give you a job and leave his brother out.'[123] In 1928 Lieutenant-Colonel A. H. Lane asserted that 'every alien at work in this country has ousted a Briton', citing a *Times* correspondent who claimed that 'unemployment is disastrously prevalent among the British population in the East End of London, *but not among the aliens there*'.[124] In a letter, published on 5 February 1930 in the *Listener*, A. J. MacGregor of Ottery St Mary explained that the 'chief and *steady* wrong' in Scotland was the immigration of Poles and Lithuanians into mining districts and the immigration of Irish into industrial districts, creating 'unemployment for the natives, taking the bread out of their mouths, lowering the tone of life, *creating* the slums'. He promised that, if 'aliens' were banished, Scotland would 'revive in trade, status, and general well-being'.[125] Such sentiments maintained 'aliens' in lowly occupations. Thus, the Pole Janusz Kowalewski recalled his first visit to the Labour Exchange after the war:

I entered the cubicle, the walls of which were covered with posters exhorting the reader to become a postman.
'I want to be a postman.'
'I'm extremely sorry, but unfortunately that's a job you can't have.'
'Why not? I'm a former soldier. And, after all, former combatants have priority.'
'Yes, but unfortunately you are not British.'
'That's true, but I fought as a soldier of the British 8th Army.'
The elderly gentleman on the other side of the glass smiled

sympathetically but did not reply. Clearly he was waiting for a more realistic proposal from me.

He became a kitchen porter instead.[126] Jews in the East End were at the centre of these accusations relating to employment. They were blamed for 'sweated labour' and Parliament passed legislation attempting to protect 'English mothers and sisters' against Jewish exploitation. For the East End furniture makers, Jewish immigration threatened their livelihood. Walter Southgate's father-in-law was a furniture master in Bethnal Green in the 1920s. Although he 'had no objection' to a person's colour, creed, or nationality, he argued passionately for the regulation of Jewish immigration: 'To talk to him about the brotherhood of man and the granting of asylum to the oppressed as a noble idea was one thing. When you came to experience, as he and others did, that your standard of living was menaced and pride in your craft going down the drain because of this unregulated influx of penniless people, who were being exploited, this was quite another thing, which no professional body of people would tolerate.' Thus, as children, Southgate and his friends would kick in the door of a rabbi living in their district: 'There was no rhyme or reason for it, except that he was a Jew and they had invaded the East End.'[127]

This metaphor of 'invasion' was equally potent in the context of housing. In Anthony Richmond's survey, 60 per cent of respondents in Bristol blamed 'black' immigrants for the deterioration of local housing.[128] It was infuriating to have people from outside the community 'take' houses which had been reserved (in the minds of locals) for particular families. In the words of one Eastender in the first decade of the twentieth century: 'Let them go to Cable Street and see house after house, and street after street, once filled with happy English families, now filled with foreigners.'[129] Others were thankful that their streets were free of Jews and 'foreigners', and were willing to ensure that immigrants stayed away: 'they would have had a rough reception and their life mad [*sic*] a misery had they attempted to live in "our street" '.[130]

It was an issue willingly adopted by politicians such as the Tory William Evans Gordon, arguing in 1902 in favour of tighter immigration controls on the grounds that: 'Not a day passes but English families are ruthlessly turned out to make room for foreign workers. . . . It is only a matter of time before the population becomes entirely foreign.' He claimed that the working class resented the erection of new buildings to benefit 'strangers from abroad'.[131] In the words of

Lieutenant-Colonel A. H. Lane in 1928: 'Like the locust [the immigrant] destroys wherever he alights. In the east-end of London there are numbers of large tenement buildings (flats) comparatively new, and well and conveniently built. The money for some of these buildings came from charitable sources, benefactions, etc., and a few years ago they were cleanly habitations occupied by decent English people. But to-day these buildings are crowded by aliens and have become sordid dens.'[132] This idea that immigrants were actually creating the slums provided an argument for the segregation of 'black' housing from 'white'. One conservative Alderman from Birmingham asserted that 'They seem to be happy to live in the most distressing conditions, but there's no harm in that. They live with their own people. They also live where they want. That's not a ghetto. It's a place where they live. This mixing up is wholly wrong.'[133]

Local councils recognized housing to be a sensitive area, and were anxious to reassure 'white' residents that they would be allocated housing before any 'coloured person'.[134] This belief that immigrants posed a great threat to the housing market was exacerbated by slum clearance programmes from the 1950s. Denied or restricted access to state housing schemes, immigrants from the 1950s began buying large houses near the inner-city slums. 'White' working-class residents regarded this with bitterness: 'We're been living in these slums for years waiting rehousing. We couldn't afford to buy big houses and would even have tried to buy those big houses across the road. But while we're been waiting to be rehoused these coloured immigrants have come in and bought what are the best houses in the neighbourhood and turned them into slums.'[135] Leaflets saying 'House Britons, not Blacks' struck a receptive chord in these districts. In 1964, Peter Griffiths, a Tory candidate, defeated Labour in the elections with the slogan, 'If you want a Nigger for a neighbour vote Labour'. Blaming immigrants for creating slum conditions was widespread. Thus, in Parliament in 1957, Eric Fletcher argued that while it was 'nobody's fault that people from overseas are content to live in conditions different from those sought by white people', overcrowding exacerbated racial tensions.[136] Local councils remained unconcerned. In 1966 the Birmingham Borough Labour Conference rejected an appeal to allocate council housing to 'blacks'.[137] Overcrowding provisions in the Public Health Act were ignored for fear that the evicted 'black' families would thereby gain priority on any housing list.[138] Sheila Patterson, in *Dark Strangers*, found that by 1957 few 'black' families were living in council tenancies, and the Mayor of Lambeth even boasted that 'only six West Indian families have been rehoused in the worse type of requisitioned property – because no-one else would take it'.[139] Such forms of discrimination were particularly effective: in the 1960s, only 6 per cent of the overseas-born 'black' population were accommodated in the state sector, compared with approximately one-third of the Irish and English-born populations. 'White' households were twenty-six times more likely to be allocated a council house than their 'black' counterparts.[140] Discrimination was openly practised at every level. Building societies invented 'blue zones' to exclude areas of 'black' settlement from the mortgage loan market.[141] In the 1965 Milner–Holland Report on housing in London, it was estimated that only 11 per cent of private lettings that were publicly advertised were not explicitly racist.[142] This report also reported that only one-third of all private landlords would consider renting to 'black' tenants.[143] The publicity afforded to these forms of discrimination was inhibited by the 1965 and 1968 Race Relations Acts which set up the Race Relations Board and the Community Relations Commission to deal with racial discrimination and to educate the population about race relations.

As we have already seen, a principal source of grievance concerned the distribution of welfare benefits. It was argued that 'foreigners' had no entitlement to scarce welfare provisions. Thus, the 1908 Pension Act legislated that pensioners had to have been both a resident and a British subject for twenty years. The National Insurance Act also decreed that people who had not been resident in the country for five years would receive only seven-ninths of the benefit, even if they had paid full contributions. Under the National Insurance Act of 1918, this stipulation was repealed on practical grounds. Sir E. Cornwall reassured Parliament in the following words: 'I dare say some people will be rather alarmed at our proposals that ['aliens'] should receive ordinary benefits but I can assure the House that it is not from any love of aliens. It is simply a business proposition. We find the arrangements in the original Act very complicated and it costs a great deal more than if we gave them ordinary benefits.'[144] Equally, welfare legislation of the 1940s seemed to avoid the discriminatory provisions of their forerunners. Residence in the United Kingdom qualified a person for benefits under the National Health Service Act of 1946 and the National Assistance Act of 1948. The fact that these welfare provisions were granted to everyone irrespective of nationality could only be maintained because of confidence in the efficiency of the 1948 immigration laws in screening entrants. Thus, the Minister for Health, Aneurin Bevan, boasted that he had 'rearranged for immigration officers to turn back aliens who were coming to this country to secure benefits off the health service'.[145] By focusing on employment, housing, and welfare entitlements in the postwar period, the conservatives touched a receptive chord within sections of the 'white' working class.

Throughout the century, however, it is mistaken to speak simply in terms of 'white' versus 'the rest'. Within and between each ethnic group there were notable divisions. In the East End, children of foreign-born Jews ('Polacks') fought children of English-born Jews ('Choots').[146] Immigrant groups were divided along class lines. For instance, one Irishman interviewed about his life in the building trade in London during the 1930s recalled that there was little contact between middle- and working-class Irish: 'There was simply no meaningful contact. We stuck to our circuit and they stuck to theirs. . . . Mind you, I was from Mayo, and these people would be from a city such as Dublin or Cork. . . . You ask me if there was any Community help? Ah, you're jokin' using phrases like that. What Community? We relied on ourselves.'[147] Ethnicity may be regarded as less important than regional identities. Chaim Bermont, a Jew from Glasgow, was evacuated to Annan (Dumfriesshire) during the Second World War. Shortly after arriving, he was attacked by local boys and thrashed. Deeply shocked by what he interpreted as his first serious experience of anti-semitism, he attended school the following day only to discover that half of his schoolmates had also suffered: 'My injuries were not incurred from the fact that I was Jewish, but that I was a town boy, a Glaswegian. It was the most reassuring revelation of my young life. I glorified in the name of Glaswegian, and I have not ceased to glory in it since.'[148] The sense of belonging to a 'nation' or a 'locality' was constantly shifting.

The insider–outsider dichotomy also ignores tensions between 'outsider' groups. The absence of any longstanding anti-racist 'black' organizations was the result of continuous factionalism, leading Anthony Richmond to complain in 1956 that 'It appears that any organization which attempts to weld together the diverse interests of the various national groups within the coloured population is likely to disintegrate unless the sense of external threat is great enough to overcome the lack of common sentiments among people from as far afield as the West Indies, Africa, and Asia. In the case of specifically West Indian organizations, status competition between individuals is often so acute as to prevent effective leadership from emerging.'[149] Racialist violence was perpetrated by other ethnic groups, such as the Irish, who were also at the bottom of the social hierarchy. In the East End, for example, the strongest manifestations of anti-semitism came from Irish Catholics in the dockland areas of Shadwell and Wapping. During the anti-'black' riots in Cardiff during 1919, one-third of men arrested for attacking 'blacks' had Irish surnames.[150] Fights frequently broke out between European Volunteer Workers and Poles, Irish, and Caribbean workers sharing hostels administered by the National Service Hostels Corporation during the 1940s.[151] There were also serious tensions between Jewish and 'black' immigrants. In 1922 Alexander Hartog was born to a Jewish family in the East End. His father was a barrowman and his mother kept a market stall. His autobiography relates his experiences of anti-semitism from childhood when his best friend was told that Jews were dirty and 'certainly not British', to adulthood when soldiers serving with him in the British army reminded him that though he was born and bred in England, he remained 'a dirty Jew'. With the growing popularity of fascism in the East End, Hartog joined the radical anti-fascist '43 Group', helped publish *On Guard*, and broke up fascist meetings. By the end of the 1950s, however, fascist attention in the East End had switched from the Jews to the 'blacks'. At this stage in the autobiography, a distinct change of tone takes place. Declaring that he wanted to speak about the new wave of 'black' immigrants 'from a humanitarian point of view', Hartog began:

> When ['black' immigrants] came here, they came with hatred in their hearts, they said that they'd been exploited. Somebody ought to explain to them that the white people of this country were exploited just as much as they were. The Establishment here, who had their representatives abroad, *they* took the cream, *they* raped these countries, the working class didn't. And, now the chickens have come home to roost, who is supporting them? The average ratepayer, the average working man who gets taxed whether he likes it or not. And who are we workers keeping? People who think we are the people who exploited them because we are the only people they see. Yet we are victims the same as them. They've come in like an invading army and they will not integrate. The Jews were proud to come to this country. They set up little businesses and there is no racial prejudice in a Jewish firm – whether you're Jew, Gentile, black, white, green, Martian, Venus, the Moon, most Jewish guvnors [*sic*], not all, will pay you a living wage. . . . The Jews are now integrated with the British people. We are patriotic. We are loyal. We are law-abiding. Ask for the prison-records of the Jewish population of the United Kingdom. The figures would amaze you. Thieving is for people who have no brains or are lazy. Jews have always worked. England has had the benefit of their trade and they have set new standards in the City. Yet many of the coloured people

are behaving like parasites with resentment in their hearts and at the same time breeding like rabbits.[152]

The rhetoric of this prominent working-class anti-fascist conforms to the sentiments expressed by any editor of *Bulldog*.

CONCLUSION

'Englishness is a fragile identity', began Miranda Chaytor. She continued: 'It relies on nostalgia for emotional power, feeds off our childhood memories of smaller, less abstract forms of belonging – to a household, neighbourhood, landscape. Patriotism draws on these images (part memories, part fantasies), exploiting our homesickness, which is probably why I am immune to it – or would like to be. But then I have no sense of being English that I can separate from my early experience of class.'[153] If in times of external crisis there was little cross-class or cross-racial agreement on the nature of the 'nation' which was being defended, confusion was even greater when the threat was perceived to be within the 'nation'. The individual's concentration on the home and local territories provided a conceptual basis for identifying with what was national. This may be illustrated by the Mass Observation research in the eighteen months prior to September 1938. This research showed that until the last week in September, the mass of the working people were uninterested in the national crisis, expressing interest only when the national and international crisis threatened to enter their own homes (in the form of gas). In the words of Tom Harrisson and Charles Madge, 'Through all our research results, the interest in oneself and one's own home has predominated far and away, over international and general political concerns except in the upper middle class.'[154] It was precisely this intimacy which has sustained the rhetoric of the 'working class' in twentieth-century Britain.

SELECTIVE BIBLIOGRAPHY

Fitzpatrick, David, *Irish Emigration 1801-1921* (Dublin, 1984).
A summary of trends, with a critical analysis of the historiography. Divided into three parts: profile, determinants, and consequences.

Harrison, Brian, *Peaceable Kingdom: Stability and Change in Modern Britain* (Oxford, 1982).
An illuminating interpretation of 'consensus' in British society since 1780 through an examination of different types of violence in British politics, humanitarian and philanthropic movements, religion, and political cohesion.

Holmes, Colin, *John Bull's Island: Immigration and British Society 1871-1971* (London, 1988).
A valuable history of immigration from the 'Age of Imperialism' to the postwar years. Focuses on the process of migration, the characteristics of the migrants, their reception in Britain, and their responses.

Kushner, Tony and Kenneth Lunn (eds), *Traditions of Intolerance: Historical Perspectives on Fascism and Race Discourse in Britain* (Manchester, 1989).
A wide range of chapters concerned with fascism and racism in British social history. All stress the need to place hostility to minority groups within a wider cultural and class context.

Samuel, Raphael (ed.), *Patriots: The Making and Unmaking of British National Identity*, 3 volumes (London, 1989).
The three volumes deal with a diversity of topics, including patriotic movements, imperialism, militarism, racism, John Bull, Britannia, music, landscape, literature, theatre, cinema, childhood, class, religion, women, nations within nations, and minorities.

Smout, T. C., *A Century of the Scottish People 1830-1950* (London, 1986).
A general social history of Scotland, with particularly useful chapters on industry, drink, temperance, recreation, sex, churchgoing, and education.

Solomos, John, *Race and Racism in Contemporary Britain* (London, 1989).
The best analysis of the politics of immigration and race relations since 1945.

Swift, Roger and Sheridan Gilley (eds), *The Irish in Britain 1815-1939* (London, 1989).
Includes chapters on the residential experience of the Irish in Britain, political participation of Irish migrants, employment, and crime. The chapter by David Fitzpatrick is an elegant analysis of the experience of Irish migrants between 1871 and 1921.

Epilogue

Despite radical economic and social shifts since the mid-1960s, the identification of 'working-class' has scarcely changed from the period we have been examining in this book. From the 1970s, the relationship between 'class' and social characteristics such as wealth, social status, and security eroded further in response to spiralling unemployment amongst previously secure professions, the collapse of economic markets which sustained middle-class and upper-class life styles, and the fragmentation of institutions dedicated to the well-being of waged workers. In recent elections, two-thirds of skilled workers, 60 per cent of trade union members, and over half of all unskilled and semi-skilled workers voted for political parties other than the self-proclaimed 'Labour' Party. This shift was due not only to the declining importance of old-style industrial labour, nor was it due simply to changing political ideologies. As in the earlier decades of the twentieth century, 'class' identification remained potent outside of the political arena and its language remained a powerful self-defining metaphor which referred less to the individual in the present, and more to perceptions of historical construction. Men and women identifying themselves as 'working-class' today draw their imagery from the first sixty years of the twentieth century. Then, as now, 'class' identification was a reality located in the intimate locale of the body, the home, and the locality.

Notes

1 INTRODUCTION

1 F. M. Martin, 'Some Subjective Aspects of Social Stratification', in D. V. Glass (ed.), *Social Mobility in Britain* (London, 1954), 58.
2 P. Hiller, 'Continuities and Variations in Everyday Conceptual Components of Class', *Sociology*, 9 (1975), 255 and H. F. Moorhouse, 'Attitudes to Class and Class Relationships in Britain', *Sociology*, 10 (1976), 469.
3 Alfred Willener, *L'image-action de la société ou la politisation culturelle* (Paris, 1970), 63.
4 Edward Short, *I Knew My Place* (London, 1983), 38.
5 Jilly Cooper, *Class: A View from Middle England* (London, 1979), 14.
6 Eric Hobsbawm, *Labouring Men* (London, 1964) and J. Foster, *Class Struggle in the Industrial Revolution* (London, 1974).
7 Eric Hobsbawm, 'The Forward March of Labour Halted?', in M. Jacques and F. Mulhern (eds), *The Forward March of Labour Halted?* (London, 1981), 3.
8 'Mass Observation', *War Factory* (London, 1943), 70.
9 Sir John Boyd Orr, *Food, Health and Income* (London, 1936), 39–41.
10 Elizabeth Fanshawe, *Penkhull Memories* (Stafford, 1983), 17.
11 Kenneth Leech, *Struggle in Babylon* (London, 1988), 1–2.
12 Johnny Speight, *It Stands to Reason* (Walton-on-Thames, 1973), 20.
13 E. P. Thompson, *The Making of the English Working Class* (New York, 1966), 9–10.
14 Louis Heren, *Growing Up Poor In London* (London, 1973), 13.
15 Asa Briggs, 'The Language of "Class" in Early Nineteenth Century England', in Asa Briggs and John Seville (eds), *Essays in Labour History* (London, 1967) and E. P. Thompson, *The Making of the English Working Class* (New York, 1966).
16 E. Slater and M. Woodside, *Patterns of Marriage* (London, 1951), 255.
17 John Benson, *The Working Class in Britain, 1850–1939* (London, 1989), 55. For further discussion, see Geoffrey Best, *Mid-Victorian Britain 1851–1875* (London, 1971); A. L. Bowley, *Wages and Income in the United Kingdon Since 1860* (Cambridge, 1937), 30 and 122; S. G. Checkland, *The Rise of Industrial Society in England, 1815–1885* (London, 1964); G. D. H. Cole, *A Short History of the British Working-Class Movement 1789–1947* (London, 1948), 140; Eric Hopkins, 'Small Town Aristocrats of Labour and their Standard of Living, 1840–1914', *Economic History Review*, second series, xxviii (May 1975), 222–42; E. A. Hunt, *British Labour History 1815–1914* (London, 1981), 73–6; H. Perkin, *The Origins of Modern English Society, 1780–1880* (London, 1969). Charles Feinstein has questioned the sharpness of the change in real wages in 'A New Look at the Cost of Living, 1870–1914', in James Foreman-Peck (ed.), *New Perspectives on the Late Victorian Economy* (Cambridge, 1991), 151–79.
18 B. Seebohm Rowntree, *A Study of Town Life* (London, 1901).

19 H. Llewellyn Smith (ed.), *The New Survey of London Life and Labour* (London, 1974).
20 Dudley Seers, *Changes in the Cost of Living and the Distribution of Income Since 1938* (Oxford, 1949), 8–9.
21 John Benson, *The Working Class in Britain, 1850–1939* (London, 1989), 98.
22 F. B. Smith, 'Health', in John Benson (ed.), *The Working Class in England, 1875–1914* (London, 1985), 53.
23 Ibid., 47.
24 Richard M. Titmuss, *Birth, Poverty and Wealth* (London, 1943), 26. For an historical summary of trends and causes, see Valerie Fildes, Lara Marks and Hilary Marland (eds), *Women and Children First* (London, 1992).
25 Richard M. Titmuss, *Birth, Poverty and Wealth*, 32 and 53.
26 Paul Addison, *Now the War is Over* (London, 1985), 199.
27 *New Society*, survey, no. 13 (1962).
28 M. Young and P. Willmott, *The Symmetrical Family* (London, 1973), 23.
29 Ibid., 23.
30 Brian Harrison, *Peaceable Kingdom* (Oxford, 1982), 248–9.
31 Ibid., 247.
32 *Report of the Royal Commission on Physical Training (Scotland)*, para 85, 165 and 176, 1903.
33 Quoted in J. M. Mackintosh, *Trends of Opinion About the Public Health 1901–1951* (London, 1953), 29.
34 Philip Snowden, *The Living Wage* (London, 1912), 49.
35 Lionel Rose, *Massacre of the Innocents* (London, 1986), 18–19.
36 British Institute of Public Opinion, *The Beveridge Report and the Public* (London, 1944), 5.
37 Ned Buckley, 'The Mother That Didn't Die', in Jack Lane and Drendan Clifford (eds), *Ned Buckley's Poems* (Aubane, 1987), 23. Buckley was a Duhallow poet, 1880–1954.
38 Gary Cross, *A Quest for Time* (Berkeley, 1989), 44–5.
39 E. Llewelyn Lewis, *The Children of the Unskilled* (London, 1924), 11.
40 Gary Cross, *A Quest for Time*, 134–6.
41 Calculated from the Department of Employment and Productivity, *British Labour Statistics: Historical Abstract 1886–1968* (London, 1971), 96–7 and 104–5.
42 H. Llewellyn Smith (ed.), *The New Survey of London Life and Labour*, 116–17.
43 Dr F. E. Larkins, 'The Influence of Wages on Children's Nutrition', *The Medical Officer*, 17 December 1910.
44 Richard M. Titmuss, *Birth, Poverty and Wealth*, 33–4.
45 Gavin Weightman and Steve Humphries, *The Making of Modern London 1914–1939* (London, 1984), 103.
46 Ibid., 104.
47 Paul Oliver, 'Introduction', in Paul Oliver, Ian David and Ian Bentley (eds), *Dunroamin* (London, 1981), 13.
48 John Lowerson, 'Battles for the Countryside', in Frank Goldsmith (ed.), *Class, Culture and Social Change* (Brighton, 1980), 258.
49 John Benson, *The Working Class in Britain, 1850–1939*, 73.
50 A. H. Halsey (ed.), *Trends in British Society Since 1900* (London, 1972), 308.
51 Sidney Pollard, *The Development of the British Economy 1914–1950* (London, 1962), 242–3.
52 Richard Croucher, *We Refuse to Starve in Silence* (London, 1987), 26.
53 M. E. Rose, *The English Poor Law 1780–1930* (London, 1971).
54 Alan Deacon, *In Search of the Scrounger* (London, 1976), 10–11.
55 Ibid., 13.
56 Richard Croucher, *We Refuse to Starve in Silence*, 108.
57 Alan Deacon, *In Search of the Scrounger*, 9.
58 Ibid., 82.

59 E. Wight Bakke, *The Unemployed Man* (London, 1935), 191.
60 Ibid., 191.
61 H. L. Beales and R. S. Lambert (eds), *Memoirs of the Unemployed* (London, 1934), 105.
62 Richard Croucher, *We Refuse to Starve in Silence*, 164.
63 Ibid., 154.
64 Ellen Wilkinson, *The Town that was Murdered* (London, 1939), 209.
65 Paul Addison, *Now the War is Over*, 1.
66 Peter Baker, 'The Great Disillusion', *New Generation*, no. 2 (Winter 1947), 9. Historians also sometimes argue that during the Second World War 'class-specific interests and preoccupations were, in large part, forgotten': E. Ellis Cashmore, *United Kingdom?* (London, 1989), 14.
67 E. Slater and M. Woodside, *Patterns of Marriage*, 254.
68 For a discussion of health, see Wartime Social Survey, *Public Attitudes to Health and to the Autumn Health Campaign*, Report no. 21, new series, part 2 (1942), 9.
69 Quoted in John Osmond, *The Divided Kingdom* (London, 1988), 153–5.
70 Peter Baker, 'The Great Disillusion', 9.
71 E. Slater and M. Woodside, *Patterns of Marriage*, 77.
72 Margaret Hewitt, *Wives and Mothers in Victorian Industry* (London, 1958), 165–6.
73 British Institute of Public Opinion, *The Beveridge Report and the Public*, 8.
74 Cited in John Saville, 'Labour and Income Redistribution', *Socialist Register*, 1965, 151ff.
75 B. Seebohm Rowntree and G. R. Lavers, *Poverty and the Welfare State* (London, 1951), 43–8.
76 Carolyn Steedman, 'Landscape for a Good Woman', in Liz Heron (ed.), *Truth, Dare, Promise* (London, 1985), 118.
77 Denis Potter, *The Glittering Coffin* (London, 1960), 13 and 16.
78 Richard Hoggart, *The Uses of Literacy* (Harmondsworth, 1957).

2   BODY

1 Anon., 'Crossing Peckham Rye', in William Margrie (compiler), *The Poets of Peckham*, second edition (London, 1956), 22.
2 Anon., 'He Meant Business', in *The Love Book* (Dundee, 1911), 9.
3 Women's Co-Operative Guild, *Working Women and Divorce* (London, 1911), 21.
4 Geoffrey Gorer, *Exploring English Character* (London, 1955), 86.
5 E. C. Urwin, *Can the Family Survive?* (London, 1944), 18–19.
6 Beatrice Webb, 'Preface', in Richard Titmuss and Kathleen Titmuss, *Parents Revolt* (London, 1942), 10. Also see 55.
7 Howard Association, *Juvenile Offenders* (London, 1898), 22.
8 Lawrence Stone, *The Family, Sex and Marriage in England 1500–1800* (London, 1977), 659 and Arthur Marwick, 'The 1960s. Was There a "Cultural Revolution"?', *Contemporary Record*, 2.3 (Autumn 1988). This was believed by working-class commentators as well: for instance, see Jim Wolveridge, *Ain't It Grand* (London, 1976), 47.
9 Robert Graves and Alan Hodges, *The Long Weekend* (London, 1950), 13 and 38.
10 Stephen Humphries, *A Secret World of Sex* (London, 1988), 217.
11 Philippe D'Albo-Julienne, *The Crisis of Marriage* (London, 1943), 7. Also see E. C. Urwin, *Can the Family Survive?*, 7–8.
12 Ellen M. Holtzman, in 'The Pursuit of Married Love: Women's Attitudes Towards Sexuality and Marriage in Great Britain, 1918–1939', *Journal of Social History*, 16.2 (Winter 1982), 41.
13 H. Mainwaring Holt, 'The Decay of Family Life', *Health Education Journal*, ix.4 (October 1951), 183.

14 E. C. Urwin, *Can the Family Survive?*, 20–1 and Hannen Foss, 'Foreword', in Hannen Foss, *Come Home With Me* (London, 1945), 5.

15 For some excellent summaries of the uses of autobiographies as historical evidence, see John Burnett (ed.), *Destiny Obscure: Autobiographies of Childhood, Education, and Family from the 1820s to the 1920s* (Harmondsworth, 1982), 9–17 and his *Useful Toil: Autobiographies of Working People from the 1820s to the 1920s* (Harmondsworth,1984), 9–19. The best theoretical discussion can be found in David Vincent, *Bread, Knowledge, and Freedom: A Study of Nineteenth-Century Working-Class Autobiographies* (London, 1981). Many of the arguments used to defend oral history are also applicable. For instance, see Elizabeth Roberts, *A Woman's Place* (Oxford, 1984) and any issue of *Oral History*.

16 Dr Eustace Chesser, *The Sexual, Marital and Family Relationships of the English Woman* (London, 1956), 311 and 316.

17 Moya Woodside, 'Health and Happiness in Marriage', *Health Education Journal*, iv.4 (October 1946), 147.

18 D. Wright and E. Cox, 'Changes in Moral Belief Among Sixth Form Boys and Girls', *British Journal of Clinical Psychology*, 10 (1971).

19 Family Planning Association, 'Medical Newsletter, no. 10' (1961), 2.

20 Ted Walker, *The High Path* (London, 1982), 125.

21 Mary Craddock, *A North Country Maid* (London, 1960), 88–9.

22 Editor's Foreword in Lena M. Jeger (ed.), *Illegitimate Children and Their Parents* (London, 1951), x.

23 Letter from 'Mrs B. A.' in Marie C. Stopes, *Mother England* (London, 1929), 9.

24 Marjorie Graham, *Love, Dears!* (London, 1980), 13.

25 Nancy Sharman, *Nothing to Steal* (London, 1977), 86 and Kathleen Price, *Looking Back* (Nottingham, 1980), 16.

26 Molly Weir, *Best Foot Forward* (Bath, 1979), 78.

27 Elizabeth Ring, *Up the Cockneys!* (London, 1975), 23; Jimmy Boyle, *A Sense of Freedom* (Long Preston, North Yorkshire, 1988), 27; Stella Entwistle of Marshchapel, Lincolnshire, in John Burnett (ed.), *Destiny Obscure*, 102.

28 Grace Foakes, *Between High Walls* (London, 1972), 69. A similar belief was held by the foster-mother of May Hobbs, *Born to Struggle* (London, 1973), 5.

29 Edward Short, *I Knew My Place* (London, 1983), 178.

30 Catherine Cookson, *Our Kate* (London, 1969), 37. Also see Nancy Sharman, *Nothing to Steal*, 18 and Phyllis Willmott, *A Green Girl* (London, 1983), 55–6.

31 Marjorie Graham, *Love, Dears!*, 13. Also see Phyllis Willmott, *Growing Up in a London Village* (London, 1979), 101–2.

32 Michael Schofield, *The Sexual Behaviour of Young People* (London, 1965), 98.

33 Ibid., 32, 36, 84–7.

34 Royal College of Midwives, *Preparation for Parenthood* (London, 1964), 7.

35 Catholic Church, *Joint Pastoral Letter of the Hierarchy of England and Wales on the Catholic Attitude to Sex Education* (London, 1944), 5 and 7.

36 Eileen Slade, *Middle Child* (Andover, 1979), 51–2.

37 Edith Hall, *Canary Girls and Stockpots* (Luton, 1977), 9.

38 Van de Velde, *Ideal Marriage* (London, 1961), first published 1928, 6.

39 E. Slater and M. Woodside, *Patterns of Marriage* (London, 1951), 143.

40 Elizabeth Ring, *Up the Cockneys!*, 78.

41 E. Slater and M. Woodside, *Patterns of Marriage*, 78.

42 Eileen Slade, *Middle Child*, 51–2.

43 Joan Bellam, *Them Days* (Padstow, 1982), 20.

44 Angela Rodaway, *A London Childhood* (Bath, 1985), 110.

45 Tory Reform Committee, *To-Morrow's Children* (London, 1944), 18.

46 J. P. Mayer, *British Cinemas and Their Audiences* (London, 1948), 116.

47 Ibid., 74.

48 Ibid., 101.

49 Geoffrey Gorer, *Exploring English Character*, 84.

50 A. J. Jenkinson, *What Do Boys and Girls Read?* (London, 1940), 218.
51 Stella Entwistle of Marshchapel, Lincolnshire, in John Burnett (ed.), *Destiny Obscure*, 109.
52 Edna Bold of Beswick, Manchester, in John Burnett (ed.), *Destiny Obscure*, 119. Also see Kathleen Price, *Looking Back*, 16.
53 Sam Clarke, *An East End Cabinet-Maker* (London, 1983), 28.
54 Gladys Teal, *Grasp the Nettle* (Leeds, c.1980), 15.
55 For a sensitive analysis of these letters, see Leslie Hall, *Hidden Anxieties* (Cambridge, 1991).
56 *Natural Science in Education*, section 52 (London, 1918), 67.
57 William Henry Hadow, *Board of Education. Report of the Consultative Committee on the Education of the Adolescent* (London, 1926), 224–5.
58 Louis Moss, *Education and the People* (London, 1945), 17–18.
59 William Henry Hadow, *Report on the Education of the Adolescent* (London, 1926); Lord Geoffrey Crowther of Headingly, *Report of the Central Advisory Council for Education, England* (London, 1959); Sir J. H. Newsam, *Half Our Future: Report of the Central Advisory Council for Education (England)* (London, 1963) and Lady B. H. Plowden, *Children and Their Primary Schools: A Report of the Central Advisory Council for Education (England). Vol. 1: The Report* (London, 1967), 260.
60 F. P. Crozier, *A Brass Hat in No-Man's Land* (London, 1930), 48.
61 George Ryley Scott, *Sex Problems and Dangers in War-Time* (London, 1940), 40 and 42.
62 Judith R. Walkowitz, *Prostitution and Victorian Society* (Cambridge, 1980).
63 S. A. B. Rogers, *Four Acres and a Donkey* (London, 1979), 47.
64 C. H. Rolph, *Women of the Streets* (London, 1955), 138, 146, and 162.
65 B. Seebohm Rowntree and G. R. Lavers, *English Life and Leisure* (London, 1951), 210–11.
66 C. H. Rolph, *Women of the Streets*, 166.
67 Charlie Potter, *On the Tramp in the 1930s* (Nottingham, 1983), 17.
68 B. Seebohm Rowntree and G. R. Lavers, *English Life and Leisure*, 210.
69 C. H. Rolph, *Women of the Streets*, 137, 143, 154, 171, and 177.
70 F. Zweig, *Labour, Life and Poverty* (London, 1948), 145–6.
71 'Civic', 'A Word about Venereal Disease', *The English Review*, 23 (May 1916), 511.
72 Otto May, *Venereal Diseases and Their Effects* (London, 1924), 9.
73 National Council of Public Morals, *Prevention of VD* (London, 1921), 4.
74 Evidence by Dr A. Mearns Fraser, Medical Officer of Health, Portsmouth, in National Council on Public Morals, Special Committee on Venereal Disease, *Prevention of VD*, 27–8.
75 Sir Thomas Barlow, *The Incidence of Venereal Diseases and its Relation to School Life and School Teaching* (London, 1917), 5.
76 Charles C. Osborne, *Ignorance: The Great Enemy* (London, 1916), 3.
77 *Royal Commission on Venereal Diseases: Economic Effects of Venereal Diseases* (London, 1916), 1.
78 Cited in Otto May, *Venereal Diseases and Their Effects*, 10.
79 Women's Co-Operative Guild, *Working Women and Divorce*, 7.
80 Evidence by Dr A. Mearns Fraser, Medical Officer of Health, Portsmouth, in National Council on Public Morals, Special Committee on Venereal Disease, *Prevention of VD*, 28.
81 George Ryley Scott, *Sex Problems and Dangers in War-Time*, 77–8.
82 Pixie J. Wilson assisted by Virginia Barker, *The Campaign Against Venereal Diseases*, Central Office of Information, Wartime Social Survey, new series no. 42 (January 1944), 29.
83 Dr F. E. Larkins, 'The Influence of Wages on Children's Nutrition', *Medical Officer*, 17 December 1910. Larkins was the Assistant Medical Officer of Health in Warwickshire.

84 Institute of Child Health, *The Health and Growth of the Under-Fives* (London, 1951), 9.
85 Ibid., 11.
86 Wartime Social Survey, *Sanitary Towels*, new series 11 (March 1942), 2.
87 J. C. Flugel, *Men and Their Motives* (London, 1934), 65.
88 *Health and Strength Annual* (1908), 3.
89 *Health and Strength Annual* (1910), 5.
90 Data from annual issues of the *Health and Strength Annual*.
91 Part of the official 'Objects', see *Health and Strength Annual* (1911), 6 and all subsequent issues.
92 *Health and Strength Annual* (1911), 6.
93 *Health and Strength Annual* (1908), 4.
94 Rose Gamble, *Chelsea Child* (Bath, 1980), 151-2.
95 'Uncle Bob', *How To Increase Your Height* (London, 1957), 8-9.
96 Anon., *Health Culture for Busy Men* (London, 1912); Anon., *How To Gain Five Inches Chest Expansion* (Burnley, 1960); Anon., *The Muscles of the Body: Their Uses and Development* (London, 1908); Anon., *The Muscles of the Body and How To Develop Them* (London, 1942), 7; 'Uncle Bob', *How To Develop the Arm* (London, 1910); Charles T. Trevor, *How To Develop Powerful Arms* (London, 1944); Anon., *How To Develop Strong Muscular Arms* (London, 1962); Edward Aston, *How To Develop a Powerful Grip* (Lonon, 1946); Edward Aston, *How To Develop Massive Arms* (London, 1937); and Charles T. Trevor, *How To Develop a Powerful Abdomen*, (Kenton, 1943).
97 Gladys Teal, *Grasp the Nettle*, 23.
98 *Health and Strength: Leaguers' Guide* (London, c.1935), 7-10.
99 Ibid., 11-12.
100 John D. Vose, *Diary of a Tramp* (St Ives, 1981), 23-4.
101 Michael Schofield, *The Sexual Behaviour of Young People*, 27 and Alexander Comfort, *Sex in Society* (London, 1963), 100-1.
102 For the clearest analysis, see John R. Gillis in 'The Evolution of Juvenile Delinquency in England, 1890-1914', *Past and Present*, 67 (1975), 96-126 and in his *Youth and History* (New York, 1981).
103 Cyril Burt, *The Young Delinquent* (London, 1925), 68-9.
104 Michael Schofield, *The Sexual Behaviour of Young People*, 6-7.
105 Winifred Elkin, *English Juvenile Courts* (London, 1938), 6.
106 Michael Schofield, *The Sexual Behaviour of Young People*, 6-7.
107 Mark Abrams, *Teenage Consumer Spending in 1959* (London, 1959).
108 Ibid.
109 Bernice Martin, *A Sociology of Contemporary Cultural Change* (Oxford, 1981), 138-9. Also see Paul Rock and Stanley Cohen, 'The Teddy Boy', in Vernon Bogdanor and Robert Skidelsky (eds), *The Age of Affluence 1951-1964* (London, 1970), 288-320.
110 Women's Co-Operative Guild, *Working Women and Divorce*, 7, 11-12, 23, 26, and 42-3.
111 E. L. Packer, 'Aspects of Working-Class Marriage', *Pilot Papers: Social Essays and Documents*, 2.1 (March 1947), 93.
112 Women's Co-Operative Guild, *Working Women and Divorce*, 9.
113 Ibid., 11-12.
114 E. L. Packer, 'Aspects of Working-Class Marriage', 93-4.
115 Arthur Marwick, 'A Social History of Britain 1945-1983', in David Punter (ed.), *Introduction to Contemporary Cultural Studies* (London, 1986), 28-9.
116 E. Slater and M. Woodside, *Patterns of Marriage*, 168-9.
117 F. Zweig, *Labour, Life and Poverty*, 174. Also see 169-70 for example of a 42-year-old glass worker.
118 Ibid., 137.
119 Family Planning Association, 'Medical Newsletter, no. 12' (1962), 2.

120 J. F. Tuthill, 'Impotence', *The Lancet*, 15 January 1955, 127.
121 *Maternity in Great Britain* (Oxford, 1948), 83.
122 Moya Woodside, 'Courtship and Mating in an Urban Community', *Eugenics Review*, xxxviii.1 (April 1946), 36.
123 Marie C. Stopes, *Mother England*, 14.
124 Ibid., 20.
125 Moya Woodside, 'Courtship and Mating in an Urban Community', 31.
126 E. Slater and M. Woodside, *Patterns of Marriage*, 140.
127 'Mass Observation', *Britain and Her Birth Rate* (London, 1945), 109.
128 James Allen Bullock, *Bowers Row* (East Ardsley, 1976), 63 and Elizabeth Ring, *Up the Cockneys!*, 120.
129 Margaret Powell, *My Children and I* (London, 1977), 36.
130 A. A. Philip and H. R. Murray, *Knowledge a Young Husband Should Have* (London, 1911), 116–17.
131 Elizabeth Ring, *Up the Cockneys!*, 133.
132 E. L. Packer, 'Aspects of Working-Class Marriage', 103.
133 Moya Woodside, 'Health and Happiness in Marriage', 149.
134 'Mrs A. A.', married 14 years to a man earning a wage of £3 1s, in Marie C. Stopes, *Mother England*, 7.
135 'A. J. B.' to Marie C. Stopes, punctuation and spelling as in original, in Stopes, *Mother England*, 36–7.
136 Audrey Leathard, *The Fight for Family Planning* (London, 1980), 103. The sample size was 2,336 couples.
137 Ibid., 86–7.
138 Family Planning Association, 'Medical Newsletter no. 2' (1959), 5 and 6.
139 George Ryley Scott, *Birth Control* (London, 1933), 10–12.
140 Ministry of Health and Home Office, *Report of the Inter-Departmental Committee on Abortion* (London, 1939), 8.
141 Vivien Seal, *Whose Choice?* (London, 1990), 376.
142 Elizabeth Ring, *Up the Cockneys!*, 79.
143 Audrey Leathard, *The Fight for Family Planning*, 105.
144 M. S. Soutar, E. H. Wilkins and P. Sargant Florence, *Nutrition and the Size of Family* (London, 1942), 30.
145 E. Slater and M. Woodside, *Patterns of Marriage*, 181.
146 Ibid., 290.

3   HOME

1 Margaret Powell, *My Children and I* (London, 1977), 18.
2 Lydia Morris, *The Workings of the Household* (Cambridge, 1990), 16. Also see Rosemary Collins, ' "Horses for Courses": Ideology and the Division of Labour', in Paul Close and Rosemary Collins (eds), *Family and Economy in Modern Society* (London, 1985), 66; R. Davies, *Women and Work* (London, 1985).
3 Michele Barrett, *Women's Oppression Today* (London, 1980); Heidi Hartmann, 'The Historical Roots of Occupational Segregation: Capitalism, Patriarchy and Job Segregation by Sex', *Signs*, 1.3 (Spring 1976), 137–69; Ellen Jordan, 'The Exclusion of Women from Industry in Nineteenth-Century Britain', *Comparative Studies in Society and History*, 31.3 (April 1989), 273–96; Judy Lown, 'Not So Much a Factory, More a Form of Patriarchy: Gender and Class During Industrialization', in Eva Gamarnikow (ed.), *Gender, Class and Work* (London, 1985), 36–43.
4 Sally Alexander, 'Women's Work in Nineteenth Century London', in Juliet Mitchell and Ann Oakley (eds), *The Rights and Wrongs of Women* (Harmondsworth, 1976); Cynthia Cockburn, *Brothers: Male Dominance and Technological Changes* (London, 1983); Sonya O. Rose, 'Gender Antagonism and

Class Conflict: Exclusionist Strategies of Male Trade Unionists in Nineteenth-Century Britain', *Social History*, 13 (1988), 191–208; Sonya O. Rose, 'Gender at Work: Sex, Class and Industrial Capitalism', *History Workshop*, 21 (Spring 1986), 119–27; Sylvia Walby, *Patriarchy at Work* (London, 1986).

5 See Ann Oakley, *Women's Work: The Housewife, Past and Present* (New York, 1974).

6 June Purvis, *Hard Lessons* (Oxford, 1989), 46.

7 Terry Fee, 'Domestic Labour: An Analysis of Housework and its Relation to the Production Process', *Review of Radical Political Economics*, 8 (Spring 1976) and Wally Seccombe, 'The Housewife and Her Labour Under Capitalism', *New Left Review*, no. 83 (1974), 8 and 19.

8 Notable exceptions are Paul Johnson, *Saving and Spending* (Oxford, 1985) and Melanie Tebbutt, *Making Ends Meet* (London, 1983).

9 Rosemary Collins, ' "Horses for Courses": Ideology and the Division of Labour', 66.

10 Jean Comaroff, *Body of Power, Spirit of Resistance* (Chicago, 1985), 1.

11 Elizabeth Ring, *Up the Cockneys!* (London, 1975), 93.

12 Geoffrey Thomas, *The Social Survey* (London, 1948), 5.

13 *Royal Commission on Labour. The Agricultural Labourer. Vol. I. England. Part III. Reports by Mr. Arthur Wilson Fox (Assistant Commissioner), Upon Certain Districts in the Counties of Cumberland, Lancaster, Norfolk, Northumberland, and Suffolk, With Summary Report Prefixed* [C-6894-III], H. C. 1893–4, xxxv, 97 (413), labourer from Swaffham, Norfolk.

14 For justification for choosing the 21s to 30s level as the threshold, see D. J. Oddy, 'Working-Class Diets in Late-Nineteenth-Century Britain', *Economic History Review*, second series, xxiii (1970), 314–23 and B. Seebohm Rowntree, *Poverty: A Study of Town Life* (London, 1901).

15 Christopher Bliss, 'The Labour Market: Theory and Experience', in Michael Beenstock (ed.), *Modelling the Labour Market* (London, 1988), 4.

16 See *Royal Commission on Labour. The Agricultural Labourer. Vol. I. England. Part III. Reports by Mr. Arthur Wilson Fox (Assistant Commissioner), Upon Certain Districts in the Counties of Cumberland, Lancaster, Norfolk, Northumberland, and Suffolk, With Summary Report Prefixed* [C-6894-III], H. C. 1893–4, xxxv, 86 (402), letter from Dr H. G. Foster, medical officer of health for Wayland and Swaffham; *Royal Commission on Labour. The Agricultural Labourer. Vol. V. Part I. General Report by Mr. William C. Little (Senior Assistant Agricultural Commissioner)* [C-6894-xxv], H. C. 1893–4, 55 (67), comment for Glendale Union, Northumberland.

17 *Royal Commission on Labour. The Agricultural Labourer. Vol. V. Part I. General Report by Mr. William C. Little (Senior Assistant Agricultural Commissioner)* [C-6894-xxv], H. C. 1893–4, 55 (67), Glendale Union (Northumberland).

18 Paul Johnson, 'Credit and Thrift and the British Working Class, 1870-1939', in Jay Winter (ed.), *The Working Class in Modern British History* (Cambridge, 1983), 148.

19 For an example, see Ben Turner, *About Myself, 1863–1930* (London, 1930), 19–20.

20 Edith Hall, *Canary Girls and Stockpots* (Luton, 1977), 17.

21 For two examples, see Gary Becker, *A Treatise on the Family* (Cambridge, Mass., 1981) and Jacob Mincer, 'Labour Force Participation of Married Women', *Aspects of Labour Economics* (New York, 1975), 63–97.

22 Eric Hobsbawm, 'Peasants and Politics', *Journal of Peasant Studies*, 1 (1973), 3–22.

23 Arthur Barton, *The Penny World* (London, 1969), 173 and Edward Ezard, *Battersea Boy* (London, 1979), 48.

24 See Walter Southgate, *That's the Way it Was* (London, 1982), 67.

25 Allan Jobson, *The Creeping Hours of Time* (London, 1977), 15. Also see Alfred

Green, *Growing Up in Attercliffe* (Sheffield, 1981), 55; John Blake, *Memories of Old Poplar* (London, 1977), 8.

26 'P. P.', 'Padded Houses', *Daily Herald*, 25 October 1922, 7.

27 See the weekly column 'Home Rulings', in the *Daily Herald*, 1922.

28 Neville Cardus, *Autobiography* (London, 1955), first pub. 1947, 24; Kay Pearson, *Life in Hull from Then Till Now* (London, 1980), 39; Arthur Barton, *The Penny World*, 97; Kate Jenkins, 'Co-Operative Housekeeping', *Women and Progress*, 30 November 1906, 78.

29 *Royal Commission on Agriculture. England. Report by Mr. R. Henry Rew (Assistant Commissioner) on the County of Norfolk* [C-7915], H. C. 1895, xvii, 45 (369).

30 For a summary of these arguments, see my 'How to be Happy though Married: Housewifery in Working-Class Britain, 1880–1914', *Past and Present* (1993).

31 Joseph Toole, *Fighting Through Life* (London, 1935), 61–2; Robert Tressell, *The Ragged Trousered Philanthropist* (London, 1914), 44; Margaret Llewlyn Davies (ed.), *Maternity* (London, 1989), first pub. 1915, 151; Nigel Gray, *The Worst of Times* (London, 1985), 177.

32 *Board of Education. General Report on the Teaching of Domestic Subjects to Public Elementary School Children in England and Wales, by the Chief Woman Inspector of the Board of Education* (London, 1912), 38; Fanny L. Calder, 'The Training of Teachers in Cookery', *Journal of Education*, 1 December 1894, 712; *Board of Education. Special Report on the Teaching of Cookery to Public Elementary School Children* (1907), i.

33 Dena Attar, *Wasting Girls' Time* (London, 1990); Anna Davin, ' "Mind That You Do as You Are Told": Reading Books for Board School Children, 1870–1902', *Feminist Review*, 3 (1979); Carol Dyhouse, *Girls Growing Up in Late Victorian and Edwardian England* (London, 1981); June Purvis, 'Domestic Subjects Since 1870', in Ivor Goodson (ed.), *Social Histories of the Secondary Curriculum* (Falmer, 1985); Annmarie Turnbull, 'Learning Her Womanly Work: The Elementary School Curriculum, 1870–1914', in Felicity Hunt (ed.), *Lessons for Life* (London, 1987).

34 See the reports in the Public Record Office in London [hereafter P.R.O. (Kew)] ED.164-3, ED.77-8, ED.96-198. For autobiographical accounts from women who enjoyed cookery classes between 1910 and 1940, see Molly Weir, *Best Foot Forward* (Bath, 1979), 182–3; A. P. Jephcott, *Girls Growing Up* (London, 1942), 46; Marjory Todd, *Snakes and Ladders* (London, 1960), 52; Maureen Bell, *Portwood Girl* (Stockport, 1987), 32; Dorothy Scannell, *Mother Knows Best* (Bath, 1974), 223.

35 Emily Glencross, *Breakfast at Windsor* (Swinton, 1983), 35.

36 *Board of Education. Report of the Consultative Committee on Practical Work in Secondary Schools* [Cd.6849], H. C. 1913, xx, 302 (608), evidence by Miss S. A. Burstall, Headmistress of the Manchester High School, on 9 December 1909; Miss Rowland, 'Wales (With Monmouthshire) Domestic Subjects in Public Elementary Schools Annual Report 1911-1912', P.R.O. (Kew) ED.92-10.

37 *Board of Education. General Report on the Teaching of Domestic Subjects*, 10, 32 and 36 and Rowland, 'Wales (With Monmouthshire) Domestic Subjects', P.R.O. (Kew) ED.92-10.

38 *Report of the Committee of Council on Education (England and Wales); with Appendix 1883-84* [C.4091-I], H. C. 1884, xxiv, 387 (387) and *Report of the Committee of Council on Education (England and Wales); with Appendix 1897-98* [C.8987], H. C. 1898, xxii, 296 (430).

39 *Report of the Committee of Council on Education (England and Wales); with Appendix 1885-86* [C-4849-I], H. C. 1886, xxiv, 284 (284).

40 *Report of the Committee of Council on Education (England and Wales); with Appendix 1892-93* [C-7089-I], H. C. 1893–94, xxvi, 87 (135).

41 *General Report for the Year 1894, by Rev. C. H. Parez, One of Her Majesty's Chief*

Inspectors on the Schools in the North Central Division of England [C-7814-II], H. C. 1895, xxviii, 22 (244).

42 Horace Plunkett, 'Agricultural Education', in The Countess of Warwick (ed.), *Progress in Women's Education in the British Empire* (London, 1898), 124.

43 Lilian K. Buckpitt, 'For the Sake of the Child', *The Child*, II (1912), 893.

44 Flora Klickmann, *The Mistress of the Little House* (London, 1912); *Board of Education: General Report on the Teaching of Domestic Subjects*, 15–16; Sophia H. E. Landmaid, *A Woman's Work and How to Lighten It* (London, 1904), 11.

45 *Board of Education, Interim Memorandum on the Teaching of Housecraft in Girls' Secondary Schools* (London, 1911), 35–6; Mary Lovett Cameron, 'How To Train Housewives', *Journal of Education* (February 1898), 107; Mary Harrison, *Simple Lessons in Cookery* (London, 1898), vii–viii.

46 E. A. Hunt, *British Labour History 1815–1914* (London, 1981), 90–9.

47 For a review of the literature, see ibid., 85–7. Also see T. E. Kebbell, *The Agricultural Labourer* (London, 1893); A. Wilson Fox, 'Agricultural Wages in England and Wales During the Last Fifty Years', *Journal of the Royal Statistical Society*, lxvi (1903), 295.

48 For a contemporary discussion, see Flora Klickmann, *The Mistress of the Little House*, 1.

49 Gavin Weightman and Steve Humphries, *The Making of Modern London 1914–1939* (London, 1984), 129; Norman Page, *The Thirties in Britain* (London, 1990), 10; 'Mass Observation', *People and Paints* (Slough, Bucks, 1950), 37.

50 Eric Gill, *Autobiography* (London, 1944), 38–9.

51 Wil Jon Edwards, *From the Valley I Came* (London, 1956), 116.

52 P.R.O. (Kew) HO.45-9839 1310432, letters between the Shipmasters' Society and the Commission of Council on Education, April 1891; Committee of Management of the National Training School for Cookery, 16 February 1904, 205–7, P.R.O. (Kew) ED.164-3; Committee of Management of the National Training School for Cookery, 4 April 1911, no page number, P.R.O. (Kew) ED.164-4; Rowland, 'Wales (With Monmouthshire) Domestic Subjects', P.R.O. (Kew) ED.92-10; Alexander Quinlan and N. E. Mann, *Cookery for Seamen* (Liverpool, 1894).

53 Anna Martin, *Married Working Women* (London, 1911), 29–30.

54 Maurice Ridley, 'Making a Contribution', in Durham 'Strong Words' Collective (eds), *But the World Goes on the Same* (Whitley Bay, 1979), 61. Also see Richard Church, *Over the Bridge* (London, 1955), 210 and Henry Tanner, *Jack's Education* (London, 1879), 9ff.

55 Lucy H. M. Soulsby, *Home Rule* (Oxford, 1894), 14.

56 P. A. Sheehan, *Glenanaar* (New York, 1905), 161–3.

57 Robert Lynd, *Home Life in Ireland* (London, 1909), 22. For other examples, see Margaret E. Loane, *From Their Point of View* (London, 1908), 50 and Robert Roberts, *A Ragged Schooling* (Manchester, 1976), 88.

58 Catherine Cookson, *Our Kate* (London, 1969), 37.

59 Nancy Sharman, *Nothing to Steal* (London, 1977), 37.

60 John Benson, *The Working Class in Britain, 1850–1939* (London, 1989) and Nancy Tomes, 'A "Torrent of Abuse"', *Journal of Social History*, 11 (Spring 1978); Peter N. Stearns, 'Working Class Women', in Martha Vinicus (ed.), *Suffer and Be Still* (London, 1972).

61 Nancy Tomes, 'A "Torrent of Abuse"', 330.

62 Archie Hill, *An Empty Glass* (London, 1984), 10.

63 Pat O'Mara, *The Autobiography of a Liverpool Irish Slummy* (London, 1972), first pub. 1934, 31.

64 Elizabeth Ring, *Up the Cockneys!*, 12.

65 Vera Alsop, 'A Woman's Part', in Durham 'Strong Words' Collective (eds), *But the World Goes on the Same*, 71.

66 Pat O'Mara, *The Autobiography of a Liverpool Irish Slummy*, 36.

67 'Tiger' O'Reilly, *The Tiger of the Legion* (London, 1936), 26.

68 Vera Alsop, 'A Woman's Part', 71.
69 Winifred Foley, *A Child in the Forest* (Bath, 1978), 162.
70 Molly Weir, *Best Foot Forward*, 39–40.
71 Vera Alsop, 'A Woman's Part', 71.
72 Pat O'Mara, *The Autobiography of a Liverpool Irish Slummy*, 33.
73 Stephen Reynolds, *Seems So!* (London, 1911), 254.
74 Pat O'Mara, *The Autobiography of a Liverpool Irish Slummy*, 34 and 36.
75 Stephen Reynolds, *Seems So!*, 254–5.
76 Elizabeth Ring, *Up the Cockneys!*, 12.
77 Edward Ezard, *Battersea Boy*, 710.
78 Robert Roberts, *A Ragged Schooling*, 22.
79 Wally Ward, 'Fit For Anything: Early Days', *Bristol Writes*, 1 (1982), 27–8.
80 Grace Foakes, *My Part of the River* (London, 1974), 53. Also see Nancy Dobrin, *Happiness* (London, 1980), 29; James Allen Bullock, *Bowers Row* (East Ardsley, 1976), 14; Ernest Martin, *The Best Street in Rochdale* (Rochdale, 1985), 2.
81 Women's Co-Operative Guild, *Working Women and Divorce* (London, 1911), 40.
82 E. P. Thompson, 'Patrician Society, Plebeian Culture', *Journal of Social History*, 7 (1974).
83 *Housewife*, 5 (1890), 217–18, 443, 535–6, 679–80, and 757.
84 Margaret E. Loane, *The Queen's Poor* (London, 1906), 1, the first sentence in this book. Also see Celia Davies, *Clean Clothes on Sunday* (Lavenham, 1974), 17.
85 Maurice Levinson, *The Trouble With Yesterday* (London, 1946), 50.
86 Margaret E. Loane, *From Their Point of View*, 120–1.
87 Albert S. Jasper, *A Hoxton Childhood* (London, 1969), 17–18.
88 Jack Lawson, *A Man's Life* (London, 1932), 20. For other examples, see George Edwards, *From Crow-Scaring to Westminster* (London, 1922), 26 and *Commission on the Employment of Children, Young Persons and Women in Agriculture (1867), Appendix II to the First Report, Evidence from the Assistant Commissioners* [4068-I], H. C. 1867–8, xvii, 199 (437), evidence by Robert Webb of Ingoldisthorpe, farm labourer.
89 Molly Weir, *Best Foot Forward*, 39; 'Tiger' O'Reilly, *The Tiger of the Legion*, 26; Vera Alsop, 'A Woman's Part', 71; Ted Willis, *Whatever Happened to Tom Mix?* (London, 1970), 92; Albert S. Jasper, *A Hoxton Childhood*, 33; Elizabeth Ring, *Up the Cockneys!*, 103; George Hitchin, *Pit-Yacker* (London, 1962), 11.
90 Elizabeth Ring, *Up the Cockneys!*, 135.
91 Ted Willis, *Whatever Happened to Tom Mix?*, 102–3; Bim Andrews, 'Making Do', in John Burnett (ed.), *Destiny Obscure* (Harmondsworth, 1982), 127.
92 Jim Hooley, *A Hillgate Childhood* (Stockport, 1981), n.p. approx. 29; Albert S. Jasper, *A Hoxton Childhood*, 112–13; James Allen Bullock, *Bowers Row*, 55.
93 E. L. Packer, 'Aspects of Working-Class Marriage', *Pilot Papers: Social Essays and Documents*, 2.1 (March 1947), 101.
94 Alice Linton, *Not Expecting Miracles* (London, 1982), 53–4.
95 Bob Cooper, *Early to Rise* (London, 1976), 222. For other cases of stealing from husbands (in each case, the wife justifies her actions), see Nancy Tomes, 'A "Torrent of Abuse" ', 332; Albert S. Jasper, *A Hoxton Childhood*, 31; Nancy Sharman, *Nothing to Steal*, 15; Bessie Wallis, 'Yesterday', in John Burnett (ed.), *Destiny Obscure*, 309; S. A. B. Rogers, *Four Acres and a Donkey* (London, 1979), 33.
96 Cited in Melanie Tebbutt, *Making Ends Meet*, 60.
97 Both quotations from Margaret E. Loane, *From Their Point of View*, 95.
98 'H. S. G.', *Autobiography of a Manchester Cotton Manufacturer* (London, 1887), 21.
99 D. F. Delderfield, *Bird's Eye View* (London, 1954), 3; Jack Common, *Seven Shifts* (London, 1938), 170; Celia Davies, *Clean Clothes on Sunday*, 17.
100 Edward Ezard, *Battersea Boy*, 24.
101 Nancy Tomes, 'A "Torrent of Abuse" ', 328–45.

102 Kathleen Behan, *Mother of all Behans* (London, 1985), 80.
103 Winifred Brown, *Under Six Planets* (London, 1955), 36–7 and Mollie Harris, *A Kind of Magic* (Oxford, 1985), 135. For similar examples, see Archie Hill, *An Empty Glass*, 10 and Mary Craddock, *A North Country Maid* (London, 1960), 43–4.
104 E. P. Thompson, 'C18 English Society: Class Struggle Without Class', *Social History*, 3.2 (May 1978), 158–9.
105 For examples, see Peter Fletcher, *The Long Sunday* (London, 1958), 20 and Dorothy Scannell, *Mother Knows Best*, 5–6.
106 Jack Lawson, *A Man's Life*, 144.
107 L. Stoddart, 'What Can the Girls Do?', *Housewife*, 5 (1890), 288.
108 Nancy Dobrin, *Happiness*, 25.
109 Ibid., 19.
110 Robert Roberts, *A Ragged Schooling*, 76.
111 Ibid., 76 and Evelyn Haythorne, *On Earth to Make the Numbers Up* (Pontefract, 1981), 21.
112 Margaret Llewlyn Davies (ed.), *Maternity*, 50.
113 Edith Hall, *Canary Girls and Stockpots*, 16. Also see Rose Neighbour, *All of Me* (London, 1979), 61.
114 'Strategy with Husbands', *Housewife*, 5 (1890), 443.
115 Richard Church, *Over the Bridge*, 110–11.
116 Hannah Mitchell, *The Hard Way Up* (London, 1968), 114.
117 Peter Fletcher, *The Long Sunday*, 61.
118 Robert Roberts, *A Ragged Schooling*, 61.
119 She had tried to protest by her silence first: Richard Church, *Over the Bridge*, 116.
120 Ibid., 61.
121 For an excellent justification for calling these actions acts of resistance, see James C. Scott, *Weapons of the Weak* (New Haven, 1985).
122 Eileen Green, Sandra Hebron and Diana Woodward, *Women's Leisure, What Leisure?* (London, 1990), 49.
123 Folklore Archive, University College Dublin, MSS McCarthy, 62 years, January 1938, 228, Mss., 462.
124 Peter Willmott, *The Evolution of a Community* (London, 1963), 94.
125 Geoffrey Crossick, *An Artisan Elite in Victorian Society* (London, 1978), 146.
126 Jane Rendall, *Women in an Industrializing Society: England 1750–1880* (Oxford, 1990), 89.
127 Roger Langdon, *The Life of Roger Langdon Told By Himself* (London, 1909), 80; Margaret Brown, 'Reminiscences', Coventry Record Office, n.d., 21–2; Ben Turner, *About Myself*, 33–4; Eleanor Ackland, *Good-Bye for the Present* (London, 1935), 87–8; Arthur Harding, *East End Underworld* (London, 1981), 65; George A. Cook, *A Hackney Memory Chest* (London, 1983), 3; Richard Heaton, *Salford* (Swinton, 1983), 9; Allan Jobson, *The Creeping Hours of Time*, 17; Elizabeth Bryson, *Look Back in Wonder* (Dundee, 1966), 7; Harry Pollitt, *Serving My Time* (London, 1940), 21; Wil Jon Edwards, *From the Valley I Came*, 116; Lillian Hine, 'A Poplar Childhood', *East London Record*, 3 (1980), 40; Nigel Gray, *The Worst of Times*, 12; 'Nora James', *A Derbyshire Life* (South Normanton, 1981), 30; Daisy England, *Daisy Daisy* (London, 1981), 47ff.; Lilian Slater, *Think On! Said Many* (Swinton, 1984), 6; Margaret Wharton, *Recollections of a G. I. War Bride* (Gloucester, 1984), 19–21; John D. Vose, *Diary of a Tramp* (St Ives, 1981), 10; Winifred Foley, *A Child in the Forest*, 16; Bim Andrews of Cambridge in John Burnett (ed.), *Destiny Obscure*, 127; Kathleen Price, *Looking Back* (Nottingham, 1980), 25; Jo Barnes, *Arthur and Me* (Bristol, 1979), 6; James Kirkup, *The Only Child* (London, 1957), 51; Angus Fish, *The Family Chatton* (Manchester, 1983), 15; John Blake, *Memories of Old Poplar*, 13; Dorothy Tildsley, *Remembrance* (Swinton, 1985), 5; Angela Rodaway, *A London Childhood* (Bath, 1985), 3; Marjory Todd, *Snakes and Ladders*, 56–7; B. Seebohm Rowntree and May Kendall, *How the Labourer*

Lives (London, 1917), 143; Mrs Pember Reeves, *Round About a Pound a Week*, first published 1913 (London, 1979), 157–66.

128 Marie C. Stopes, *Mother England* (London, 1929).

129 James Whittaker, *I, James Whittaker* (London, 1934), 289.

130 Jacqueline Sarsby, *Missuses and Mouldrunners* (Milton Keynes, 1988), 84.

131 Bob Cooper, *Early to Rise*, 13.

132 Margaret E. Loane, *From Their Point of View*, 145. Also see Nigel Gray, *The Worst of Times*, 12–13 and Richard Heaton, *Salford: My Home Town*, 11.

133 George Anderson, *Down the Mine at Twelve* (Hamilton, 1985), 24 and Joan Bellam, *Them Days* (Padstow, 1982), 23.

134 Ernest Egerton Wood, *Is This Theosophy?* (London, 1936), 17, 48 and Ted Walker, *The High Path* (London, 1982), 18.

135 Winifred Foley, *A Child in the Forest*, 130.

136 Gary Cross (ed.), *Worktowners at Blackpool* (London, 1990), 156–7.

137 Ernest Egerton Wood, *Is This Theosophy?*, 16; Margaret Brown, 'Reminiscences', 21; B. L. Coombes, *These Poor Hands* (London, 1939), 25; Elizabeth Fanshawe, *Penkhull Memories* (Stafford, 1983), 13; Grace Foakes, *My Part of the River*, 18; Isaac C. Johnson, *Autobiography* (London, 1912), 10–11; Nigel Gray, *The Worst of Times*, 14; Dick Field, *Up and Down the Valley* (Cirencester, 1985), 105; Elsie Gadsby, *Black Diamonds, Yellow Apples* (Ilkeston, 1978), 12; Tom Harrisson (ed.), *War Factory* (London, 1943), 35; Felix Greene (ed.), *Time to Spare* (London, 1935), 116.

138 Mentioned by Brian Harrison, 'Class and Gender in Modern British Labour History', *Past and Present*, 124 (1989), 130.

139 Jenni Calder, *The Victorian Home* (London, 1977), 70.

140 Hannah Mitchell, *The Hard Way Up*, 43 cf. 44.

141 Rosamond Jevons and John Madge, *Housing Estates* (Bristol, 1946), 35.

142 Gillian C. Rose, 'Locality, Politics and Culture', Ph.D. thesis, Queen Mary College (1989), 230.

143 Bolton Oral History Project, Tape no. 85, 10, Female, born 1903 in Halliwell, Bolton, a cardroom weaver.

144 J. M. Mogey, 'Changes in Family Life', *Marriage and Family Living*, xvii.2 (May 1955), 125.

145 Gitta Meier, 'A Neighbourhood Study', *The Good Neighbour*, 2.6 (November, 1950), 122–3.

146 *Houses: Hovels or Homes?*, no. 18 (June 1939), 13–14.

147 Peter Willmott, *The Evolution of a Community*, 92.

148 Ibid., 92–3.

149 Letter signed 'Mrs. O' of St James's House, in *Houses: Hovels or Homes?*, no. 10 (June 1935), 10.

150 E. Wight Bakke, *The Unemployed Man* (London, 1933), 153–4.

151 Arthur W. Ashby, *Allotments and Small Holdings in Oxfordshire* (Oxford, 1917).

152 Cited in David Crouch and Colin Ward, *The Allotment* (London, 1988), 70.

153 C. R. Fay and H. C. Fay, *The Allotment Movement in England and Wales* (London, 1942), 18.

154 Ibid., 15; David Crouch and Colin Ward, *The Allotment*, 71–3.

155 David Crouch and Colin Ward, *The Allotment*, 73.

156 'Mass Observation', *An Enquiry into People's Homes* (London, 1943), 161–2.

157 6 June 1924, Bolton City Archives, AK-6-83-1, Bolton County Council Papers [Applications], 6 in family, including 3 adults and 3 children under 10 years. Spelling and punctuation as in original.

158 *Second Annual Report and Year Book of the National Allotments Society Ltd. for the Year Ended December 31st., 1931* (London, 1932), 10–11.

159 Peter Willmott, *The Evolution of a Community*, 91.

160 B. Seebohm Rowntree and May Kendall, *How the Labourer Lives*, 306–7.

161 *Second Annual Report and Year Book of the National Allotments Society Ltd. for the Year Ended December 31st., 1931*, 10–11.

162 Jack Hardy and S. Foxman, *Food Production in the School Garden* (London, 1940), n.p., preface.

163 B. Seebohm Rowntree and May Kendall, *How the Labourer Lives*, 129 and 331.

164 Arthur Barton, *The Penny World*, 95.

165 Arthur W. Ashby, *Allotments and Small Holdings in Oxfordshire*, 75.

166 *Annual Report of the National Allotments Society Limited. For the Years 1943–44* (London, 1944), 13; Friends Allotment Committee, *Diggers and Producers* (London, 1945), no page numbers.

167 B. Seebohm Rowntree and May Kendall, *How the Labourer Lives*, 118–19.

168 Nellie Hoare, *A Winton Story* (Bournemouth, 1982), 37–8.

169 Margaret E. Loane, *From Their Point of View*, 168.

170 Ibid., 155.

171 Ibid., 39 and Arthur Barton, *The Penny World*, 96. Also see Peter Willmott, *The Evolution of a Community*, 63; Leo Kuper (ed.), *Living in Towns* (London, 1953), 24; J. M. Mogey, 'Changes in Family Life', 126; C. B. Purdom, *The Garden City* (London, 1913), 105.

172 See William Good, *Allotment Gardening* (London, 1922), 2.

173 'Nora James', *A Derbyshire Life*, 5; John Howlett, *The Guv'nor* (London, 1973), 28; John Edwin, *I'm Going – What Then?* (Bognor Regis, 1978), 14–15; William Waddington, *Rossendale Reflections* (Rossendale, 1983), 20; Bob Cooper, *Early to Rise*, 175–6 and 184; Bill Harrocks, *Reminiscences of Bolton* (Swinton, 1984), 35; John Blake, *Memories of Old Poplar*, 23–4.

174 Jack Lawson, *A Man's Life*, 50–1; Nigel Gray, *The Worst of Times*, 128; Ethelwyn Rolfe, *The Soul of the Slum Child* (London, 1929), 23–4; John Burnett (ed.), *Destiny Obscure*, 295; John McGovern, *Neither Fear Nor Favour* (London, 1960), 15; Richard Heaton, *Salford*, 11; Harry Pollitt, *Serving My Time*, 19 and 21; Sir Reader Bullard, *The Camels Must Go* (London, 1961), 27; Ernest Egerton Wood, *Is This Theosophy?*, 23; Richard Church, *Over the Bridge*, 9, 85, and 123; Sid Knight, *Cotswold Lad* (London, 1960), 31–2; H. J. Bennett, *I Was a Walworth Boy* (London, 1980), 57–8; Hannah Mitchell, *The Hard Way Up*, 59 and 109–10; Lillian Hine, 'A Poplar Childhood', 40; James Whittaker, *I, James Whittaker*, 37.

175 Margaret E. Loane, *From Their Point of View*, 170–1.

176 Ben Turner, *About Myself*, 38–9.

177 Benedict Anderson, *Imagined Communities* (London, 1983), 30.

178 Philip Magnus, 'Manual Training in School Education', *The Contemporary Review*, 1 (November 1886), 697–700 and John Lubbock, 'Manual Instruction', *Fortnightly Review*, ccxxxviii, new series (October 1886), 464–7.

179 National Association of Manual Training Teachers, *Report on the Examination of Handicraft and Technical Drawing in Secondary Schools* (London, 1947), 2.

180 *Congested Districts Board for Ireland: Twentieth Report* [Cd. 6553], H. C. 1912–13, xvii, 30.

181 *Department of Agriculture and Technical Instruction for Ireland: Fourth Report*, H. C. 1905, xxi, 6.

182 Quoted in Philip Magnus, 'Manual Training in School Education', 701.

183 *Royal Commission on Congestion, First Appendix to the Seventh Report*, H. C. 1908, xl, 138, evidence by the Rev. Patrick Finegan.

184 Margaret Powell, *My Children and I*, 72. Also see George Henry Hewins, *The Dillen* (London, 1981), 67.

185 *Manual Training*, xiii.145 (October 1913), 25, extract from the *Yorkshire Observer*.

186 Cited in Trevor Lummis, 'The Historical Dimension of Fatherhood: A Case Study 1890–1914', in Lorna McKee and Margaret O'Brien (eds), *The Father Figure* (London, 1982), 46.

187 Robert Roberts, *A Ragged Schooling*, 53–4.

188 Norman Dennis, Fernando Henriques and Clifford Slaughter, *Coal is Our Life* (London, 1956), 181.

189 For a superb chapter on domestic violence, see Carl Chinn, *They Worked All Their Lives* (Manchester, 1988), 155–66.

190 Margaret E. Loane, *Neighbours and Friends* (London, 1910), 296.

191 Dorothy Scannell, *Mother Knows Best*, 5.

192 Margaret Powell, *My Children and I*, 45–6.

193 Elizabeth K. Blackburn, *In and Out of Windows* (Burnley, 1980), 48; Mary Chamberlain, *Fenwomen* (London, 1975), 77; Mollie Harris, *A Kind of Magic*, 133; Lilian Slater, *Think On! Said Many*, 6; T. A. Westwater, *The Early Life of T. A. Westwater* (Oxford, 1979), 9; Frederick C. Wigby, *Just a Country Boy* (Wymondham, 1976), 4; Margaret E. Loane, *Simple Sanitation* (London, 1905), 13 and 18; Bessie Harvey, 'Youthful Memories', *Suffolk Review*, 2 (September 1960), 73; Ernest Egerton Wood, *Is This Theosophy?*, 48.

194 Richard Heaton, *Salford*, 11; Sid Knight, *Cotswold Lad*, 31–2; Jack Lawson, *A Man's Life*, 50–1; Richard Church, *Over the Bridge*, 123; Ben Turner, *About Myself*, 38–9; 'The Co-Operation of Children', *Housewife*, 5 (1890), 58; John McGovern, *Neither Fear Nor Favour*, 15; Sir Reader Bullard, *The Camels Must Go*, 27; Wil Jon Edwards, *From the Valley I Came*, 116; Charles Welch, *An Autobiography* (Banstead, 1960), 36; Harry Pollitt, *Serving My Time*, 19.

195 For instance, by 1950 fewer than one in ten men earning less than £5 a week owned a lawnmower (compared with over one-fifth of men earning between £5 10s and £10): 'Mass Observation', *People and Paints*, 43.

196 Kathleen Dayus, *Her People* (London, 1982), 6–7.

197 Margaret Powell, *My Children and I*, 19.

198 Kay Pearson, *Life in Hull From Then Till Now*, 98. She concluded her speech with the words: 'Allow me to state here that I had three other girls during my marriage, and through each of those pregnancies my husband's health was affected the same (plus salmon) – don't say it's an old wives tale – it really happened.'

199 Evelyn Haythorne, *On Earth to Make the Numbers Up*, 6.

200 B. Seebohm Rowntree and May Kendall, *How the Labourer Lives*, 94; John Burnett (ed.), *Destiny Obscure*, 295; Aida Hayhoe, in Mary Chamberlain, *Fenwomen*, 77; Elizabeth K. Blackburn, *In and Out of Windows*, 48; Mollie Harris, *A Kind of Magic*, 133.

201 Hannah Mitchell, *The Hard Way Up*, 59.

202 Ted Walker, *The High Path*, 12; Gladys Teal, *Grasp the Nettle* (Leeds, c.1980), 4; John Blake, *Memories of Old Poplar*, 15–17; Leo Kuper (ed.), *Living in Towns*, 18 and 59.

203 B. Seebohm Rowntree and May Kendall, *How the Labourer Lives*, 94; Mrs Pember Reeves, *Round About a Pound a Week*, 63–4.

204 Richard Church, *Over the Bridge*, 107–8; Edward Ezard, *Battersea Boy*, 24 and 26.

205 A. D. K. Owen, *A Survey of Juvenile Employment and Welfare in Sheffield*, Sheffield Social Survey Committee, Pamphlet no. 6, April 1933, 17. Also see E. Llewelyn Lewis, *The Children of the Unskilled* (London, 1924), 74–97.

206 Basil Kingsley Martin, *Father Figures* (London, 1966), 27; 'A Workaday Mother', *What Every Mother Should Tell Her Children* (London, 1938), 14.

207 Charles Welch, *An Autobiography*, 36.

208 Margaret E. Loane, *From Their Point of View*, 147–8.

209 Ibid., 146–7.

210 Geoffrey Gorer, *Exploring English Character* (London, 1955), 153.

211 Walter Southgate, *That's the Way it Was*, 12 and Arthur Barton, *The Penny World*, 169.

212 Cited in George Henry Hewins, *The Dillen*, 92.

213 Unemployed London house-painter, in H. L. Beales and R. S. Lambert (eds), *Memoirs of the Unemployed* (London, 1934), 171–2.

214 S. P. B. Mais, *S. O. S. Talks on Unemployment* (London, 1933), 12.

215 H. L. Beales and R. S. Lambert (eds), *Memoirs of the Unemployed*, 180.
216 Phyllis Willmott, *Growing Up in a London Village* (London, 1979), 109 and Elizabeth Ring, *Up the Cockneys!*, 100.
217 Letter from 'Clerk', 'The Home Parliament', in *Daily Herald*, 31 October 1919, 8; Women's Group on Public Welfare, *Loneliness* (London, 1955), 11 and 20; *The Island* (London, 1979), 33; John Blake, *Memories of Old Poplar*, 45–6; Alice Linton, *Not Expecting Miracles*, 53.
218 Ivy Willis in Gavin Weightman and Steve Humphries, *The Making of Modern London 1914–1939*, 126–7.
219 Elizabeth Bryson, *Look Back in Wonder*, 7.
220 Margaret Llewlyn Davies (ed.), *Maternity*, 121.

4 MARKETPLACE

1 *Daily Mirror*, 25 June 1945, 1.
2 Blue-collar jobs are defined as SEG 7, 9–11, 15 while white-collar jobs are SEG 1–6, 8, 12–14.
3 John H. Goldthorpe, *Social Mobility and Class Structure in Modern Britain* (Oxford, 1980), 72, 75–6, 84.
4 Jim Wolveridge, *Ain't It Grand* (London, 1976), 19.
5 Mrs M. G. Fawcett, *The Women's Victory and After* (London, 1920), 106.
6 J. McCalman, 'The Impact of the First World War on Female Employment in England', *Labour History* (1972), 39.
7 Isobel M. Pizzey, 'Home Parliament', *Daily Herald*, 31 October 1919, 8.
8 Jane Lewis, 'In Search of a Real Equality: Women Between the Wars', in Frank Gloversmith (ed.), *Class, Culture and Social Change* (Brighton, 1980), 214–15.
9 N. Branson and M. Heinemann, *Britain in the 1930s* (London, 1971), 145.
10 Gavin Weightman and Steve Humphries, *The Making of Modern London 1914–1939* (London, 1984), 125.
11 Ibid., 23.
12 E. Slater and M. Woodside, *Patterns of Marriage* (London, 1951), 82.
13 Stephen Nickell, *Research Into Unemployment*, Centre for Labour Economics, London School of Economics, Discussion Paper no. 131 (June 1982), 1.
14 Daniel K. Benjamin and Levis A. Kochin, 'Searching for an Explanation of Unemployment in Interwar Britain', *Journal of Political Economy*, 87.3 (June 1979) and follow-up discussions in 90.2 (April 1982).
15 Richard Croucher, *We Refuse to Starve in Silence* (London, 1987), 15.
16 Geoff Payne, *Mobility and Change in Modern Society* (Basingstoke, 1987), 144.
17 Harry Hendrick, *Images of Youth* (Oxford, 1990), 34.
18 Barclay Baron, *The Growing Generation* (London, 1911), 58.
19 A. D. K. Owen, *A Survey of Juvenile Employment and Welfare in Sheffield* (Sheffield, 1933), 22.
20 John Jewkes and Sylvia Jewkes, *The Juvenile Labour Market* (London, 1938), 42–3.
21 N. B. Dearle, 'The Organisation of Boy Labour', *Clare Market Review*, 5.3 (June 1910), 102.
22 Rev. Spencer J. Gibb, *The Boy and His Work* (London, 1911), 80.
23 Jack Lawson, *A Man's Life* (London, 1932), 39.
24 Gwynne Meara, *Juvenile Unemployment in South Wales* (Cardiff, 1936), 65.
25 Ministry of Labour, *Report on Juvenile Employment*, 1933, 6, cited in Gwynne Meara, *Juvenile Unemployment in South Wales*, 65.
26 For example, see Social Survey, *Scottish Mining Communities*, Report New Series, no. 61 (Autumn 1946), 21.
27 Allan Winterbottom, *An Enquiry into the Employment of Juveniles in Lancashire* (Manchester, 1932), 21.

28 Reginald A. Bray, 'The Apprenticeship Question', *Economic Journal*, xix.75 (September 1909), 411.
29 A. D. K. Owen, *A Survey of Juvenile Employment and Welfare in Sheffield*, 17.
30 *Board of Education. Report of the Consultative Committee of Attendance, Compulsory or Otherwise, at Continuation Schools* [Cd. 4757–8], H. C. 1909, 62.
31 E. Llewelyn Lewis, *The Children of the Unskilled* (London, 1924), 55.
32 Frederic Keeling, *The Labour Exchange in Relation to Boy and Girl Labour* (London, 1910), 10.
33 Gwynne Meara, *Juvenile Unemployment in South Wales*, 64.
34 Social Survey, *Scottish Mining Communities*, 25.
35 A. D. K. Owen, *A Survey of Juvenile Employment and Welfare in Sheffield*, 17; Arthur Greenwood and John E. Kettlewell, 'Some Statistics of Juvenile Employment and Unemployment', *Journal of the Royal Statistical Society*, lxxv (June 1912), 753; Political and Economic Planning, *The Entrance to Industry*, May (London, 1935), 26; John Jewkes and Sylvia Jewkes, *The Juvenile Labour Market*, 32–4.
36 Frederic Keeling, *The Labour Exchange in Relation to Boy and Girl Labour*, 14, 18–19, and 22–3.
37 A. H. Halsey, *Change in British Society* (Oxford, 1981), 117.
38 Jonathan Rose, *The Edwardian Temperament 1895–1919* (Ohio, 1986), 178.
39 B. Seebohm Rowntree, *Poverty and Progress: A Second Social Study of York* (London, 1941), 196.
40 See Henry Hadow, *Board of Education. Report of the Consultative Committee on the Education of the Adolescent* (London, 1936) and R. H. Tawney (ed.), *Secondary Education for All* (London, 1922).
41 Kirsten Drotner, *English Children and Their Magazines 1751–1945* (New Haven, 1988), 197–8.
42 J. E. Floud, 'The Educational Experience of the Adult Population of England and Wales as at July, 1949', in D. V. Glass (ed.), *Social Mobility in Britain* (London, 1954).
43 Stuart Laing, *Representations of Working-Class Life 1957–1964* (London, 1986), 24–5.
44 Adam Collier, 'Social Origins of a Sample of Entrants to Glasgow University', *Sociological Review*, xxx (1939), 276.
45 Ian J. McDonald, 'Untapped Reservoirs of Talent?', *Scottish Educational Studies*, 1.1 (June 1967), 53.
46 A. H. Halsey, 'Higher Education', in A. H. Halsey, *Trends in British Society*, second edition (Oxford, 1981).
47 Alan Sinfield, *Literature, Politics and Culture in Postwar Britain* (Oxford, 1989), 234–5.
48 E. Slater and M. Woodside, *Patterns of Marriage*, 67 and Phyllis Willmott, *A Green Girl* (London, 1983), 12. Also see George Scott, *Time and Place* (London, 1956), 24–5 and Elsie Gadsby, *Black Diamonds, Yellow Apples* (Ilkeston, 1978), 43.
49 Ray Lowe, *Education in the Postwar Years* (London, 1988), 53.
50 A. H. Halsey, *Change in British Society*, third edition (Oxford, 1986), 40.
51 Valerie Walkerdine, 'Dreams from an Ordinary Childhood', in Liz Heron (ed.), *Truth, Dare, Promise* (London, 1985), 74.
52 E. Slater and M. Woodside, *Patterns of Marriage*, 70.
53 Margaret Neville Keynes, *The Problem of Boy Labour in Cambridge* (Cambridge, 1911), 13.
54 Ron Barnes, *Coronation Cups and Jam Jars* (London, 1976), 56–7.
55 Len Wincott, *Invergordon Mutineer* (London, 1974), 5.
56 Jack Goodwin, *Myself and My Boxers* (London, 1924), 8.
57 Stephen Humphries, 'Steal to Survive: The Social Crime of Working Class Children 1890–1940', *Oral History*, 9.1 (Spring 1981), 71.
58 Mrs Hylton Dale, *Child Labour Under Capitalism* (London, 1908), 17.

59 *Annual Report in 1915 of the Chief Medical Officer of the Board of Education* [Cd. 8338], H. C. 1916, v.

60 Industrial Christian Fellowship, *Children at Work* (London, 1943), 7–8.

61 John Jewkes and Sylvia Jewkes, *The Juvenile Labour Market*, 133–4.

62 Ibid., 132.

63 Jane Lewis, *Women in England 1870–1950* (Brighton, 1984).

64 Bolton County Borough Papers, 'General Correspondence', ABCF-9-60, letter from Miss Norah Darbyshire, 62 Morris Green Lane, Bolton, 15 November 1935, to Mr Kinlay, Public Assistance Officer.

65 Alice Foley Collection, Bolton City Library Archives ZFO-17, 'Married Women Weavers. Are They Surplus to Industry?', typescript, no date, 5.

66 Cited in review by James Hinton in *Society for the Study of Labour History*, 42 (Spring 1981), 51.

67 Geoffrey Thomas, *The Social Survey* (London, 1948), 17–19.

68 Gertrude Wagner, *Cakes – Buying and Baking*, Wartime Social Survey, new series 40 (November–December 1943), 1–2.

69 Richard Church, *Over the Bridge* (London, 1955), 77. Also see Mrs Bayly, *Home Rule* (London, 1886), 38.

70 Elizabeth Roberts, *A Woman's Place* (Oxford, 1984).

71 C. Matheson, 'Women's Labour and the Home', *Birmingham Street Children's Union Magazine*, no. 11 (April 1911), 210.

72 Geoffrey Thomas, *The Social Survey*, 1.

73 Lincolnshire: *Commission on the Employment of Children, Young Persons and Women in Agriculture (1867). Appendix Part II to the First Report. Evidence from the Assistant Commissioners* [4068–I], H. C. 1867–8, xvii, 301 (539); Berkshire: *Commission on the Employment of Children, Young Persons and Women in Agriculture (1867). First Report of the Commissioners, with Appendix. Part I* [4068], H. C. 1867–8, xvii, Appendix, 17 (44): in this case, it is 4d a year difference. For very similar statements, see *Commission on the Employment of Children, Young Persons and Women in Agriculture (1867). Appendix Part II to the First Report. Evidence from the Assistant Commissioners* [4068–I], H. C. 1867–8, xvii, 441–2 (679–80), comments by John Jervis and James Marriott, labourers from Islip and Stanwick, Northamptonshire; *Commission on the Employment of Children, Young Persons and Women in Agriculture (1867). Appendix Part II to Second Report. Evidence from the Assistant Commissioners* [4202–I], H.C. 1868–9, xiii, 136, 292–3 and 295 (366, 522–3 and 525), comments by Mrs Finnimore, wife of a labourer in Broadclyst, Devonshire; William Muggleton, gardener in Byfleet, Surrey; and Mrs Hook, wife of a carter in Sanderstead, Surrey.

74 Albert S. Jasper, *A Hoxton Childhood* (London, 1969), 9.

75 Pat O'Mara, *The Autobiography of a Liverpool Irish Slummy* (London, 1972), first pub. 1934, 52.

76 Elizabeth Ring, *Up the Cockneys!* (London, 1975), 112.

77 Denise Riley, *War in the Nursery* (London, 1983), 92–108 and Elizabeth Vallance, *Women in the House* (London, 1979), 130–1.

78 *Hansard*, 5 March 1942, vol. 378, 49.

79 V. Klein, *Britain's Married Women Workers* (London, 1965), 25.

80 Diana G. Gittens, 'Married Life and Birth Control Between the Wars', *Oral History*, 2 (1975), 53.

81 R. M. Titmuss, 'The Position of Women and Some Vital Statistics', in M. W. Flinn and T. C. Smout (eds), *Essays in Social History* (Oxford, 1974), 278–9.

82 Arthur Marwick, 'A Social History of Britain 1945–1983', in David Punter (ed.), *Introduction to Contemporary Cultural Studies* (London, 1986), 28–9.

83 Michael Anderson, 'The Emergence of the Modern Life Cycle in Britain', *Social History*, 10.1 (January 1985), 73–4.

84 Jack Common, *Seven Shifts* (London, 1938), 7.

85 Nigel Gray, *The Worst of Times* (London, 1985), 137; Jack Lanigan, 'Incidents in

the Life of a Citizen', in John Burnett (ed.), *Destiny Obscure* (Harmondsworth, 1982), 99; Ted Willis, *Whatever Happened to Tom Mix?* (London, 1970), 98–9; Bob Cooper, *Early to Rise* (London, 1976), 124.

86 Jack Common, *Seven Shifts*, 15–16.

87 Winifred Foley, *A Child in the Forest* (Bath, 1978), 133. Also see Jim Hooley, *A Hillgate Childhood* (Stockport, 1981), n.p. approx. 12.

88 Nigel Gray, *The Worst of Times*, 137; Jack Lanigan, 'Incidents in the Life of a Citizen', in John Burnett (ed.), *Destiny Obscure*, 99.

89 Nancy Dobrin, *Happiness* (London, 1980), 24; Vera Alsop, 'A Woman's Part', in Durham 'Strong Words' Collective (eds), *But the World Goes on the Same* (Whitley Bay, 1979), 71; Margaret Powell, *My Children and I* (London, 1977), 50–1.

90 Mary Craddock, *A North Country Maid* (London, 1960), 42–3. Also see the testimony of an unemployed London house-painter in H. L. Beales and R. S. Lambert (eds), *Memoirs of the Unemployed* (London, 1934), 172 and 215–16, and Horace B. Pointing, *Unemployment is Beating Us?* (London, 1934), 23.

91 Alexander Paterson, *Across the Bridges* (New York, 1980), first published 1911, 22.

92 Jack Common, *Seven Shifts*, 208.

93 Mary Craddock, *A North Country Maid*, 43–4. Also see Margaret Powell, *My Children and I*, 66; Felix Greene (ed.), *Time to Spare* (London, 1935), 31; S. P. B. Mais, *S. O. S. Talks on Unemployment* (London, 1933), xxii; Horace B. Pointing, *Unemployment is Beating Us?*, 23; Rose Neighbour, *All of Me* (London, 1979), 11–12; H. L. Beales and R. S. Lambert (eds), *Memoirs of the Unemployed*, 97–8 and 180.

94 E. Wight Bakke, *The Unemployed Man* (London, 1933), 69–70.

95 S. P. B. Mais, *S. O. S. Talks on Unemployment*, 40.

96 Nigel Gray, *The Worst of Times*, 68–9.

97 Rose Neighbour, *All of Me*, 58.

98 H. L. Beales and R. S. Lambert (eds), *Memoirs of the Unemployed*, 73–4.

99 Ibid., 180.

100 Eileen Slade, *Middle Child* (Andover, 1979), 49.

101 H. L. Beales and R. S. Lambert (eds), *Memoirs of the Unemployed*, 94 and 97–8.

102 Ibid., 171–2.

103 Arthur Barton, *Two Lamps in Our Street* (London, 1967), 145.

104 H. L. Beales and R. S. Lambert (eds), *Memoirs of the Unemployed*, 104–5.

105 Mary Craddock, *A North Country Maid*, 43–4; Felix Greene (ed.), *Time to Spare*, 31; Rose Neighbour, *All of Me*, 11–12; S. P. B. Mais, *S. O. S. Talks on Unemployment*, xxii; F. Zweig, *Men in the Pits* (London, 1948), 153; Nigel Gray, *The Worst of Times*, 110–11; Jack Common, *Seven Shifts*, 138.

106 Note the use of the term 'house-father' in the Ladies Sanitary Association, *24th Annual Report of the Ladies Sanitary Association*, April 1882, 17.

107 Cited in Gavin Weightman and Steve Humphries, *The Making of Modern London 1914–1939*, 126–7.

108 F. Zweig, *The Worker in an Affluent Society* (London, 1961).

5 LOCALITY

1 Mrs Annie Hukin, 'Some Memories of the Early 1900s' (1974), 3, in Alice Foley Collection, Bolton City Library Archives.

2 Margaret Brown, 'Reminiscences of My Childhood, 1896–1910' (n.d.), Coventry Record Office, 3.

3 Dorothy Tildsley, *Remembrance* (Swinton, 1985), 2.

4 John Blake, *Memories of Old Poplar* (London, 1977), 12.

5 Charles Forman, *Industrial Town* (London, 1978), 142.

6 George A. Hillery, 'Definitions of Community. Areas of Agreement', *Rural Sociology*, 20 (1955), 111–23.

7 G. Lansbury, *Looking Backwards – and Forwards* (London, 1935), 134; G. Lansbury, *My Life* (London, 1928), 287; 'The Future of Socialism', *Socialist Review*, 24 (1924), 85.

8 For examples, see the Bolton County Council Papers for the 1920s, in the Bolton City Library Archives, AK-6-83-1.

9 Alice Foley, 'Shift Working in Cotton Mills. A Woman's Point of View', typescript article, n.d., Alice Foley Collection, Bolton City Library Archives, ZFO-5, no. 5, 3.

10 For example, the Watling estate was established in 1927. It had a difficult few years: amenities were poor and bordering neighbourhoods were hostile. To defend the residents, a local paper, the *Watling Resident*, started. In 1928, it was bought by four-fifths of all houses in Watling. As the estate settled and amenities improved, sales began declining, so that, within eight years, sales had declined to one-quarter of households and the editor could write: 'Watlingitis, common disease after 8–10 months residence on this Estate. The patient is attacked with a sudden desire to do nothing, see nothing, help no-one and go nowhere': Ruth Durant, *Watling* (London, 1939), 43 and 46.

11 Jeremy Seabrook, *The Idea of Neighbourhood* (London, 1984), 3–4 and 22.

12 Martin Bulmer, *The Occupational Community of the Traditional Worker* (London, 1973), 20.

13 Robert E. Park, 'Community Organisation and Juvenile Delinquency', in Robert E. Park and E. W. Burgess (eds), *The City* (Chicago, 1925), 6.

14 For a discussion of the 'defended neighbourhood', see Gerald D. Suttles, *The Social Construction of Communities* (Chicago, 1972), 21.

15 Standish Meacham, *A Life Apart* (London, 1977); Michael Young and Peter Willmott, *Family and Kinship in East London* (London, 1990), first published 1957, 104; Ellen Ross, 'Survival Networks: Women's Neighbourhood Sharing in London Before World War I', *History Workshop*, 15 (Spring 1983); Elizabeth Roberts, *A Woman's Place* (Oxford, 1984).

16 Gillian C. Rose, 'Locality, Politics and Culture', Ph.D. thesis, Queen Mary College (1989), 230.

17 Sir Hubert Llewellyn Smith (ed.), *New Survey of London Life and Labour. Vol. VI. Survey and Social Conditions (2) The Western Area (Text)* (London, 1934), 265.

18 Michael Young and Peter Willmott, *Family and Kinship in East London*, 104.

19 Geoffrey Gorer, *Exploring English Character* (London, 1955), 44.

20 Sandra Wallman (ed.), *Living in South London* (London, 1982), 110–11.

21 Standish Meacham, *A Life Apart*, 47.

22 Dennis Chapman, *Sound in Dwellings*, Wartime Social Survey, new series Region S6 (November 1943), 28.

23 Leo Kuper, 'Blueprint for Living Together', in Leo Kuper (ed.), *Living in Towns* (London, 1953), 22.

24 W. White, *Life in a Court: How to Stop Neighbours' Quarrels* (Birmingham, 1890), 2.

25 Hackney and Stoke Newington Social Workers' Group, *What Kind of Homes?* (London, 1944), 9.

26 Mark W. Hodges and Cyril S. Smith, 'The Sheffield Estate', in University of Liverpool Social Science Department, *Neighbourhood and Community* (Liverpool, 1954), 90.

27 Bertram Hutchinson, *Willesden and the New Towns* (London, 1947), 3, 69, and 71.

28 Hackney and Stoke Newington Social Workers' Group, *What Kind of Homes?*, 9–10.

29 Dennis Chapman, *The Location of Dwellings in Scottish Towns*, Wartime Social Survey, new series no. 34 (September 1943), 27.

30 For two examples – one from Armagh and the other from Sheffield – see Jack

Fallon's memoirs in typescript at the Ulster Folk and Transport Museum G4-1-15, 15 March 1976 and Kay Pearson, *Life in Hull From Then to Now* (Hull, 1980), 110.

31 Leo Kuper, 'Blueprint for Living Together', 15.

32 Ibid., 19.

33 Ibid., 15.

34 Jo Barnes, *Arthur and Me* (Bristol, 1979), 2 and Jane Walsh, *Not Like This* (London, 1953), 12.

35 Elizabeth K. Blackburn, *In and Out of Windows* (Burnley, 1980), 15.

36 Leo Kuper, 'Blueprint for Living Together', 15.

37 Ibid., 55.

38 Ibid., 52.

39 G. Duncan Mitchell and Thomas Lipton, 'The Liverpool Estate', in University of Liverpool Social Science Department, *Neighbourhood and Community* (Liverpool, 1954), 54.

40 Leo Kuper, 'Blueprint for Living Together', 52 and 59.

41 'A Worker's Family. Life From the Inside', in Sir Hubert Llewellyn Smith (ed.), *The New Survey of London Life and Labour. Vol. IX. Life and Leisure* (London, 1935), 396.

42 G. Duncan Mitchell and Thomas Lipton, 'The Liverpool Estate', in University of Liverpool Social Science Department, *Neighbourhood and Community*, 46.

43 Mark W. Hodges and Cyril S. Smith, 'The Sheffield Estate', in University of Liverpool Social Science Department, *Neighbourhood and Community*, 93.

44 'Mass Observation', *The Pub and the People*, first pub. 1943 (Welwyn Garden City, 1970), 130-1 and their *Contemporary Churchgoing* (n.p., 1949), 13-14.

45 Mark W. Hodges and Cyril S. Smith, 'The Sheffield Estate', in University of Liverpool Social Science Department, *Neighbourhood and Community*, 95.

46 Jimmy Reid, *Reflections of a Clyde-Built Man* (London, 1976), 3.

47 Alan Haig, *The Victorian Clergy* (London, 1984).

48 Brian Harrison, *Peaceable Kingdom* (Oxford, 1982), 123.

49 *Christian World*, 31 October 1901, 10.

50 Kenneth D. Brown, 'Ministerial Recruitment and Training. An Aspect of the Crisis of Victorian Nonconformity', *Victorian Studies*, 30.3 (Spring 1987), 367.

51 Jonathan Rose, *The Edwardian Temperament 1895-1919* (Ohio, 1986), 1.

52 M. Blanch, 'Imperialism, Nationalism and Organised Youth', in J. Clarke, C. Critcher and R. Johnson (eds), *Working Class Culture* (London, 1979), 117.

53 B. Seebohm Rowntree and G. R. Lavers, *English Life and Leisure* (London, 1951), 343-4.

54 Keith Sword, Norman Davies and Jan Ciechanowski, *The Formation of the Polish Community in Great Britain, 1939-50* (London, 1989), 367.

55 'Mass Observation', *Puzzled People* (London, 1947), 83.

56 Ibid., 86-7.

57 Commission on Evangelism, reported in *Christian Newsletter*, supplement 172, 10 February 1943.

58 Tory Reform Committee, *To-Morrow's Children* (London, 1944), 18.

59 Cited in Kevin O'Connor, *The Irish in Britain* (London, 1972), 73-4.

60 B. Seebohm Rowntree and G. R. Lavers, *English Life and Leisure*, 355.

61 Ibid., 346.

62 Margaret E. Loane, *The Queen's Poor* (London, 1905), 28-9.

63 Margaret E. Loane, *From Their Point of View* (London, 1908), 94.

64 Victor Bailey, 'Bibles and Dummy Rifles: The Boys' Brigade', *History Today*, 33 (October 1983).

65 Ibid., 7.

66 John Springhall, *Youth, Empire and Society* (London, 1977), 25.

67 John R. Gillis, *Youth and History* (New York, 1981), 147.

68 B. Seebohm Rowntree and G. R. Lavers, *English Life and Leisure*, 346.

69 Tom Burns, 'Social Development in New Neighbourhoods', *Pilot Papers. Social Essays and Documents*, 2.4 (December 1947), 22–3.

70 Unnamed female textiles worker, born in Farnsworth in 1914, Bolton Oral History Project, Tape no. 95, in the Bolton City Library Archives, 360. Also see Tapes nos. 85 and 55e.

71 G. Duncan Mitchell and Thomas Lipton, 'The Liverpool Estate', in University of Liverpool Social Science Department, *Neighbourhood and Community*, 56–7.

72 John Barron Mays, *Growing Up in the City* (Liverpool, 1954), 73.

73 University of Liverpool Social Science Department, *Neighbourhood and Community*, 135.

74 Marie C. Stopes, *Mother England* (London, 1929), 47–8, spelling and punctuation as in original.

75 Joan Mills, 'The Tenement Housewife', in *The Good Neighbour*, 2.6 (November 1950), 135. For an interesting sidelight to this, see the work by Bertram Hutchinson, *Willesden and the New Towns*, 42–3 and Dennis Chapman, *A Social Survey of Middlesbrough*, part iv (London, 1945), 5–6 which show the level of dissatisfaction between residents in a street or area – a sizeable proportion wishing to move to a neighbourhood slightly better than the one she or he is presently living in.

76 Gerald D. Suttles, *The Social Construction of Communities*.

77 'Our Street', Alice Foley Collection, Bolton City Library Archive, typescript, n.d., ZFO-32, 1.

78 Bernard Gainer, *The Alien Invasion* (London, 1972), 49.

79 Jane Walsh, *Not Like This*, 12.

80 Louis Battye, *I Had a Little Nut Tree* (London, 1959), 93.

81 National Council of Social Services, *Out of Adversity* (London, 1939), 47.

82 This chapter deals with urban communities only. For studies of the importance of kinship and neighbourhood in isolated rural communities, see C. M. Arensberg and S. T. Kimball, *Family and Community in Ireland* (Cambridge, Mass., 1940); R. Frankenberg, *Communities in Britain* (Harmondsworth, 1966); R. Frankenberg, *Villages on the Border* (London, 1957); H. Newby, *England's Green and Pleasant Land* (London, 1979); Svend Riemer, 'Villages in Metrolis', *British Journal of Sociology*, II.1 (March 1951), 31–43; A. Rees, *Life in the Welsh Countryside* (Cardiff, 1950); and W. M. Williams, *The Sociology of an English Village: Gosforth* (London, 1956).

83 Madeline Kerr, *The People of Ship Street* (London, 1958), 40.

84 E. L. Packer, 'Aspects of Working-Class Marriage', *Pilot Papers: Social Essays and Documents*, 2.1 (March 1947), 102–3.

85 Madeline Kerr, *The People of Ship Street*, 40.

86 Geoffrey Gorer, *Exploring English Character*, 45. For the closeness of kin, also see Peter Willmott, *The Evolution of a Community* (London, 1963), 25.

87 Mark W. Hodges and Cyril S. Smith, 'The Sheffield Estate', in University of Liverpool Social Science Department, *Neighbourhood and Community*, 109. For a similar study, see Peter Willmott, *The Evolution of a Community*, 29.

88 Margaret E. Loane, *From Their Point of View*, 37.

89 R. Firth and J. Djamour, 'Kinship in South Borough', in R. Firth (ed.), *Two Studies of Kinship in London*, London School of Economics Monograph on Social Anthropology, no. 15 (London, 1956), 40.

90 Bertram Hutchinson, *Willesden and the New Towns*, 43 and Peter Willmott, *The Evolution of a Community*, 32.

91 Michael Young and Peter Willmott, *Family and Kinship in East London*, 29.

92 J. M. Mogey, 'Changes in Family Life Experienced by English Workers Moving From the Slums to Housing Estates', *Marriage and Family Living*, xvii.2 (May 1955), 126.

93 'Mass Observation', *Britain and Her Birth Rate* (London, 1945), 63.

94 Madeline Kerr, *The People of Ship Street*, 43.

95 Peter Willmott, *The Evolution of a Community*, 32.
96 For the distance between the relatives, see Geoffrey Gorer, *Exploring English Character*, 45–6. For other discussions of the importance of the mother's mother, see R. Firth and J. Djamour, 'Kinship in South Borough', in R. Firth (ed.), *Two Studies of Kinship in London*, 35–7 and Madeline Kerr, *The People of Ship Street*, 22.
97 Lulie A. Shaw, 'Impressions of Family Life in a London Suburb: Studies of a General Practice IV', *Sociological Review*, 2.2 (1954), 184. This was not the case in the Liverpool slum studied by Madeline Kerr, *The People of Ship Street*, 43.
98 See the breakdown of childcare arrangements for mothers working at a Bermondsey biscuit factory in 1955, in London School of Economics and Political Science, The Social Sciences Department, *Woman, Wife, Worker* (London, 1960), 26.
99 Lulie A. Shaw, 'Impressions of Family Life in a London Suburb', 184.
100 R. Firth and J. Djamour, 'Kinship in South Borough', in R. Firth (ed.), *Two Studies of Kinship in London*, 41.
101 Lulie A. Shaw, 'Impressions of Family Life in a London Suburb', 184.
102 Peter Willmott, *The Evolution of a Community*, 29.
103 Ibid., 32–3 and J. M. Mogey, 'Changes in Family Life Experienced by English Workers Moving From the Slums to Housing Estates', 126.
104 Gillian C. Rose, 'Locality, Politics and Culture', 193.
105 Mark W. Hodges and Cyril S. Smith, 'The Sheffield Estate', in University of Liverpool Social Science Department, *Neighbourhood and Community*, 108.
106 Leo Kuper, 'Blueprint for Living Together', 50.
107 J. M. Mogey, 'Changes in Family Life Experienced by English Workers Moving From the Slums to Housing Estates', 126.
108 Ronald Goldman (ed.), *Breakthrough* (London, 1968), 2–3.
109 Peter Willmott, *The Evolution of a Community*, 27.
110 Ibid., 27.
111 J. M. Mogey, 'Changes in Family Life Experienced by English Workers Moving From the Slums to Housing Estates', 125 and 127.
112 'Mass Observation', *An Enquiry into People's Homes* (London, 1943), 173–4.
113 Peter Willmott, *The Evolution of a Community*, 64 and Michael Young and Peter Willmott, *Family and Kinship in East London*, 84.
114 Michael Young and Peter Willmott, *Family and Kinship in East London*, 148.
115 Gitta Meier, 'A Neighbourhood Study', *The Good Neighbour*, 2.6 (November 1950), 122–3.
116 'Mass Observation', *An Enquiry into People's Homes*, 208.
117 Madeline Kerr, *The People of Ship Street*, 101.
118 Ibid., 23–4 and 101–2.
119 Lulie A. Shaw, 'Impressions of Family Life in a London Suburb', 192–3.
120 'Mass Observation', *An Enquiry into People's Homes*, 191.
121 See the Bolton City Library Archives, Bolton County Council Papers, AK-6-83-1 and 3 – Applications 2 and 3. Spelling as in original.
122 'Mass Observation', *An Enquiry into People's Homes*, 185.
123 Ibid., 189.
124 B. M. Osbourne, *The Glasgow and North Lanarkshire Housing and New Towns Survey*, The Social Survey, new series 102 (April 1948).
125 Dennis Chapman, *A Social Survey of Middlesbrough. Part II. Attitudes to Middlesbrough*, and *Part III. Public Opinion in Relation to Planning and Housing in Middlesbrough*, The Social Survey, new series no. 50 (January 1950), 3 and 27–8.
126 Bertram Hutchinson, *Willesden and the New Towns*, 3–4.
127 Ibid., 2, 44, and 99–100. Nearly half of the housewives whose chief breadwinner earned up to £4 a week said they did not help their neighbours, compared with between 35 and 40 per cent of housewives with wealthier husbands; 83 per cent of

the poorer housewives would not visit neighbours, compared with between 68 and 75 per cent of wealthier housewives.

128 Letters to the Bolton Council, Application 3, AK-6-15-1, at Bolton City Council Archives.
129 W. White, *Life in a Court: How to Stop Neighbours' Quarrels*, 2.
130 Bolton Oral History Project, Tape no. 158a.
131 Peter Willmott, *The Evolution of a Community*, 79.
132 Faith Dorothy Osgerby, unpublished autobiography, entitled 'My Memoirs', in John Burnett (ed.), *Destiny Obscure* (Harmondsworth, 1982), 90; Kathleen Dayus, *Her People* (London, 1982), 76; Catherine Cookson, *Our Kate* (London, 1969), 22; Joyce Ayres, 'Memories of Bethnal Green 1935-1945', *East London Record*, 6 (1983), 3; Kathleen Price, *Looking Back* (Nottingham, 1980), 9; James Allen Bullock, *Bowers Row* (East Ardsley, 1976), 16; Mary Wade, *To the Miner Born* (Stocksfield, 1984), 10; Alice Linton, *Not Expecting Miracles* (London, 1982), 2; Grace Foakes, *My Part of the River* (London, 1974), 20.
133 Nancy Dobrin, *Happiness* (London, 1980), 32.
134 Grace Foakes, *My Part of the River*, 13.
135 Leo Kuper, 'Blueprint for Living Together', 46.
136 Harry Blacker, *Just Like It Was* (London, 1974), 165-6.
137 Peter Russell, *Butler Royal* (London, 1982), 13; Arthur Barton, *The Penny World* (London, 1969), 33-4 and 173; Harry Blacker, *Just Like It Was*, 163; E. R. Manley, *Meet the Miner* (Nr. Wakefield, 1947), 66.
138 Catherine Cookson, *Our Kate*, 117.
139 'Mass Observation', *People and Paints* (Slough, 1950), 42.
140 For examples of competition between women, see Louie Stride, *Memoirs of a Street Urchin* (Bath, 1984), 32.
141 Rose Neighbour, *All of Me* (London, 1979), 7.
142 Peter C. Vigor, *Memories are Made of This* (Luton, 1983), 8.
143 Ronald Goldman (ed.), *Breakthrough*, 148 and Louis Heren, *Growing Up Poor In London* (London, 1973), 49.
144 Charles Madge, 'Wartime Patterns of Saving and Spending', National Institute of Economic and Social Research, Occasional Papers IV (Cambridge, 1943), 77.
145 Doris M. Bailey, *Children of the Green* (London, 1981), 9.
146 Molly Weir, *Best Foot Forward* (Bath, 1979), 77. For a similar story, see Mary Wade, *To The Miner Born*, 44.
147 Max Bygraves, *I Wanna Tell You a Story!* (London, 1976), 28.
148 Catherine Cookson, *Our Kate*, 52.
149 James Allen Bullock, *Bowers Row*, 89.
150 H. J. Bennett, *I Was a Walworth Boy* (London, 1980), 23.
151 James Kirkup, *The Only Child* (London, 1957), 76-7. For very similar reminiscences, see James Allen Bullock, *Bowers Row*, 45-6.
152 Elsie Oman, *Salford Stepping Stones* (Swinton, 1983), 9; James Kirkup, *The Only Child*, 76-7; James Allen Bullock, *Bowers Row*, 45-6.
153 James Allen Bullock, *Bowers Row*, 45-6.
154 Henry Brown, *Them Days is Gone* (Sleaford, 1988), 24. Also see Charles Forman, *Industrial Town*, 144-5.
155 Tom Harrisson and Charles Madge, *Britain By Mass Observation* (London, 1986), 219.
156 Bolton Oral History Project, Tape no. 55b.
157 Leo Kuper, 'Blueprint for Living Together', 74-82.
158 Ibid., 18.
159 W. M. Williams, *The Sociology of an English Village: Gosforth*, 143.
160 John Blake, *Memories of Old Poplar*, 45-6.
161 Mark W. Hodges and Cyril S. Smith, 'The Sheffield Estate', in University of Liverpool Social Science Department, *Neighbourhood and Community*, 92.
162 Reginald Lee, *The Town That Died* (London, 1975), 33.

163 See Bolton City Library Archive, AK-6-60-9, 'Miners' Welfare Survey' 1947, for the Kearsley Urban District where it lists all community services. The services listed above were the only ones provided: in this mining area, there were no licensed bars, billiard halls, cinemas, ice rinks, reading rooms, swimming pools, golf courses, greyhound courses, or putting courses.
164 John Barron Mays, *Growing Up in the City*, 49–50.
165 Peter Willmott, *The Evolution of a Community*, 70.
166 Scottish Housing Advisory Committee, *The Housing of Special Groups* (Edinburgh, 1952), 66.
167 Mark W. Hodges and Cyril S. Smith, 'The Sheffield Estate', in University of Liverpool Social Science Department, *Neighbourhood and Community*, 120.
168 Ibid., 111.
169 Lillian Hine, 'A Poplar Childhood', *East London Record*, no. 3 (1980), 41.
170 Margaret E. Loane, *Englishman's Castle* (London, 1909), 57.
171 Mark W. Hodges and Cyril S. Smith, 'The Sheffield Estate', in University of Liverpool Social Science Department, *Neighbourhood and Community*, 108–9.
172 Peter Willmott, *The Evolution of a Community*, 59–60.
173 B. Seebohm Rowntree and May Kendall, *How the Labourer Lives* (London, 1917), 100.
174 E. Llewelyn Lewis, *The Children of the Unskilled* (London, 1924), 58.
175 For regional differences, see Stefan Muthesius, *The English Terraced House* (New Haven, 1982), 75–6.
176 John Cullen, aged 71, a labourer of Bailieborough (County Cavan), speaking to folklore collector P. J. Gaynor of Bailieborough, January 1948, 38–41, Irish Folklore Collection, MSS 1024.
177 Frank Deegan, *There's No Other Way* (Liverpool, 1980), 13.
178 Robert Roberts, *A Ragged Schooling* (Manchester, 1976), 53–4.
179 William Margrie (compiler), *The Poets of Peckham* (London, 1956), 38 and Howard Spring, *Heaven Lies About Us* (London, 1956), 12.
180 Dorothy Tildsley, *Remembrance*, 22. Also see Mary Craddock, *A North Country Maid* (London, 1960), 25; Harry Gibbs, '*Box On*' (London, 1981), 64.
181 Gracie Fields, *Sing As We Go* (London, 1960), 38. For other studies emphasizing the importance of local working-class identities, see J. Urry, 'Paternalism, Management and Localities', *Lancaster Regionalism Group. Working Paper No. 2* (Lancaster, 1980); D. Howell, *British Workers and the Independent Labour Party 1886–1906* (Manchester, 1983); D. Massey, *Spatial Divisions of Labour* (London, 1984); M. Savage, *The Dynamics of Working Class Politics* (Cambridge, 1987); and H. Wainwright, *Labour: A Tale of Two Parties* (London, 1987).
182 *The Island* (London, 1979), 55.
183 For example, see Reginald L. Lee, *The Town That Died*, 33–4.
184 Sarah Shears, *Tapioca for Tea* (London, 1971), 130–1.
185 James Allen Bullock, *Bowers Row*, 46.
186 Johnny Speight, *It Stands to Reason* (Walton-on-Thames, 1973), 23 and 25. Also see Sarah Shears, *Tapioca for Tea*, 131.
187 Evelyn Haythorne, *On Earth to Make the Numbers Up* (Pontefract, 1981), 8.
188 E. R. Manley, *Meet the Miner*, 63.
189 Geoffrey Gorer, *Exploring English Character*, 57.
190 Doris M. Bailey, *Children of the Green*, 6. For similar fights, see Nigel Gray, *The Worst of Times* (London, 1985), 13; Ian MacDougall (ed.), *Voices from the Hunger Marches*, vol. 1 (Edinburgh, 1990), 40; A. S. Neill, '*Neill! Neill! Orange Peel!*' (London, 1972), 19.
191 For examples of the tensions which develop when a man 'poaches' a woman from another district, see Edward Ezard, *Battersea Boy* (London, 1979), 30–1; Evelyn Haythorne, *On Earth to Make the Numbers Up*, 8; James Allen Bullock, *Bowers Row*, 85.
192 *The Island*, 41.

193 Dorothy Rockett, 'A Streatham Childhood in the Twenties', in *Two Streatham Childhoods* (London, 1980), 3.
194 Humphrey Jennings and Charles Madge (eds), *May the Twelfth* (London, 1937), 42–3 and 169.

6 NATION

1 Sir Thomas Browne (1605–1682).
2 M. E. Carrington, 'Stepney Memories', *East London Record*, no. 9 (1986), 4.
3 Louis Heren, *Growing Up Poor in London* (London, 1973), 103, 79, 13, and 59. Emphasis added.
4 Peter Boerner (ed.), *Concepts of National Identity* (Baden-Baden, 1986), his introduction, 14. For a defence of Boerner's position, see Alfred Fouillée, *Esquisse psychologique des peuples Européens* (Paris, 1903), 547. For other examples of books on British national identity which ignore either the working classes or regionalism, see A. Siegfried, *The Character of Peoples* (London, 1952); R. W. Emerson, *English Traits* (London, 1856); Alfred Leslie Rowse, *The English Spirit* (London, 1944); Ernest Barker, *National Character* (London, 1927); Ernest Barker (ed.), *The Character of England* (Oxford, 1947); Richard Faber, *High Road to England* (London, 1985); Ulf Hedetoft, *British Colonialism and Modern Identity* (Aalborg, 1985); Charles St Lawrence Duff, *England and the English* (London, 1954); T. H. Pear, *English Social Differences* (London, 1955); and G. Gorer, *Exploring English Character* (London, 1955).
5 *Daily Telegraph*, 7 May 1937, cited by Humphrey Jennings and Charles Madge (eds), *May the Twelfth* (London, 1937), 42.
6 Donald Read (ed.), *Edwardian England* (London, 1979), 363.
7 *Interdepartmental Committee on Physical Deterioration: Evidence*, H. C. 1904, 13–14, and Appendix 1.
8 Arnold White, *Efficiency and Empire* (London, 1901), 100.
9 R. S. Churchill, *Winston Spencer Churchill: Young Statesman* (London, 1967), 32.
10 W. H. Barrett, *A Fenman's Story* (London, 1965), 10.
11 C. Delisle Burns, 'National Prejudices and International Necessities', *The Listener*, 12 February 1930, 288.
12 Doris Langley Moore, *The Vulgar Heart* (London, 1945), 144.
13 Quoted in Paul Addison, *Road to 1945* (London, 1977).
14 For example, see Nikolaus Pevsner, *The Englishness of English Art* (Harmondsworth, 1978), 206.
15 Jim Wolveridge, *Ain't It Grand* (London, 1976), 59.
16 Humphrey Jennings and Charles Madge (eds), *May the Twelfth*, 143.
17 Geoffrey Gorer, 'Some Notes on the British Character', *Horizon*, xx, no. 120 (December 1949), 370.
18 Margaret Pease, *True Patriotism and Other Lessons on Peace and Internationalism* (London, 1911), 36–7.
19 Elizabeth K. Blackburn, *In and Out of Windows* (Burnley, 1980), 9.
20 Daniel Kirkwood, *My Life of Revolt* (London, 1935), 56–7; Louis Heren, *Growing Up Poor in London*, 13; J. B. Priestley, *Margin Released* (London, 1962), 7.
21 Barrie S. Morgan, 'Social Status Segregation in Comparative Perspective: The Case of the United Kingdom and the United States', University of London King's College, Occasional Paper 3, Department of Geography (October 1976).
22 Alexander Paterson, *Across the Bridges* (London, 1911), 269–70.
23 Benedict Anderson, *Imagined Communities* (London, 1983), 15.
24 Cited in John Fuller, *Popular Culture and Troop Morale in British and Dominion Forces in the First World War* (Oxford, 1990), 190.
25 *Report of the Board of Education*, H. C. 1886, 273. See the autobiographies of Mary Wade, *To the Miner Born* (Stocksfield, 1984), 57 and Winifred Foley, *A*

Child in the Forest (Bath, 1978), 136. However, the young labourer's daughter from Scotter, Lancashire, who said: 'I live in Scotter; it's in Lancashire. Don't know England nor London. I've been to school every year a little' might have been only slightly less ignorant than other children: Mr. Stanhope's report in *Commission on the Employment of Children, Young Persons and Women in Agriculture (1867). Appendix. Part II to the First Report. Evidence from the Assistant Commissioners* [4068-I], H. C. 1867-8, xvii, 297 and 535. Also see Edith Hall, *Canary Girls and Stockpots* (Luton, 1977), 23 and Louis Heren, *Growing Up Poor in London*, 57-8.

26　Mary Wade, *To the Miner Born*, 57-8.

27　Phyllis Willmott, *A Green Girl* (London, 1983), 10.

28　Elizabeth Fanshawe, *Penⱥ ull Memories* (Stafford, 1983), 2 and 11.

Շ 9　Cited in K. L. Little, *Negroes in Britain* (London, 1947), 217. Also see Sheila Patterson, *Dark Strangers* (Harmondsworth, 1965), 212.

30　Louis Heren, *Growing Up Poor in London*, 57-8.

31　Ralph Waldo Emerson, *English Traits*, 94. For an example of a historian making this sort of statement, see Raphael Samuel (ed.), *Patriotism*, vol. III (London, 1989), his introduction, xxv.

32　Cited in H. J. Hanham, *Scottish Nationalism* (London, 1969), 130.

33　Joost Augusteijn, 'The Importance of Being Irish: Ideas and the Volunteers in Mayo and Tipperary', in David Fitzpatrick (ed.), *Revolution? Ireland 1917-1923* (Dublin, 1990), 31.

34　Arthur Barton, *The Penny World* (London, 1969), 87-8 and 92.

35　William Gallacher, *Revolt on the Clyde* (London, 1949), 56. For an historical analysis of this strike, see Iain McLean, *The Legend of Red Clydeside* (Edinburgh, 1983).

36　See Bernard Waites, 'The Government of the Home Front and the "Moral Economy" of the Working Class', in Peter H. Liddle (ed.), *Home Fires and Foreign Fields* (London, 1985), 180.

37　Ken Howarth (ed.), *Dark Days* (Manchester, 1978), 85-6. Also see Elsie Gadsby, *Black Diamonds, Yellow Apples* (Ilkeston, 1978), 50.

38　Thomas H. Jones, *Fingers in the Sky* (Wembley, 1949).

39　Ken Howarth (ed.), *Dark Days*, 84-6.

40　Ibid., 82.

41　Nye Bevan in *Hansard*, 28 April 1944.

42　Mass Observation Archive, File FR 1924, Woman 2906, on whether strikes should be allowed in War Industries.

43　Richard Price, *An Imperial War and the British Working Class* (London, 1972), 231.

44　'A South African Trip', *Club Life*, 4 May 1901, 1, cited in Richard Price, *An Imperial War and the British Working Class*, 231-2. Also see William Gallacher, *Revolt on the Clyde*, 18-19.

45　Colonel A. C. T. White, *The Story of Army Education 1643-1963* (London, 1963), 43.

46　Ibid., 74.

47　Ibid., 74.

48　M. D. Blanch, 'British Society and the War', in Peter Warwick (ed.), *The South African War* (Harlow, 1980), 215.

49　B. S. Johnson, *All Bull* (London, 1973), 3, 14 and 289.

50　Jimmy Reid, *Reflections of a Clyde-Built Man* (London, 1976), 27-8.

51　Cited in Sidney Jacobs, 'Race, Empire and the Welfare State: Council Housing and Racism', *Critical Social Policy*, 13 (Summer 1985), 11.

52　Evelyn Haythorne, *On Earth to Make the Numbers Up* (Pontefract, 1981), 37 and George Henry Hewins, *The Dillen* (London, 1981), 57.

53　George Scott, *Time and Place* (London, 1956), 90.

54　David Morgan, '*It Will Make a Man of You*' (Manchester, 1987), 50-1.

55　Marjory Todd, *Snakes and Ladders* (London, 1960), 57-8.

56 Chris Cook and John Stevenson, *The Longman Handbook of Modern British History* (London, 1983), 201–2.
57 Stephen Reynolds and Bob and Tom Woolley, *Seems So! A Working-Class View of Politics* (London, 1911), xvii.
58 Dr Harry Roberts, 'The East-Ender's Point of View', *Listener*, 16 December 1931, 1063.
59 Valerie Chancellor, *History for Their Masters* (Bath, 1970), 137.
60 W. H. Webb, 'History, Patriotism and the Child', *History*, 2.1 (1913), 54.
61 See Valerie E. Chancellor, *History for Their Masters*, especially 112–38 and M. D. Blanch, 'British Society and the War', especially 212–13.
62 For an analysis, see S. Humphries, ' "Hurrah for England": Schooling and the Working Class in Bristol, 1870–1914', *Southern History*, 1 (1979), 171–207.
63 Peter C. Vigor, *Memories are Made of This* (Luton, 1983), 59.
64 Ibid., 59.
65 Elizabeth Fanshawe, *Penkhull Memories*, 10; Lilian Slater, *Think On! Said Many* (Swinton, 1984), 30–1; Louis Heren, *Growing Up Poor in London*, 10–11.
66 Eileen Green, Sandra Hebron and Diana Woodward, *Women's Leisure, What Leisure?* (London, 1990), 48–9 and Asa Briggs, *Mass Entertainment* (Adelaide, 1960), 18.
67 *An Ordinary Lot*, written collectively (Leeds, 1985), 5.
68 Ibid., 5.
69 Stuart Laing, *Representations of Working-Class Life 1957–1964* (London, 1986), 109–10.
70 See Paddy Scannell and David Cardiff, *A Social History of British Broadcasting* (Oxford, 1991) and Raymond Williams, *Television, Technology, and Cultural Form* (London, 1974), 21.
71 James Walvin, *Beside the Seaside* (London, 1978), 137–8.
72 Eileen Green, Sandra Hebron and Diana Woodward, *Women's Leisure, What Leisure?*, 49. For examples in working-class autobiographies of the inter-war period, see Dorothy Tildsley, *Remembrance* (Swinton, 1985), 13; Jo Barnes, *Arthur and Me* (Bristol, 1979), 29–31; Jim Wolveridge, *Ain't It Grand*, 52; Kathlyn Davenport, *My Preston Yesterdays* (Swinton, 1984), 32; Arthur Potts, *Whitsters Lane* (Swinton, 1985), 38.
73 Paddy Scannell and David Cardiff, *A Social History of British Broadcasting*, 277.
74 Humphrey Jennings and Charles Madge (eds), *May the Twelfth*, 7.
75 Felix Greene (ed.), *Time to Spare* (London, 1935), 116.
76 Humphrey Jennings and Charles Madge (eds), *May the Twelfth*, 12.
77 John C. W. Reith, *Broadcasting Over Britain* (London, 1924), 15.
78 Eric Midwinter, *Fair Game* (London, 1986), 108 and Stuart Laing, *Representations of Working-Class Life 1957–1964*, 141–2.
79 Morag Shiach, *Discourse on Popular Culture* (Cambridge, 1989), 176.
80 Kirsten Drotner, *English Children and Their Magazines 1751–1945* (New Haven, 1988), 199.
81 Mary Wade, *To the Miner Born*, 109–10 and Kathlyn Davenport, *My Preston Yesterdays*, 32.
82 Humphrey Jennings and Charles Madge (eds), *May the Twelfth*, 317.
83 'Mass Observation', *The Voters' Choice* (London, 1950), 4.
84 John Osmond, *The Divided Kingdom* (London, 1988), 123–4.
85 For a more detailed analysis, see Keith Robbins, 'The Grubby Wreck of Old Glories: The United Kingdom and the End of the British Empire', *Journal of Contemporary History*, 15 (1980), 91.
86 Charles W. J. Withers, *Gaelic in Scotland* (Edinburgh, 1984), 238.
87 See Bryan S. Turner, 'Marginal Politics, Cultural Identities and the Clergy in Scotland', *International Journal of Sociology and Social Policy*, 1.1 (1981), 94–5 and Charles W. J. Withers, *Gaelic in Scotland*.
88 Anne O'Dowd, *Spalpeens and Tattie Hokers* (Blackrock, 1991), 73.

89 Gisela C. Lebzelter, 'Anti-Semitism – A Focal Point for the British Radical Right', in Paul Kennedy and Anthony Nicholls (eds), *Nationalist and Racialist Movements in Britain and Germany Before 1914* (London, 1981), 89–90.

90 See the excellent book on these workers: Diana Kay and Robert Miles, *Refugees or Migrant Workers? European Volunteer Workers in Britain 1946-1951* (London, 1992).

91 Alan Sinfield, *Literature, Politics and Culture in Postwar Britain* (Oxford, 1989), 126.

92 'Report on Investigation into Conditions of the Coloured Colonial Men in a Stepney Area', 1944–45, in PRO CO 876/39.

93 *Jewish Chronicle*, 2 April 1926, 21.

94 Cited in Steve Cohen, 'Anti-Semitism, Immigration Controls and the Welfare State', *Critical Social Policy*, 13 (1985), 76.

95 *Jewish Chronicle*, 24 June 1910.

96 Steve Cohen, 'Anti-Semitism, Immigration Controls and the Welfare State', 81.

97 J. Bush, *Behind the Lines* (London, 1984), 170–3.

98 'Justitia', 'The Alien in Our Midst: The Bondage of the East End', in Douglas Halliday Macartney, *Boy Welfare* (London, 1917), 30–1.

99 Richard A. Voeltz, 'A Good Jew and a Good Englishman: The Jewish Lads' Brigade, 1894–1922', *Journal of Contemporary History*, 23.1 (1988), 120.

100 Steve Cohen, 'Anti-Semitism, Immigration Controls and the Welfare State', 87.

101 Jacqueline Bhabha, Francesca Klug and Sue Shutter, *Worlds Apart: Women Under Immigration and Nationality Law* (London, 1985).

102 Gisela C. Lebzelter, 'Anti-Semitism – A Focal Point for the British Radical Right', 95 and *Easter Post*, 2 November 1901, cited in Steve Cohen, 'Anti-Semitism, Immigration Controls and the Welfare State', 79.

103 Mosley, 'Fascism is not Anti-Semitic', *Jewish Economic Forum*, 1.9, 28 July 1933, 3 and *Blackshirt*, 30 September 1933, 1.

104 *Blackshirt*, 2 November 1934, 1–2.

105 D. S. Lewis, *Mosley, Fascism and British Society 1931-81* (Manchester, 1987), 107.

106 Richard Thurlow, *Fascism in Britain* (Oxford, 1987), 122.

107 *Cavalcade*, 13 November 1937.

108 Quoted by John D. Brewer, *Mosley's Men* (Aldershot, 1984), 9.

109 Tom Gallagher, *Glasgow* (Manchester, 1987), 153 and 155.

110 Steve Cohen, 'Anti-Semitism, Immigration Controls and the Welfare State', 76–7.

111 Anthony Richmond, *Migration and Race Relations in an English City* (London, 1973), 62 and 127.

112 Lilian Slater, *Think On! Said Many*, 52.

113 Sam Clarke, *An East End Cabinet-Maker* (London, 1983), 13.

114 Sheila Patterson, *Dark Strangers*, 317.

115 *Jewish Chronicle*, 23 October 1936, 8.

116 *The Circle*, December 1934, 5.

117 'Mass Observation', 'Anti-Semitism', *Mass Observation Reprint*, 1.23 (May 1951), 1.

118 Tony Kushner, *The Persistence of Prejudice* (Manchester, 1989), 53.

119 Lieutenant-Colonel A. H. Lane, *The Alien Menace* (London, 1928), 37.

120 Andrew Dewar Gibb, *Scotland in Eclipse* (London, 1930), 55. For statistics on crime, see David Fitzpatrick, 'A Curious Middle Place', in Roger Swift and Sheridan Gilley (eds), *The Irish in Britain* (London, 1989), 25–6.

121 Sir E. J. Russell, 'Introduction', in Alan G. Ogilvie (ed.), *Great Britain* (Cambridge, 1928), xxx.

122 Tom Gallagher, *Glasgow*, 28–9.

123 Ernest Marke, *In Troubled Waters* (London, 1986), 26.

124 Lieutenant-Colonel A. H. Lane, *The Alien Menace*, 25.

125 *Listener*, 5 February 1930, 260, letter from A. J. MacGregor of Ottery St Mary.

126 Keith Sword, Norman Davies and Jan Ciechanowski, *The Formation of the Polish Community in Great Britain 1939–50* (London, 1989), 381.
127 Walter Southgate, *That's the Way it Was* (London, 1982), 33–4.
128 Anthony Richmond, *Migration and Race Relations in an English City*, 62 and 127.
129 Cited in Bernard Gainer, *The Alien Invasion* (London, 1972), 42. Also see pages 36–59.
130 Walter Southgate, *That's the Way it Was*, 33.
131 *Hansard*, 29 January 1902, cited in Steve Cohen, 'Anti-Semitism, Immigration Controls and the Welfare State', 74. Also see B. Smithies and P. Fiddick, *Enoch Powell on Immigration* (London, 1969), 40.
132 Lieutenant-Colonel A. H. Lane, *The Alien Menace*, 36–7.
133 Cited in Paul Rich, 'The Politics of Race and Segregation in British Cities With Reference to Birmingham, 1945–76', in Susan J. Smith and John Mercer (eds), *New Perspectives on Race and Housing in Britain* (Glasgow, 1987), 98. Also see Elaine R. Smith, 'Jewish Responses to Political Anti-Semitism and Fascism in the East End of London 1920–1939', in Tony Kushner and Kenneth Lunn (eds), *Traditions of Intolerance* (Manchester, 1989), 80.
134 For examples, see Sidney Jacobs, 'Race, Empire and the Welfare State: Council Housing and Racism', 20.
135 John Rex, 'Race in the Inner City', in *Five Views of Multi-Racial Britain* (London, 1978), 13–14.
136 Cited in Elaine R. Smith, 'Jewish Responses to Political Anti-Semitism and Fascism in the East End of London 1920–1939', 113.
137 Ibid., 93.
138 Sheila Patterson, *Dark Strangers*, 159.
139 Ibid., 159.
140 Elaine R. Smith, 'Jewish Responses to Political Anti-Semitism and Fascism in the East End of London 1920–1939', 52 and 93.
141 M. Boddy, *The Building Societies* (London, 1980), 69.
142 W. W. Daniel, *Racial Discrimination in Britain* (Harmondsworth, 1968), 154.
143 Elaine R. Smith, 'Jewish Responses to Political Anti-Semitism and Fascism in the East End of London 1920–1939', 81–2.
144 *Hansard*, 22 November 1917.
145 *Hansard*, 19 September 1949.
146 Ralph L. Finn, *Spring in Aldgate* (London, 1968), 16.
147 Cited in Kevin O'Connor, *The Irish in Britain* (London, 1972), 73–4.
148 Chaim Bermont, *Coming Home* (London, 1976), 62–3.
149 Anthony Richmond, 'Immigration as a Social Process: The Case of Coloured Colonials in the United Kingdom', *Social and Economic Studies*, 5.2 (1956), 190.
150 Neil Evans, 'The South Wales Race Riots of 1919', *Llafur*, iii.1 (1980), 2.
151 Diana Kay and Robert Miles, *Refugees or Migrant Workers? European Volunteer Workers in Britain 1946–1951*, 169–70.
152 Alexander Hartog, *Born to Sing* (London, 1978), 19, 58–62 and 77–9.
153 Miranda Chaytor, 'Martyrs of Class', in Raphael Samuel (ed.), *Patriotism*, vol. II, 39.
154 Tom Harrisson and Charles Madge (arranged and written by), *Britain by Mass Observation* (London, 1986), 217.

Bibliography

Contents of bibliography:

AUTOBIOGRAPHIES AND ORAL HISTORIES

Ackland, Eleanor, *Good-Bye for the Present: The Story of Two Childhoods* (London, 1935).

An Ordinary Lot: Recollections of the 1930s and World War II, written collectively (Leeds, 1985).

Anderson, George, *Down the Mine at Twelve* (Hamilton, 1985).

Ayres, Joyce, 'Memories of Bethnal Green 1935–1945', *East London Record*, no. 6 (1983).

Bailey, Doris M., *Children of the Green: A True Story of Childhood in Bethnal Green 1922–1937* (London, 1981).

Barnes, Jo, *Arthur and Me: Docker's Children* (Bristol, 1979).

Barnes, Ron, *Coronation Cups and Jam Jars: A Portrait of an East End Family Through Three Generations* (London, 1976).

Barrett, W. H., *A Fenman's Story* (London, 1965).

Barton, Arthur, *Two Lamps in Our Street: A Time Remembered* (London, 1967).

Barton, Arthur, *The Penny World: A Boyhood Recalled* (London, 1969).

Battye, Louis, *I Had a Little Nut Tree* (London, 1959).

Beales, H. L. and R. S. Lambert (eds), *Memoirs of the Unemployed* (London, 1934).

Behan, Kathleen, *Mother of all Behans: The Autobiography of Kathleen Behan* (London, 1985).

Bell, Maureen, *Portwood Girl: A Forties Childhood* (Stockport, 1987).

Bellam, Joan, *Them Days* (Padstow, 1982).

Bennett, H. J., *I Was a Walworth Boy* (London, 1980).

Bermont, Chaim, *Coming Home* (London, 1976).

Blackburn, Elizabeth K., *In and Out of Windows: A Story of the Changes in Working-Class Life 1902–1977 in a Small East Lancashire Community* (Burnley, 1980).

Blacker, Harry, *Just Like It Was: Memoirs of the Mittel East* (London, 1974).

Blake, John, *Memories of Old Poplar* (London, 1977).

Boyle, Jimmy, *A Sense of Freedom* (Long Preston, 1988).

Brown, Henry, *Them Days is Gone* (Sleaford, 1988).

Brown, Margaret, 'Reminiscences of My Childhood, 1896–1910', Coventry Record Office, n.d.

Brown, Winifred, *Under Six Planets* (London, 1955).

Bryson, Elizabeth, *Look Back in Wonder* (Dundee, 1966).

Bullard, Sir Reader, *The Camels Must Go: An Autobiography* (London, 1961).

Bullock, James Allen, *Bowers Row: Recollections of a Mining Village* (East Ardsley, 1976).

Burnett, John (ed.), *Destiny Obscure: Autobiographies of Childhood, Education and Family from the 1820s to the 1920s* (Harmondsworth, 1982).

Bygraves, Max, *I Wanna Tell You a Story!* (London, 1976).

Cardus, Neville, *Autobiography* (London, 1955), first pub. 1947.

Carrington, M. E., 'Stepney Memories', *East London Record*, no. 9 (1986).

Chamberlain, Mary, *Fenwomen: A Portrait of Women in an English Village* (London, 1975).

Church, Richard, *Over the Bridge: An Essay in Autobiography* (London, 1955).

Clarke, Sam, *An East End Cabinet-Maker* (London, 1983).

Common, Jack, *Seven Shifts* (London, 1938).

Cook, George A., *A Hackney Memory Chest* (London, 1983).

Cookson, Catherine, *Our Kate* (London, 1969).

Coombes, B. L., *These Poor Hands* (London, 1939).

Cooper, Bob, *Early to Rise: A Sussex Boyhood* (London, 1976).

Craddock, Mary, *A North Country Maid* (London, 1960).

Crozier, F. P., *A Brass Hat in No-Man's Land* (London, 1930).

Davenport, Kathlyn, *My Preston Yesterdays* (Swinton, 1984).

Davies, Celia, *Clean Clothes on Sunday* (Lavenham, 1974).

Dayus, Kathleen, *Her People* (London, 1982).

Deegan, Frank, *There's No Other Way* (Liverpool, 1980).

Delderfield, D. F., *Bird's Eye View* (London, 1954).

Dobrin, Nancy, *Happiness: A Twinge of Conscience is a Glimpse of God* (London, 1980).

Durham 'Strong Words' Collective (eds), *But the World Goes on the Same: Changing Times in Durham Pit Mines* (Whitley Bay, 1979).

Edwards, George, *From Crow-Scaring to Westminster: An Autobiography* (London, 1922).

Edwards, Wil Jon, *From the Valley I Came* (London, 1956).

Edwin, John, *I'm Going – What Then?* (Bognor Regis, 1978).

England, Daisy, *Daisy Daisy* (London, 1981).

Ezard, Edward, *Battersea Boy* (London, 1979).

Fanshawe, Elizabeth, *Penkhull Memories* (Stafford, 1983).

Field, Dick, *Up and Down the Valley* (Cirencester, 1985).

Fields, Gracie, *Sing As We Go: The Autobiography of Gracie Fields* (London, 1960).

Finn, Ralph L., *Spring in Aldgate* (London, 1968).

Fish, Angus, *The Family Chatton* (Manchester, 1983).

Fletcher, Peter, *The Long Sunday* (London, 1958).

Foakes, Grace, *Between High Walls* (London, 1972).

Foakes, Grace, *My Part of the River* (London, 1974).

Foley, Winifred, *A Child in the Forest* (Bath, 1978).

Forman, Charles, *Industrial Town: Self Portrait of St Helens in the 1920s* (London, 1978).

Forrester, Helen, *By the Waters of Liverpool* (London, 1981).

Gadsby, Elsie, *Black Diamonds, Yellow Apples: A Working-Class Derbyshire Childhood Between the Wars* (Ilkeston, 1978).

Gallacher, William, *Revolt on the Clyde: An Autobiography* (London, 1949).

Gamble, Rose, *Chelsea Child* (Bath, 1980).

Gibbs, Harry, *'Box On'. The Autobiography of Harry Gibbs* (London, 1981).

Gibney, Josephine, *Joe McGarrigle's Daughter* (Kineton, 1977).

Gill, Eric, *Autobiography* (London, 1944).

Glencross, Emily, *Breakfast at Windsor: Memories of a Salford Childhood 1914–1928* (Swinton, 1983).

Goldman, Ronald (ed.), *Breakthrough: Autobiographical Account of the Education of Some Socially Disadvantaged Children* (London, 1968).

Goodwin, Jack, *Myself and My Boxers* (London, 1924).

Gordon, Isaac, *It Can Happen* (London, 1985).

Graham, Marjorie, *Love, Dears!* (London, 1980).

Gray, Nigel, *The Worst of Times: An Oral History of the Great Depression in Britain* (London, 1985).

Green, Alfred, *Growing Up in Attercliffe* (Sheffield, 1981).

Greene, Felix (ed.), *Time to Spare: What Unemployment Means, by Seven Unemployed* (London, 1935).

Hall, Edith, *Canary Girls and Stockpots* (Luton, 1977).

Harding, Arthur (edited by Raphael Samuel), *East End Underworld* (London, 1981).

Harris, Mollie, *A Kind of Magic: An Oxfordshire Childhood in the 1920s* (Oxford, 1985).

Harrocks, Bill, *Reminiscences of Bolton* (Swinton, 1984).

Hartog, Alexander, *Born to Sing* (London, 1978).

Harvey, Bessie, 'Youthful Memories of my Life in a Suffolk Village', *Suffolk Review*, 2 (September 1960).

Haythorne, Evelyn, *On Earth to Make the Numbers Up* (Pontefract, 1981).

Heaton, Richard, *Salford: My Home Town* (Swinton, 1983).

Heren, Louis, *Growing Up Poor In London* (London, 1973).

Hewins, George Henry, *The Dillen* (London, 1981).

Hill, Archie, *An Empty Glass* (London, 1984).

Hine, Lillian, 'A Poplar Childhood', *East London Record*, no. 3 (1980).

Hitchin, George, *Pit-Yacker* (London, 1962).

Hoare, Nellie, *A Winton Story* (Bournemouth, 1982).

Hobbs, May, *Born to Struggle* (London, 1973).

Hooley, Jim, *A Hillgate Childhood, Myself When Young* (Stockport, 1981).

Howarth, Ken (ed.), *Dark Days: Memories of the Lancashire and Cheshire Coalmining Industry* (Manchester, 1978).

Howlett, John, *The Guv'nor* (London, 1973).

'H. S. G.', *Autobiography of a Manchester Cotton Manufacturer* (London, 1887).

Hukin, Annie, 'Some Memories of the Early 1900s' (1974), in Alice Foley Collection, Bolton City Library Archives.

The Island: The Life and Death of an East London Community 1870-1970 (London, 1979).

'James, Nora', *A Derbyshire Life* (South Normanton, 1981).

Jasper, Albert S., *A Hoxton Childhood* (London, 1969).

Jobson, Allan, *The Creeping Hours of Time: An Autobiography of Allan Jobson* (London, 1977).

Johnson, B. S., *All Bull: The National Servicemen* (London, 1973).

Johnson, Isaac C., *Autobiography* (London, 1912).

Jones, Thomas H., *Fingers in the Sky: A Miner's Life Story* (Wembley, 1949).

Kirkup, James, *The Only Child: An Autobiography of Infancy* (London, 1957).

Kirkwood, Daniel, *My Life of Revolt* (London, 1935).

Knight, Sid, *Cotswold Lad* (London, 1960).

Langdon, Roger, *The Life of Roger Langdon Told By Himself* (London, 1909).

Lansbury, G., *My Life* (London, 1928).

Lansbury, G., *Looking Backwards - and Forwards* (London, 1935).

Lawson, Jack, *A Man's Life* (London, 1932).

Lee, Reginald, *The Town That Died* (London, 1975).

Leech, Kenneth, *Struggle in Babylon* (London, 1988).

Levinson, Maurice, *The Trouble With Yesterday* (London, 1946).

Linton, Alice, *Not Expecting Miracles* (London, 1982).

MacDougall, Ian (ed.), *Voices from the Hunger Marches: Personal Recollections by Scottish Hunger Marchers of the 1920s and 1930s* (Edinburgh, 1990).

McGovern, John, *Neither Fear Nor Favour* (London, 1960).

Manley, E. R., *Meet the Miner* (Nr Wakefield, 1947).

Marke, Ernest, *In Troubled Waters* (London, 1986).

Martin, Basil Kingsley, *Father Figures* (London, 1966).

Martin, Ernest, *The Best Street in Rochdale* (Rochdale, 1985).

Mitchell, Hannah, *The Hard Way Up* (London, 1968).

Morgan, David, *'It Will Make a Man of You': Notes on National Service, Masculinity, and Autobiography* (Manchester, 1987).

Neighbour, Rose, *All of Me: The True Story of a London Rose* (London, 1979).

Neill, A. S., *'Neill! Neill! Orange Peel!'. A Personal View of 90 Years* (London, 1972).

Oman, Elsie, *Salford Stepping Stones* (Swinton, 1983).

O'Mara, Pat, *The Autobiography of a Liverpool Irish Slummy* (London, 1972), first pub. 1934.

O'Reilly, 'Tiger', *The Tiger of the Legion* (London, 1936).

Pearson, Kay, *Life in Hull from Then Till Now* (London, 1980).
Pollitt, Harry, *Serving My Time: An Apprenticeship to Politics* (London, 1940).
Potter, Charlie, *On the Tramp in the 1930s* (Nottingham, 1983).
Potts, Arthur, *Whitsters Lane: Recollections of Pendleton and the Manchester Cotton Trade* (Swinton, 1985).
Powell, Margaret, *My Children and I* (London, 1977).
Price, Kathleen, *Looking Back* (Nottingham, 1980).
Priestley, J. B., *Margin Released: A Writer's Reminiscences and Reflections* (London, 1962).
Reid, Jimmy, *Reflections of a Clyde-Built Man* (London, 1976).
Ring, Elizabeth, *Up the Cockneys!* (London, 1975).
Roberts, Robert, *A Ragged Schooling: Growing Up in the Classic Slum* (Manchester, 1976).
Rockett, Dorothy, 'A Streatham Childhood in the Twenties', in *Two Streatham Childhoods* (London, 1980).
Rodaway, Angela, *A London Childhood* (Bath, 1985).
Rogers, S. A. B., *Four Acres and a Donkey* (London, 1979).
Russell, Peter, *Butler Royal* (London, 1982).
Sarsby, Jacqueline, *Missuses and Mouldrunners: An Oral History of Women Pottery Workers at Work and at Home* (Milton Keynes, 1988).
Scannell, Dorothy, *Mother Knows Best: An East End Childhood* (Bath, 1974).
Scott, George, *Time and Place* (London, 1956).
Sharman, Nancy, *Nothing to Steal: The Story of a Southampton Childhood* (London, 1977).
Shears, Sarah, *Tapioca for Tea: Memories of a Kentish Childhood* (London, 1971).
Short, Edward, *I Knew My Place* (London, 1983).
Slade, Eileen, *Middle Child: The Autobiography of Eileen Slade* (Andover, 1979).
Slater, Lilian, *Think On! Said Many: A Childhood in Bradford, Manchester 1911–1919* (Swinton, 1984).
Southgate, Walter, *That's the Way it Was: A Working Class Autobiography 1890–1950* (London, 1982).
Speight, Johnny, *It Stands to Reason: A Kind of Autobiography* (Walton-on-Thames, 1973).
Spring, Howard, *Heaven Lies About Us* (London, 1956).
Stride, Louie, *Memoirs of a Street Urchin* (Bath, 1984).
Teal, Gladys, *Grasp the Nettle* (Leeds, c.1980).
Tildsley, Dorothy, *Remembrance: Recollections of a Wartime Childhood in Swinton* (Swinton, 1985).
Todd, Marjory, *Snakes and Ladders: An Autobiography* (London, 1960).
Toole, Joseph, *Fighting Through Life* (London, 1935).
Turner, Ben, *About Myself, 1863–1930* (London, 1930).
Vigor, Peter C., *Memories are Made of This* (Luton, 1983).
Vose, John D., *Diary of a Tramp* (St Ives, 1981).
Waddington, William, *Rossendale Reflections* (Rossendale, 1983).
Wade, Mary, *To the Miner Born* (Stocksfield, 1984).

Walker, Ted, *The High Path* (London, 1982).
Walsh, Jane, *Not Like This* (London, 1953).
Ward, Wally, 'Fit For Anything: Early Days', *Bristol Writes*, 1 (1982).
Weir, Molly, *Best Foot Forward* (Bath, 1979).
Welch, Charles, *An Autobiography* (Banstead, 1960).
Westwater, T. A., *The Early Life of T. A. Westwater: Railway Signalman, Trade Unionist and Town Councillor in County Durham* (Oxford, 1979).
Wharton, Margaret, *Recollections of a G. I. War Bride: A Wiltshire Childhood* (Gloucester, 1984).
Whittaker, James, *I, James Whittaker* (London, 1934).
Wigby, Frederick C., *Just a Country Boy* (Wymondham, 1976).
Willis, Ted, *Whatever Happened to Tom Mix? The Story of One of My Lives* (London, 1970).
Willmott, Phyllis, *Growing Up in a London Village* (London, 1979).
Willmott, Phyllis, *A Green Girl* (London, 1983).
Wincott, Len, *Invergordon Mutineer* (London, 1974).
Wolveridge, Jim, *Ain't It Grand (Or This Was Stepney)* (London, 1976).
Wood, Ernest Egerton, *Is This Theosophy?* (London, 1936).

MANUSCRIPTS AND TYPESCRIPTS

Bolton City Library Archives, Oral History Tapes.
Bolton City Library Archive, AK-6-60-9, 'Miners' Welfare Survey' (1947).
Bolton County Borough Papers, General Correspondence, ABCF-9-60.
Bolton County Council Papers for the 1920s, in the Bolton City Library Archives, AK-6-83-1.
Colonial Office Papers, 'Report on Investigation into Conditions of the Coloured Colonial Men in a Stepney Area', 1944–45, in P.R.O. CO 876/39.
Department of Education Papers, P.R.O. (Kew) HO.45-9839 1310432, Shipmasters' Society and the Commission of Council on Education, April 1891; Committee of Management of the National Training School for Cookery, 16 February 1904, 205-7, P.R.O. (Kew) ED.164-3; Committee of Management of the National Training School for Cookery, 4 April 1911, no page number, P.R.O. (Kew) ED.164-4; Rowland, 'Wales (With Monmouthshire) Domestic Subjects', P.R.O. (Kew) ED.92-10.
Fallon, Jack, memoirs in typescript at the Ulster Folk and Transport Museum G4-1-15, 15 March 1976.
Family Planning Association, 'Medical Newsletter', all issues.
Foley, Alice, Collection, Bolton City Library Archives ZFO-17, 'Married Women Weavers. Are They Surplus to Industry?', typescript, no date.
Foley, Alice, 'Shift Working in Cotton Mills. A Woman's Point of View', typescript article, n.d., Alice Foley Collection, Bolton City Library Archives, ZFO-5.
Folklore Archive, University College Dublin, MSS McCarthy, 62 years, January 1938, 228, MSS.
Hukin, Mrs Annie, 'Some Memories of the Early 1900s' (1974), 3, in Alice Foley Collection, Bolton City Library Archives.

PERIODICALS AND NEWSPAPERS CONSULTED FOR A SERIES OF YEARS

Blackshirt, 30 September 1933 and 1934.
Cavalcade, 13 November 1937.
Christian World, 1901–1905.
Circle, December 1934.
Daily Herald, 1919, 1922, 1925, 1928, 1931, 1934, 1936.
Daily Mirror, 25 June 1945.
Economic Journal, xix, no. 75, September 1909.
English Review, 1916.
Health and Strength Annual, all issues.
Houses: Hovels or Homes? A Journal of Housing in the East End, all issues.
Housewife, all issues.
Jewish Chronicle, 2 April 1926.
Jewish Chronicle, 24 June 1910 and 1936.
Jewish Economic Forum, 1.9, 28 July 1933.
Listener, 5 February 1930.
Manual Training: A Review of School Handiwork and Practical Education, all issues.
New Society, 1962.
Socialist Review, 24, 1924.
Women and Progress, all issues.

BOOKS, PAMPHLETS, AND ARTICLES PUBLISHED PRIOR TO 1970

Able-Smith, B. and P. Townsend, *The Poor and the Poorest* (London, 1965).
Abrams, Mark, *Teenage Consumer Spending in 1959* (London, 1959).
Anon., *Health Culture for Busy Men* (London, 1912).
Anon., *How To Develop Strong Muscular Arms* (London, 1962).
Anon., *How To Gain Five Inches Chest Expansion* (Burnley, 1960).
Anon., *The Love Book* (Dundee, 1911).
Anon., *The Muscles of the Body: Their Uses and Development* (London, 1908).
Anon., *The Muscles of the Body and How to Develop Them* (London, 1942).
Arensberg, C. M. and S. T. Kimball, *Family and Community in Ireland* (Cambridge, Mass., 1940).
Ashby, Arthur W., *Allotments and Small Holdings in Oxfordshire* (Oxford, 1917).
Aston, Edward, *How To Develop Massive Arms* (London, 1937).
Aston, Edward, *How To Develop a Powerful Grip* (London, 1946).
Baker, Peter, 'The Great Disillusion', *New Generation*, no. 2 (Winter 1947).
Bakke, E. Wight, *The Unemployed Man: A Social Study* (London, 1933).
Barker, Ernest, *National Character and the Factors in its Formation* (London, 1927).
Barker, Ernest (ed.), *The Character of England* (Oxford, 1947).
Barlow, Sir Thomas, *The Incidence of Venereal Diseases and its Relation to School Life and School Teaching* (London, 1917).

Baron, Barclay, *The Growing Generation: A Study of Working Boys and Girls in Our Cities* (London, 1911).

Bayly, Mrs, *Home Rule: An Old Mother's Letter to Parents* (London, 1886).

Benson, Margaret, 'The Political Economy of Women's Liberation', *Monthly Review* (September 1969).

Beveridge, Sir William, *Changes in Family Life* (London, 1932).

Board of Education. General Report on the Teaching of Domestic Subjects to Public Elementary School Children in England and Wales, by the Chief Woman Inspector of the Board of Education (London, 1912).

Booth, Charles, 'Occupations of the People of the UK, 1801–1881', *Journal of the Royal Statistical Society*, xlix (1886).

Bowley, A. L., *Wages and Income in the United Kingdom Since 1860* (Cambridge, 1937).

Bransby, E. R. and Barbara Osbourne, 'A Social and Food Survey of the Elderly, Living Alone or in Married Couples', *British Journal of Nutrition*, 7 (1953).

Bray, Reginald A., 'The Apprenticeship Question', *Economic Journal*, xix.75 (September 1909).

Briggs, Asa, *Mass Entertainment: The Origins of a Modern Industry* (Adelaide, 1960).

Briggs, Asa, 'The Language of "Class" in Eearly Nineteenth Century England', in Asa Briggs and John Seville (eds), *Essays in Labour History* (London, 1967).

British Institute of Public Opinion, *The Beveridge Report and the Public* (London, 1944).

Buckpitt, Lilian K., 'For the Sake of the Child', *The Child*, II (1912).

Burns, C. Delisle, 'National Prejudices and International Necessities', *The Listener* (12 February 1930).

Burns, Tom, 'Social Development in New Neighbourhoods', *Pilot Papers. Social Essays and Documents*, 2.4 (December 1947).

Burt, Cyril, *The Young Delinquent* (London, 1925).

Calder, Fanny L., 'The Training of Teachers in Cookery', *Journal of Education* (1 December 1894).

Cameron, Mary Lovett, 'How To Train Housewives', *Journal of Education* (February 1898).

Catholic Church, *Joint Pastoral Letter of the Hierarchy of England and Wales on the Catholic Attitude to Sex Education. April 1944* (London, 1944).

Chapman, Dennis, *The Location of Dwellings in Scottish Towns*, Wartime Social Survey, new series no. 34 (September 1943).

Chapman, Dennis, *Sound in Dwellings*, Wartime Social Survey, new series Region S6 (November 1943).

Chapman, Dennis, *A Social Survey of Middlesbrough*, part iv (London, 1945).

Chapman, Dennis, *A Social Survey of Middlesbrough: Part II. Attitudes to Middlesbrough, and Part III. Public Opinion in Relation to Planning and Housing in Middlesbrough*, The Social Survey, new series no. 50 (January 1950).

Checkland, S. G., *The Rise of Industrial Society in England, 1815–1885* (London, 1964).

Chesser, Eustace, *The Sexual, Marital and Family Relationships of the English Woman* (London, 1956).

Churchill, R. S., *Winston Spencer Churchill: Young Statesman* (London, 1967).

'Civic', 'A Word about Venereal Disease', *The English Review*, 23 (1916).

Cole, G. D. H., *A Short History of the British Working-Class Movement 1789–1947* (London, 1948).

Collet, Clara C., 'The Collection and Utilization of Official Statistics Bearing on the Extent and Effects of Industrial Employment on Women', *Journal of the Royal Statistical Society*, cxi (June 1898).

Collet, Clara C., *Women in Industry* (London, *c.*1900).

Collier, Adam, 'Social Origins of a Sample of Entrants to Glasgow University', *Sociological Review*, xxx (1939).

Comfort, Alexander, *Sex in Society* (London, 1963).

Cosens, Marjorie E., 'Evacuation: A Social Revolution', *Social Work: A Quarterly Review of Family Casework*, 1.3 (January 1940).

Crowther, Lord Geoffrey, *Report of the Central Advisory Council for Education, England* (London, 1959).

Cunnison, J. and J. B. S. Gilfillan, *The City of Glasgow* (Glasgow, 1958).

Curtis, S. J., *History of Education in Great Britain*, seventh edition (London, 1967).

D'Albo-Julienne, Philippe, *The Crisis of Marriage* (London, 1943).

Dale, Mrs Hylton, *Child Labour Under Capitalism* (London, 1908).

Daniel, W. W., *Racial Discrimination in Britain* (Harmondsworth, 1968).

Davies, Margaret Llewlyn (ed.), *Maternity: Letters From Working Women* (London, 1989), first pub. 1915.

Dearle, N. B., 'The Organisation of Boy Labour', *The Clare Market Review*, 5.3 (June 1910).

Dennis, Norman, Fernando Henriques and Clifford Slaughter, *Coal is Our Life: An Analysis of a Yorkshire Mining Community* (London, 1956).

Duff, Charles St Lawrence, *England and the English* (London, 1954).

Durant, Ruth, *Watling: A Survey of Social Life on a New Housing Estate* (London, 1939).

Elkin, Winifred, *English Juvenile Courts* (London, 1938).

Emerson, Ralph Waldo, *English Traits* (London, 1856).

Faning, E. Lewis, *Report on an Enquiry into Family Limitation and Its Influence on Human Fertility During the Past Fifty Years* (London, 1949).

Fawcett, M. G., *The Women's Victory and After* (London, 1920).

Fay, C. R. and H. C. Fay, *The Allotment Movement in England and Wales* (London, 1942).

Firth, R. (ed.), *Two Studies of Kinship in London*, London School of Economics Monograph on Social Anthropology, no. 15 (London, 1956).

Firth, R. and J. Djamour, 'Kinship in South Borough', in R. Firth (ed.), *Two Studies of Kinship in London*, London School of Economics Monograph on Social Anthropology, no. 15 (London, 1956).

Flugel, J. C., *Men and Their Motives: Psycho-Analytical Studies* (London, 1934).

Foss, Hannen, *Come Home With Me* (London, 1945).

Fouillée, Alfred, *Esquisse psychologique des peuples Européens* (Paris, 1903).

Fox, A. Wilson, 'Agricultural Wages in England and Wales During the Last Fifty Years', *Journal of the Royal Statistical Society*, lxvi (1903).

Frankenberg, R., *Villages on the Border* (London, 1957).

Frankenberg, R., *Communities in Britain* (Harmondsworth, 1966).

Friends Allotment Committee, *Diggers and Producers: Annual Report of the Friends Allotments Committee and the Allotment Gardens for the Unemployed Central Committee for the Year Ended 31st August, 1945* (London, 1945).

Gibb, Andrew Dewar, *Scotland in Eclipse* (London, 1930).

Gibb, Rev. Spencer J., *The Problem of Boy-Work* (London, 1906).

Gibb, Rev. Spencer J., *The Boy and His Work* (London, 1911).

Glass, D. V. (ed.), *Social Mobility in Britain* (London, 1954).

Good, William, *Allotment Gardening* (London, 1922).

Gorer, Geoffrey, 'Some Notes on the British Character', *Horizon*, xx, no. 120 (December 1949).

Gorer, Geoffrey, *Exploring English Character* (London, 1955).

Graves, Robert and Alan Hodges, *The Long Weekend* (London, 1950).

Greenwood, Arthur and John E. Kettlewell, 'Some Statistics of Juvenile Employment and Unemployment', *Journal of the Royal Statistical Society*, lxxv (June 1912).

Hackney and Stoke Newington Social Workers' Group, *What Kind of Homes? An Enquiry in a London Borough* (London, 1944).

Hadow, Henry, *Board of Education: Report of the Consultative Committee on the Education of the Adolescent* (London, 1926).

Hanham, H. J., *Scottish Nationalism* (London, 1969).

Hardy, Jack and S. Foxman, *Food Production in the School Garden* (London, 1940).

Harrison, Mary, *Simple Lessons in Cookery for the Use of Teachers of Elementary and Technical Classes* (London, 1898).

Health and Strength: Leaguers' Guide (London, c.1935).

Hewitt, Margaret, *Wives and Mothers in Victorian Industry* (London, 1958).

Hillery, George A., 'Definitions of Community. Areas of Agreement', *Rural Sociology*, 20 (1955).

Hobsbawm, Eric, *Labouring Men: Studies in the History of Labour* (London, 1964).

Hodges, Mark W. and Cyril S. Smith, 'The Sheffield Estate', in University of Liverpool Social Science Department, *Neighbourhood and Community* (Liverpool, 1954).

Hoggart, Richard, *The Uses of Literacy* (Harmondsworth, 1957).

Holt, H. Mainwaring, 'The Decay of Family Life', *Health Education Journal*, ix.4 (October 1951).

Howard Association, *Juvenile Offenders* (London, 1898).

Hutchinson, Bertram, *Willesden and the New Towns* (London, 1947).

Industrial Christian Fellowship, *Children at Work: Hours of Young People in Industry, Shops and Agriculture* (London, 1943).

Institute of Child Health, *The Health and Growth of the Under-Fives* (London, 1951).

Jeger, Lena M. (ed.), *Illegitimate Children and Their Parents* (London, 1951).

Jenkins, Kate, 'Co-Operative Housekeeping', *Women and Progress* (30 November 1906).

Jenkinson, A. J., *What Do Boys and Girls Read? An Investigation into Reading Habits* (London, 1940).

Jennings, Humphrey and Charles Madge (eds), *May the Twelfth: Mass Observation Day Surveys 1937 By Over 200 Observers* (London, 1937).

Jephcott, A. P., *Girls Growing Up* (London, 1942).

Jevons, Rosamond and John Madge, *Housing Estates: A Study of Bristol Corporation Policy and Practice Between the Wars* (Bristol, 1946).

Jewkes, John and Sylvia Jewkes, *The Juvenile Labour Market* (London, 1938).

Kebbell, T. E., *The Agricultural Labourer* (London, 1893).

Keeling, Frederic, *The Labour Exchange in Relation to Boy and Girl Labour* (London, 1910).

Kerr, Madeline, *The People of Ship Street* (London, 1958).

Keynes, Margaret Neville, *The Problem of Boy Labour in Cambridge* (Cambridge, 1911).

Klein, V., *Britain's Married Women Workers* (London, 1965).

Klickmann, Flora, *The Mistress of the Little House: What She Should Know and What She Should Do When She Has an Untrained Servant* (London, 1912).

Kuper, Leo (ed.), *Living in Towns* (London, 1953).

Ladies Sanitary Association, *24th Annual Report of the Ladies Sanitary Association* (April 1882).

Laird, Sydney M., *Venereal Disease in Britain* (Harmondsworth, 1943).

Landmaid, Sophia H. E., *A Woman's Work and How to Lighten It* (London, 1904).

Lane, Lieutenant-Colonel A. H., *The Alien Menace: A Statement of the Case* (London, 1928).

Larkins, Dr F. E., 'The Influence of Wages on Children's Nutrition', *The Medical Officer* (17 December 1910).

Lewis, E. Llewelyn, *The Children of the Unskilled: An Economic and Social Survey* (London, 1924).

Little, K. L., *Negroes in Britain: A Study of Race Relations in English Society* (London, 1947).

Loane, Margaret E., *Simple Sanitation: The Practical Application of Laws of Health to Small Dwellings* (London, 1905).

Loane, Margaret E., *The Queen's Poor: Life As They Find It in Town and Country* (London, 1905), new and cheaper edition, 1906.

Loane, Margaret E., *From Their Point of View* (London, 1908).

Loane, Margaret E., *Englishman's Castle* (London, 1909).

Loane, Margaret E., *Neighbours and Friends* (London, 1910).

London School of Economics and Political Science, The Social Sciences Department, *Woman, Wife, Worker* (London, 1960).

Lubbock, John, 'Manual Instruction', *Fortnightly Review*, ccxxxviii, new series (October 1886).

Lynd, Robert, *Home Life in Ireland* (London, 1909).

Macartney, Douglas Halliday, *Boy Welfare* (London, 1917).

McCrone, G., *Regional Policy in Britain* (London, 1969).

McDonald, Ian J., 'Untapped Reservoirs of Talent? Social Class and Opportunities in Scottish Higher Education, 1910–1960', *Scottish Educational Studies*, 1.1 (June 1967).

Mackintosh, J. M., *Trends of Opinion About the Public Health 1901–51* (London, 1953).

Madge, Charles, 'Wartime Patterns of Saving and Spending', National Institute of Economic and Social Research, Occasional Papers IV (Cambridge, 1943).

Magnus, Philip, 'Manual Training in School Education', *The Contemporary Review*, 1 (November 1886).

Mais, S. P. B., *S. O. S. Talks on Unemployment* (London, 1933).

Margrie, William (compiler), *The Poets of Peckham*, second edition (London, 1956).

Martin, Anna, *Married Working Women* (London, 1911).

Martin, F. M., 'Some Subjective Aspects of Social Stratification', in D. V. Glass (ed.), *Social Mobility in Britain* (London, 1954).

'Mass Observation', *War Factory* (London, 1943).

'Mass Observation', *An Enquiry into People's Homes* (London, 1943).

'Mass Observation', *Britain and Her Birth Rate* (London, 1945).

'Mass Observation', *Puzzled People: A Study in Popular Attitudes to Religion, Ethics, Progress, and Politics in a London Borough* (London, 1947).

'Mass Observation', *Contemporary Churchgoing* (n.p., 1949).

'Mass Observation', *People and Paints: The Housewife's Viewpoint on Paints and Finishes* (Slough, Bucks, Imperial Chemical Industries Ltd., 1950).

'Mass Observation', *The Voters' Choice: A Mass Observation Report on the General Election of 1950* (London, 1950).

'Mass Observation', 'Anti-Semitism', *Mass Observation Reprint*, 1.23 (May 1951).

'Mass Observation', *The Pub and the People: A Worktown Study*, first pub. 1943 (Welwyn Garden City, 1970), 130–1.

Maternity in Great Britain: A Survey of Social and Economic Aspects of Pregnancy and Childbirth Undertaken by a Joint Committee of the Royal College of Obstetricians and Gynaecologists and the Population Investigation Committee (Oxford, 1948).

Matheson, C., 'Women's Labour and the Home', *Birmingham Street Children's Union Magazine*, no. 11 (April 1911).

May, Otto, *Venereal Diseases and Their Effects* (London, 1924).

Mayer, J. P., *British Cinemas and Their Audiences* (London, 1948).

Mays, John Barron, *Growing Up in the City: A Survey of Juvenile Delinquency in an Urban Neighbourhood* (Liverpool, 1954).

Meara, Gwynne, *Juvenile Unemployment in South Wales* (Cardiff, 1936).

Meier, Gitta, 'A Neighbourhood Study', *The Good Neighbour: A Woman's Magazine of Public Welfare*, 2.6 (November 1950).

Mills, Joan, 'The Tenement Housewife', *The Good Neighbour: A Woman's Magazine of Public Welfare*, 2.6 (November 1950).

Ministry of Health and Home Office, *Report of the Inter-Departmental Committee on Abortion* (London, 1939).

Ministry of National Service, *Report Vol. I Upon the Physical Examination of Men of Military Age by National Service Medical Boards From November 1st, 1917 – October 31st, 1918* [Cmd. 504], P. P. 1919, xxvi.

Mitchell, G. Duncan and Thomas Lipton, 'The Liverpool Estate', in

University of Liverpool Social Science Department, *Neighbourhood and Community* (Liverpool, 1954).

Mogey, J. M., 'Changes in Family Life Experienced by English Workers Moving From the Slums to Housing Estates', *Marriage and Family Living*, xvii.2 (May 1955).

Moore, Doris Langley, *The Vulgar Heart: An Enquiry into the Sentimental Tendencies of Public Opinion* (London, 1945).

Moss, Louis, *Education and the People: A Study of Public Attitudes Towards Education and the Education Act* (London, 1945).

National Allotments Society, *Second Annual Report and Year Book of the National Allotments Society Ltd. for the Year Ended December 31st, 1931* (London, 1932).

National Association of Manual Training Teachers, *Report on the Examination of Handicraft and Technical Drawing in Secondary Schools* (London, 1947).

National Council of Public Morals, *Prevention of VD* (London, 1921).

National Council of Social Services, *Out of Adversity: A Survey of the Clubs for Men and Women Which Have Grown Out of the Needs of Unemployment* (London, 1939).

National Union of Allotment Holders, *Allotment Holders' Yearbook for 1923* (London, 1923).

Natural Science in Education, section 52 (London, 1918).

Newsam, Sir J. H., *Half our Future: Report of the Central Advisory Council for Education (England)* (London, 1963).

Oliver, T., 'The Diet of Toil', *Lancet* (29 June 1895).

Orr, Sir John Boyd, *Food, Health and Income: Report on a Survey of Adequacy of Diet in Relation to Income* (London, 1936).

Osborne, Charles C., *Ignorance: The Great Enemy* (London, 1916).

Osbourne, B. M., *The Glasgow and North Lanarkshire Housing and New Towns Survey*, The Social Survey, new series 102 (April 1948).

Owen, A. D. K., *A Survey of Juvenile Employment and Welfare in Sheffield* (Sheffield, 1933).

'P. P.', 'Padded Houses', *Daily Herald* (25 October 1922).

Packer, E. L., 'Aspects of Working-Class Marriage', *Pilot Papers: Social Essays and Documents*, 2.1 (March 1947).

Park, Robert E. and E. W. Burgess (eds), *The City* (Chicago, 1925).

Paterson, Alexander, *Across the Bridges: Life By the South London River-Side* (New York, 1980), first pub. 1911.

Patterson, Sheila, *Dark Strangers: A Study of West Indians in London* (Harmondsworth, 1965).

Pear, T. H., *English Social Differences* (London, 1955).

Pease, Margaret, *True Patriotism and Other Lessons on Peace and Internationalism* (London, 1911).

Perkin, H., *The Origins of Modern English Society, 1780–1880* (London, 1969).

Philip, A. A. and H. R. Murray, *Knowledge a Young Husband Should Have* (London, 1911).

Pizzey, Isobel M., 'Home Parliament', *Daily Herald* (31 October 1919).

Plowden, Lady B. H., *Children and Their Primary Schools: A Report of the Central Advisory Council for Education (England)* (London, 1967).

Plunkett, Horace, 'Agricultural Education for Women in Great Britain, Ireland, and the Colonies', in The Countess of Warwick (ed.), *Progress in Women's Education in the British Empire. Being the Report of the Education Section, Victorian Era Exhibition 1897* (London, 1898).

Pointing, Horace B., *Unemployment is Beating Us? Is It Our Concern?* (London, 1934).

Political and Economic Planning, *The Entrance to Industry*, May (London, 1935).

Pollard, Sidney, *The Development of the British Economy 1914–1950* (London, 1962).

Potter, Denis, *The Glittering Coffin* (London, 1960).

Purdom, C. B., *The Garden City* (London, 1913).

Quinlan, Alexander and N. E. Mann, *Cookery for Seamen* (Liverpool, 1894).

Rees, A., *Life in the Welsh Countryside* (Cardiff, 1950).

Reeves, Mrs Pember, *Round About a Pound a Week* (London, 1979), first pub. 1913.

Reith, John C. W., *Broadcasting Over Britain* (London, 1924).

Reynolds, Stephen, Bob Woolley and Tom Woolley, *Seems So! A Working-Class View of Politics* (London, 1911).

Richmond, Anthony, 'Immigration as a Social Process: The Case of Coloured Colonials in the United Kingdom', *Social and Economic Studies*, 5.2 (1956).

Riemer, Svend, 'Villages in Metrolis', *British Journal of Sociology*, II.1 (March 1951).

Rolfe, Ethelwyn, *The Soul of the Slum Child* (London, 1929).

Rolph, C. H., *Women of the Streets: A Sociological Study of the Common Prostitute* (London, 1955).

Rowntree, B. Seebohm, *Poverty: A Study of Town Life* (London, 1901).

Rowntree, B. Seebohm, *Poverty and Progress: A Second Social Study of York* (London, 1941).

Rowntree, B. Seebohm and May Kendall, *How the Labourer Lives: A Study of the Rural Labour Problem* (London, 1917).

Rowntree, B. Seebohm and G. R. Lavers, *English Life and Leisure: A Social Study* (London, 1951).

Rowntree, B. Seebohm and G. R. Lavers, *Poverty and the Welfare State* (London, 1951).

Rowse, Alfred Leslie, *The English Spirit: Essays in History and Literature* (London, 1944).

Royal College of Midwives, *Preparation for Parenthood* (London, 1964).

Royal Commission on Venereal Diseases: Economic Effects of Venereal Diseases (London, 1916).

Russell, Sir E. J., 'Introduction', in Alan G. Ogilvie (ed.), *Great Britain: Essays in Regional Geography* (Cambridge, 1928).

Saville, John, 'Labour and Income Redistribution', *Socialist Register* (1965).

Schofield, Michael, *The Sexual Behaviour of Young People* (London, 1965).

Scott, George Ryley, *Birth Control: A Practical Guide for Working Women* (London, 1933).

Scott, George Ryley, *Sex Problems and Dangers in War-Time: A Book of Practical Advice for Men and Women on the Fighting and Home Fronts* (London, 1940).

Scottish Housing Advisory Committee, *The Housing of Special Groups* (Edinburgh, 1952).

Seers, Dudley, *Changes in the Cost of Living and the Distribution of Income Since 1938* (Oxford, 1949).

Shaw, Lulie A., 'Impressions of Family Life in a London Suburb: Studies of a General Practice IV', *Sociological Review*, 2.2 (1954).

Sheehan, P. A., *Glenanaar* (New York, 1905).

Siegfried, A., *The Character of Peoples* (London, 1952).

Slater, E. and M. Woodside, *Patterns of Marriage: A Study of Marriage Relationships in the Urban Working Classes* (London, 1951).

Smith, Sir Hubert Llewellyn (ed.), *New Survey of London Life and Labour: Vol. VI. Survey and Social Conditions (2) The Western Area (Text)* (London, 1934).

Smith, Sir Hubert Llewellyn (ed.), *New Survey of London Life and Labour: Vol. IX. Life and Leisure* (London, 1935).

Smithies, B. and P. Fiddick, *Enoch Powell on Immigration* (London, 1969).

Snowden, Philip, *The Living Wage* (London, 1912).

Social Survey, *Scottish Mining Communities: An Enquiry Made by the Social Survey for the Department of Health for Scotland, the Cly Valley Planning Advisory Department, and the Central and South-East Scotland Planning Advisory Committee*, Report New Series, no. 61 (Autumn 1946).

Soulsby, Lucy H. M., *Home Rule, Or Daughters To-Day* (Oxford, 1894).

Soutar, M. S., E. H. Wilkins and P. Sargant Florence, *Nutrition and the Size of Family: Report on a New Housing Estate – 1939* (London, 1942).

Stopes, Marie C., *Married Love* (London, 1918).

Stopes, Marie C., *Mother England* (London, 1929).

Sturdee, R. J., 'The Ethics of Football', *Westminster Review*, 159 (1903).

Tanner, Henry, *Jack's Education or How He Learnt Farming* (London, 1879).

Tawney, R. H. (ed.), *Secondary Education for All* (London, 1922).

Thomas, Geoffrey, *The Social Survey: Women and Industry* (London, 1948).

Thompson, E. P., *The Making of the English Working Class* (New York, 1966).

Titmuss, Richard M., *Birth, Poverty and Wealth* (London, 1943).

Titmuss, Richard M. and Kathleen Titmuss, *Parents Revolt: A Study of the Declining Birth-Rate in Acquisitive Societies* (London, 1942).

Tory Reform Committee, *To-Morrow's Children* (London, 1944).

Tressell, Robert, *The Ragged Trousered Philanthropist* (London, 1914).

Trevor, Charles T., *How To Develop a Powerful Abdomen* (Kenton, 1943).

Trevor, Charles T., *How To Develop Powerful Arms* (London, 1944).

Tuthill, J. F., 'Impotence', *The Lancet* (15 January 1955).

'Uncle Bob', *How To Develop the Arm* (London, 1910).

'Uncle Bob', *How To Increase Your Height* (London, 1957).

University of Liverpool Social Science Department, *Neighbourhood and Community* (Liverpool, 1954).

Urwin, E. C., *Can the Family Survive?* (London, 1944).

Velde, Van de, *Ideal Marriage* (London, 1961), first pub. 1928.

Wagner, Gertrude, *Cakes – Buying and Baking*, Wartime Social Survey, new series 40 (November–December 1943).

Ward, J. C., *Children Out of School* (London, 1948).

Wartime Social Survey, *Public Attitudes to Health and to the Autumn Health Campaign*, Report no. 21, new series, part 2 (1942).

Wartime Social Survey, *Sanitary Towels: A Survey of Housewives' Habits for the Board of Trade*, new series no. 11 (March 1942).

Webb, W. H., 'History, Patriotism and the Child', *History*, 2.1 (1913).

White, Colonel A. C. T., *The Story of Army Education 1643–1963* (London, 1963).

White, Arnold, *Efficiency and Empire* (London, 1901).

White, W., *Life in a Court: How to Stop Neighbours' Quarrels* (Birmingham, 1890).

Wilkinson, Ellen, *The Town that was Murdered: The Life Story of Jarrow* (London, 1939).

Williams, W. M., *The Sociology of an English Village: Gosforth* (London, 1956).

Willmott, Peter, *The Evolution of a Community: A Study of Dagenham After Forty Years* (London, 1963).

Wilson, Pixie J., assisted by Virginia Barker, *The Campaign Against Venereal Diseases*, Central Office of Information, Wartime Social Survey, new series no. 42 (January 1944).

Winterbottom, Allan, *An Enquiry into the Employment of Juveniles in Lancashire* (Manchester, 1932).

Women's Co-Operative Guild, *Working Women and Divorce* (London, 1911).

Women's Group on Public Welfare, *Loneliness*, 1955.

Woodside, Moya, 'Courtship and Mating in an Urban Community', *Eugenics Review*, xxxviii.1 (April 1946).

Woodside, Moya, 'Health and Happiness in Marriage', *Health Education Journal*, iv.4 (October 1946).

'A Workaday Mother', *What Every Mother Should Tell Her Children* (London, 1938).

Young, Michael and Peter Willmott, *Family and Kinship in East London* (London, 1990), first pub. 1957.

Zweig, F., *Labour, Life and Poverty* (London, 1948).

Zweig, F., *Men in the Pits* (London, 1948).

Zweig, F., *The Worker in an Affluent Society* (London, 1961).

BOOKS, PAMPHLETS, AND ARTICLES PUBLISHED SINCE 1970

Addison, Paul, *Road to 1945* (London, 1977).

Addison, Paul, *Now the War is Over: A Social History of Britain 1945–1951* (London, 1985).

Alexander, Sally, 'Women's Work in Nineteenth Century London', in Juliet Mitchell and Ann Oakley (eds), *The Rights and Wrongs of Women* (Harmondsworth, 1976).

Anderson, Benedict, *Imagined Communities: Reflections on the Origin and Spread of Nationalism* (London, 1983).

Anderson, Michael, 'The Emergence of the Modern Life Cycle in Britain', *Social History*, 10.1 (January 1985).

Attar, Dena, *Wasting Girls' Time: The History and Politics of Home Economics* (London, 1990).

Augusteijn, Joost, 'The Importance of Being Irish: Ideas and the Volunteers in Mayo and Tipperary', in David Fitzpatrick (ed.), *Revolution? Ireland 1917–1923* (Dublin, 1990).

Bailey, Victor, 'Bibles and Dummy Rifles: the Boys' Brigade', *History Today*, 33 (October 1983).

Barrett, Michele, *Women's Oppression Today* (London, 1980).

Becker, Gary, *A Treatise on the Family* (Cambridge, Mass., 1981).

Beddoe, Deirdre, *Back to Home and Duty: Women Between the Wars, 1918–1939* (London, 1989).

Benjamin, Daniel K. and Levis A. Kochin, 'Searching for an Explanation of Unemployment in Interwar Britain', *Journal of Political Economy*, 87.3 (June 1979).

Benson, John (ed.), *The Working Class in England, 1875–1914* (London, 1985).

Benson, John, *The Working Class in Britain, 1850–1939* (London, 1989).

Best, Geoffrey, *Mid-Victorian Britain 1851–1875* (London, 1971).

Bhabha, Jacqueline, Francesca Klug and Sue Shutter, *Worlds Apart: Women Under Immigration and Nationality Law* (London, 1985).

Blanch, M. D., 'Imperialism, Nationalism and Organised Youth', in J. Clarke, C. Critcher and R. Johnson (eds), *Working Class Culture* (London, 1979).

Blanch, M. D., 'British Society and the War', in Peter Warwick (ed.), *The South African War: The Anglo-Boer War 1899–1902* (Harlow, 1980).

Bliss, Christopher, 'The Labour Market: Theory and Experience', in Michael Beenstock (ed.), *Modelling the Labour Market* (London, 1988).

Boddy, M., *The Building Societies* (London, 1980).

Boerner, Peter (ed.), *Concepts of National Identity: An Interdisciplinary Dialogue* (Baden-Baden, 1986).

Bone, M., *Family Planning Services in England and Wales* (London, 1973).

Bourke, Joanna, *Husbandry to Housewifery: Women, Economic Change, and Housewifery in Ireland, 1890–1914* (Oxford, 1993).

Bourke, Joanna, 'How to be Happy though Married: Housewifery in Working-Class Britain, 1880–1914', *Past and Present* (1993).

Branson, N. and M. Heinemann, *Britain in the 1930s* (London, 1971).

Brewer, John D., *Mosley's Men: The British Union of Fascists in the West Midlands* (Aldershot, 1984).

Brown, Kenneth D., 'Ministerial Recruitment and Training: An Aspect of the Crisis of Victorian Nonconformity', *Victorian Studies*, 30.3 (Spring 1987).

Buckley, Ned, 'The Mother That Didn't Die', in Jack Lane and Drendan Clifford (eds), *Ned Buckley's Poems* (Aubane, 1987).

Bulmer, Martin, *The Occupational Community of the Traditional Worker* (London, 1973).

Burnett, John (ed.), *Destiny Obscure: Autobiographies of Childhood, Education and Family from the 1820s to the 1920s* (Harmondsworth, 1982).

Burnett, John, *Useful Toil: Autobiographies of Working People from the 1820s to the 1920s* (Harmondsworth, 1984).

Bush, J., *Behind the Lines: East London Labour 1914–1919* (London, 1984).

Calder, Jenni, *The Victorian Home* (London, 1977).

Cashmore, E. Ellis, *United Kingdom? Class, Race and Gender Since the War* (London, 1989).

Chancellor, Valerie, *History for Their Masters: Opinion in the English History Textbook: 1800–1914* (Bath, 1970).

Chaytor, Miranda, 'Martyrs of Class', in Raphael Samuel (ed.), *Patriotism: The Making and Unmaking of British National Identity*. Vol. II: *Minorities and Outsiders* (London, 1989).

Chinn, Carl, *They Worked All Their Lives: Women of the Urban Poor in England, 1880–1939* (Manchester, 1988).

Clarkson, L. A. (ed.), *British Trade Union and Labour History: A Compendium* (London, 1990).

Cockburn, Cynthia, *Brothers: Male Dominance and Technological Changes* (London, 1983).

Cohen, Steve, 'Anti-Semitism, Immigration Controls and the Welfare State', *Critical Social Policy*, 13 (1985).

Collins, Rosemary, ' "Horses for Courses": Ideology and the Division of Labour', in Paul Close and Rosemary Collins (eds), *Family and Economy in Modern Society* (London, 1985).

Comaroff, Jean, *Body of Power, Spirit of Resistance: The Culture and History of a South African People* (Chicago, 1985).

Constantine, Stephen, *Unemployment in Britain Between the Wars* (London, 1980).

Cook, Chris and John Stevenson, *The Longman Handbook of Modern British History 1714–1980* (London, 1983).

Cooper, Jilly, *Class: A View from Middle England* (London, 1979).

Costello, John, *Love, Sex and War: Changing Values 1939–1945* (London, 1985).

Cronin, James E., *Labour and Society in Britain 1918–1979* (London, 1984).

Cross, Gary, *A Quest for Time. The Reduction of Work in Britain and France, 1840–1940* (Berkeley, 1989).

Cross, Gary (ed.), *Worktowners at Blackpool* (London, 1990).

Crossick, Geoffrey, *An Artisan Elite in Victorian Society: Kentish London 1840–1880* (London, 1978).

Crouch, David and Colin Ward, *The Allotment* (London, 1988).

Croucher, Richard, *We Refuse to Starve in Silence: A History of the National Unemployed Workers' Movement 1920–46* (London, 1987).

Currie, Robert, Alan Gilbert and Lee Horsley, *Churches and Churchgoers: Patterns of Growth in the British Isles Since 1700* (Oxford, 1977).

Daunton, M. J., *House and Home in the Victorian City: Working-Class Housing 1850–1914* (London, 1983).

Davies, Charlotte Aull, *Welsh Nationalism in the Twentieth Century: The Ethnic Option and the Modern State* (New York, 1989).

Davies, Margaret Llewlyn (ed.), *Maternity: Letters From Working Women* (London, 1989), first pub. 1915.

Davies, R., *Women and Work* (London, 1985).

Davin, Anna, ' "Mind That You Do as You Are Told": Reading Books for Board School Children, 1870–1902', *Feminist Review*, 3 (1979).

Deacon, Alan, *In Search of the Scrounger: The Administration of the Unemployed Insurance in Britain 1920–1931* (London, 1976).

Department of Employment and Productivity, *British Labour Statistics: Historical Abstract 1886-1968* (London, 1971).

Domanian, J., *Marriage in Britain 1945-1980* (London, 1980).

Drotner, Kirsten, *English Children and Their Magazines 1751-1945* (New Haven, 1988).

Durkacz, Victor Edward, *The Decline of the Celtic Languages* (Edinburgh, 1983).

Dyhouse, Carol, *Girls Growing Up in Late Victorian and Edwardian England* (London, 1981).

Edwards, John, *Language, Society and Identity* (Oxford, 1985).

Evans, Neil, 'The South Wales Race Riots of 1919', *Llafur*, iii.1 (1980).

Faber, Richard, *High Road to England* (London, 1985).

Fee, Terry, 'Domestic Labour: An Analysis of Housework and its Relation to the Production Process', *Review of Radical Political Economics*, 8 (Spring 1976).

Feinstein, Charles, 'A New Look at the Cost of Living, 1870-1914', in James Foreman-Peck (ed.), *New Perspectives on the Late Victorian Economy: Essays in Quantitative Economic History, 1860-1914* (Cambridge, 1991).

Fildes, Valerie, Lara Marks and Hilary Marland (eds), *Women and Children First: International Maternal and Infant Welfare 1870-1945* (London, 1992).

Fitzpatrick, David, *Irish Emigration 1801-1921* (Dublin, 1984).

Fitzpatrick, David, 'A Curious Middle Place: The Irish in Britain, 1871-1921', in Roger Swift and Sheridan Gilley (eds), *The Irish in Britain 1815-1939* (London, 1989).

Foster, J., *Class Struggle in the Industrial Revolution* (London, 1974).

Fuller, John, *Popular Culture and Troop Morale in British and Dominion Forces in the First World War* (Oxford, 1990).

Gainer, Bernard, *The Alien Invasion: The Origins of the Aliens Act of 1905* (London, 1972).

Gallagher, Tom, *Glasgow: The Uneasy Peace. Religious Tension in Modern Scotland* (Manchester, 1987).

Gillis, John R., 'The Evolution of Juvenile Delinquency in England, 1890-1914', *Past and Present*, 67 (1975).

Gillis, John R., *Youth and History: Tradition and Change in European Age Relations, 1770-Present* (New York, 1981).

Gittens, Diana G., 'Married Life and Birth Control Between the Wars', *Oral History*, 2 (1975).

Goldthorpe, John H., *Social Mobility and Class Structure in Modern Britain* (Oxford, 1980).

Green, Eileen, Sandra Hebron and Diana Woodward, *Women's Leisure, What Leisure?* (London, 1990).

Haig, Alan, *The Victorian Clergy* (London, 1984).

Hakim, C., *Occupational Segregation* (London, 1979).

Hall, Leslie, *Hidden Anxieties: Male Sexuality 1900-1950* (Cambridge, 1991).

Halsey, A. H. (ed.), *Trends in British Society Since 1900* (London, 1972).

Halsey, A. H., 'Higher Education', in A. H. Halsey, *Trends in British Society*, second edition (Oxford, 1981).

Halsey, A. H. (ed.), *Change in British Society*, third edition (Oxford, 1986).

Harrison, Brian, *Peaceable Kingdom: Stability and Change in Modern Britain* (Oxford, 1982).

Harrison, Brian, 'Class and Gender in Modern British Labour History', *Past and Present*, 124 (1989).

Harrisson, Tom and Charles Madge, *Britain By Mass Observation* (London, 1986).

Hartmann, Heidi, 'The Historical Roots of Occupational Segregation: Capitalism, Patriarchy and Job Segregation by Sex', *Signs*, 1.3 (Spring 1976).

Hawkins, Alun, 'The Discovery of Rural England', in Robert Colls and Philip Dodd (eds), *Englishness: Politics and Culture 1880-1920* (London, 1986).

Hedetoft, Ulf, *British Colonialism and Modern Identity* (Aalborg, 1985).

Hendrick, Harry, *Images of Youth: Age, Class and the Male Youth Problem, 1880-1920* (Oxford, 1990).

Hiller, P., 'Continuities and Variations in Everyday Conceptual Components of Class', *Sociology*, 9 (1975).

Hinton, James, 'Review', *Society for the Study of Labour History*, 42 (Spring 1981).

Hobsbawm, Eric, 'Peasants and Politics', *Journal of Peasant Studies*, 1 (1973).

Hobsbawm, Eric, 'The Forward March of Labour Halted?', in M. Jacques and F. Mulhern (eds), *The Forward March of Labour Halted?* (London, 1981).

Holmes, Colin, *John Bull's Island: Immigration and British Society 1871-1971* (London, 1988).

Holt, Richard, *Sport and the British: A Modern History* (Oxford, 1989).

Holtzman, Ellen M., 'The Pursuit of Married Love: Women's Attitudes Towards Sexuality and Marriage in Great Britain, 1918-1939', *Journal of Social History*, 16.2 (Winter 1982).

Hopkins, Eric, 'Small Town Aristocrats of Labour and their Standard of Living, 1840-1914', *Economic History Review*, second series, xxviii (May 1975).

Hopkins, Eric, *The Rise and Decline of the English Working Classes 1918-1990: A Social History* (London, 1991).

Howell, D., *British Workers and the Independent Labour Party 1886-1906* (Manchester, 1983).

Humphries, S., ' "Hurrah for England": Schooling and the Working Class in Bristol, 1870-1914', *Southern History: A Review of the History of Southern England*, 1 (1979).

Humphries, Stephen, *Hooligans or Rebels? An Oral History of Working-Class Childhood and Youth 1889-1939* (Oxford, 1981).

Humphries, Stephen, 'Steal to Survive: The Social Crime of Working Class Children 1890-1940', *Oral History*, 9.1 (Spring 1981).

Humphries, Stephen, *A Secret World of Sex: Forbidden Fruit: The British Experience 1900-1950* (London, 1988).

Hunt, E. A., *British Labour History 1815-1914* (London, 1981).

Jacobs, Sidney, 'Race, Empire and the Welfare State: Council Housing and Racism', *Critical Social Policy*, 13 (Summer 1985).

Jeffery, Keith and Peter Hennessy, *States of Emergency: British Governments and Strikebreaking Since 1919* (London, 1983).

John, Angela (ed.), *Unequal Opportunities: Women's Employment in England, 1800-1918* (Oxford, 1986).

Johnson, Paul, 'Credit and Thrift and the British Working Class, 1870–1939', in Jay Winter (ed.), *The Working Class in Modern British History: Essays in Honour of Henry Pelling* (Cambridge, 1983).

Johnson, Paul, *Saving and Spending: The Working-Class Economy in Britain, 1870–1939* (Oxford, 1985).

Jones, Gareth Stedman, *Languages of Class: Studies in English Working-Class History 1832–1982* (Cambridge, 1983).

Jones, H. J., *Second Abstract of British Historical Statistics* (Cambridge, 1971).

Jordan, Ellen, 'The Exclusion of Women from Industry in Nineteenth Century Britain', *Comparative Studies in Society and History*, 31.3 (April 1989).

Kay, Diana and Robert Miles, *Refugees or Migrant Workers? European Volunteer Workers in Britain 1946–1951* (London, 1992).

Kushner, Tony, *The Persistence of Prejudice: Antisemitism in British Society During the Second World War* (Manchester, 1989).

Kushner, Tony and Kenneth Lunn (eds), *Traditions of Intolerance: Historical Perspectives on Fascism and Race Discourse in Britain* (Manchester, 1989).

Laing, Stuart, *Representations of Working-Class Life 1957–1964* (London, 1986).

Laslett, Peter, 'Introduction: Comparative Illegitimacy Over Time and Between Cultures', in Peter Laslett, Karla Oosterveen and Richard M. Smith (eds), *Bastardy and Its Comparative History* (London, 1980).

Leathard, Audrey, *The Fight for Family Planning: The Development of Family Planning Services in Britain 1921–74* (London, 1980).

Lebzelter, Gisela C., 'Anti-Semitism – A Focal Point for the British Radical Right', in Paul Kennedy and Anthony Nicholls (eds), *Nationalist and Racialist Movements in Britain and Germany Before 1914* (London, 1981).

Lewis, D. S., *Mosley, Fascism and British Society 1931–81* (Manchester, 1987).

Lewis, Jane, 'In Search of a Real Equality: Women Between the Wars', in Frank Gloversmith (ed.), *Class, Culture and Social Change: A New View of the 1930s* (Brighton, 1980).

Lewis, Jane, *The Politics of Motherhood: Child and Maternal Welfare in England, 1900–1939* (London, 1980).

Lewis, Jane, *Women in England 1870–1950* (Brighton, 1984).

Lewis, Jane (ed.), *Labour and Love: Women's Experience of Home and Family, 1850–1940* (Oxford, 1986).

Lowe, Ray, *Education in the Postwar Years: A Social History* (London, 1988).

Lowerson, John, 'Battles for the Countryside', in Frank Goldsmith (ed.), *Class, Culture and Social Change: A New View of the 1930s* (Brighton, 1980).

Lown, Judy, 'Not So Much a Factory, More a Form of Patriarchy: Gender and Class During Industrialization', in Eva Gamarnikow (ed.), *Gender, Class and Work* (London, 1985).

Lummis, Trevor, 'The Historical Dimension of Fatherhood: A Case Study 1890–1914', in Lorna McKee and Margaret O'Brien (eds), *The Father Figure* (London, 1982).

McCalman, J., 'The Impact of the First World War on Female Employment in England', *Labour History* (1972).

MacDougall, Ian (ed.), *Voices from the Hunger Marches: Personal Recollections by Scottish Hunger Marchers of the 1920s and 1930s*, vol. 1 (Edinburgh, 1990).

McKibbin, Ross, *The Ideologies of Class: Social Relations in Britain 1880-1950* (Oxford, 1990).

McLean, Iain, *The Legend of Red Clydeside* (Edinburgh, 1983).

Martin, Bernice, *A Sociology of Contemporary Cultural Change* (Oxford, 1981).

Marwick, Arthur, 'A Social History of Britain 1945-1983', in David Punter (ed.), *Introduction to Contemporary Cultural Studies* (London, 1986).

Marwick, Arthur, 'The 1960s: Was There a "Cultural Revolution"?', *Contemporary Record*, 2.3 (Autumn 1988).

'Mass Observation', *The Pub and the People: A Worktown Study*, first pub. 1943 (Welwyn Garden City, 1970).

Massey, D., *Spatial Divisions of Labour: Social Structure and the Geography of Production* (London, 1984).

Meacham, Standish, *A Life Apart* (London, 1977).

Midwinter, Eric, *Fair Game: Myth and Reality in Sport* (London, 1986).

Miles, Peter and Malcolm Smith, *Cinema, Literature and Society: Elite and Mass Culture in Interwar Britain* (London, 1987).

Mincer, Jacob, 'Labour Force Participation of Married Women', *Aspects of Labour Economics* (New York, 1975).

Mitchell, B. R. and Phyllis Deane, *Abstract of British Historical Statistics* (Cambridge, 1971).

Mitchell, B. R. and H. G. Jones, *Second Abstract of British Historical Statistics* (Cambridge, 1971).

Moorhouse, H. F., 'Attitudes to Class and Class Relationships in Britain', *Sociology*, 10 (1976).

Morgan, Barrie S., 'Social Status Segregation in Comparative Perspective: The Case of the United Kingdom and the United States', University of London King's College, Occasional Paper 3, Department of Geography (October 1976).

Morgan, David, *'It Will Make a Man of You': Notes on National Service, Masculinity, and Autobiography* (Manchester, 1987).

Morris, Lydia, *The Workings of the Household: A US-UK Comparison* (Cambridge, 1990).

Muthesius, Stefan, *The English Terraced House* (New Haven, 1982).

Newby, H., *England's Green and Pleasant Land* (London, 1979).

Nickell, Stephen, *Research Into Unemployment: A Partial View of the Economics Literature*, Centre for Labour Economics, London School of Economics, Discussion Paper no. 131 (June 1982).

Oakley, Ann, *Women's Work: The Housewife, Past and Present* (New York, 1974).

O'Connor, Kevin, *The Irish in Britain* (London, 1972).

Oddy, D. J., 'Working-Class Diets in Late Nineteenth Century Britain', *Economic History Review*, second series, xxiii (1970).

O'Dowd, Anne, *Spalpeens and Tattie Hokers: History and Folklore of the Irish Migratory Agricultural Worker in Ireland and Britain* (Blackrock, 1991).

Oliver, Paul, 'Introduction', in Paul Oliver, Ian David and Ian Bentley (eds), *Dunroamin: The Suburban Semi and Its Enemies* (London, 1981).

Osmond, John, *The Divided Kingdom* (London, 1988).

Page, Norman, *The Thirties in Britain* (London, 1990).

Payne, Geoff, *Mobility and Change in Modern Society* (Basingstoke, 1987).

Pevsner, Nikolaus, *The Englishness of English Art* (Harmondsworth, 1978).

Price, Richard, *An Imperial War and the British Working Class* (London, 1972).

Purvis, June, 'Domestic Subjects Since 1870', in Ivor Goodson (ed.), *Social Histories of the Secondary Curriculum* (Falmer, 1985).

Purvis, June, *Hard Lessons* (Oxford, 1989).

Read, Donald (ed.), *Edwardian England* (London, 1979).

Rendall, Jane, *Women in an Industrializing Society: England 1750-1880* (Oxford, 1990).

Rex, John, 'Race in the Inner City', in *Five Views of Multi-Racial Britain* (London, 1978).

Rice, Margery Spring, *Working-Class Wives: Their Health and Conditions* (London, 1981), first pub. 1939.

Rich, Paul, 'The Politics of Race and Segregation in British Cities With Reference to Birmingham, 1945-76', in Susan J. Smith and John Mercer (eds), *New Perspectives on Race and Housing in Britain* (Glasgow, 1987).

Richards, Eric, 'Women in the British Economy Since About 1700: An Interpretation', *History*, 59.197 (October 1974).

Richmond, Anthony, *Migration and Race Relations in an English City* (London, 1973).

Riley, Denise, *War in the Nursery: Theories of the Child and Mother* (London, 1983).

Robbins, Keith, 'The Grubby Wreck of Old Glories: The United Kingdom and the End of the British Empire', *Journal of Contemporary History*, 15 (1980).

Roberts, Elizabeth, *A Woman's Place: An Oral History of Working-Class Women 1890-1940* (Oxford, 1984).

Rock, Paul and Stanley Cohen, 'The Teddy Boy', in Vernon Bogdanor and Robert Skidelsky (eds), *The Age of Affluence 1951-1964* (London, 1970).

Rodger, Richard (ed.), *Scottish Housing in the Twentieth Century* (Leicester, 1989).

Rose, Gillian C., 'Locality, Politics and Culture: Poplar in the 1920s', Ph.D. thesis, Queen Mary College (1989).

Rose, Jonathan, *The Edwardian Temperament 1895-1919* (Ohio, 1986).

Rose, Lionel, *Massacre of the Innocents: Infanticide in Britain 1800-1939* (London, 1986).

Rose, M. E., *The English Poor Law 1780-1930* (London, 1971).

Rose, Sonya O., 'Gender at Work: Sex, Class and Industrial Capitalism', *History Workshop*, 21 (Spring 1986), 119-27.

Rose, Sonya O., 'Gender Antagonism and Class Conflict: Exclusionist Strategies of Male Trade Unionists in Nineteenth-Century Britain', *Social History*, 13 (1988).

Ross, Ellen, 'Survival Networks: Women's Neighbourhood Sharing in London Before World War I', *History Workshop*, 15 (Spring 1983).

Samuel, Raphael (ed.), *Patriotism: The Making and Unmaking of British National Identity*, 3 volumes (London, 1989).

Sarsby, Jacqueline, *Missuses and Mouldrunners: An Oral History of Women Pottery Workers at Work and at Home* (Milton Keynes, 1988).

Savage, M., *The Dynamics of Working Class Politics* (Cambridge, 1987).

Scannell, Paddy and David Cardiff, *A Social History of British Broadcasting: Volume One 1922-1939. Serving the Nation* (Oxford, 1991).

Scott, James C., *Weapons of the Weak: Everyday Forms of Resistance* (New Haven, 1985).

Seabrook, Jeremy, *The Idea of Neighbourhood: What Local Politics Should be About* (London, 1984).

Seal, Vivian, *Whose Choice? Working-Class Women and the Control of Fertility* (London, 1990).

Seccombe, Wally, 'The Housewife and Her Labour Under Capitalism', *New Left Review*, no. 83 (1974).

Seccombe, Wally, 'Patriarchy Stabilized: The Construction of the Male Breadwinner Wage Norm in Nineteenth Century Britain', *Social History*, 11 (1986).

Shiach, Morag, *Discourse on Popular Culture: Class, Gender and History in Cultural Analysis, 1730 to the Present* (Cambridge, 1989).

Sinfield, Alan, *Literature, Politics and Culture in Postwar Britain* (Oxford, 1989).

Smith, Elaine R., 'Jewish Responses to Political Anti-Semitism and Fascism in the East End of London 1920-1939', in Tony Kushner and Kenneth Lunn (eds), *Traditions of Intolerance* (Manchester, 1989).

Smith, F. B., 'Health', in John Benson (ed.), *The Working Class in England, 1875-1914* (London, 1985).

Smith, H. Llewellyn (ed.), *The New Survey of London Life and Labour* (London, 1974).

Smout, T. C., *A Century of the Scottish People 1830-1950* (London, 1986).

Solomos, John, *Race and Racism in Contemporary Britain* (London, 1989).

Springhall, John, *Youth, Empire and Society: British Youth Movements 1883-1940* (London, 1977).

Stearns, Peter N., 'Working Class Women', in Martha Vinicus (ed.), *Suffer and Be Still* (London, 1972).

Steedman, Carolyn, 'Landscape for a Good Woman', in Liz Heron (ed.), *Truth, Dare, Promise: Girls Growing Up in the 50s* (London, 1985).

Stevenson, J., *British Society 1914-45* (Harmondsworth, 1984).

Stewart, M., 'Racial Discrimination and Occupational Achievement', Centre for Labour Economics, Working Paper, London School of Economics, no. 89 (n.d.).

Stone, Lawrence, *The Family, Sex and Marriage in England 1500-1800* (London, 1977).

Stone, Lawrence, *Road to Divorce: England 1530-1987* (Oxford, 1990).

Suttles, Gerald D., *The Social Construction of Communities* (Chicago, 1972).

Swift, Roger and Sheridan Gilley (eds), *The Irish in Britain 1815-1939* (London, 1989).

Sword, Keith, Norman Davies and Jan Ciechanowski, *The Formation of the Polish Community in Great Britain, 1939-50* (London, 1989).

Tebbutt, Melanie, *Making Ends Meet: Pawnbroking and Working-Class Credit* (London, 1983).

Thane, Pat, *Foundation of the Welfare State* (London, 1982).

Thompson, E. P., 'Patrician Society, Plebeian Culture', *Journal of Social History*, 7 (1974).

Thompson, E. P. 'C18 English Society: Class Struggle Without Class', *Social History*, 3.2 (May 1978).

Thurlow, Richard, *Fascism in Britain: A History 1918-1985* (Oxford, 1987).

Tilly, Louise A. and Joan W. Scott, *Women, Work, and Family* (New York, 1978).

Titmuss, R. M., 'The Position of Women and Some Vital Statistics', in M. W. Flinn and T. C. Smout (eds), *Essays in Social History* (Oxford, 1974).

Tomes, Nancy, 'A "Torrent of Abuse": Crimes of Violence Between Working-Class Men and Women in London, 1840-1875', *Journal of Social History*, 11 (Spring 1978).

Treble, James H., *Urban Poverty in Britain, 1830-1914* (London, 1979).

Turnbull, Annmarie, 'Learning Her Womanly Work: The Elementary School Curriculum, 1870-1914', in Felicity Hunt (ed.), *Lessons for Life: The Schooling of Girls and Women 1850-1950* (London, 1987).

Turner, Bryan S., 'Marginal Politics, Cultural Identities and the Clergy in Scotland', *International Journal of Sociology and Social Policy*, 1.1 (1981).

Urry, J., 'Paternalism, Management and Localities', *Lancaster Regionalism Group. Working Paper No. 2* (Lancaster, 1980).

Vallance, Elizabeth, *Women in the House: A Study of Women Members of Parliament* (London, 1979).

Vincent, David, *Bread, Knowledge and Freedom. A Study of Nineteenth Century Working-Class Autobiographies* (London, 1981).

Voeltz, Richard A., 'A Good Jew and a Good Englishman: The Jewish Lads' Brigade, 1894-1922', *Journal of Contemporary History*, 23.1 (1988).

Wainwright, H., *Labour: A Tale of Two Parties* (London, 1987).

Waites, Bernard, 'The Government of the Home Front and the "Moral Economy" of the Working Class', in Peter H. Liddle (ed.), *Home Fires and Foreign Fields: British Social and Military Experience in the First World War* (London, 1985).

Walby, Sylvia, *Patriarchy at Work: Patriarchal and Capitalist Relations in Employment* (London, 1986).

Walkerdine, Valerie, 'Dreams from an Ordinary Childhood', in Liz Heron (ed.), *Truth, Dare, Promise* (London, 1985).

Walkowitz, Judith R., *Prostitution and Victorian Society: Women, Class, and the State* (Cambridge, 1980).

Wallman, Sandra (ed.), *Living in South London: Perspectives on Battersea 1871-1981* (London, 1982).

Walvin, James, *Beside the Seaside: A Social History of the Popular Seaside Holiday* (London, 1978).

Webb, Michael, 'Sex and Gender in the Labour Market', in Ivan Reid and Erica Stratta (eds), *Sex Differences in Britain*, second edition (Aldershot, 1989).

Webber, G., 'Patterns of Membership and Support for the British Union of Fascists', *Journal of Contemporary History*, 19 (1984).

Weeks, Jeffrey, *Sex, Politics and Society: The Regulation of Sexuality Since 1800*, second edition (London, 1989).

Weightman, Gavin and Steve Humphries, *The Making of Modern London 1914-1939* (London, 1984).

Whiteside, Noel, *Bad Times: Unemployment in British Social and Political History* (London, 1991).

Willener, Alfred, *L'image-action de la société ou la politisation culturelle* (Paris, 1970).

Williams, Gwylmore Prys and George Thomas Brake, *Drink in Great Britain, 1900 to 1979* (London, 1980).

Williams, Raymond, *Television, Technology, and Cultural Form* (London, 1974).

Winter, Jay M. (ed.), *The Working Class in Modern British History: Essays in Honour of Henry Pelling* (Cambridge, 1983).

Winter, Jay M., *The Great War and the British People* (London, 1987).

Winter, Jay M., 'Some Paradoxes of the First World War', in Richard Wall and Jay M. Winter (eds), *The Upheaval of War: Family, Work and Welfare in Europe, 1914-1918* (Cambridge, 1988).

Winter, Jay M., *The Experience of World War I* (London, 1989).

Withers, Charles W. J., *Gaelic in Scotland 1698-1981* (Edinburgh, 1984).

Wright, D. and E. Cox, 'Changes in Moral Belief Among Sixth Form Boys and Girls', *British Journal of Clinical Psychology*, 10 (1971).

Yeo, Eileen and Stephen Yeo (eds), *Popular Culture and Class Conflict 1590-1914: Explorations in the History of Labour and Leisure* (Brighton, 1981).

Young, Michael and Peter Willmott, *The Symmetrical Family* (London, 1973).

Young, Michael and Peter Willmott, *Family and Kinship in East London* (London, 1990), first pub. 1957.

Index